TEST PREP SERIES

GRE®
QUANTITATIVE PRACTICE QUESTIONS
2025-2026

> 2 Full Quantitative Tests

> All Question Types Covered

> Categorized by Difficulty Level

> Detailed Answer Explanations

Scan the QR Code to access Online Resources
bit.ly/GRE-QPQ

GRE® Quantitative Practice Questions
First Edition

Copyright © 2025, by Vibrant Publishers LLC, USA. All rights reserved. No part of this publication may be reproduced or distributed in any form or by any means, or stored in a database or retrieval system, without the prior permission of the publisher.

Published by Vibrant Publishers LLC, USA, **www.vibrantpublishers.com**

Paperback ISBN 13: 978-1-63651-440-6

Ebook ISBN 13: 978-1-63651-565-6

Library of Congress Control Number: 2025939625

This publication is designed to provide accurate and authoritative information regarding the subject matter covered. The Author has made every effort in the preparation of this book to ensure the accuracy of the information. However, information in this book is sold without warranty, either expressed or implied. The Author or the Publisher will not be liable for any damages caused or alleged to be caused either directly or indirectly by this book.

All trademarks and registered trademarks mentioned in this publication are the property of their respective owners. These trademarks are used for editorial and educational purposes only, without intent to infringe upon any trademark rights. This publication is independent and has not been authorized, endorsed, or approved by any trademark owner.

Vibrant Publishers' books are available at special quantity discounts for sales promotions, or for use in corporate training programs. For more information, please write to **bulkorders@vibrantpublishers.com**

Please email feedback/corrections (technical, grammatical, or spelling) to **spellerrors@vibrantpublishers.com**

Vibrant publishes in a variety of print and electronic formats and by print-on-demand. Some material included with standard print versions of this book may not be included in e-books or in print-on-demand. To access the complete catalog of Vibrant Publishers, visit **www.vibrantpublishers.com**

GRE® is the registered trademark of the Educational Testing Service (ETS) which neither sponsors nor endorses this product.

GRE® Books in Test Prep Series

GRE® VERBAL PRACTICE QUESTIONS

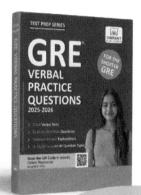

Paperback ISBN:
978-16365-144-1-3

PRACTICE TESTS FOR THE GRE®

Paperback ISBN:
978-1-63651-439-0

GRE® WORDS IN CONTEXT: THE COMPLETE LIST

Paperback ISBN:
978-1-63651-206-8

GRE® MASTER WORDLIST: 1535 WORDS FOR VERBAL MASTERY

Paperback ISBN:
978-1-63651-196-2

For more practice, visit www.vibrantpublishers.com

Dear Test Taker

Thank you for choosing GRE® Quantitative Practice Questions by Vibrant Publishers. We are truly honored to support you in this significant stage of your academic and professional journey. Preparing for the GRE is both a challenge and an opportunity—one that demands not just hard work but also the right guidance and resources. At Vibrant Publishers, we aim to be that reliable support system by creating books that are:

- **Content-rich** – Covers key GRE topics in a way that's clear, practical, and easy to absorb
- **Concise** – Designed to focus on what really matters, without unnecessary distractions
- **Approachable** – Written in a clear, accessible manner to ease your learning process
- **Strategic** – Built to mirror the test format and sharpen your skills for the actual GRE

How This Book Supports Your Success:

- Helps you identify strengths and areas for improvement
- Builds the confidence you need to tackle challenging questions
- Trains you to manage time effectively under test conditions
- Encourages a step-by-step approach to mastering quantitative reasoning

Tips for Getting the Most Out of This Book:

✓ Set a regular practice schedule and stick to it

✓ Take notes and track recurring errors or patterns

✓ Use the answer explanations as learning tools—not just to check accuracy

✓ Stay patient and persistent—progress comes with consistent effort

We also recognize that every learner's journey is unique. If you have questions, feedback, or suggestions as you work through this book, we warmly invite you to connect with us. Your input helps us create better resources for all learners.

Email us anytime at reachus@vibrantpublishers.com

As you take on this challenge, we hope this book proves to be a valuable companion and that your preparation opens doors to exciting new academic and professional opportunities.

Wishing you focus, clarity, and success on your GRE journey!

Warm regards,
The Vibrant Publishers Team

Table of Contents

How to Use This Book — vii

Focused Book Plan — xii

Chapter 1   Overview of the GRE General Test — 1

Chapter 2   Introduction to Quantitative Reasoning — 13

Chapter 3   **Arithmetic** — 19
- Practice Set 1: Easy   20
- Practice Set 2: Medium   25
- Practice Set 3: Hard   37
- Answer Key   40
- Answers & Explanations   41

Chapter 4   **Algebra** — 69
- Practice Set 1: Easy   70
- Practice Set 2: Medium   75
- Practice Set 3: Hard   86
- Answer Key   90
- Answers & Explanations   91

Chapter 5   **Geometry** — 125
- Practice Set 1: Easy   126
- Practice Set 2: Medium   133
- Practice Set 3: Hard   150
- Answer Key   154
- Answers & Explanations   155

Chapter 6   Data Analysis   187

    Practice Set 1: Easy   188

    Practice Set 2: Medium   194

    Practice Set 3: Hard   212

    Answer Key   216

    Answers & Explanations   217

Chapter 7   Practice Test #1   243

    Section 1   244

    Section 2 (Easy)   246

    Section 2 (Hard)   248

    Answer Key   251

    Answers & Explanations   252

Chapter 8   Practice Test #2   265

    Section 1   266

    Section 2 (Easy)   268

    Section 2 (Hard)   270

    Answer Key   273

    Answers & Explanations   274

How to Use This Book

GRE® Quantitative Practice Questions is your complete guide to mastering the Quantitative Reasoning section of the GRE. Whether you're starting your preparation or refining your skills for test day, this book provides the right blend of foundational knowledge and realistic practice to help you succeed.

1. Why This Book?

This book is carefully designed to replicate the real GRE in terms of structure, content, and difficulty level.

You can use this book in two effective ways:

- **Option 1:** Begin with a targeted practice on individual question types.
- **Option 2:** Start with a full test to identify your strengths and weaknesses, then zero in on areas that need improvement.

2. Understand the Test Before You Start

Before jumping into practice questions, it's crucial to:

- Review the **GRE General Test structure** and understand where Quantitative Reasoning fits.
- Learn about the **key question types:**
  - ❑ Quantitative Comparison Questions
  - ❑ Multiple-choice Questions — Select One Answer Choice
  - ❑ Multiple-choice Questions — Select One or More Answer Choices
  - ❑ Numeric Entry Questions
- Read the **strategies and tips** in the section to build a strong foundation and avoid common pitfalls.

3. Practice by Question Type and Topic

Each question type is broken down into manageable, focused sections. The questions are also organized by four core content areas tested on the GRE, which include:

- Arithmetic
- Algebra
- Geometry
- Data Analysis

This topic-based approach ensures you're exposed to a wide variety of mathematical scenarios. Each practice question includes a **detailed explanation,** helping you understand the reasoning behind the correct answer and learn from any mistakes.

After mastering individual topics and question types, you'll get the opportunity to test your skills with two full quantitative practice tests.

4. Simulate Real Testing Conditions

Taking practice tests is most effective when you simulate the actual test environment. This not only helps you become familiar with the test format but also builds focus that is required for the real exam.

How to Create a Test-Like Environment?

- **Follow the official timing:** Stick to the time limits for each section. Use a timer to practice pacing yourself.
- **Avoid distractions:** Put away your phone, turn off notifications, and choose a quiet place where you won't be interrupted.

The Quantitative practice tests in this book are made up of 3 modules instead of 2 to give you an adaptive test experience **on paper.** It will look like this:

- Section 1 (mix of easy, medium, and hard questions)
- Section 2 (easier questions)
- Section 2 (harder questions)

Attempt Section 1 and note down the number of answers you get right. If you get less than 7 questions right, move to Section 2 (Easy), and if you get 7 or more questions right, move to Section 2 (Hard).

5. Review Your Performance Thoroughly

The most valuable part of your preparation lies in analyzing your results.

Steps to Review Your Test:

- **Check your answers:** Use the answer key to score your test. Note both correct and incorrect responses.
- **Understand mistakes:** For every incorrect answer, refer to the detailed explanations in this book. Identify whether the mistake was due to a lack of knowledge, a misinterpretation of the question, or a timing issue for the tests.
- **Revisit challenging questions:** Redo the questions you answered incorrectly without looking at the solutions. This helps reinforce your learning.
- **Identify patterns:** Look for recurring types of mistakes. For example, are certain topics consistently difficult? Are word problems your weak point?

Use Mistakes as Learning Opportunities

Remember, mistakes are a normal part of the learning process. Treat them as opportunities to refine your skills and deepen your understanding of the test.

6. Track Your Progress

Preparation for the GRE is a journey, and tracking your progress helps you stay motivated and focused. Use this book as a tool to monitor your improvement over time.

Why Track Progress?

- It allows you to see tangible improvements in your scores.
- It helps you adjust your study plan based on your evolving needs.
- It builds confidence as you approach your target score.

How to Track Progress?

- **Analyze trends:** Look for consistent improvements or recurring issues.
- **Set goals:** Break down your target score into smaller, achievable milestones.

Remember, progress may not always be linear. Some tests may feel harder than others, but consistency in practice is key.

7. Use Effective Test-Taking Strategies

Success on the GRE isn't just about knowing the content; it's also about applying the right strategies.

- **Time management:** Learn how to pace yourself to complete each section without rushing.
- **Eliminate wrong answers:** Narrow down your choices, especially on multiple-choice questions.
- **Guess wisely:** There's no penalty for guessing on the GRE, so make sure to answer every question.
- **Focus on high-value questions:** Prioritize questions you're more confident about before tackling harder ones.

By practicing these strategies during your preparation, you'll feel more prepared and less anxious on test day.

8. Prepare for the Real Exam

As your test date approaches, use the *Practice Tests for the GRE®* for a full-length simulation. This will help you fine-tune your readiness and reduce any last-minute nerves.

Tips for Final Preparation

- **Review key formulas and concepts:** Know geometry rules, exponent laws, percent formulas, and data interpretation basics.
- **Practice pacing:** Take at least one full test under strict timed conditions.
- **Build confidence:** Use your previous successes to boost your morale. Remind yourself of how much you've improved.
- **Consistency is key:** GRE preparation is most effective when done consistently over time. Avoid cramming in the weeks leading up to the test. Instead, set aside regular study sessions and stick to a schedule.

The final days before the test should focus on reviewing rather than learning new material. This will help you feel calm and prepared.

A Final Word

This book is more than just a collection of practice questions—it's a comprehensive tool to help you achieve your best GRE score. By solving all the questions here, staying consistent in your practice, and reviewing your progress regularly, you'll be well on your way to success. With the right preparation and mindset, you can confidently approach this challenge and open doors to your future aspirations.

Good luck on your GRE journey!

Online Resources

With our test prep books, we also provide Online Resources to help you in your test prep journey! The online resources of this book include:

1. **A Stress Management E-book**

    The book, titled *Conquer the GRE: Stress Management and a Perfect Study Plan*, is designed for test takers to manage the commonly experienced stress during GRE prep. It includes:

    - Stress Management Techniques
    - A 6-month Deep Study Plan
    - An 8-week Sprint Plan
    - Practical Tips to Get a Good Score on the GRE
    - GRE Score Scale Parameters

2. **GRE Quantitative Reasoning Cheat Sheet**

    Mastering math fundamentals is key to scoring well on the GRE Quantitative section. This exclusive Cheat Sheet compiles the most essential formulas, rules, and shortcuts. It includes:

    - **Arithmetic rules** – (number types, divisibility, GCF/LCM, absolute values)
    - **Algebra essentials** – (equations, inequalities, exponents, roots, identities)
    - **Geometry formulas** – (area, volume, angles, triangle properties, coordinate geometry)
    - **Data analysis tools** – (mean, median, mode, range, standard deviation, probability)

How to Access the Online Resources

Step 1: Scan the QR code

Step 2: Fill in your details and submit to request the online resources

Step 3: Check your email inbox to download the resources

Have fun learning !

bit.ly/GRE-QPQ

Focused Book Plan

> **Which plan is right for you?**
>
> Want to study both Verbal and Quant quickly?
> ✓ **8-Week Sprint Plan (Online)**
>
> Prefer a slower pace with deeper study?
> ✓ **6-Month Deep Study Plan (Online)**
>
> Only interested in Quantitative Reasoning?
> ✓ **6-Week Focused Book Plan**

If you're aiming to master the Quantitative Reasoning section and prefer a dedicated, streamlined approach, this focused 6-week plan is for you. Whether you're brushing up on forgotten math concepts or targeting specific weak spots, this plan helps you build a strong foundation, boost problem-solving accuracy, and develop the strategies needed to handle every GRE Quant question type confidently.

Week 1: Foundation Review

Day 1-3: Begin by reviewing the structure and scoring of the GRE Quant section. Understand the four core content areas: Arithmetic, Algebra, Geometry, and Data Analysis. Familiarize yourself with the question formats.

Day 4: Take a GRE Quant test under timed conditions to establish your baseline performance.

Day 5-7: Analyze the test results. Identify which topic areas need the most attention and set goals for skill improvement over the coming weeks.

Week 2: Content Review – Arithmetic & Algebra

Day 1-3: Focus on Arithmetic topics, including number properties, fractions, percentages, ratios, and absolute value. Complete targeted practice sets and review explanations in detail.

Day 4: Shift to Algebra topics such as linear equations, inequalities, exponents, roots, and word problems.

Day 5-7: Continue working on Algebra, focusing on more complex expressions and translating word problems into equations. Use the cheat sheet provided in the *Online Resources* to memorize key formulas.

Week 3: Content Review – Geometry & Data Analysis

Day 1-3: Dive into Geometry topics including lines, angles, triangles, circles, and coordinate geometry.

Day 4: Focus on Data Analysis topics such as interpreting graphs, tables, statistics (mean, median, standard deviation), and probability.

Day 5-7: Complete mixed practice sets from both Geometry and Data Analysis. Track error patterns and continue refining through continuous practice.

Week 4: Strategy Development & Topic Reinforcement

Day 1-3: Revisit your weakest content area based on earlier practice questions. Solve 20–25 questions from that topic under timed conditions.

Day 4: Study strategic approaches for Quant: plugging in numbers, working backwards from answer choices, estimation, and pacing techniques.

Day 5-7: Apply these strategies to timed sets across all topics. Focus on improving accuracy while staying within the time limit.

Week 5: Mixed Practice & Accuracy Training

Day 1-3: Solve a mixed set covering all topics (10-15 questions each from Arithmetic, Algebra, Geometry, and Data Analysis). Pay attention to transitions between question types and maintain pace.

Day 4: Take the second Quantitative practice test to simulate the real exam experience.

Day 5-7: Assess the test in detail. Review the in-depth explanations for every incorrect answer to strengthen conceptual understanding.

Week 6: Final Review & Test Readiness

Day 1-3: Focus your review on high-yield topics and formulas. Re-do tough questions from earlier weeks.

Day 4: Take a break from intense studying. Rest well, eat healthy, and reduce stress to be in peak mental shape for test day.

Day 5-7: Light review only—skim the cheat sheet, review top error types, and do a few warm-up questions each day.

Adjust the study plan according to your individual needs and schedule, ensuring a balance between content review, practice, and relaxation. Stay committed, stay focused, and trust in your preparation as you approach the GRE.

Icons in this Book and Their Meanings:

 — Key points to remember

 — Quick glance

 — Solved examples

 — Expert tips to help you excel

Chapter 1
Overview of the GRE® General Test

The **Graduate Record Examinations (GRE) General Test** has traditionally been a key component in graduate admissions. While its role is now part of a broader evaluation process, a strong GRE score remains a valuable asset—it can serve as evidence of a strong scholarship on an application. This book is designed to prepare you thoroughly for the GRE General Test, formerly known as the GRE revised General Test (renamed in 2016). While the name has changed, the test's structure and scoring have remained consistent.

It's important to note that some graduate programs may also require GRE Subject Tests. These are designed to assess knowledge in specific academic disciplines and are not covered in this book. Before beginning your GRE preparation, review the admissions criteria of your target programs to determine whether a Subject Test is also required. For more information, visit the Subject Tests section on ets.org.

What the GRE Measures

The GRE General Test is not designed to measure your knowledge of specific fields. It does not measure your ability to be successful in your career or even in school. It does, however, give a reasonably accurate indication of your capabilities in certain key areas such as:

- Comprehending and analyzing complex written material
- Understanding basic mathematical concepts
- Interpreting and evaluating data
- Applying logical reasoning and critical thinking

By preparing for the GRE using this book, you'll not only enhance your test performance but also strengthen foundational skills that are crucial for success in graduate studies.

Format of the GRE General Test

The GRE General Test is offered as a computer-delivered test throughout the year. Post-COVID, ETS provides test-takers with the option to take the test from home. Whether you are taking the GRE General Test at the testing center or at home, the format of the test will essentially be the same. The total time for the test will be about **1 hour and 58 minutes**. The test consists of three main components:

- Analytical Writing
- Verbal Reasoning
- Quantitative Reasoning

Note: The unscored section has also been removed for the shorter GRE General Test, along with the 10-minute scheduled break, which was granted to the students after the 2-hour mark of the 3-hour 45-minute test.

Inside the GRE: What's Tested

The Verbal Reasoning and Quantitative Reasoning sections of the GRE General Test are **section-level adaptive**. This means that the computer will adapt the test to your performance. Since there are two sections, each for Verbal Reasoning and Quantitative Reasoning, the difficulty of the second section will depend on how well you did in the first section. The overall format of the GRE General Test will be as follows:

Measure	Number of Questions	Time Allowed
Analytical Writing (1 section)	1 Analyze an Issue	30 minutes
Verbal Reasoning (2 sections)	12 questions (first section) 15 questions (second section)	18 minutes (first section) 23 minutes (second section)
Quantitative Reasoning (2 sections)	12 questions (first section) 15 questions (second section)	21 minutes (first section) 26 minutes (second section)
		Total Time: 1 hour 58 minutes

1. Analytical Writing Measure

The first section of the GRE General Test is the Analytical Writing measure. This section of the GRE is designed to test your ability to use basic logic and critical reasoning to make and assess arguments. The Analytical Writing measure comprises a singular assignment, which must be completed within 30 minutes. You will be given an issue and a prompt with some specific instructions on how to approach the assigned issue. You will be expected to take a position on the issue and then write a clear, persuasive, and logically sound essay defending your position in correct English.

The tasks in the Analytical Writing measure are designed to reflect a wide range of subject areas—from the arts and humanities to the social and physical sciences—but they do **not require specialized content knowledge.**

To support your preparation, the GRE Program has published the complete pool of **Issue topics** from which the prompts are drawn—you can access this resource as a downloadable PDF from the official ETS website.

 Quick Glance at the Analytical Writing Measure

- **Duration:** The task must be completed within 30 minutes.
- **Task format:** A short essay must be written in response to an issue of general interest. The prompt should be addressed clearly and thoughtfully.
- **Skills measured:** This task assesses the ability to develop complex ideas coherently, structure writing in a focused and organized way, support claims with relevant evidence, and demonstrate a strong command of standard written English.
- **Subject knowledge:** The task is designed to measure reasoning, writing, and analytical skills, not familiarity with specific academic topics.
- **Evaluation criteria:** Responses are evaluated based on clarity of argument, depth of reasoning, use of evidence, organization, and language proficiency.

2. Verbal Reasoning Measure

The Verbal Reasoning measure of the GRE assesses your reading comprehension, ability to draw inferences, and vocabulary skills. You will encounter two Verbal Reasoning sections containing 12 and 15 questions, with time limits of 18 and 23 minutes, respectively.

Most questions are multiple-choice and fall into three main types:

- **Reading Comprehension (RC):** You will read a short passage (1 to 3 paragraphs) and answer questions that test your understanding of the content.

- **Text Completion (TC):** These questions present a brief passage with one to three blanks. You will select the best choices from multiple options to fill in the blanks appropriately.

- **Sentence Equivalence (SE):** You will complete a sentence by selecting two words that both fit the blank and produce sentences with similar meanings.

Together, these question types assess how well you understand and analyze written material, as well as your command of vocabulary in context.

 Quick Glance at the Verbal Reasoning Measure

- **Duration:** The section is split into 12 questions with a 18-minute time limit and 15 questions with a 23-minute limit.

- **Question types:** This section includes Reading Comprehension, Text Completion, and Sentence Equivalence questions.

- **Choices:** RC questions may require selecting one or more correct answers or highlighting a relevant portion of the text. TC questions involve choosing the correct words to fill one or more blanks in a passage. SE questions ask for two answer choices that produce sentences with similar meanings.

- **Skills measured:** The section tests the ability to understand complex texts, apply vocabulary in context, and make logical inferences based on written material.

3. Quantitative Reasoning Measure

The Quantitative Reasoning section of the GRE tests your ability to apply basic math skills, interpret data, and reason with numbers. You'll face two sections: one with 12 questions in 21 minutes, and another with 15 questions in 26 minutes.

Questions may be set in real-world or purely mathematical contexts, with many presented as word problems that require mathematical modeling. The section covers **four** content areas: Arithmetic, Algebra, Geometry, and Data Analysis.

You'll encounter four types of questions:

- **Quantitative Comparison**
- **Multiple Choice — Select One Answer**
- **Multiple Choice — Select One or More Answers**
- **Numeric Entry**

Quick Glance at the Quantitative Reasoning Measure

- **Time Allotted:** The section is split into 12 questions with a 21-minute time limit and 15 questions with a 26-minute limit.

- **Question Types:** This section includes Multiple Choice, Numeric Entry, Quantitative Comparison, and Data Interpretation questions.

- **Skills Measured:** This section tests the ability to use Arithmetic, Algebra, Geometry, and Statistics, interpret and analyze quantitative data, and apply mathematical reasoning to real-world problems..

Features of the Computer-delivered Test

1. **Review and Preview Questions**
   Test takers can review and preview questions within a section, which allows them to manage their time effectively and focus on the most challenging questions first.

2. **Mark and Return to Questions**
   Questions can be marked within a section and revisited later. This enables moving past difficult questions and returning to them, as long as the time limit for the section is respected.

3. **Change or Edit Answers**
   Answers can be changed or edited within a section. If a mistake is noticed, test takers can correct their responses before the section time expires.

4. **On-Screen Calculator**
   An on-screen calculator is provided during the Quantitative Reasoning measure, facilitating quick and accurate calculations. However, you should only use the calculator for complex equations that will take a longer time to do manually, such as square roots, addition, subtraction, and multiplication of numbers with several digits.

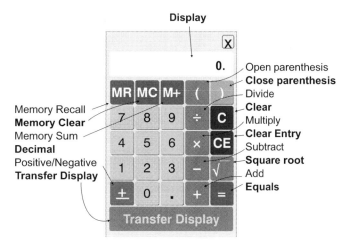

Guidelines for using the on-screen calculator

- The on-screen calculator follows the order of operations (PEMDAS). This means that it computes equations in the following order - parentheses, exponentiation (including square roots), multiplication and division (left to right), addition and subtraction (left to right). So, for an equation like 2 + 3 * 6, the on-screen calculator will give the answer 20 but some calculators will give the answer 30 as they first add 2 and 3 and get 5 which is multiplied by 6 to get the final answer 30.

- The Transfer Display button will be useful for Numeric Entry questions. The button will transfer the number on your calculator display to the numeric entry answer box. But remember to check the transferred answer as sometimes you may be required to round up your answer; adjust it accordingly.

- The Memory Recall (MR), Memory Clear (MC), and Memory Sum (M+) buttons work as per normal calculators.

Registering for the GRE

Before you register to take the GRE, be sure to consider your schedule and any special accommodations that you may need. Be aware that the availability of testing dates may vary according to your location. Be sure to give yourself plenty of time to prepare for the GRE and be sure that you know the deadlines for score reporting and application deadlines for all the schools you are applying to. For general information about deadlines and the GRE, visit the GRE section at ets.org. For more information on how to register for the GRE, visit the Registration section at ets.org. For information on special accommodations for disabled students, visit the Disability Accommodations section on ets.org.

If you are taking the GRE General Test at home, there are certain equipment, environment, and testing space requirements that you need to fulfill before you can start the registration process. For more information on these requirements, read the At Home Testing section on ets.org.

How the GRE General Test is Scored
Scoring for the Analytical Writing Section

In the Analytical Writing section, you will be scored on a scale of 0-6 in increments of 0.5. The Analytical Writing measure emphasizes your ability to engage in reasoning and critical thinking over your facility with the finer points of grammar. The highest scores of 5.5-6.0 are given to work that is generally superior in every respect - sustained analysis of complex issues, coherent argumentation, and excellent command of the English language. The lowest scores of 0.0-0.5 are given to work that is completely off-topic or so poorly composed as to be incoherent.

Scoring for the Verbal and Quantitative Reasoning Sections

The Verbal and Quantitative Reasoning sections are now scored on a scale of 130-170 in 1-point increments.

Preparing for Test Day

How you prepare for the test is completely up to you and will depend on your own test-taking preferences and the amount of time you can devote to studying for the test. At the very least, before you take the test, you should know the basics of what is covered on the test along with the general guidelines for taking the GRE. This book is designed to provide you with the basic information you need and give you the opportunity to prepare thoroughly for the GRE General Test.

Remember, you don't need to spend an equal amount of time on each of these areas to do well on the GRE - allot your study time to your own needs and preferences. Following are some suggestions to help you make the final preparations for your test, and help you through the test itself.

- In the time leading up to your test, practice, then practice some more. Practice until you are confident with the material.

- Know when your test is, and when you need to be at the testing center or in front of your computer at home.

- Make a "practice run" to your testing center, so that you can anticipate how much time you will need to allow to get there. For the at home test, make sure to sign in at least 15 minutes before the test.

- Understand the timing and guidelines for the test and plan accordingly. Remember that you are not allowed to eat or drink while taking the GRE, although you will be allowed to snack or drink during some of the short breaks during testing. Plan accordingly.

- Know exactly what documentation you will need to bring with you to the testing center. If you are testing at home, you will have to provide a valid government-issued identification document as well.

- Relax, especially on the day or night before your test. If you have studied and practiced wisely, you will be well prepared for the test. You may want to briefly glance over some test preparation materials but cramming the night before will not be productive.

- Eat well and get a good night's sleep. You will want to be well-rested for the test.

The Test Day

- Wake up early to give yourself plenty of time to eat a healthy breakfast, gather the necessary documentation, pack a snack and a water bottle, and make it to the testing center well before your test is scheduled to start.

- Have confidence; you've prepared well for the test, and there won't be any big surprises. You may not know the answers to some questions, but the format will be exactly like what you've been practicing.

- While you are taking the test, don't panic. The test is timed, and students often worry that they will run out of time and miss too many questions. The sections of the test are designed so that many students will not finish them, so don't worry if you don't think you can finish a section on time. Just try to answer as many questions as you can, as accurately as possible.

- If there's a question you're not sure of, don't panic—the GRE test allows you to skip and return to questions when you are ready, so take advantage of that. Remember, the value of each easy question is the same as the hard questions!

- Remember the strategies and techniques that you learn from this book and apply them wherever possible.

General Strategies for Taking the GRE

The following is a list of strategies that will help to improve your chances of performing well on the GRE:

- Learn the basics about the test - what is being tested, the format, and how the test is administered.

- Familiarize yourself with the specific types of questions that you will see on the GRE General Test.

- Review basic concepts in math, logic, and writing.

- Work through the test-taking strategies offered in this book.

- Work through mock GRE tests until you feel thoroughly comfortable with the types of questions you will see.

- As you are studying for the GRE, focus your energy on the types of questions that give you the most difficulty.

- Learn to guess wisely. For many of the questions in the Verbal and Quantitative Reasoning Sections, the correct answer is in front of you - you only need to correctly identify it. Especially for questions that you find difficult, you should hone your ability to dismiss the options that are clearly wrong and make an educated guess about which one is right.

- Answer every question. You won't lose any points for choosing the wrong answer, so even a wild guess that might or might not be right is better than no answer at all.

Frequently Asked Questions

General Questions

1. **What changes have been made to the GRE General Test after the announcement on May 31, 2023?**

   The main changes to the test are a reduction in the time (from 3 hours 45 minutes to 1 hour 58 minutes), and the removal of the "Analyze an Argument" essay task (which was a part of the Analytical Writing section) and the unscored section. The time has been curtailed by decreasing the number of questions in each section, reducing the total number of questions from 40 to 27. Furthermore, the removal of the "Analyze an Argument" task and the unscored section also aided in shortening the total duration. The official scores will also be delivered more promptly and will now take 8-10 calendar days, facilitating faster applications to their desired institutes by the students. For more information on the changes, visit the GRE section at ets.org.

2. **Can I take the GRE test at home?**

    Yes. ETS now provides students with the option to take the test from home. If your local test centers are closed or you prefer a familiar testing environment, you can take the GRE from home. You will have to check the equipment, environment, and testing space requirements for the at home test and whether it's an option for you. For detailed information on the requirements for the home test, check the At Home Testing section at ets.org.

3. **How do I get ready to take the GRE General Test?**

    To take the GRE General Test, there are several steps you'll need to take:

    - Find out what prospective graduate/professional programs require: Does the program you're interested in require additional testing beyond the GRE General Test? What is the deadline for receipt of scores?

    - Sign up for a test date. You need to sign up for any GRE testing. Act in a timely manner so that you have plenty of time to prepare and are guaranteed that your scores will be sent and received on time. For the in-center test, testing dates are much more restricted, so if you know that you will need to take the GRE General Test at the center, make arrangements well in advance of the application deadline for your program. There are additional requirements if you're taking the test at home, so make sure to check the requirements well in advance.

    - Use resources provided by ETS and Vibrant Publishers to familiarize yourself with the format of the GRE and the types of questions you will face. Even if you are confident about taking the test, it is essential to prepare for the test.

4. **Does the GRE General Test measure my proficiency in specific subject areas?**

    No. The GRE General Test is designed to measure general proficiency in reading, critical reasoning, and working with data, all abilities that are critical to graduate work. However, you won't be tested on your knowledge of any specific field.

5. **Where can I get additional information on the GRE General Test?**

    Educational Testing Service (ETS), the organization that administers the GRE, has an informative website entirely devoted to information about the test in the GRE section at ets.org. There, you can find links that further explain how to sign up for testing, fees, score reporting, and much more.

Preparing for the Test

1. **How should I start to prepare for the test?**

    The first thing you should do is thoroughly familiarize yourself with the format of the GRE General Test. Read about each section of the test, how many questions are there per section, and the required format for answers. You can find general information about the structure of the test earlier in this chapter.

2. **How do I prepare for the questions I will be asked on the GRE General Test?**

    There are plenty of resources by Vibrant Publishers, including this book to help you prepare for the questions you will face on the GRE General Test. A list of books is provided at the beginning of this book. For the most updated list, you may visit the Test Prep Series section on www.vibrantpublishers.com.

3. **How much should I study/practice for the GRE?**

   Study and practice until you feel comfortable with the test. Practice, practice, and practice some more until you feel confident about test day!

4. **Are there additional materials I can use to get even more practice?**

   Yes. ETS offers a free full-length practice test that can be downloaded from the GRE section at ets.org. Also, after you have signed up for testing through ETS, you are eligible for some further test preparation materials free of additional charge.

Test Content

1. **What skills does the GRE test?**

   In general, the GRE is designed to test your proficiency in certain key skills that you will need for graduate-level study. More specifically:

   - **The Analytical Writing section** tests your ability to write about complex ideas in a coherent, focused fashion as well as your ability to command the conventions of standard written English, provide and evaluate relevant evidence, and critique other points of view.

   - **The Verbal Reasoning section** is an assessment of your ability to understand, interpret and analyze complex passages, use reasoning to draw inferences about written material, and use sophisticated vocabulary in context.

   - **The Quantitative Reasoning section** is an assessment of basic, high school-level mathematical skills and knowledge, as well as your ability to analyze and interpret data.

2. **What level of math is required for the Quantitative Reasoning section?**

   You will be expected to know high school-level math: arithmetic, and basic concepts in algebra and geometry. You will also be expected to be able to analyze and interpret data presented in tables and graphs.

Scoring and Score Reporting

1. **How are the sections of the GRE General Test scored?**

   The GRE General Test is scored as follows:

   - **The scores of the Verbal Reasoning section** are done in 1-point increments on a scale of 130-170.

   - **The scores of the Quantitative Reasoning section** are done in 1-point increments on a scale of 130-170.

   - **The scores of the Analytical Writing section** are done in increments of 0.5 on a scale of 0-6.

2. **When will my score be reported?**

   It depends on when you decide to take the GRE General Test. In general, scores for the test are reported in 8-10 days. You can find your scores in your official ETS account. An email notification from ETS is sent when the test scores are made available. ETS will also send an official Institution Score Report to the institutions you've chosen to send the test scores to. Check the GRE section at ets.org for updates on score reporting and deadlines.

3. **How long will my scores be valid?**

   Your score for the GRE General Test will remain valid for five years.

Other Questions

1. **Do business schools accept the GRE instead of the GMAT?**

   An increasing number of business schools accept the GRE as a substitute for the more standard test for admission to an MBA program, the GMAT. Before you decide to take the GRE instead of the GMAT, make sure that the programs you are interested in applying to will accept the GRE. You can find a list of business schools that currently accept the GRE in the GRE section at ets.org.

2. **How is the GRE administered?**

   The GRE is administered continuously year-round at designated testing centers, where you can take the test free from distractions in a secure environment that discourages cheating. The GRE Test at home is also available for those who are more comfortable in a familiar environment. For information on testing centers in your area and important dates, visit the GRE section at ets.org.

3. **I have a disability that requires me to ask for special accommodation while taking the test - what sort of accommodation is offered?**

   ETS does accommodate test-takers with disabilities. For information on procedures, visit the GRE Disability Accomodations section at ets.org.

4. **Will there be breaks during testing?**

   No. There are no breaks. If you take an unscheduled break, testing time will not stop.

5. **Will I be given scratch paper?**

   Yes. The test administrator will provide you with scratch paper to use during the test, which has to be returned to the testing center staff without any pages missing.

   For the at home test, you cannot use regular notepaper. You may use either of the following materials:

   - One small desktop whiteboard with an erasable marker.

   - A sheet of paper placed inside a transparent sheet protector. You can write on this with an erasable marker.

   At the end of the test, you will need to show the proctor that all the notes you took during the test have been erased.

6. **Should I bring a calculator to the test?**

   No. There will be an on-screen calculator for you to use.

This page is intentionally left blank

Chapter 2
Introduction to Quantitative Reasoning

Overview

The Quantitative Reasoning Section of the GRE is designed to measure and test the ability to solve problems that require fundamental skills in arithmetic, algebra, geometry, and data analysis. The section consists of three modules:

- Quantitative Comparison, which involves fewer computations or calculations than the other modules but requires reasoning ability and the skills to describe problems in a logical manner. The module is about 35% of the GRE Quantitative Section.

- Math Problem Solving, which tests basic mathematical skills. Problems in this module are usually multiple-choice questions that can be solved fairly quickly.

- The Numeric Entry module requires entering solutions to math problems into an answer box.

Some of the questions in the quantitative reasoning section are based in real-world settings, while others are placed in formal mathematical contexts. Solving these problems requires basic mathematical skills.

Question Types

There are four types of questions in the Quantitative Reasoning Section. In general, the questions test your ability to:

- Understand and apply basic mathematical skills
- Understand fundamental mathematical concepts
- Use quantitative methods to logically reason and model practical problems

1. Quantitative Comparison Questions

Quantitative Comparison (QC) Questions are a subset of the Quantitative Reasoning Section.
In Quantitative Comparison questions, you will be provided with information on two quantities, such as Quantity A and Quantity B. From the given information, you should compare Quantity A and Quantity B, and select an answer that is based on these choices:

- (A) Quantity A is greater.
- (B) Quantity B is greater.
- (C) The two quantities are equal.
- (D) The relationship cannot be determined from the information given.

Hints for answering QC questions:

- Carefully examine answers (A) through (C), before selecting choice (D).

- Avoid unnecessary and lengthy computations. Sometimes, you need to simplify the results of the computation in order to find the answer in choices (A) through (C).

- Keep in mind that geometric figures may not be drawn to scale.

- If quantities A and B are mathematical expressions, plug your answer into the expressions in order to validate your choice of answer.

- You may need to simplify the mathematical expressions for quantities in order to use them effectively.

Example:

Quantity A	Quantity B
The number of prime numbers between 1 and 100	The number of odd numbers between 1 and 100

- (A) Quantity A is greater.
- (B) Quantity B is greater.
- (C) The two quantities are equal.
- (D) The relationship cannot be determined from the information given.

2. Multiple-Choice Select One Answer Questions

The Multiple-Choice Select One Answer Questions form a subset of the Quantitative Reasoning Section. In the MCSO (Multiple-Choice Select One) section, you will be asked to select only one answer to a question from a list of choices.

Hints for answering MCSO questions:

- Carefully compute to validate the selected answer.
- Avoid unnecessary and lengthy computations but check your calculations to avoid careless errors.
- Keep in mind that geometric figures may not be drawn to scale.
- If you need to guess the answer, you should perform validation tests (such as plugging the selected answer into the problem).
- The answer is present there; so make use of that fact. Work 'backward' by substituting each option in the problem and see if it fits.
- The answer to some questions is in the question itself. Some direct questions specifically ask for a property that you will be able to answer by looking at the choices and the relationships between them.
- You may need to simplify the mathematical expressions for quantities in order to use them effectively.

Example:

If the average (arithmetic mean) of four distinct positive integers is 11, what is the greatest possible value of any one of the integers?

- (A) 35
- (B) 38
- (C) 40
- (D) 41
- (E) 44

3. Multiple-Choice-Select Multiple Answers Questions

The Multiple-Choice Select Multiple Answers Section of the GRE is a subset of the Quantitative Reasoning Section. In the MCSM (Multiple-Choice Select Multiple) Section, you will be asked to select one or more answers to a question from a list of choices. Keep in mind that a question may not specify the number of choices that need to be selected.

Hints for answering MCSM questions:

- If the question hasn't specified how many choices need to be selected, you will have to consider each answer carefully and choose all that apply.

- Try to avoid lengthy numerical calculations as far as possible. Look for numerical patterns and make a wise, educated guess.

Example:

Which of the following decimals are greater than 5.04078 and less than 6.1035?
Indicate all that apply.

- [A] 5.1703
- [B] 5.0405
- [C] 5.709
- [D] 5.00231
- [E] 6.123
- [F] 6.046

4. Numeric Entry Questions

Numeric Entry (NE) questions are one of the four types of questions in the Quantitative Reasoning Section of the GRE. Questions of the NE type require you to answer a question by typing your answer into a box. Your answers may be in the form of integers, decimals, or fractions, and they could be negative quantities.

Because there are no answer choices for an NE question, it is necessary to read the question carefully, and to answer the question in the form that is expected. It is also important to pay attention to units (such as feet, yards, miles/hour, km/hour, and so on), and to give answers that are fractions or percentages, if requested. You may be asked to round up an answer to a certain number of decimal places.

Because NE questions do not allow you to guess at an answer, it is necessary to check your answer carefully after you have expended some time to obtain it.

Example:

What is 21% of 19? Write your answer in the answer box up to two significant digits.

☐

Hints for answering NE questions:

- Read the question carefully. Since there are no answer choices to act as a guide, you need to understand what exactly is required.

- Keep aside a larger margin of time for this section, as the computations may take time.

- Make sure that you round up your answer to the exact degree of accuracy specified in the question. If no instructions are given, enter the exact number.

- Your answer should be reasonable in terms of the question and what it is asking.

This page is intentionally left blank

Chapter 3
Arithmetic

Chapter 3: Arithmetic

Practice Set 1: Easy

1. a, and c are consecutive even integers.

Quantity A	Quantity B
$a + b + c$	$3a + 6$

A) Quantity A is greater.
B) Quantity B is greater.
C) The two quantities are equal.
D) The relationship cannot be determined from the information given.

2.

Quantity A	Quantity B
42% of 165	The number that 80 is 20% of

A) Quantity A is greater.
B) Quantity B is greater.
C) The two quantities are equal.
D) The relationship cannot be determined from the information given.

3.

Quantity A	Quantity B
$\dfrac{11!}{5!}$	The sum of the smallest 3 digit prime numbers.

A) Quantity A is greater.
B) Quantity B is greater.
C) The two quantities are equal.
D) The relationship cannot be determined from the information given.

4. A two–pound box of brand A costs $7.88. A three pound box of brand B costs $11.79.

Quantity A	Quantity B
Cost per pound of Brand A	Cost per pound of Brand B

A) Quantity A is greater.
B) Quantity B is greater.
C) The two quantities are equal.
D) The relationship cannot be determined from the information given.

5. An apartment building has 5 floors, one of which has only 2 apartments. Each of the other floors have 4 apartments.

Quantity A	Quantity B
3 times the number of floors in the building	The number of apartments in the building

A) Quantity A is greater.
B) Quantity B is greater.
C) The two quantities are equal.
D) The relationship cannot be determined from the information given.

6.

$$\frac{x}{y} = \frac{z}{x} \text{ and } x > 0$$

Quantity A	Quantity B
$y + z$	$2x$

A) Quantity A is greater.
B) Quantity B is greater.
C) The two quantities are equal.
D) The relationship cannot be determined from the information given.

Practice Set 1: Easy

7 The relationship between the cost and the pounds of laundry washed by two different laundry services is shown below. Compare Quantity A and Quantity B for 30 pounds of laundry.

Laundry A	
Laundry washed (lbs)	Cost ($)
1	16
2	18
3	20
4	22

Laundry B	
Laundry washed (lbs)	Cost ($)
1	6
2	10
3	14
4	18

Quantity A   **Quantity B**

Laundry A   Laundry B

Ⓐ Quantity A is greater.
Ⓑ Quantity B is greater.
Ⓒ The two quantities are equal.
Ⓓ The relationship cannot be determined from the information given.

8 The ratio of IT staff to administrative staff to legal staff is 3:4:7. Twenty-five percent of the IT staff, thirty percent of the administrative staff, and fifty percent of the legal staff are enrolled in the company's healthcare plan. There are 28 legal staff members.

Quantity A   **Quantity B**

The number of IT staff not enrolled in the company's health care plan.   3

Ⓐ Quantity A is greater.
Ⓑ Quantity B is greater.
Ⓒ The two quantities are equal.
Ⓓ The relationship cannot be determined from the information given.

9 x is an odd negative integer

Quantity A   **Quantity B**

$\left(-\dfrac{1}{816}\right)^x$ -2^x

Ⓐ Quantity A is greater
Ⓑ Quantity B is greater
Ⓒ The two quantities are equal.
Ⓓ The relationship cannot be determined from the information given.

10

Quantity A   **Quantity B**

24.6×10^3 0.246×10^5

Ⓐ Quantity A is greater.
Ⓑ Quantity B is greater.
Ⓒ The two quantities are equal.
Ⓓ The relationship cannot be determined from the information given.

11

Quantity A   **Quantity B**

$\dfrac{1}{3} \div \dfrac{5}{9} + \dfrac{2}{5} \times \dfrac{4}{7}$ $\dfrac{1}{3} \div \dfrac{5}{7} + \dfrac{4}{5} \times \dfrac{4}{7}$

Ⓐ Quantity A is greater.
Ⓑ Quantity B is greater.
Ⓒ The two quantities are equal.
Ⓓ The relationship cannot be determined from the information given.

Chapter 3: Arithmetic

12. On a number line, the distance from *x* to *y* is 8 and the distance from *x* to *z* is 12. The position of *y* is not between *x* and *z*.

Quantity A	Quantity B
The distance from *y* to *z*	20

Ⓐ Quantity A is greater.
Ⓑ Quantity B is greater.
Ⓒ The two quantities are equal.
Ⓓ The relationship cannot be determined from the information given.

13.

$$\left\{\frac{m}{n} = \frac{2}{3}; n \neq 3\right\}$$

Quantity A	Quantity B
$\dfrac{m+3}{n+3}$	$\dfrac{5}{6}$

Ⓐ Quantity A is greater.
Ⓑ Quantity B is greater.
Ⓒ The two quantities are equal.
Ⓓ The relationship cannot be determined from the information given.

14. The ratio of the length and the width of a rectangle is 4:3. The area of the rectangle is 108 square inches.

Quantity A	Quantity B
The width of the rectangle	The square of the difference between the length and the width

Ⓐ Quantity A is greater.
Ⓑ Quantity B is greater.
Ⓒ The two quantities are equal.
Ⓓ The relationship cannot be determined from the information given.

15. Charles takes 40 minutes to cycle to his office.

Quantity A	Quantity B
Additional time taken by Charles to reach his office when his speed is 80% of his usual speed	10 minutes

Ⓐ Quantity A is greater.
Ⓑ Quantity B is greater.
Ⓒ The two quantities are equal.
Ⓓ The relationship cannot be determined from the information given.

16. *p*, *q* and *r* are three distinct positive integers such that their product *pqr* = 385.

Quantity A	Quantity B
The value of $p + q + r$	22

Ⓐ Quantity A is greater.
Ⓑ Quantity B is greater.
Ⓒ The two quantities are equal.
Ⓓ The relationship cannot be determined from the information given.

17. A is the decimal value of $\dfrac{5}{7}$ and B is the decimal value of $\dfrac{5}{11}$.

Quantity A	Quantity B
The 18th digit to the right of the decimal place in A	The 20th digit to the right of the decimal place in B

Ⓐ Quantity A is greater.
Ⓑ Quantity B is greater.
Ⓒ The two quantities are equal.
Ⓓ The relationship cannot be determined from the information given.

Practice Set 1: Easy

18 For 6 hours, a computer uploaded files at a constant rate of 7 files every 4 seconds.

Quantity A	Quantity B
The number of files the computer uploaded in 6 hours	40,000

- Ⓐ Quantity A is greater.
- Ⓑ Quantity B is greater.
- Ⓒ The two quantities are equal.
- Ⓓ The relationship cannot be determined from the information given.

19 Sequence S is defined as $S_n = 3S_{n-1} - 3$. If $S_1 = 3$ then $S_5 - S_4 = ?$

- Ⓐ 79
- Ⓑ 80
- Ⓒ 81
- Ⓓ 82
- Ⓔ 83

20 What is the product of 4.23×10^4 and 8.53×10^5 in scientific notation?

- Ⓐ 3.608×10^9
- Ⓑ 3.608×10^{10}
- Ⓒ 36.08×10^9
- Ⓓ 360.8×10^8
- Ⓔ 3.608×10^8

21 What is the sum of all the odd factors of 45?

- Ⓐ 45
- Ⓑ 46
- Ⓒ 77
- Ⓓ 78
- Ⓔ 2025

22 The ratio of the arithmetic mean of two numbers to one of the numbers is 3 : 5. What is the ratio of the smaller number to the larger?

- Ⓐ 1 : 5
- Ⓑ 1 : 4
- Ⓒ 1 : 3
- Ⓓ 1 : 2
- Ⓔ 2 : 3

23 What is the value of $\dfrac{c}{d}$ when $\dfrac{4}{\dfrac{2}{c}+\dfrac{5}{c}} = \dfrac{6}{\dfrac{9}{3d}+\dfrac{16}{4d}}$?

- Ⓐ $\dfrac{2}{7}$
- Ⓑ $\dfrac{4}{7}$
- Ⓒ $\dfrac{2}{3}$
- Ⓓ $\dfrac{7}{6}$
- Ⓔ $\dfrac{3}{2}$

24 If $(2^{2x+1})(3^{2y-1}) = 2^{3x}3^{3y}$, then $x + y = ?$

- Ⓐ -2
- Ⓑ -1
- Ⓒ 0
- Ⓓ 1
- Ⓔ 2

25 What is the least common multiple of the largest composite factors of 48 and 64 (excluding 48 and 64)?

- Ⓐ 12
- Ⓑ 16
- Ⓒ 32
- Ⓓ 96
- Ⓔ 512

Chapter 3: Arithmetic

26 Peter, a salesman, bought a laptop at $320. While selling the laptop, he offered a 2.5 % discount on the marked price. If the discounted price gave him a profit of 21.875%, what was the marked price?

- (A) 328
- (B) 380
- (C) 390
- (D) 400
- (E) 410

27 Mike's coin collection consists of quarters, dimes, and nickels. If the ratio of the number of quarters to the number of dimes is 5:2, and the ratio of the number of dimes to the number of nickels is 3:4, what is the ratio of the number of quarters to the number of nickels?

- (A) 5:4
- (B) 7:5
- (C) 10:6
- (D) 12:7
- (E) 15:8

28 $\frac{1}{4}$ boys and $\frac{1}{6}$ girls play soccer at the Union High School, The ratio of boys : girls is 2 : 1. Calculate the fraction of students playing soccer.

- (A) $\frac{1}{24}$
- (B) $\frac{5}{24}$
- (C) $\frac{2}{9}$
- (D) $\frac{1}{3}$
- (E) $\frac{5}{12}$

29 If a sweater sells for $48 after a 25 percent markdown, what was its original price?

- (A) $56
- (B) $60
- (C) $64
- (D) $65
- (E) $72

30 George requires 10 days to completely build a house, while his friend requires 8 days to do the same job. If two masons who work at the same rate as George are allowed to work together with him and his friend, how long will it take them to complete the same job?

- (A) 2.4 days
- (B) 2.5 days
- (C) 9.8 days
- (D) 18 days
- (E) 38 days

31 The average laptop price today is $700. If the average laptop price 5 years ago was 75% of the average laptop price today, what was the percentage increase in the average laptop price over the past 5 years?

- (A) 15%
- (B) 20%
- (C) $33\frac{1}{3}$%
- (D) 36%
- (E) 50%

32 If 780 is decreased by 75% and then increased by x percent, the resulting value would be 234. What is the value of x?

- (A) 20%
- (B) 40%
- (C) 60%
- (D) 80%
- (E) 120%

33 What is the eighth term in a series in which the nth term is $n^2(n-1)$?

- (A) 56
- (B) 324
- (C) 448
- (D) 512
- (E) 674

34 When $\frac{y}{x} > y$, which of the following statements could be true?

Indicate all that apply.

- [A] y is infinite
- [B] x is infinite
- [C] $y < 0$ and $x < 0$
- [D] $y > 1$ and $x > 1$
- [E] $y > 0$ and $0 < x < 1$
- [F] None of the above

35 The product of two different non-negative integers less than 10 is the square of another integer less than 10. The difference of these numbers is 6. Which is the larger number?

☐

36 If $\frac{x}{y} = \frac{5}{8}$, then what is the value of $\dfrac{y(x+y)(\frac{x}{y}-1)}{x(x-y)(\frac{x}{y}+1)}$?

☐

37 150 regular size chocolate bars include 10 lbs. of sugar total. When promotional size bars are made 20% more sugar is needed. How many pounds of sugar will be required to make 250 promotional size chocolates?

☐ lbs

Practice Set 2: Medium

38 Integers m and n when individually divided by the number 5, their remainders are 2 and 1 respectively.

Quantity A	**Quantity B**
Remainder obtained when sum of m and n is divided by 5	Remainder obtained when product of m and n is divided by 5

- Ⓐ Quantity A is greater.
- Ⓑ Quantity B is greater.
- Ⓒ The two quantities are equal.
- Ⓓ The relationship cannot be determined from the information given.

39 The positive numbers A and B are not divisible by 9.

Quantity A	**Quantity B**
The remainder when A + B is divided by 9	0

- Ⓐ Quantity A is greater.
- Ⓑ Quantity B is greater.
- Ⓒ The two quantities are equal.
- Ⓓ The relationship cannot be determined from the information given.

40 The LCM of the numbers x and y is xy and the LCM of the numbers x and z is xz where x, y, and z are all positive.

Quantity A	**Quantity B**
LCM of y and z	yz

- Ⓐ Quantity A is greater.
- Ⓑ Quantity B is greater.
- Ⓒ The two quantities are equal.
- Ⓓ The relationship cannot be determined from the information given.

Chapter 3: Arithmetic

41 Use the expression $\sqrt{x^2 - 3x - 18}$

Quantity A	Quantity B
The minimum value of a positive solution for x to create a real number for the expression.	The absolute value of maximum value of a negative solution for x to create a real number for the expression.

- (A) Quantity A is greater.
- (B) Quantity B is greater.
- (C) The two quantities are equal.
- (D) The relationship cannot be determined from the information given.

42 x is a positive integer.

Quantity A	Quantity B
$\dfrac{\dfrac{3x}{8}}{\dfrac{6}{(x+2)}}$	$\dfrac{x^2}{16} + \dfrac{x}{8}$

- (A) Quantity A is greater.
- (B) Quantity B is greater.
- (C) The two quantities are equal.
- (D) The relationship cannot be determined from the information given.

43 A field grows three different types of trees: oak, maple, and walnut. The ratio of oak to maple trees is 2:3 and the ratio of maple to walnut is 4:5. There are a total of 105 trees.

Quantity A	Quantity B
Number of walnut trees	35

- (A) Quantity A is greater.
- (B) Quantity B is greater.
- (C) The two quantities are equal.
- (D) The relationship cannot be determined from the information given.

44 Anna, Beatrice and Charlotte have $2,200 between them. After Anna spends 50% of her money, Beatrice spends 75% of her money and Charlotte spends 80% of hers, they are each left with similar amounts.

Quantity A	Quantity B
The initial amount of money owned by Beatrice	The amount of money spent by Charlotte

- (A) Quantity A is greater.
- (B) Quantity B is greater.
- (C) The two quantities are equal.
- (D) The relationship cannot be determined from the information given.

45 The price of product A is $\dfrac{2}{3}$ the price of product B. The sales revenue of product B was $\dfrac{6}{13}$ of the total sales revenue of product A and B combined.

Quantity A	Quantity B
Amount of product A sold	Twice the amount of product B sold

- (A) Quantity A is greater.
- (B) Quantity B is greater.
- (C) The two quantities are equal.
- (D) The relationship cannot be determined from the information given.

46

Quantity A	Quantity B
$(2)^4 (8)^{-\frac{2}{3}}$	$(4)^{\frac{5}{2}} (16)^{-\frac{3}{4}}$

- (A) Quantity A is greater.
- (B) Quantity B is greater.
- (C) The two quantities are equal.
- (D) The relationship cannot be determined from the information given.

47 A is the unit digit of the decimal 0.A and B is the hundredth digit of the decimal 0.10B where A and B are nonzero integers.

Quantity A   **Quantity B**

$\dfrac{0.A}{0.10B}$ 9

(A) Quantity A is greater.
(B) Quantity B is greater.
(C) The two quantities are equal.
(D) The relationship cannot be determined from the information given.

48 a, b, and c are positive integers

$(b+c)^a = 81$

$a \neq b \neq c$

Quantity A   **Quantity B**

a $b+c$

(A) Quantity A is greater.
(B) Quantity B is greater.
(C) The two quantities are equal.
(D) The relationship cannot be determined from the information given.

49

```
   R
  +S
  +T
  ---
  1W
```

In the addition problem above, R, S, and T are different digits that are multiples of 3, and W is a digit.

Quantity A   **Quantity B**

W 8

(A) Quantity A is greater.
(B) Quantity B is greater.
(C) The two quantities are equal.
(D) The relationship cannot be determined from the information given.

50 Series A is defined as $A_n = A_{n-1} - 4(n-5)$ and $A_1 = 5$.

Quantity A   **Quantity B**

The sum of A_1 to A_4 The sum of A_5 to A_8

(A) Quantity A is greater.
(B) Quantity B is greater.
(C) The two quantities are equal.
(D) The relationship cannot be determined from the information given.

51 Jeremy goes for a walk in the countryside at a speed of 4 mph. If he had walked at 6 mph he would have walked 9 miles more in the same time.

Quantity A   **Quantity B**

The time that Jeremy   The time it would take
walked   Jeremy to walk
                        22 miles at 5 mph

(A) Quantity A is greater.
(B) Quantity B is greater.
(C) The two quantities are equal.
(D) The relationship cannot be determined from the information given.

52

Given: $A = \dfrac{3}{4} - \dfrac{5}{4} + \dfrac{9}{4}$, $B = \dfrac{3}{6} - \dfrac{5}{12} + \dfrac{7}{24}$, and $C = \dfrac{3}{8} + \dfrac{1}{8}$.

Quantity A   **Quantity B**

C% of (A + B) $\dfrac{17}{160}$

(A) Quantity A is greater.
(B) Quantity B is greater.
(C) The two quantities are equal.
(D) The relationship cannot be determined from the information given.

Chapter 3: Arithmetic

53. Manny's weekly income is 72 percent of Fran's weekly income. Manny's weekly income is $648.

Quantity A	Quantity B
Fran's weekly income	$900

Ⓐ Quantity A is greater.
Ⓑ Quantity B is greater.
Ⓒ The two quantities are equal.
Ⓓ The relationship cannot be determined from the information given.

54. The total cost of 2 pencils, a notebook, and 5 erasers is $6.25. The total cost of 1 pencil, 2 notebooks, and 3 erasers is $7.75. The ratio of the cost of an eraser to a pencil is 1:4.

Quantity A	Quantity B
The cost of a notebook	$2

Ⓐ Quantity A is greater.
Ⓑ Quantity B is greater.
Ⓒ The two quantities are equal.
Ⓓ The relationship cannot be determined from the information given.

55.

$n \neq 0$

$n \neq -\dfrac{1}{2}$

$n \neq -1$

Quantity A	Quantity B
$\dfrac{1}{1+\dfrac{1}{1+\dfrac{1}{n}}}$	$\dfrac{n+1}{2n+1}$

Ⓐ Quantity A is greater.
Ⓑ Quantity B is greater.
Ⓒ The two quantities are equal.
Ⓓ The relationship cannot be determined from the information given.

56. The sum of an arithmetic series is 85, with $a_1 = 4$ and $a_n = 6$.

Quantity A	Quantity B
The number of terms in the series	15

Ⓐ Quantity A is greater.
Ⓑ Quantity B is greater.
Ⓒ The two quantities are equal.
Ⓓ The relationship cannot be determined from the information given.

57. If x is an odd integer and if y is an even integer, then $x^2 - y^2$ is always which of the following?

I. An odd integer
II. An even integer
III. The square of an integer

Ⓐ I only
Ⓑ II only
Ⓒ III only
Ⓓ I and III
Ⓔ II and III

58. Stella has some coins with her. She can bundle the coins equally into 6 bags with no coins left over. She can also pack the coins equally into 4 bags with no coins left over. However, when she bundles them into 7 bags, she has one coin left over. What is the least number of coins Stella could have?

Ⓐ 12
Ⓑ 25
Ⓒ 29
Ⓓ 36
Ⓔ 48

Practice Set 2: Medium

59. Integers are related as follows, $a = 2b$, $c = -3b$, and b is a negative integer.

    Quantity A $\quad\quad$ **Quantity B**

    $\dfrac{a^2 b^4}{c^3}$ $\quad\quad\quad$ $\dfrac{(-a)^2(-b)^4}{(-c)^3}$

    (A) Quantity A is greater.
    (B) Quantity B is greater.
    (C) The two quantities are equal.
    (D) The relationship cannot be determined from the information given.

60. On a sale, John bought one tie at 60% off and one pair of shoes at 30% off. If he paid $64 less for the tie than for the shoes and he spent a total of $104, what was the initial price of the tie?

    (A) 46
    (B) 50
    (C) 52
    (D) 54
    (E) 56

61. In the last 5 years, the price of new Brand x car increased 30 percent. If it is assumed that the percent increase in the next 5 year period will be the same, then what will be the percent increase in the price of a new Brand x car over the entire 10 year period?

    (A) 15%
    (B) 30%
    (C) 39%
    (D) 60%
    (E) 69%

62. Which month will it be after 132 weeks of September? (Assume 4 weeks = 1 month)

    (A) June
    (B) August
    (C) September
    (D) October
    (E) November

63. Of the total number of days in a week, what fraction of them occurs only 52 times in a leap year?

    (A) $\dfrac{1}{7}$
    (B) $\dfrac{2}{7}$
    (C) $\dfrac{3}{7}$
    (D) $\dfrac{4}{7}$
    (E) $\dfrac{5}{7}$

64. Pam makes pies and jam pints with strawberries. This year, Pam had s grams of strawberries, of which she utilized 40% to make pies and the rest for jam pints. Each pie needs p grams of strawberries while each jam pint needs j grams. Choose the following option that gives the total jam pints Pam can make?

    (A) $\dfrac{2s}{5p}$
    (B) $\dfrac{2s}{5j}$
    (C) $\dfrac{3s}{5j}$
    (D) $\dfrac{3p}{5s}$
    (E) $\dfrac{3sj}{5}$

Chapter 3: Arithmetic

65 A chest of drawers is shaped like a rectangular prism. It has a height of 42 inches, a length of 38 inches and a width of 30 inches. There are 5 identical drawers in total inside the chest. The ratio of the drawers height: length: width is 2:9:7. What are the height, length and width of the drawers if only 7,560 cubic inches of the chest's volume are not occupied by drawers?

- A) Height = 7 inches, Length = 37 inches, Width = 29 inches
- B) Height = 7 inches, Length = 36 inches, Width = 29 inches
- C) Height = 8 inches, Length = 36 inches, Width = 28 inches
- D) Height = 8 inches, Length = 36 inches, Width = 29 inches
- E) Height = 8 inches, Length = 37 inches, Width = 29 inches

66 Magazine A has a total of 28 pages, 16 of which are advertisements and 12 of which are articles. Magazine B has a total of 35 pages, all of them either articles or advertisements. If the ratio of the number of pages of advertisements to the number of pages of articles is the same for both magazines, then magazine B has how many more pages of advertisements than magazines A?

- A) 2
- B) 3
- C) 4
- D) 5
- E) 6

67 If $(x-2)^2 = (x-3)^2$, then $x = ?$

- A) $\frac{1}{2}$
- B) $\frac{3}{2}$
- C) $\frac{5}{2}$
- D) $\frac{7}{2}$
- E) $\frac{9}{2}$

68 If $\dfrac{1}{1+\dfrac{1}{1+x}} = 4$, then $x = ?$

- A) $-\frac{1}{4}$
- B) $-\frac{7}{3}$
- C) $\frac{4}{3}$
- D) $\frac{5}{2}$
- E) $\frac{7}{3}$

69 Charles works in a factory. For the first eight hours, he earns $20 per hour and for the next 2 hours, his salary is $30 per hour. Beyond 10 hours his salary is $40 per hour. In a single shift if he earns $340, how many hours long was the shift?

- A) 11 hours
- B) 12 hours
- C) 13 hours
- D) 14 hours
- E) 15 hours

Practice Set 2: Medium

70 If x, y, and z are integers such that $2xy + 3z$ is even, then which of the following CANNOT be true?

- (A) x is odd
- (B) $2x$ is even
- (C) xy is odd
- (D) z is odd
- (E) $x + y$ is even

71 If $m < -4$, which of the following has the greatest value?

- (A) $\dfrac{1}{(1-m)^2}$
- (B) $\dfrac{1}{(m-1)^2}$
- (C) $\dfrac{1}{(m+4)^2}$
- (D) $\dfrac{1}{m+6}$
- (E) $\dfrac{1}{m^2 - 8}$

72 What is the units digit of the product $(23^{31})(24^{32})(25^{33})$?

- (A) 0
- (B) 1
- (C) 2
- (D) 3
- (E) 4

73

Quantity A	Quantity B
$\sqrt{\dfrac{9^4 - 3^4}{3^8}}$	$\sqrt[2]{(3^5 + 9^2)(3^5 - 9^2)}$

- (A) Quantity A is greater.
- (B) Quantity B is greater.
- (C) The two quantities are equal.
- (D) The relationship cannot be determined from the information given.

74 If $a^2 b = 12^2$, where b is odd, then a is divisible by all of the following EXCEPT

- (A) 3
- (B) 4
- (C) 6
- (D) 9
- (E) 12

75 How many decimal places will the decimal equivalent of $\dfrac{1}{2^9 5^{12}} + \dfrac{1}{5^9 2^{12}}$ have?

- (A) 10
- (B) 12
- (C) 14
- (D) 15
- (E) 16

76 Let x be the 4023rd digit to the right of the decimal place for the decimal $0.\overline{41256}$ and y be the 89th digit to the right of the decimal place for the decimal $0.\overline{389}$. What is the value of x^y?

- (A) 1
- (B) 64
- (C) 125
- (D) 256
- (E) 65536

77 If a and b are integers and $\dfrac{a}{b} = 1.80$, which of the following CANNOT be a value of a?

- (A) −45
- (B) −27
- (C) 10
- (D) 18
- (E) 36

Chapter 3: Arithmetic

78. The ratio of SUVs to compact cars in a lot is 4:9. A new shipment of 14 SUVs arrived and now the ratio is 2:3. How many compact cars are in the lot?

- (A) 18
- (B) 21
- (C) 28
- (D) 54
- (E) 63

79. A person paid x dollars for a full tank of gasoline. The car gets 43 miles per gallon on the highway and 38 miles per gallon on regular roadways. If gas costs $3.45 per gallon, how many more miles would a person be able to travel on one tank of gas driving on a highway compared to a regular roadway?

- (A) $\dfrac{x}{345}$
- (B) $\dfrac{100x}{69}$
- (C) $\dfrac{5}{x}$
- (D) $\dfrac{69}{100x}$
- (E) $\dfrac{20x}{69}$

80. A particular vehicle dealer sells only cars and trucks. The ratio of cars to trucks is 3:4, the ratio of four-wheel-drive trucks to two-wheel-drive trucks is 7:3, and the ratio of luxury cars to non-luxury cars is 3:2? If there are 108 luxury cars, what is the ratio of two-wheel-drive trucks to non-luxury cars?

- (A) 1:1
- (B) 1:2
- (C) 2:3
- (D) 3:2
- (E) 14:9

81. At a casino there are three tables. The payoff at the first table is 10: 1; at the second, 30: 1; and at the third, 40: 1. If a woman bets $10 at each table and wins at two of the tables, what is the difference between her maximum and minimum possible gross winnings?

- (A) $200
- (B) $300
- (C) $400
- (D) $500
- (E) $600

82. Win : loss ratio of a basketball team is 3:1. After they won 6-straight games, the ratio changed to 5:1. How many games did the team win before it won the 6-straight games?

- (A) 3
- (B) 6
- (C) 9
- (D) 15
- (E) 24

83. The AM (Arithmetic Mean) of 6 numbers is 24. Find the AM of 2 numbers, if the sum of the other 4 numbers is 96.

- (A) 12
- (B) 24
- (C) 48
- (D) 72
- (E) 96

84. Tom is t years old, which is 3 times Becky's age. In terms of t, after how many years Tom will be just twice as old as Becky?

- (A) $\dfrac{t}{3}$
- (B) $\dfrac{t}{2}$
- (C) $\dfrac{2t}{2}$
- (D) t
- (E) $\dfrac{3t}{2}$

Practice Set 2: Medium

85. For which values of x is the statement $x^3 > x^2$ true?

    A) All values of x
    B) $x > 0$
    C) $x > 1$ or $x < -1$
    D) $-1 < x < 1$
    E) $x > 1$

86. Richard sold a valuable painting for $1,395, and he incurred a loss. Had he bought it for 3% less and sold it for $351 more, he would have made a 20% profit. What is the loss percentage that Richard incurred?

    A) 2%
    B) 5%
    C) 7%
    D) 10%
    E) 12%

87. 60% of the trees in a section of forest are maple and birch in a ratio of 3 :5. If there are a total of 440 trees in this section of forest, how many are birch?

    A) 33
    B) 99
    C) 165
    D) 264
    E) 275

88. 1200 kg of apples is purchased for $3000. It is sold in such a way that after selling the whole quantity, the quantum of loss is equal to the amount obtained by selling 300 kg of apples.

Quantity A	**Quantity B**
$1.80	Sales price per kg of apples

    A) Quantity A is greater.
    B) Quantity B is greater.
    C) The two quantities are equal.
    D) The relationship cannot be determined from the information given.

89. Cylinder A and Cylinder B have the same height. The ratio of the volume of a Cylinder A to Cylinder B is 36:49. What is the ratio of the surface area of Cylinder A to Cylinder B?

    A) $\dfrac{(h+6)}{(h+7)}$
    B) $\dfrac{36h}{49h}$
    C) $\dfrac{6}{7h}$
    D) $\dfrac{6(h+6)}{7(h+7)}$
    E) $\dfrac{36h+6}{49h+7}$

90. A prize of $600 is to be distributed among 20 winners, each of whom must be awarded at least $20. If $\dfrac{2}{5}$ of the prize will be distributed to $\dfrac{3}{5}$ of the winners, what is the greatest possible individual award?

    A) $20
    B) $25
    C) $200
    D) $220
    E) $300

91. If the five vowels are repeated continuously in the pattern $a, e, i, o, u, a, e, i, o, u$, and so on, what vowel will the 327th letter be?

    A) a
    B) e
    C) i
    D) o
    E) u

Chapter 3: Arithmetic

92 If $a_1 = \frac{1}{3}$ and $a_6 = 768$, what is the sum of the geometric series?

- A) $\frac{3075}{4}$
- B) 896
- C) $\frac{4095}{4}$
- D) 1024
- E) $\frac{5000}{3}$

93 A fundraiser allocated its funds to 4 different charities. Charity A received $\frac{1}{3}$ of the funds. Charity B received $\frac{2}{5}$ of what was left after Charity A's funds were disbursed. Charity C received $\frac{1}{2}$ of what was left after Charity B received their funds.

The final $9378 was given to Charity D. What was the total funds that the fundraiser gave to all 4 charities?

- A) $46,890
- B) $93,780
- C) $124,620
- D) $156,710
- E) $234,450

94 If $x(a + b)$ is an even integer, which of the following will always result in this statement being true?

I. x is odd
II. $a > b$
III. $a = b + 2$

- A) I only
- B) II only
- C) III only
- D) I and II
- E) I and III

95 Which of the following statements must be true?

I. If n^2 is even, then n^3 is even.
II. If $2n$ is even, then n is odd.
III. If n is even, then $2n - 1$ is odd.

Indicate all that apply.

- A) I only
- B) II only
- C) III only
- D) I and II only
- E) I and III only
- F) I, II and III

96 30 liters of a certain drink is to be divided between the students of 5th and 10th class. A school teacher is appointed on that duty. He gave $\frac{3}{7}$ liter drink to each of 5th class student and then the remaining drink with $\frac{3}{2}$ liters to each of 10th class student. If there are 21 students of 5th class, then what will be the number of students of 10th class and what will be their percentage to the total number of students?

Indicate all that apply.

- A) 12 students
- B) 14 students
- C) 16 students
- D) 40%
- E) 50%
- F) 60%

Practice Set 2: Medium

97 The AM (Arithmetic Mean) of 3 successive numbers is M. Which of the following statements could be true to fulfill the previous statement?

   I. One of the three numbers must be M
   II. The AM of two numbers is M
   III. M is an integer

Indicate all that apply.

[A] I
[B] II
[C] III
[D] I & II only
[E] I & III only
[F] None of the above

98 Sarah's weight is 25 pounds more than that of Tony. If together they weigh 205 pounds, what will be the weight of Sarah and Tony approximately in kilograms?

   Assume 1 pound = 0.4535 kilograms

Indicate all that apply.

[A] 41
[B] 45
[C] 48
[D] 50
[E] 52

99 For which of the following values of x is $\frac{2^x}{x^2}$ an integer?

Indicate all that apply.

[A] 1
[B] 2
[C] 3
[D] 4
[E] 5

100 If $x < 0$ and $0 < \frac{xy}{z} < 1$, which of the following must be true?

Indicate all that apply.

[A] $y < 0$
[B] $z < 0$
[C] $yz < 0$
[D] $y < x$
[E] $xy < z$

101 If the ratio of Patriots fans to Jets fans at a sports game is 6:5. Which of the following statements could be true?

Indicate all that apply.

[A] More than half of the fans at the game are Patriots fans.
[B] If there are 72 Patriots fans at the game, there are 132 total fans (for both teams) in attendance.
[C] If there are 110 total fans at the game, there are 10 more Patriots fans than Jets fans in attendance.
[D] There are more Jets fans at the game than Patriots fans.

Chapter 3: Arithmetic

102 If one of the pairs of side lengths of a rectangle is reduced by 40%, which of the following must be true?

Indicate all that apply.

- [A] the new area is 60% of the original area
- [B] the original perimeter experienced a 45% percent decrease
- [C] the new area is 60% less than the original area

103 If $x > 0$, which of the following expressions are equal to 1.8% of $\frac{4x}{5}$?

Indicate all that apply.

- [A] 9% of $\frac{4x}{5}$
- [B] 20% of $\frac{9x}{250}$
- [C] 18% of $4x$
- [D] $\frac{9x}{1250}$

104 In a survey, 70% of the 5000 respondents were of voting age and at least 35% of those respondents owned a home. Which of the following could be the number of respondents of voting age that did NOT own a home?

Indicate all such values.

- [A] 875
- [B] 1225
- [C] 2275
- [D] 2800

105 A survey reported a 5:3 ratio of votes for Candidate A compared to Candidate B. If there were at least 720 people surveyed, which of the following could be the amount of votes for Candidate B?

Indicate all such values.

- [A] 90
- [B] 270
- [C] 460
- [D] 540
- [E] 840

106 Toy train cars made of blocks of wood either 6 inches long or 7 inches long can be hooked together to make longer trains. 6 inches trains can be hooked only in pairs. Which of the following train lengths can be made by hooking together the 6-inch train cars, 7-inch train cars, or a combination of both?

Indicate all that apply.

- [A] 30 inches
- [B] 31 inches
- [C] 38 inches
- [D] 40 inches
- [E] 46 inches
- [F] 51 inches
- [G] 53 inches
- [H] 59 inches

107 A number line is divided into 5 evenly spaced tick marks. The length between each mark is x, where x is a prime number. What could be the range of values on the number line?

Indicate all such values.

- [A] 4
- [B] 5
- [C] 12
- [D] 16
- [E] 20

Practice Set 3: Hard

108. If x and y are positive integers such that the remainder is 5 when a is divided by b, what is the smallest possible value of $a + b$?

109. A survey of 100 individuals revealed that 96% are actively using Instagram and 85% are active on their Pinterest accounts. If 83% of the surveyed individuals have both Instagram and Pinterest accounts, what percent of these individuals do not use Instagram or Pinterest?

    ____%

110. What is the greatest integer value of x such that $\dfrac{36^x}{216^8} < 1?$

111. If $\dfrac{2 + \dfrac{4}{n}}{4 + \dfrac{2}{n}} = \dfrac{3}{8}$, what is the value of n?

112.

    A and B form $\dfrac{1}{2}$ of the square, while C and D form the other $\dfrac{1}{2}$ of the square. The area of A is $\dfrac{1}{2}$ the area of B, while the area of C is $\dfrac{2}{5}$ the area of D. What fraction of the square is the area of C? Give the ratio in the simplest form.

    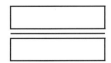

113. If a, b, and c are consecutive odd integers such as $a < b < c$ and $abc = 9177$, what is the value of c?

114. If a is 70% of b, b is 60% of c, and c is 80% of d, then d is what percent of $3a$?

115. If $\dfrac{16x}{5} = \dfrac{5}{4y}$ and $\dfrac{4x}{3} = \dfrac{a}{2y}$, then what is the value of a?

Practice Set 3: Hard

116. When an integer a is divided by 3, the remainder is 2. When an integer b is divided by 6, the remainder is 1. What is the remainder when $a^2 + b^2$ is divided by 6?

    A) 1
    B) 2
    C) 3
    D) 4
    E) 5

117. If x, y, z, and w are four consecutive integers where $x^{y+z} = w$, what is the lowest possible value of $x + y + z + w$?

    A) −3
    B) −2
    C) 0
    D) 2
    E) 6

Chapter 3: Arithmetic

118 For every positive integer n, the nth term of the sequence is given by $a_n = -\dfrac{1}{n+1} + \dfrac{1}{n}$. What is the sum of the first 50 terms?

- A) $\dfrac{1}{50}$
- B) 1
- C) $\dfrac{51}{50}$
- D) $\dfrac{26}{25}$
- E) $\dfrac{53}{50}$

119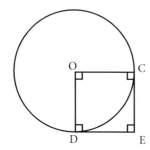

Circumference of the circle O is 12π. What is the ratio of the area bounded by the circle, CE, and DE to the area of the square?

- A) $4\pi - 1$
- B) $1 - \dfrac{\pi}{4}$
- C) $\dfrac{\pi}{4} - 1$
- D) $\dfrac{1}{4} + 1$
- E) $4\pi + 1$

120 Given A is the least common multiple of 80, 450, and 735, which of the following is NOT a factor of A?

- A) 245
- B) 315
- C) 980
- D) 1512
- E) 3528

121 The population of a school increased *a*% from 1990 to 2000 and *b*% from 2000 to 2010. If the total population increased by 75% of the original amount and the increase in the second decade was double the increase in the first, what is the value of *b*?

- A) 20
- B) 25
- C) 40
- D) 50
- E) 60

122 A scientist purchases two compounds to create a solution. Compound A and compound B cost the same one year and the next year the price of compound A increased by 40% and the price of compound B decreased by 15%. A solution of equal parts compound A and compound B cost the scientist $22.50 per 5 ounces. What is the new price of compound A?

- A) $4.00
- B) $4.50
- C) $5.60
- D) $6.50
- E) $7.60

123 If $a < 0 < b < 1$, which of the following is the least?

- A) ab
- B) $\dfrac{a}{b^2}$
- C) $a - b$
- D) $\dfrac{a}{b}$
- E) $\dfrac{a}{a-b}$

124 Two integers *x* and *y* are in the ratio 7:8. Which of the following must be true?

Indicate all such options.

- A) The greatest prime factor of $x + y$ is 5
- B) $x + y$ is odd
- C) xy is even
- D) x must be less than y
- E) y must be divisible by 4

Practice Set 3: Hard

125 If n and m are even integers, which of the following are even integers?

Indicate all that apply.

- [A] $3mn$
- [B] $(3m+2)(3n-2)$
- [C] $3(2m-3)(3n-1)$
- [D] $5(5m+2)(5n-6)$
- [E] $\frac{1}{64}m^3n^3$
- [F] m^2n^3

126 The remainder when x is divided by 2 is a. The remainder when y is divided by 3 is b. Which of the following would be sufficient to solve for the relationship between a and b to determine which one is greater?

Indicate all such options.

- [A] a is an odd integer
- [B] ab is greater than 1
- [C] a is odd and b is even
- [D] $a + b$ is a nonzero

127 For which of the integers n, where $0 < n < 25$, is $(n-1)!$ a multiple of n?

Indicate all such options.

- [A] 2
- [B] 6
- [C] 12
- [D] 15
- [E] 23

128 If $A = \frac{2}{3}$ of $(\frac{3}{4}+x)$, $B = \frac{3}{5}$ of $(\frac{1}{2}+y)$, and $C = \frac{5}{8}$ of $(\frac{x}{y}+1)$, which of the following statements are true?

Indicate all such statements.

- [A] $30(A + B) = 20x + 18y + 24$
- [B] $10(B + C) = 6y + 6xy + 6$
- [C] $(B + A) = 4x + 4y + 5$
- [D] $24y(A + C) = 16xy + 15x + 27y$

129 The price of a product was originally $P. It was reduced by x% and then reduced by x% again. Which of the following are true?

Indicate all such options.

- [A] The final price of the book after both discounts is $P\left(\frac{x}{100}\right)^2$
- [B] The final price of the book after both discounts is $P\left(1-\frac{x}{100}\right)^2$
- [C] The total percentage decrease in the price of the book after both discounts is $2\left(\frac{x}{100}\right)$
- [D] The total percentage decrease in the price of the book after both discounts is $2\left(\frac{1}{x}\right)-\frac{x}{100x}$

130 There are 25 red jelly beans and 25 yellow jelly beans in a jar. What is the least possible number of jellybeans that can be removed to get a ratio of 1:3 red jelly beans to yellow jelly beans?

[   ]

Answer Key

Q. No.	Correct Answer	Your Answer
1	C	
2	B	
3	A	
4	A	
5	B	
6	D	
7	B	
8	A	
9	B	
10	C	
11	B	
12	C	
13	D	
14	C	
15	C	
16	A	
17	C	
18	B	
19	C	
20	B	
21	D	
22	A	
23	E	
24	C	
25	D	
26	D	
27	E	
28	C	
29	C	
30	A	
31	C	
32	A	
33	C	
34	C,E	

Q. No.	Correct Answer	Your Answer
35	8	
36	$\frac{8}{5}$	
37	20	
38	A	
39	D	
40	D	
41	A	
42	C	
43	A	
44	C	
45	B	
46	C	
47	B	
48	D	
49	D	
50	C	
51	A	
52	B	
53	C	
54	A	
55	C	
56	A	
57	A	
58	D	
59	A	
60	B	
61	E	
62	A	
63	E	
64	C	
65	C	
66	C	
67	C	

Q. No.	Correct Answer	Your Answer
68	B	
69	C	
70	D	
71	C	
72	A	
73	B	
74	D	
75	E	
76	D	
77	C	
78	E	
79	B	
80	A	
81	B	
82	B	
83	B	
84	A	
85	E	
86	C	
87	C	
88	A	
89	D	
90	D	
91	B	
92	C	
93	A	
94	C	
95	E	
96	B,D	
97	A,B,C	
98	A,E	
99	A,B,D	
100	C,E	

Q. No.	Correct Answer	Your Answer
101	A,B,C	
102	A,B	
103	B,D	
104	A,B,C	
105	B,D,E	
106	B,C,D,H	
107	C	
108	17	
109	2%	
110	11	
111	$-\frac{13}{2}$	
112	$\frac{1}{7}$	
113	23	
114	100.8	
115	$\frac{24}{25}$	
116	E	
117	B	
118	C	
119	B	
120	D	
121	C	
122	C	
123	B	
124	C,D,E	
125	A,B,D,F	
126	B,C	
127	B,C,D	
128	A,D	
129	B,D	
130	30	

Practice Set 1 (Easy): Answers & Explanations

1 **Choice C is correct.** The values of a, b, and c differ by 2 as they are consecutive even integers.
Let $a = a$, $b = a + 2$, $c = a + 4$.

Now substitute these variables into Quantity A, simplify, and compare.

Quantity A:
$a + b + c$
$a + (a + 2) + (a + 4)$
$3a + 6$

Quantity B:
$3a + 6$

Choice A is incorrect because Quantity A is not greater than Quantity B. **Choice B** is incorrect because Quantity B is equal to Quantity A. **Choice D** is incorrect because it is possible to use the given information to make a comparison between Quantity A and Quantity B.

2 **Choice B is correct** because Quantity B is larger than Quantity A. Compare Quantity A and Quantity B.

Quantity A:
42% of 165 is 1650.42 = 69.3.

Quantity B: The number which 80 is 20% is $N \times 0.20 = 80$, or $N = \dfrac{80}{0.20} = 400$.

Choice A is incorrect because Quantity A is less than Quantity B. **Choice C** is incorrect because it is not possible for the two quantities to be equal. **Choice D** is incorrect because it is possible to use the given information to make a comparison between Quantity A and Quantity B.

3 **Choice A is correct** because Quantity A is greater than Quantity B. Quantity A can be simplified by using factorial properties.
$\dfrac{11!}{5!} = \dfrac{11 \times 10 \times 9 \times 8 \times 7 \times 6 \times 5!}{5!} = 11 \times 10 \times 9 \times 8 \times 7 \times 6 = 332640$

Quantity B can be solved by finding the smallest 3 digit prime numbers. 101, 103 and 107. Their sum is 311.

Choice B is incorrect because Quantity B is less than Quantity A. **Choice C** is incorrect because it is not possible for the two quantities to be equal. **Choice D** is incorrect because it is possible to use the given information to make a comparison between Quantity A and Quantity B.

4 **Choice A is correct** because Quantity A is greater than Quantity B.

Quantity A: $7.88 divided by 2 equals $3.94.

Quantity B: $11.79 divided by 3 equals $3.93.

Choice B is incorrect because Quantity B is less than Quantity A. **Choice C** is incorrect because it is not possible for the two quantities to be equal. **Choice D** is incorrect because it is possible to use the given information to make a comparison between Quantity A and Quantity B.

5 **Choice B is correct** because Quantity B is greater than Quantity A. First, Quantity A must be 15 since 5 × 3 = 15. As for Quantity B, since there is 1 floor with 2 apartments and 4 floors with 4 apartments, the total number of apartments in the building is 18. So, Quantity B is greater.

Choice A is incorrect because Quantity A is less than Quantity B. **Choice C** is incorrect because it is not possible for the two quantities to be equal. **Choice D** is incorrect because it is possible to use the given information to make a comparison between Quantity A and Quantity B.

6 **Choice D is correct** because it is possible to get a situation where Quantity A is greater than or equal to Quantity B.

To get an answer where Quantity A is greater than Quantity B, you can use $x = 2$, $y = 4$, and $z = 1$ since the statement $\dfrac{x}{y} = \dfrac{z}{x}$ would be true, $\dfrac{2}{4} = \dfrac{1}{2}$. Therefore Quantity A being $y + z$ would equal $4 + 1$ which is 5.

Quantity B as $2x$ would equal $2(2) = 4$. In this scenario Quantity A is greater.

To get an answer where Quantity A is equal to Quantity B, you can use $x = 1$, $y = 1$, and $z = 1$ since the statement $\dfrac{x}{y} = \dfrac{z}{x}$ would be true, $\dfrac{1}{1} = \dfrac{1}{1}$. Therefore Quantity A being $y + z$ would equal $1 + 1$ which is 2. Quantity B as $2x$ would equal $2(1) = 2$. In this scenario Quantity A and Quantity B are equal.

Choice A is incorrect because Quantity A is only sometimes greater than Quantity B. **Choice B** is incorrect because Quantity B is never greater than Quantity A. **Choice C** is incorrect because Quantity A is only sometimes equal to Quantity B.

Chapter 3: Arithmetic

7. **Choice B is correct** because Quantity B is greater than Quantity A. Analyzing the data given in the two tables, we can see that the costs charged by both the laundries are in arithmetic progression.

At Laundry A, the cost progresses with weight as: $16, $18, $20, $22…

First term $a = \$16$

Common difference $d = \$18 - \$16 = \$2$

The cost of washing 30 pounds of cloth at Laundry A = 30th term

$$= a + (n - 1)d$$
$$= 16 + (30 - 1) \cdot 2$$
$$= 16 + 29 \times 2$$
$$= 16 + 58$$
$$= \$74$$

At Laundry B, the cost progresses with weight as: $10, $14, $18…

First term $a = \$6$

Common difference $d = 10 - 6 = \$4$

The cost of washing 30 pounds of cloth at Laundry B = 30th term

$$= a + (n - 1)d$$
$$= 6 + (30 - 1) \cdot 4$$
$$= 16 + 29 \times 4$$
$$= 16 + 116$$
$$= \$132$$

Laundry A charges $74 for washing 30 pounds of clothes, while Laundry B charges $132 for the same weight. Hence, Laundry B charges more for washing 30 pounds of clothes.

Choice A is incorrect because Quantity A is less than Quantity B. **Choice C** is incorrect because it is not possible for the two quantities to be equal. **Choice D** is incorrect because it is possible to use the given information to make a comparison between Quantity A and Quantity B.

8. **Choice A is correct** because there are 9 employees on the IT staff that are not enrolled in the company's health care which makes Quantity A greater than Quantity B.

To find out the value of Quantity A, use the fact that there are 28 legal staff members to complete the ratio of 3:4:7. If there are 28 legal staff members the ratio can be found to be 12:16:28. To find this use the ratio $\frac{3}{7} = \frac{x}{28}$ to get $84 = 7x$. Divide by 7 to get $x = 12$. Then use the fraction $\frac{4}{7} = \frac{y}{28}$ to get $112 = 7y$. Divide by 7 to get $y = 16$.

Since there are 12 IT staff members, you can find the number not enrolled by finding the percent not enrolled and multiplying it by 12. Since 25% are enrolled, that would mean 75% are not enrolled ($100\% - 25\% = 75\%$). To find 75% of 12, multiply 12 by 0.75 to get 9.

Choice B is incorrect because Quantity A is greater than Quantity B. **Choice C** is incorrect because the two quantities are not equal. **Choice D** is incorrect because it is possible to determine a relationship.

9. **Choice B is correct** because rewriting Quantity A as base 2 will allow for a comparison that concludes Quantity B will be less negative and therefore greater than Quantity A for all values of x that are odd negative integers.

Rewriting $\left(-\frac{1}{816}\right)^x$ as a base 2 would give you $\left(-2^{-34}\right)^x$.

In comparison to Quantity B, Quantity A will always be a negative integer raised to an odd power while Quantity B will always be a negative fraction. Any negative fraction will always be greater than a negative integer making Quantity B always greater than Quantity A.

Choice A is incorrect because a negative integer will always be less than a negative fraction. **Choice C** is incorrect because Quantity A does not equal Quantity B. **Choice D** is incorrect because there is a clear relationship between the two quantities.

10. **Choice C is correct** because both quantities are equal. To determine which quantity is greater we need to change both values back to scientific notation. Therefore, Quantity A can be written as $24.6 \times 10^3 = 2.46 \times 10^4$ and Quantity B can be written as $0.246 \times 10^5 = 2.46 \times 10^4$.

Choice A is incorrect because Quantity A is equal to Quantity B. **Choice B** is incorrect because Quantity B equals Quantity A. **Choice D** is incorrect because it is possible to use the given information to make a comparison between Quantity A and Quantity B.

11. **Choice B is correct** because Quantity B is greater than Quantity A. Evaluate each expression for Quantity A and Quantity B to determine the answer. We are adding, subtracting, multiplying, and dividing fractions.

- Add/Subtracting Fractions: Get a common denominator for both fractions, combine the numerators, and simplify the fraction.
- Multiplying Fractions: Multiply straight across the numerator and denominator to obtain your answer.
- Dividing Fractions: Keep the first fraction. Change the division to multiplication and take the reciprocal of the second fraction.

Simplify.

Quantity A: $\frac{1}{3} \div \frac{5}{9} + \frac{2}{5} \times \frac{4}{7} = \frac{1}{3} \times \frac{9}{5} + \frac{2}{5} \times \frac{4}{7}$

$= \frac{9}{15} + \frac{8}{35} = \frac{63}{105} + \frac{24}{105} = \frac{87}{105}$

Lowest common denominator is 105.

Quantity B: $\frac{1}{3} \div \frac{5}{7} + \frac{4}{5} \times \frac{4}{7} = \frac{1}{3} \times \frac{7}{5} + \frac{4}{5} \times \frac{4}{7}$

$= \frac{7}{15} + \frac{16}{35} = \frac{49}{105} + \frac{48}{105} = \frac{97}{105}$

Lowest common denominator is 105.

Both answers have the same denominator, the numerator is greater in Quantity B.

Choice A is incorrect because Quantity A is less than Quantity B. **Choice C is incorrect** because it is not possible for the two quantities to be equal. **Choice D is incorrect** because it is possible to use the given information to make a comparison between Quantity A and Quantity B.

12 **Choice C is correct** because since y is not between x and z it must be before or after x or before or after z. Due to the lengths of the segments, it is only possible for y to be before or after x. It cannot be after z since the length of segment xz is 12 and segment xy is 8 so segment xzy is not possible.

Since y must go before or after x, you could do segment zxy or yxz. In either case, the length between x and z would be 12 and the length between x and y would be 8. Add these values together to get 12 + 8 = 20 as the length from y to z.

Choice A is incorrect because Quantity A is equal to Quantity B. **Choice B is incorrect** because Quantity A is equal to Quantity B. **Choice D is incorrect** because it is possible to find a relationship between the quantities.

13 **Choice D is correct** because with the given information it is not possible to make a comparison between Quantity A and Quantity B.
This question has variables in it, so we should plug in.

Practice Set 1 (Easy): Answers & Explanations

We simply have to obey the rules that $\frac{m}{n} = \frac{2}{3}$ and $n \neq 3$. Let's start with $m = 4$ and $n = 6$. In this case, Quantity A becomes $\frac{7}{9}$ which is less than $\frac{5}{6}$, so we can eliminate A and C. Now let's try some weird numbers. How about $m = -6$ and $n = -9$? These satisfy the condition that $\frac{m}{n} = \frac{2}{3}$. In this case Quantity A becomes $\frac{-3}{-6}$, which is equal to $\frac{1}{2}$. This is larger than Quantity B, so we can eliminate B and our answer must be D.

Choice A is incorrect because Quantity A can be either less or greater than Quantity B. **Choice B is incorrect** because Quantity B can be either less or greater than Quantity A. **Choice C is incorrect** because the two quantities are not equal.

14 **Choice C is correct** because both quantities are equal.

Let the length be l and the width be w; $l:w = 4:3$, so

$$\frac{l}{w} = \frac{4}{3}$$

Expressing the length in terms of the width, we have

$$l = \frac{4}{3}w$$

The area is $l \times w = \frac{4}{3}w \times w = 108$

$$\frac{4}{3}w^2 = 108$$

$$w^2 = 108 \times \frac{3}{4} = 81; \ w = \pm 9$$

Since the length of a side must be a positive value, $w = 9$ inches

Length, $l = \frac{4}{3}w = \frac{4}{3} \times 9 = 12$ inches

Quantity A: The width of the rectangle = 9 inches
Quantity B: The square of the difference between the length and the width = $(12 - 9)^2 = 3^2 = 9$ inches

Choice A is incorrect because Quantity A is equal to Quantity B. **Choice B is incorrect** because Quantity B is equal to Quantity A. **Choice D is incorrect** because it is possible to use the given information to make a comparison between Quantity A and Quantity B.

Chapter 3: Arithmetic

15 **Choice C is correct** because Quantity A and Quantity B are equal. Usual time = 40 minutes
When his speed is 80% of his usual speed, new speed = 0.80 of usual speed = $\frac{4}{5}$ of usual speed.

Since the distance is the same, new time
= $\frac{5}{4}$ of Usual Time
= $\frac{5}{4}$ (40 minutes) = 50 minutes

Additional time = 50 – 40 = 10 minutes

Choice A is incorrect because Quantity A is equal to Quantity B. **Choice B** is incorrect because Quantity B is equal to Quantity A. **Choice D** is incorrect because it is possible to use the given information to make a comparison between Quantity A and Quantity B.

16 **Choice A is correct** because Quantity A is greater than Quantity B.
385 can be factorized into 385 = 5 × 7 × 11. This being the prime factorization it is unique. So $p = 5$, $q = 7$, $r = 11$.
$p + q + r = 5 + 7 + 11 = 23$

Choice B is incorrect because Quantity B is less than Quantity A. **Choice C** is incorrect because it is not possible for the two quantities to be equal.
Choice D is incorrect because it is possible to use the given information to make a comparison between Quantity A and Quantity B.

17 **Choice C is correct** because the 18th digit in $\frac{5}{7}$ is 5 and the 20th digit in $\frac{5}{11}$ is 5.
To find the 18th digit in $\frac{5}{7}$, look for a pattern in the decimals. The decimal version of the fraction is $0.\overline{714285}$ with digits repeating every 6 numbers. Divide 18 by 6 to find what number is in the 18th place and you will get a whole number. This means the 6th number is in the 18th place which would be 5.

To find the 20th digit in $\frac{5}{11}$, look for a pattern in the decimals. The decimal version of the fraction is $0.\overline{45}$ with digits repeating every 2 numbers. Divide 20 by 2 to find what number is in the 20th place and you will get a whole number. This means the 2nd number is in the 20th place which would be 5.

Choice A is incorrect because Quantity A is equal to Quantity B. **Choice B** is incorrect because Quantity A is equal to Quantity B. **Choice D** is incorrect because it is possible to find a relationship between the quantities.

18 **Choice B is correct** because the number of files the computer uploaded in 6 hours can be found to be 37,800 files. Convert 6 hours into seconds by multiplying by 3600 since there are 60 seconds in a minute and 60 minutes in an hour. This would give you 21,600 seconds. Divide this by 4 to figure out how many groups of 7 files were uploaded within the time frame to get 5400. Then multiply this number by 7 to get the total number of files uploaded which would be 37,800. Quantity B is 40,000 which is greater than 37,800.

Choice A is incorrect because 40,000 is larger than 37,800 **Choice C** is incorrect because the two quantities do not equal each other. **Choice D** is incorrect because it is possible to find a relationship between the quantities.

19 **Choice C is correct** because the obtained answer is 81. We can use the formula to calculate the first 10 values of S:

$S_1 = 3$
$S_2 = 3(3) – 3 = 6$
$S_3 = 3(6) – 3 = 15$
$S_4 = 3(15) – 3 = 42$
$S_5 = 3(42) – 3 = 123$
$S_5 – S_4 = 123 – 42 = 81$.

Alternatively, we could solve this problem by noticing the following pattern in the sequence:

$S_2 – S_1 = 3$ or 3^1
$S_3 – S_2 = 9$ or 3^2
$S_4 – S_3 = 27$ or 3^3

We could extrapolate this pattern to see that $S_5 – S_4 = 81$.

Choice A is incorrect because 79 less than the obtained value of $S_5 – S_4$. **Choice B** is incorrect because 80 is 1 less than the obtained value of $S_5 – S_4$. **Choice D** is incorrect because 82 overapproximates the obtained value of $S_5 – S_4$. **Choice E** is incorrect because 83 is greater than the obtained value of $S_5 – S_4$.

Practice Set 1 (Easy): Answers & Explanations

20 **Choice B is correct** because the obtained answer is 3.608×10^{10}. Multiply using the properties of exponents.
$(4.23 \times 10^4)(8.53 \times 10^5) = (4.23 \times 8.53) \times (10^4 \times 10^5)$
$36.08 \times 10^9 = 3.608 \times 10^{10}$

Choice A is incorrect because 3.608109 is not equivalent to the obtained value. **Choice C is incorrect** because 36.08×10^9 is less than the obtained value. **Choice D is incorrect** because 360.8×10^8 is less than the obtained value. **Choice E is incorrect** because 3.608×10^8 is not equivalent to the obtained value.

21 **Choice D is correct** because the odd factors of 45 are 1, 3, 5, 9, 15, and 45. When these values are added together, you get 78.

Choice A is incorrect because 45 is not a possible sum of all the odd factors of 45. **Choice B is incorrect** because 46 is a possible sum of only 2 odd factors of 1 and 45. **Choice C is incorrect** because 77 is less than the obtained value. **Choice E is incorrect** because 2025 overapproximates the possible sum of the odd factors.

22 **Choice A is correct** because calling the number x and y, $\frac{x+y}{2} = x\frac{3}{5}$, that is $\frac{x+y}{2x} = \frac{3}{5}$

Cross multiplying: $5x + 5y = 6x$, $5y = x$

Hence, one number is five times as large as the other, so their ratio is 1 : 5.

Alternatively, AM is 3 parts and One number is 5 parts. We know that 2 times AM = Sum of the two numbers. So, Sum = 6 parts, hence the smaller number is (6 – 5) parts = 1 part. Hence the ratio is 1 : 5

Choice B is incorrect because 1:4 is greater than the obtained ratio. **Choice C is incorrect** because 1:3 is greater than the obtained ratio. **Choice D is incorrect** because 1:2 is greater than the obtained ratio. **Choice E is incorrect** because 2:3 is not a possible ratio.

23 **Choice E is correct** because $\frac{c}{d} = \frac{3}{2}$.

Multiply the left side of the equation by $\frac{c}{c}$ and the right side by $\frac{d}{d}$.

$$\frac{c}{c} \times \frac{4}{\frac{2}{c} + \frac{5}{c}} = \frac{6}{\frac{9}{3d} + \frac{16}{4d}} \times \frac{d}{d}$$

Simplify.

$$\frac{4c}{2+5} = \frac{6d}{3+4}$$

$$\frac{4c}{7} = \frac{6d}{7}$$

Multiply both sides by 7.

$$4c = 6d$$

Divide by $4d$ on both sides.

$$\frac{c}{d} = \frac{6}{4}$$

Simplify

$$\frac{c}{d} = \frac{3}{2}$$

Choice A is incorrect because $\frac{2}{7}$ less than the obtained value. **Choice B is incorrect** because $\frac{4}{7}$ less than the obtained value. **Choice C is incorrect** because $\frac{2}{3}$ is the reciprocal of the obtained value. **Choice D is incorrect** because $\frac{7}{6}$ less than the obtained value.

24 **Choice C is correct** because $x + y = 0$.

Since both bases in either side of the equation are different primes, we can set the exponents of each respective base equal to one another:

$2x + 1 = 3x$, so $x = 1$
$2y - 1 = 3y$, so $y = -1$
Therefore, $x + y = 1 + (-1) = 0$.

Choice A is incorrect because –2 is less than the obtained value of $x + y$. **Choice B is incorrect** because –1 is not the obtained value of $x + y$. **Choice D is incorrect** because 1 is greater than the obtained value of $x + y$. **Choice E is incorrect** because 2 is greater than the obtained value of $x + y$.

25 **Choice D is correct** because the least common multiple of 24 and 32 is 96.

First, find the largest composite factors of 48 and 64. The factors of 48 are 1, 2, 3, 4, 6, 8, 12, 16, 24, and 48. The largest composite factor of 48 is 24. The factors of 64 are 1, 2, 4, 8, 16, 32 and 64. The largest composite factor of 64 is 32. The least common multiple of 24 and 32 is 96.

Choice A is incorrect because 12 is not a possible LCM of 24 and 32. **Choice B is incorrect** because 16 is less than the obtained value. **Choice C is incorrect** because 32 is less than the obtained value. **Choice E is incorrect** because 512 is an overapproximation of the obtained value.

Chapter 3: Arithmetic

26 **Choice D is correct** because the marked price is $400.

The buying price = $320 = 100%

Selling price percentage = buying price + profit
= 100% + 21.875%
= 121.875%

The selling price = 121.875/100 × 320 = $390

The selling price is 100% − 2.5% = 97.5% of the marked price

If the marked price percentage = 100%,

The marked price = $\frac{100}{97.5} \times 390 = \$400$

Choice A is incorrect because 328 is less than the obtained value. **Choice B** is incorrect because 380 is less than the obtained value. **Choice C** is incorrect because 390 is less than the obtained value. **Choice E** is incorrect because 410 is greater than the obtained value.

27 **Choice E is correct** because the obtained answer is 15:8. Parts of different ratios don't always refer to the same whole. In the classic ratio trap, two different ratios each share a common part that is represented by two different numbers. The two ratios do not refer to the same whole, so they are not in proportion to each other. To solve this type of problem, restate both ratios so that the numbers representing the common part (in this case dimes) are the same. Then all the parts will be in proportion and can be compared to each other. To find the ratio of quarters to nickels, restate both ratios so that the number of dimes is the same in both. We are given two ratios:

quarters: dimes = 5:2 *and dimes: nickels* = 3:4

The number corresponding to dimes in the first ratio is 2.

The number corresponding to dimes in the second ratio is 3.

To restate the ratios, find the least common multiple of 2 and 3.

The least common multiple of 2 and 3 is 6.

Restate the ratios with the number of dimes as 6:

quarters : dimes = 15 : 6 *and dimes: nickels* = 6:8

The ratios are still in their original proportions, but now they're in proportion to each other and they refer to the same whole.

The ratio of quarters to dimes to nickels is

15:6:8, so the ratio of quarters to nickels is 15:8, which is answer Choice E.

Choice A is incorrect because 5:4 is not a possible ratio of quarters to nickels. **Choice B** is incorrect because 7:5 does not correspond to the ratio of quarters to nickel. **Choice C** is incorrect because 10:6 less than the ratio of quarters to nickel. **Choice D** is incorrect because 12:7 less than the ratio of quarters to nickel.

28 **Choice C is correct** because $\frac{2}{9}$ of the student body play soccer.

The student body is $\frac{2}{3}$ male and $\frac{1}{3}$ female. So

$\left(\frac{1}{4} \times \frac{1}{3}\right) + \left(\frac{1}{6} \times \frac{1}{3}\right) = \frac{1}{6} + \frac{1}{8} = \frac{2}{9}$ of the student body plays soccer.

Choice A is incorrect because $\frac{1}{24}$ is less than the obtained fraction of the student playing soccer. **Choice B** is incorrect because $\frac{5}{24}$ is less than the obtained fraction of the student playing soccer. **Choice D** is incorrect because $\frac{1}{3}$ is greater than the obtained fraction of the student playing soccer. **Choice E** is incorrect because $\frac{5}{12}$ is greater than the obtained fraction of students playing soccer, which is $\frac{2}{9}$.

29 **Choice C is correct** because the original price is $64. We want to solve for the original price, i.e. price before the markdown. The percent markdown is 25 percent, so $48 is percent of the whole.

Percent × Whole = Part

75 Percent × Original price = $48

Original price = $48/0.75 = $64

Choice A is incorrect because $56 is less than the original price. **Choice B** is incorrect because $60 is less than the original price. **Choice D** is incorrect because $65 is greater than the original price. **Choice E** is incorrect because $72 is greater than the original price.

30 **Choice A is correct** because the obtained answer is 2.4 days.

We have three masons with a rate of 10 days, so each mason completes $\frac{1}{10}$ of the work in one day. George's friend takes 8 days to complete the job, so he completes $\frac{1}{8}$ of the work in one day. If all the masons begin to work together on that particular house, they will complete

$\left(\frac{1}{10} \times 3\right) + \frac{1}{8} = \frac{17}{40}$ in one day. So, the total time required to complete the job is $\frac{40}{70} = 2.4$ days.

Choice B is incorrect because 2.5 days is greater than the obtained time to complete the job. **Choice C** is incorrect because 9.8 days is greater than the obtained time to complete the job. **Choice D** is incorrect because 18 days is too long to complete the job. **Choice E** is incorrect because 38 days is an overapproximation of the time to complete the job.

31 **Choice C is correct** because the obtained answer is $33\frac{1}{3}\%$.

The formula for percentage change is change/original × 100. In this case, the average laptop price five years ago represents the original amount = 75% of $700 or 75% × $700 = $525.

The change is the difference between the original and new prices = $700 − $525 = $175.

Thus, the percentage increase = $175/$525 × 100 = $33\frac{1}{3}\%$.

Choice A is incorrect because 15% is less than the obtained percentage increase. **Choice B** is incorrect because 20% is less than the obtained percentage increase. **Choice D** is incorrect because 36% is almost but not an accurate approximation of the percentage increase. **Choice E** is incorrect because 50% is greater than the obtained percentage increase.

32 **Choice A is correct** because 780 decreased by 75% would give you 195 which should be increased by 20% to get 234.

To find what 780 decreased by 75% equals, multiply 780 by 25% since a decrease of 75% is the same as finding 25% of the original. 25% of 780 would be 195 (780 × 0.25).

Use 195 and 234 to set-up the relationship that 195x = 234 where x is the amount that 195 must be increased by to get to 234. Divide both sides by 195 to get x=1.2 which means 195 was increased by 20% (1.2 − 1 = 0.2 which is 20%).

Choice B is incorrect because you would get this answer if you found 75% of 780, not 75% decrease. **Choice C** is incorrect because this would result from a calculation error. **Choice D** is incorrect because this would be the result if you divided incorrectly. **Choice E** is incorrect because this is the total percent change, but it needs to be reduced by 100% to get the percent increase.

33 **Choice C is correct** because any term in the series can be found by plugging the position of the term into the given formula $n^2(n-1)$. By plugging in 8 for n you will get $8^2(8-1)$ which simplifies to be 64(7) which equals 448.

Choice A is incorrect because this is the answer if you forget to square 8. **Choice B** is incorrect because this answer results from a calculation error. **Choice D** is incorrect because this results from forgetting to subtract 1 from 8. **Choice E** is incorrect because this answer results from a calculation error.

34 **Choices C and E** are correct because in order for $\frac{y}{x} > y$, either both x and y should be negative numbers (as in Choice C) or y is not negative and x must be a decimal number between 0 and 1 (as in Choice E).

Choice A is incorrect because y is not infinite. **Choice B** is incorrect because x is not infinite. **Choice D** is incorrect because $y > 1$ and $x > 1$ does not satisfy the condition that x and y should be negative numbers. **Choice F** is incorrect because Choice C and Choice E satisfies the given statement.

35 **The correct answer is 8.** Let the two numbers be x and y with $x < 10$ and $y < 10$. Since their difference is 6, the possible pairs are 1 and 7, 2 and 8, or 3 and 9.

1 × 7 = 7, 2 × 8 = 16 and 3 × 9 = 27.

Of these three sets, only 2 and 8 have a product that is the square of another integer ($4^2 = 16$).

Since the problem asks for the larger number, the solution is 8.

36 **The correct answer is $\frac{8}{5}$** because you can substitute in $x = 5$ and $y = 8$ to simplify the expression and get

$$\frac{y(x+y)\left(\frac{x}{y}-1\right)}{x(x-y)\left(\frac{x}{y}+1\right)} \text{ to be } \frac{8(5+8)\left(\frac{5}{8}-1\right)}{5(5-8)\left(\frac{5}{8}+1\right)}. \text{ Simplifying}$$

further would get you $\dfrac{8(13)\left(-\frac{3}{8}\right)}{5(-3)\left(\frac{13}{8}\right)}$ and then again will get

Chapter 3: Arithmetic

you $\dfrac{(104)\left(-\dfrac{3}{8}\right)}{(-15)\left(\dfrac{13}{8}\right)}$. Simplifying one more time would get

you the fraction $\dfrac{(-39)}{\left(-\dfrac{195}{8}\right)}$ which would become $\dfrac{8}{5}$

if you keep, change, and flip the fraction to be $-39 \times -\dfrac{8}{195}$ which would simplify to be $\dfrac{312}{195}$ which simplifies to be $\dfrac{8}{5}$.

37 **The correct answer is 20.** If 150 promotional size chocolates are made they need $10 \times 1.2 = 12$ lbs. of sugar. (1.2 represents a quantity increased by 20% in decimal form). Using simple ratio proportion,
$$\dfrac{12}{15} = \dfrac{x}{250}$$
$$x = 20$$

Practice Set 2 (Medium): Answers & Explanations

38 **Choice A is correct** because the variable m can be any integer that ends in either a 2 or a 7. n can be any integer that ends in either a 1 or a 6. Plugging in will show that in any case, $m + n$ will leave a remainder of 3 when divided by 5, and mn will leave a remainder of 2 when divided by 5, so Quantity A is greater.

Choice B is incorrect because Quantity B is less than Quantity A. **Choice C is incorrect** because it is not possible for the two quantities to be equal. **Choice D is incorrect** because it is possible to use the given information to make a comparison between Quantity A and Quantity B.

39 **Choice D is correct** because it is possible to get a remainder greater than 0, but it is also possible to get a remainder of 0.

To get a remainder greater than 0 try out numbers for A and B that meet the condition. If A = 3 and B = 10, then the remainder when A + B is divided by 9 would be found by adding 3 + 10 to get 13 and then dividing by 9 to get 1 remainder 4. This would mean Quantity A is 4 which is greater than 0.

To get a remainder equal to 0, find two numbers that add up to a multiple of 9. If A = 7 and B = 20, then A + B would be 7 + 20 = 27. When you divide 27 by 9, you will get a remainder of 0 which would make Quantity A equal to Quantity B.

Choice A is incorrect because Quantity A is sometimes greater than Quantity B, but not always. **Choice B is incorrect** because Quantity B is never greater than Quantity A. **Choice C is incorrect** because Quantity A is sometimes equal to Quantity B, but not always.

40 **Choice D is correct** because there are situations where the LCM multiple of y and z is less than or equal to yz.

For example, if $x = 3$, $y = 5$, and $z = 4$, then the LCM of y and z would be 20 which is the same as yz which equals $5 \times 4 = 20$.

In another case, if $x = 3$, $y = 8$, and $z = 4$, the LCM of y and z would be 8 which is less than yz which is $8 \times 4 = 32$.

Choice A is incorrect because Quantity A cannot be greater than Quantity B. **Choice B is incorrect** because sometimes Quantity B is greater than Quantity A. **Choice C is incorrect** because sometimes Quantity A and B are equal.

41 **Choice A is correct** because Quantity A is greater than Quantity B.

To be a real number, a square root cannot be zero. Therefore, $\sqrt{x^2 - 3x - 18} \geq 0$

Square both sides and factor the trinomial to obtain $(x-6)(x+3) > 0$ The solution is therefore $x \geq 6$ or $x \leq -3$. The minimum value of a negative solution would be 6. The maximum value of a negative solution would be -3, the absolute value id 3. Therefore, Quantity A is larger and the solution is Choice A.

Choice B is incorrect because Quantity B is less than Quantity A. **Choice C is incorrect** because it is not possible for the two quantities to be equal. **Choice D is incorrect** because it is possible to use the given information to make a comparison between Quantity A and Quantity B.

42 **Choice C is correct** because if you simplify both expressions you would get $\dfrac{x^2 + 2x}{16}$.

To simplify Quantity A, use keep, change, flip to multiply the numerator by the reciprocal of the denominator.

You would get $\frac{3x}{8} \times \frac{x+2}{6}$. Multiplying the numerators and denominators would get you $\frac{3x^2+6x}{48}$. Dividing everything by 3 would simplify the fraction to $\frac{x^2+2x}{16}$.

To simplify Quantity B, multiply $\frac{x}{8}$ by $\frac{2}{2}$ to get a common denominator of 16 to get $\frac{x^2}{16} + \frac{2x}{16}$. Combining these together would yield $\frac{x^2+2x}{16}$.

Choice A is incorrect because Quantity A is equal to Quantity B. **Choice B** is incorrect because Quantity A is equal to Quantity B. **Choice D** is incorrect because it is possible to find a relationship between the quantities.

43 **Choice A is correct** because the number of walnut trees can be found to be 45 which is greater than 35.

To find this use the given information to solve for the number of trees in each species. Since there are 105 trees divided into a 2:3 and 4:5 ratio, combine the ratios to determine how the trees are split. To combine the ratio, find the least common multiple of 3 and 4 which is 12. If the amount of maple trees was 12, the ratio would be x:12:y.

To find x, use the proportion $\frac{2}{3} = \frac{x}{12}$. Cross multiplying would get you $24 = 3x$ and dividing by 3 gives you $x = 8$.

To find y, use the proportion $\frac{4}{5} = \frac{12}{y}$. Cross multiplying would get you $60 = 4y$ and dividing by 4 gives you $y = 15$. This would make the new combine ratio 8:12:15.

Adding up the values in this ratio gives you a total of $8 + 12 + 15 = 35$. Divide 105 by 35 to get 3 which means the trees can be divided evenly into 3 groups. Multiply each of the values of the combined ratio by 3 to determine the final number of trees. For walnut trees, this would be 15 times 3 which would result in 45.

Choice B is incorrect because Quantity A is greater than Quantity B. **Choice C** is incorrect because Quantity A is not equal to Quantity B. **Choice D** is incorrect because it is possible to find a relationship between the quantities.

44 **Choice C is correct** because Quantity A and Quantity B are equal.

Let's assume:

a = initial amount of money owned by Anna

Practice Set 2 (Medium): Answers & Explanations

b = initial amount of money owned by Beatrice

c = initial amount of money owned by Charlotte

$a + b + c = \$2,200$

Anna spends 50% of her money

Amount left = $a - 50\% a = 50\% a = a/2$

Beatrice spends 75% of her money

Amount left = $b - 75\% b = 25\% b = b/4$

Charlotte spends 80% of her money

Amount left = $c - 80\% c = 20\% c = c/5$

We know that after spending some money they are each left with identical amounts of money

$a/2 = b/4 = c/5$

Let $x = a/2 = b/4 = b/4$

$a = 2x$, $b = 4x$ and $c = 5x$

We can now substitute in the first equation

$2x + 4x + 5x = \$2,200$

$11x = \$2,200$

$x = \$200$

The initial amount of money owned by Beatrice is $b = 4x = \$800$

The initial amount of money owned by Charlotte is $c = 5x = \$1,000$

The amount of money spent by Charlotte = $80\% \times \$1,000 = \$800$

The initial amount of money owned by Beatrice (\$800) is the same as the amount of money spent by Charlotte (\$800).

Choice A is incorrect because Quantity A is equal to Quantity B. **Choice B** is incorrect because Quantity B is equal to Quantity A. **Choice D** is incorrect because it is possible to use the given information to make a comparison between Quantity A and Quantity B.

45 **Choice B is correct** because the amount of product A sold is less than twice the amount of product B sold.

Let x represent the price of product B. Thus, product A's price is $\frac{2}{3}x$. Let y be the total amount of product A and B sold means the revenue of B = $\frac{6}{13}y$ and the revenue of A = $\frac{7}{13}y$.

Now to determine the amount of product A sold, you would multiply the price of the product times the amount

Chapter 3: Arithmetic

sold to get the revenue. The price of A is $\frac{2}{3}x$, the amount sold is unknown, and the revenue is $\frac{7}{13}y$. Putting this into a statement would get $\frac{2}{3}x$ times amount sold equals $\frac{7}{13}y$. Divide both sides to get the amount sold can be expressed as $\dfrac{\frac{7}{13}y}{\frac{2}{3}x}$ which simplifies to be $\frac{21y}{26x}$.

To determine the amount of product B sold, you would multiply the price of the product times the amount sold to get the revenue. The price of B is x, the amount sold is unknown, and the revenue is $\frac{6}{13}y$. Putting this into a statement would get x times amount sold equals $\frac{6}{13}y$. Divide both sides to get the amount sold can be expressed as $\dfrac{\frac{6}{13}y}{x}$ which simplifies to be $\frac{6y}{13x}$. Twice this amount would get you $\frac{12y}{13x}$.

Since product A's amount sold would be $\frac{21y}{26x}$ and twice product B's amount sold would be $\frac{12y}{13x}$, Quantity B is greater than Quantity A.

Choice A is incorrect because Quantity A is less than Quantity B. **Choice C** is incorrect because Quantity A is not equal to Quantity B. **Choice D** is incorrect because it is possible to find a relationship between the quantities.

46 **Choice C is correct** because both quantities are equal.

- $a^{-n} = \dfrac{1}{a^n}$
- $a^{m/n} = \sqrt[n]{a^m} = \left(\sqrt[n]{a}\right)^m$

Quantity A:
$$(2)^4 (8)^{-\frac{2}{3}} = \frac{(2)^4}{(8)^{\frac{2}{3}}} = \frac{16}{\left(\sqrt[3]{8}\right)^2} = \frac{16}{(2)^2} = \frac{16}{4} = 4$$

Quantity B:
$$(4)^{\frac{5}{2}} (16)^{-\frac{3}{4}} = \frac{(4)^{\frac{5}{2}}}{(16)^{\frac{3}{4}}} = \frac{\sqrt{4^5}}{\sqrt[4]{16^3}} = \frac{\left(\sqrt{4}\right)^5}{\left(\sqrt[4]{16}\right)^3} = \frac{2^5}{2^3} = \frac{32}{8} = 4$$

Choice A is incorrect because Quantity A is less than Quantity B. **Choice B** is incorrect because Quantity B is less than Quantity A. **Choice D** is incorrect because

it is possible to use the given information to make a comparison between Quantity A and Quantity B.

47 **Choice B is correct** because the greatest possible value of Quantity A would be 8.9 so Quantity B is always greater than Quantity A.

To find the greatest value for Quantity A, use 9 for A and 1 for B to get $\frac{0.9}{0.101}$. This would simplify to be 8.$\underline{9108}$ which is less than 9.

Choice A is incorrect because Quantity A is always less than Quantity B. **Choice C** is incorrect because Quantity A is not equal to Quantity B. **Choice D** is incorrect because it is possible to find a relationship between the quantities.

48 **Choice D is correct** because relationship cannot be determined from the information given.

There are only two ways for a positive integer to a positive power to equal 81 : 9^2 or 3^4. Thus, $(b + c)^a$ could be, say $(3 + 6)^2$ or it could be $(1 + 2)^4$. in the first case $b + c$ is greater than a. But in the second instance, $b + c$ is less than a. Hence, the answer is Choice D.

Choice A is incorrect because Quantity A can either be less or greater than Quantity B. **Choice B** is incorrect because Quantity B can either be less or greater than Quantity A. **Choice C** is incorrect because it is not possible for the two quantities to be equal.

49 **Choice D is correct** because a relationship cannot be determined from the information given.

Because you're told that R, S and T are digits and different multiples of 3, most people think of 3, 6, and 9, which add up to 18. That makes W equal to 8 and Columns A and B are equal.

There's another possibility that 0 is also a multiple of 3. So, the three digits could be 0, 3 and 9, or 0,6, 9, which give totals of 12 and 15, respectively. That means W could be 8,2 or 5.

Since the columns could be equal, or column B could be greater, answer choice D is correct.

Choice A is incorrect because Quantity A can either be less or greater than Quantity B. **Choice B** is incorrect because Quantity B can either be less or greater than

Quantity A. **Choice C is incorrect** because it is not possible for the two quantities to be equal.

50 **Choice C is correct** because the sum of both quantities is 105.

Find the first 8 terms by using the given formula. To find A_2, plug into $A_n = A_{n-1} - 4(n-5)$ to get $A_2 = 5 - 4(2-5) = 17$. To find A_3, plug in to get $A_3 = 17 - 4(3-5) = 25$. To find A_4, plug in to get

$A_4 = \frac{6}{13} = 29$. To find A_5, plug in to get

$A_5 = 29 - 4(5-5) = 29$. To find A_6, plug in to get

$A_6 = 29 - 4(6-5) = 25$. To find A_7, plug in to get

$A_7 = 25 - 4(7-5) = 17$. To find A_8, plug in to get

$A_8 = 17 - 4(8-5) = 5$.

Adding A_1 to A_4 would get you 5+17+25+29 which equals 105. Adding A_5 to A_8 would get you 29+25+17+5 which also equals 105

Choice A is incorrect because Quantity A is equal to Quantity B. **Choice B is incorrect** because Quantity A is equal to Quantity B. **Choice D is incorrect** because it is possible to find a relationship between the quantities.

51 **Choice A is correct** because Quantity A is greater than Quantity B.

Let the distance that Jeremy walked be x.

$$\frac{x}{4} = \frac{x+9}{6}$$

$$6x = 4x + 36$$

$$x = 18 \text{ miles}$$

The time that Jeremy walked

$$\frac{18 \text{ miles}}{4 \text{ mph}} = 4\frac{1}{2} \text{ hours} = 4 \text{ hours and } 30 \text{ minutes}$$

The time it would take Jeremy to walk 22 miles at 5 mph

$$\frac{22 \text{ miles}}{5 \text{ mph}} = 4\frac{2}{5} \text{ hours} = 4 \text{ hours and } 24 \text{ minutes}$$

4 hours and 30 minutes is greater than 4 hours and 24 minutes

Choice B is incorrect because Quantity B is less than Quantity A. **Choice C is incorrect** because it is not possible for the two quantities to be equal. **Choice D is incorrect** because it is possible to use the given information to make a comparison between Quantity A and Quantity B.

52 **Choice B is correct** because Quantity B is greater than Quantity A.

Simplify all the numerical statements of A, B, ad c first. Combine all the ratios in each expression.

$$A = \frac{3}{4} - \frac{5}{4} + \frac{9}{4}$$

$$A = \frac{-2}{4} + \frac{9}{4}$$

$$A = \frac{7}{4}$$

In (B), multiply the denominator and numerator of the first fraction by 4 and of the second fraction by 2 to make all the denominators the same, and then simplify.

$$B = \frac{12}{24} - \frac{10}{24} + \frac{7}{24}$$

$$B = \frac{3}{8}$$

In (C), denominators are the same. Keep the same denominator and add the numerators.

$$C = \frac{4}{8} = \frac{1}{2}$$

Next, find A + B. Replace A and B with their values found above.

$$A + B = \frac{7}{4} + \frac{3}{8}$$

$$A + B = \frac{17}{8}$$

Replace the values of (A + B) and C found above in the expression below:

$$C\% \text{ of } (A+B) = \left(\frac{1}{2}\%\right) \text{ of } \left(\frac{17}{8}\right)$$

$$= \left(\frac{1}{200}\right)\left(\frac{17}{8}\right)$$

$$= \frac{17}{1600}$$

Since $= \frac{17}{1600} < \frac{17}{160}$, thus Choice B is correct.

Choice A is incorrect because Quantity A is less than Quantity B. **Choice C is incorrect** because it is not possible for the two quantities to be equal. **Choice D is incorrect** because it is possible to use the given information to make a comparison between Quantity A and Quantity B. between Quantity A and Quantity B.

Chapter 3: Arithmetic

53 **Choice C is correct** because the two quantities are equal.

Define M as Manny's income and F as Fran's income.

Manny's income is 72% of Fran's so M = 0.72F, or 648 = 0.72F if you plug in 648 for Manny's income. Solving for F, divide 648 by 0.72. You find that F = 900. The two quantities are equal.

Choice A is incorrect because Quantity A is less than Quantity B. **Choice B** is incorrect because Quantity B is less than Quantity A. **Choice D** is incorrect because it is possible to use the given information to make a comparison between Quantity A and Quantity B.

54 **Choice A is correct** because it can be determined that the cost of a notebook is $3. Write out the given information as 2p + 1n + 5e = $6.25 and 1p + 2n + 3e = $7.75. Use the give ratio to create the fraction $\frac{1}{4}$ p = e.

Substitute in $\frac{1}{4}$ p = e into both equations to get 2p + 1n + 5($\frac{1}{4}$ p) = $6.25 along with the statement 1p + 2n + 3($\frac{1}{4}$ p) = $7.75. Simplify to get $\frac{13}{4}$ p + 1n = $6.25 and $\frac{7}{4}$ p + 2n = $7.75.

Solve the first expression for p to by subtracting 1n and dividing by $\frac{13}{4}$ to get p = $\frac{25}{13} - \frac{4}{13}$ n . Substitute this into the other equation to get $\frac{7}{4}$ ($\frac{25}{13} - \frac{4}{13}$ n) + 2n = $7.75.

Simplifying further will yield $\frac{175}{52} - \frac{7}{13}$ n + 2n = 7.75 which then becomes $\frac{175}{52} + \frac{19}{13}$ n = 7.75. Subtract $\frac{175}{52}$ and divide by $\frac{19}{13}$ will get you n = $3.

Choice B is incorrect because Quantity A is greater than Quantity B. **Choice C** is incorrect because Quantity A is not equal to Quantity B. **Choice D** is incorrect because it is possible to find a relationship between the quantities.

55 **Choice C is correct** because Quantity A is equal to Quantity B.

Simplifying the complex fraction in column A,

$$\frac{1}{1+\frac{1}{1+\frac{1}{n}}} = \frac{1}{1+\frac{1}{\frac{n}{n}+\frac{1}{n}}} = \frac{1}{1+\frac{1}{\frac{(n+1)}{n}}} = \frac{1}{1+\frac{n}{n+1}}$$

$$= \frac{1}{\frac{n+1}{n+1}+\frac{n}{n+1}} = \frac{1}{\frac{n+1+n}{n+1}} = \frac{1}{\frac{2n+1}{n+1}} = \frac{n+1}{2n+1}$$

Choice A is incorrect because both the quantities are equal. **Choice B** is incorrect because both the quantities are equal. **Choice D** is incorrect because it is possible to use the given information to make a comparison between Quantity A and Quantity B.

56 **Choice A is correct** because the number of terms in the series is 17 which is greater than 15. To find this use the formula for sum of a series: S = $\frac{n}{2}$ ($a_1 + a_n$). Filing this in will get you 85 = $\frac{n}{2}$ (4 + 6) which simplifies to be 85 = $\frac{n}{2}$ (10) and then 85 = 5n. Dividing both sides by 5 will give you n = 17.

Choice B is incorrect because Quantity A is greater than Quantity B. **Choice C** is incorrect because Quantity A is not equal to Quantity B. **Choice D** is incorrect because it is possible to find a relationship between the quantities.

57 **Choice A is correct** because only statement I is always true.

In these problems you must test items I, II and III for their validity. If y is even then y^2 is even. An odd number minus an even number gives you an odd number.

Choose a number for x and y. For instance, let x = 3 and y = 4. Then $3^2 - 4^2$ = 9 − 16 = −7, which is odd but not the square of an integer. The only correct choice is I. The following tables are useful for the solutions of problems of this type.

Addition Table for Odd and Even Integers

+	Odd	Even
Odd	Even	Odd
Even	Odd	Even

Multiplication Table for Odd and Even Integers

X	Odd	Even
Odd	Odd	Even
Even	Even	Even

Be careful when choosing values for the variables. In the above problems, if you had chosen $x = 5$ and $y = 4$, then $x^2 - y^2 = 5^2 - 4^2 = 25 - 16 = 9$, which would have made I and III be correct. The problem asks which answer is ALWAYS correct. Clearly I is, but III is not.

Choice B is incorrect because II is not a true statement because $x^2 - y^2$ is odd. **Choice C** is incorrect because III is not always true. **Choice D** is incorrect because I and III is statement III is not always true. **Choice E** is incorrect because II and III is statement III is not always true.

58 **Choice D is correct** because the obtained answer is 36.

Since no coins were left over when she packed them into 4 or 6 bags, the number of coins should be a multiple of their LCM.

LCM of 4 and 6 is 12.

When she packs them into 7 bags, one coin is left over.

Multiples of 12 are 12, 24, 36, 48,…….

One less than these multiples should be a multiple of 7.

The least number that fulfills this condition is 36 (as 36 – 1 = 35 is indeed a multiple of 7).

Hence, the least number of coins Stella has is 36.

Choice A is incorrect because 12 is less than the least number of coins Stella has. **Choice B** is incorrect because 25 is less than the least number of coins Stella has. **Choice C** is incorrect because 29 is less than the least number of coins Stella has. **Choice E** is incorrect because 48 is greater than the least number of coins Stella has.

59 **Choice A is correct** because Quantity A is greater than Quantity B.

When you substitute in the given values of a and c for Quantity A, you get the following expressions:

$$\frac{a^2 b^4}{c^3} = \frac{(2b)^2 b^4}{(-3b)^3} = \frac{4b^6}{-27b^3} = \frac{-4}{27}b^3$$

When you substitute in the given values of a and c for Quantity B, you get the following expressions:

$$\frac{(-a)^2(-b)^4}{(-c)^3} = \frac{(-2b)^2(-b)^4}{(3b)^3} = \frac{4b^6}{27b^3} = \frac{4}{27}b^3$$

Practice Set 2 (Medium): Answers & Explanations

Therefore, Quantity A is bigger since b is a negative integer (and thus, b^3 is a negative integer), so Quantity A is a positive and Quantity B is a negative.

Choice B is incorrect because Quantity B is less than Quantity A. **Choice C** is incorrect because both quantities are not equal. **Choice D** is incorrect because it is possible to use the given information to make a comparison between Quantity A and Quantity B.

60 **Choice B is correct** because initial price of the tie is $50.

Let the initial price of a tie be x and that of one pair of shoes be y.

Let the discounted price of a tie be t and that of pair of shoes be s.

Now $t + s = 104$…………(1)

$t + 64 = s$…………(2)

Also $t = 0.4x$…………(3) and
$s = 0.7y$…………(4)

Substituting (3) and (4) in (1) and (2) we get

$0.4x + 0.7y = 104$…………(5)

$0.4x + 64 = 0.7y$…………(6)

Substituting (6) in (5) we get

$0.4x + 0.4x + 64 = 104$…………(7)

$0.8x = 40$

$\therefore x = \dfrac{40}{0.8} = 50$

Choice A is incorrect because 46 is less than the initial price of the tie. **Choice C** is incorrect because 52 is greater than the initial price of the tie. **Choice D** is incorrect because 54 is greater than the initial price of the tie. **Choice E** is incorrect because 56 is greater than the initial price of the tie.

61 **Choice E is correct** because the obtained percentage increase is 69%.

Percent means $\dfrac{x}{100}$ so 30 percent would be $\dfrac{30}{100}$.

If the car originally costs y dollars, it would cost $y + \dfrac{30}{100}y$ after 5 years.

Simplify: $y + \dfrac{30}{100}y = 1y + \dfrac{3}{10}y = 1.3y$.

Chapter 3: Arithmetic

The car's cost will increase another 30 percent over the next 5 years. Car's cost then would be:

$(1.3y) + \frac{30}{100}(1.3y) = (1.3y) + \frac{3}{10}(1.3y)$

$= 1.3y + (.3)(1.3y)$

$= (1.3y) + .39y = 1.69y$

If the car originally cost y dollar and after 10 year costs 1.69y dollars, the increase was 69 y or $\frac{69}{100}y$. This is an increase of 69 percent.

Choice A is incorrect because 15% is less than the obtained percentage increase. **Choice B** is incorrect because 30% is less than the obtained percentage increase. **Choice C** is incorrect because 39% is less than the obtained percentage increase. **Choice D** is incorrect because 60% is less than the obtained percentage increase.

62 **Choice A is correct** because 9 months later from September will be June.

$\frac{132}{4} = 33$ months

$\frac{33}{12} = 2$ years and 9 months

Choice B is incorrect because August is not the month that's 9 months after September. **Choice C** is incorrect because September is not the month that's 9 months after September. **Choice D** is incorrect because October is not the month that's 9 months after September. **Choice E** is incorrect because November is not the month that's 9 months after September.

63 **Choice E is correct** because the ratio of days that occur 52 times is $\frac{5}{7}$.

There are 366 days in a leap year. $\frac{366}{52} = 7$, with a remainder of 2. Therefore, 2 of the 7 days in the week occur 53 times in a leap year, and the remaining 5 occur 52 times, so choice (E) is correct.

Choice A is incorrect because $\frac{1}{7}$ is less than the obtained fraction. **Choice B** is incorrect because $\frac{2}{7}$ is less than the obtained fraction. **Choice C** is incorrect because $\frac{3}{7}$ is less than the obtained fraction. **Choice D** is incorrect because $\frac{4}{7}$ is less than the obtained fraction.

64 **Choice C is correct** because the obtained answer is $\frac{3s}{5j}$.

To determine how many pints of jam Pam can make, simply divide the amount of berries set aside for jam by the number of grams required for each pint. If she uses 40 percent of the strawberries for pies, that means she has 60 percent or $\frac{3}{5}s$ to use for jam. Each pint requires j grams.

$\frac{3}{5}s \div j = \frac{3s}{5j}$

Choice A is incorrect because $\frac{2s}{5p}$ both the numerator and denominator are incorrect. **Choice B** is incorrect because $\frac{2s}{5j}$ has an incorrect numerator. **Choice D** is incorrect because $\frac{3p}{5s}$ does not correspond to the obtained expression. **Choice E** is incorrect because $\frac{3sj}{5}$ does not correspond to the obtained expression.

65 **Choice C is correct** because the obtained answer is Height = 8 inches, Length = 36 inches, Width = 28 inches.

The volume of the chest of drawers is equal to length × width × height = 38 × 30 × 42 = 47,880 cubic inches.

7,560 cubic inches of the chest's volume are not occupied by drawers.

Total volume of all the drawers = 47,880 − 7,560 = 40,320 cubic inches.

The ratio of the drawers height: length : width is 2:9:7.

Let the height = 2X, the length = 9X and the width = 7X.

$40,320 = 2X \times 9X \times 7X \times 5 = 126X^3 \times 5$

$64 = X^3 \qquad X = 4$

Drawer height = 2 × 4 = 8 inches

Drawer length = 9 × 4 = 36 inches

Drawer width = 7 × 4 = 28 inches

Choice A is incorrect because values of height, length and width are incorrect. **Choice B** is incorrect because values of height and width are incorrect. **Choice D** is incorrect because value of width is incorrect. **Choice E** is incorrect because values of length and width are incorrect.

66 **Choice C is correct** because there are four more pages in magazine B than in magazine A.

Practice Set 2 (Medium): Answers & Explanations

The Part / Whole ratio of advertisements (16) to total pages (28) in magazine A is $\frac{16}{28}$ or $\frac{4}{7}$. Magazine B has the same ratio, so if there are 35 pages in magazines B, $\frac{4}{7} \times 35$ or 20 pages are advertisements. Therefore there are four more pages of advertisements in magazine B than in magazine A.

Choice A is incorrect because 2 is less than the obtained difference in the number of pages in magazine B than in magazine A. **Choice B** is incorrect because 3 is less than the obtained difference in the number of pages in magazine B than in magazine A. **Choice D** is incorrect because 5 is greater than the obtained difference in the number of pages in magazine B than in magazine A. **Choice E** is incorrect because 6 is greater than the obtained difference in the number of pages in magazine B than in magazine A.

67 **Choice C is correct** because by distributing and simplifying, you can solve for $x = \frac{5}{2}$.

Expand $(x-2)^2$ to be $(x-2)(x-2)$ and then distribute to get $x^2 - 4x + 4$.

Expand $(x-3)^2$ to be $(x-3)(x-3)$ and then distribute to get $x^2 - 6x + 9$

Now you will have the expression $x^2 - 4x + 4 = x^2 - 6x + 9$. Subtract x^2 from both sides to get $-4x + 4 = -6x + 9$. Add $6x$ to both sides to get $2x + 4 = 9$. Subtract 4 which will give you $2x = 5$. Divide by 2 for the final answer of $x = \frac{5}{2}$.

Choice A is incorrect because this answer results from a math error. **Choice B** is incorrect because this answer results from a math error. **Choice D** is incorrect because this answer results from a math error. **Choice E** is incorrect because this answer results from a math error.

68 **Choice B is correct** because using algebraic reasoning, you can identify $x = -\frac{7}{3}$.

Start by multiplying both sides by the denominator of $\frac{1}{1+\frac{1}{1+x}}$ to get $1 = 4[1 + \left(\frac{1}{1+x}\right)]$. Distribute the 4 to get 1 $= 4 + \frac{4}{1+x}$. Subtract 4 from both sides $-3 = \frac{4}{1+x}$.

Multiply both sides by the denominator $1 + x$ to get $-3 - 3x = 4$. Then add 3 to both sides to get $-3x = 7$. Divide by -3 to get $x = -\frac{7}{3}$.

Choice A is incorrect because this answer results from a math error. **Choice C** is incorrect because this answer results from a math error. **Choice D** is incorrect because this answer results from a math error. **Choice E** is incorrect because this answer results from a math error.

69 **Choice C is correct** because the obtained answer is 14 hours.

Let Charles works for x hours in that shift.

For the first eight hours rate = $20 per hour

For the next two hours, rate = $30 per hour

For the remaining hours, rate = $40 per hour

Total earning = $340

Hence we get

Total earnings = $8 \times 20 + 2 \times 30 + (x - 10) \times 40$

$= 160 + 60 + 40x - 400$

$= 40x - 180$

By data, $40x - 180 = 340$

$40x = 520$

$x = \frac{520}{40} = 13$ hours

Choice A is incorrect because 11 hours is less than the obtained shift. **Choice B** is incorrect because 12 hours is less than the obtained shift. **Choice D** is incorrect because 14 hours is greater than the obtained shift. **Choice E** is incorrect because 15 hours is greater than the obtained shift.

70 **Choice D is correct** because $2xy$ will always be even because anything times 2 will be an even number. This means $3z$ has to be even as well in order to get an even number. To get an even number when multiplying by 3, you have to multiply by an even number since odd times an odd will never be even. Therefore, z cannot be odd.

Choice A is incorrect because if x is odd, it is still possible to get an even number with different values of y and z. **Choice B** is incorrect because if $2x$ would always be even no matter what x equals since any number times an even is an even. **Choice C** is incorrect because if xy is odd, it is still being multiplied by 2 which can still result in an even number when added to $3z$. **Choice E** is incorrect because it does not matter if x and y are even or odd since they are being multiplied by 2.

Chapter 3: Arithmetic

71 **Choice C is correct** because since $m < -4$, you would get the greatest value with the least negative and lowest value in the denominator. The answers that would like result in positive answers would be $\frac{1}{(1-m)^2}$ and $\frac{1}{(m+4)^2}$. Testing out numbers like $m = -5$ would get you $\frac{1}{(1-(-5))^2}$ which is $\frac{1}{36}$ and $(\frac{1}{-5+4})^2$ which is 1. **Choice A** is incorrect because this does not result in the largest positive possible value. **Choice B** is incorrect because this would result in a negative value. **Choice D** is incorrect because this would result in a negative value. **Choice E** is incorrect because this would result in a negative value for some instances of m.

72 **Choice A is correct** because you can use the repeated values of digits and their powers to solve. For 23, the unit value of 3 would indicate a pattern of unit digits 3, 9, 7, 1 so an exponent of 31 would give you a unit digit of 7. This can be found by dividing 31 by 4 to get 7 remainder 3. The remainder indicates which number in the pattern should be chosen.

For 24, the unit value of 4 repeats as 4, 6 so the 32nd power would get you a 6 since 32 divided by 4 goes in evenly without a remainder.

For 25, the unit value of 5 always ends in 5 so the unit value of the 33rd power would be 5.

Multiply the values of 7, 6, and 5 together to get 210 which has a units digit of .

Choice B is incorrect because the unit digit is 0 not 1.
Choice C is incorrect because the unit digit is 0 not 2.
Choice D is incorrect because the unit digit is 0 not 3.
Choice E is incorrect because the unit digit is 0 not 4.

73 **Choice B is correct** because Quantity B is greater than Quantity A.

Quantity A simplifies as follows:

$$\sqrt{\frac{9^4 - 3^4}{3^8}} = \sqrt{\frac{3^8 - 3^4}{3^8}} = \sqrt{\frac{3^4(3^4 - 1)}{3^8}} = \frac{\sqrt{80}}{9}$$

Quantity B simplifies as follows:

$$\sqrt[2]{(3^5 + 9^2)(3^5 - 9^2)} = \sqrt[2]{3^{10} - 9^4}$$
$$= \sqrt[2]{3^{10} - 3^6}$$
$$= \sqrt[2]{3^6(3^4 - 1)}$$
$$= 27\sqrt[2]{80}$$

The answer is B. Quantity B is greater by a factor of 243.

Choice A is incorrect because Quantity A is less than Quantity B. **Choice C** is incorrect because Quantity A is not equal to Quantity B. **Choice D** is incorrect because it is possible to use the given information to make a comparison between Quantity A and Quantity B.

74 **Choice D is correct** because the obtained answer is 9.

Note first this is an EXCEPT question. Now, since $a^2b = 12^2$, and b is an odd integer, let's see what we can come up with. The first value for b that occurs to us is 1, so we get the following:

$a^2b = 12^2$
$(a^2)(1) = 12^2$
$a^2 = 12^2$
$a = 12$

If a equals 12 it is divisible by 1, 2, 3, 4, 6, and 12. So the only choice that remains is D.

Choice A is incorrect because a is divisible by 3. **Choice B** is incorrect because a is divisible by 4. **Choice C** is incorrect because a is divisible by 6. **Choice E** is incorrect because a is divisible by 12.

75 **Choice E is correct** because you can simplify the expression to identify that the decimal equivalent will have 12 decimal places.

Factor out $\frac{1}{2^9 5^{12}} + \frac{1}{5^9 2^{12}}$ to get $\frac{1}{2^9 \times 5^9}(\frac{1}{5^3} + \frac{1}{2^3})$. This then would simplify to be $\frac{1}{10^9}(\frac{1}{125} + \frac{1}{8})$.

Combine the inner fractions to get $\frac{133}{1000}$ which can be rewritten as $\frac{133}{10^3}$.

Now you will have the statement $\frac{1}{10^9}(\frac{133}{10^3})$ which simplifies to be $\frac{133}{10^{12}}$. This means the expression equals 133×10^{-12}. There are 12 decimal places in total.

Choice A is incorrect because there are more than 10 digits after the decimal place. **Choice B** is incorrect because there are less than 16 digits after the decimal place. **Choice C** is incorrect because there are less than 14 digits after the decimal place.

Practice Set 2 (Medium): Answers & Explanations

76 **Choice D is correct** because the 4023rd digit of $0.\overline{41256}$ is 2 and the 89th digit of $0.\overline{389}$ is 8 and 2^8 is 256. To find the 4023rd digit of $0.\overline{41256}$ divide 4023 by 5 to get 804 remainder 3. This means the number in the 3rd position is the 4023rd digit. This would make the 4023rd digit 2 so $x = 2$. To find the 89th digit of $0.\overline{389}$, divide 89 by 3 to get 29 remainder 2 which would mean the number in the 2nd position is the 89th digit this would make the 89th digit 8 so $y = 8$. The the value of x^y would therefore be 2^8 which equals 256.

Choice A is incorrect because this is 1^1 which uses the wrong placement of digits. **Choice B is incorrect** because this is 4^3 which uses the wrong placement of digits. **Choice C is incorrect** because this is 5^3 which uses the wrong placement of digits. **Choice E is incorrect** because this is 4^8 which uses the wrong placement of digits.

77 **Choice C is correct** because if a equals 10, the b would equal $5.\overline{55}$ repeating which is not an integer. To find this you can rewrite the expression $\frac{a}{b} = 1.80$ to be $\frac{a}{b} = \frac{180}{100}$ which would simplify to be $\frac{a}{b} = \frac{18}{10} = \frac{9}{5}$. This means any multiple of 9 would work. The value 10 is not a multiple of 9.

Choice A is incorrect because −45 is a multiple of 9.
Choice B is incorrect because −27 is a multiple of 9.
Choice D is incorrect because 18 is a multiple of 9.
Choice E is incorrect because 36 is a multiple of 9.

78 **Choice E is correct** because setting up the ratios into algebraic expressions will allow you to solve for 63 compact cars on the lot.

The ratio 4:9 can be expressed as $\frac{4}{9}$ and then you know you add 14 SUVs to get to the ratio 2:3 which can be written as $\frac{2}{3}$. This means that $\frac{4x+14}{9x} = \frac{2}{3}$ with $4x$ equaling the original amount of SUVs and $9x$ equaling the original amount of compact cars.

Cross-multiplying these numbers would get you $3(4x + 14) = 2(9x)$. Simplifying would get you the expression $12x + 42 = 18x$. Subtract $12x$ on both sides to get $42 = 6x$. Divide by 6 to get 7 which is multiple that will be used to find the original amount of compact cars. Use the expression $9x$ and plug in 7 to get 63 compact cars on the lot.

Choice A is incorrect because this would be the answer if you only accounted for 14 total SUVs and used the ratio 2:3 to get 14:18. **Choice B is incorrect** because this results from a math error. **Choice C is incorrect** because this would be the number of SUVs to begin with. **Choice D is incorrect** because this would result from a math error.

79 **Choice B is correct** because you can find the difference in miles by creating a formula that connects all of the information. Since there is x dollars paid for a full tank, the total amount of gallons can be found by dividing x by the cost per gallon of $3.45. This would get you $\frac{x}{3.45}$ which simplifies to be $\frac{20x}{69}$. This should then be multiplied by the difference in miles per gallon to determine the total difference in miles. The difference in miles per gallon would be 43−38 which equals 5. $\frac{20x}{69}$ times 5 would get you $\frac{100x}{69}$.

Choice A is incorrect because this is just a variation on the equation for the number of gallons of gas that is incorrect. **Choice C is incorrect** because this results from a math simplification error. **Choice D is incorrect** because this results from a math simplification error. **Choice E is incorrect** because this is just the total number of gallons of gas and does not account for the difference in mileage.

80 **Choice A is correct** because the obtained ratio is 1:1.

Begin with what you know.

Cars:

There are 108 luxury cars which is $\frac{3}{5}$ of all cars. The total number of cars is:

$$\frac{3}{5}x = 108$$

$$x = 180 - total\ cars$$

This means there are $\frac{2}{5} \times 180$ or 72 non-luxury cars.

Trucks:

From above we know that there are a total of 180 cars which is $\frac{3}{7}$ of all vehicles. The total number of vehicles is $\frac{3}{7}x = 180 x = 420 - total\ vehicles$

This means there are $\frac{4}{7} \times 420$ or $240 \times trucks$.

Of these trucks $\frac{3}{10}$ are two-wheel drive or $240 \times \frac{3}{10} = 72$.

Chapter 3: Arithmetic

The ratio of non–luxury cars to two-wheel drive trucks is 72:72 or 1:1.

Choice B is incorrect because 1:2 is not the obtained ratio of the non-luxury cars to two-wheel drive trucks. **Choice C is incorrect** because 2:3 is not the obtained ratio of the non-luxury cars to two-wheel drive trucks. **Choice D is incorrect** because 3:2 is not the obtained ratio of the non-luxury cars to two-wheel drive trucks. **Choice E is incorrect** because 14:9 is not the obtained ratio of the non-luxury cars to two-wheel drive trucks.

81 **Choice B is correct** because the difference between her maximum and minimum possible gross winnings is $300.

The maximum winning would result from winning at the tables with 40:1 odds and 30:1 odds. Betting at $10 at the 40:1 Table and winning result in a prize of ($10)(40) = $400. Winning at the 30:1 Table yields ($10)($30) = $300, making the maximum possible winnings $400 + $300 = $700. The minimum winnings result from winnings at the 10:1 table and the 30:1 table. Winning at the 10:1 table yields ($10)(10) = $100, making the minimum winnings $100 + $300 = $400. The difference is $700−$400=$300.

Choice A is incorrect because $200 is less than the obtained difference. **Choice C is incorrect** because $400 is greater than the obtained difference. **Choice D is incorrect** because $500 is greater than the obtained difference. **Choice E is incorrect** because $600 is greater than the obtained difference.

82 **Choice B is correct** because the obtained answer is 9.

Setting up the equations.

Let w and l represent the number of wins and losses respectively.

From the given, $\frac{w}{l} = \frac{3}{1}$, $\frac{w+6}{l} = \frac{5}{1}$

Faster way to solve the problem:

Before		After	
Wins	Losses	Wins	Losses
1. 3			
2. 6			
3. 9	3(3 : 1)	15	3(5 : 1)
4. 15			
5. 24			

Choice A is incorrect because 3 is not a possible value for the change in the Win: loss ratio. **Choice C is incorrect** because 9 is not a possible value for the change in the Win: loss ratio. **Choice D is incorrect** because 15 is not a possible value for the change in the Win: loss ratio. **Choice E is incorrect** because 24 is not a possible value for the change in the Win: loss ratio.

83 **Choice B is correct** because the obtained answer is 24.

This is an average problem, so use the average formula. If the average of 6 numbers is 24, we can solve for their sum: $6 \times 24 = 144$. If four of these numbers total 96, then by subtracting 96 from 144, we get the sum of the other two numbers, 48. To find the average of these two numbers, we divide their sum by their number: $\frac{48}{2} = 24$.

Choice A is incorrect because 12 is less than the obtained average of the numbers. **Choice C is incorrect** because 48 is greater than the obtained average of the numbers. **Choice D is incorrect** because 72 is greater than the obtained average of the numbers. **Choice E is incorrect** because 96 is greater than the obtained average of the numbers.

84 **Choice A is correct** because the obtained answer is $\frac{t}{3}$.

Set up a chart.

	Now	In x years
Tom	t	$t + x$
Becky	$\frac{t}{3}$	$\frac{t}{3} + x$

Let x = the number of years from now.

If Tom is t years old he is 3 times as old as Becky, then Becky must be $\frac{t}{3}$ years old.

In x years, Tom will be $t + x$ years old and Becky will be $\frac{t}{3} + x$ years old.

Set up an equation based upon your chart.

In how many years will Tom be twice as old as Becky?

$t + x = 2\left(\frac{t}{3} + x\right)$ Distribute $t + x = \frac{2t}{3} + 2x$

Solve for x

$\frac{t}{3} = x$

Practice Set 2 (Medium): Answers & Explanations

Choice B is incorrect because $\frac{t}{2}$ has an incorrect denominator. **Choice C** is incorrect because $\frac{2t}{2}$ is not equivalent to the obtained expression. **Choice D** is incorrect because t is not equivalent to the obtained expression. **Choice E** is incorrect because $\frac{3t}{2}$ is not equivalent to the obtained expression.

85 **Choice E is correct** because $x^3 > x^2$ is only true when $x > 1$.

When $x = 0$, then $x^3 = x^2 = 0$, so choices (A) and (D) are incorrect. When x is a positive fraction, then $x^3 < x^2$; for example, $x = \frac{1}{2}, \left(\frac{1}{2}\right)^3 = \frac{1}{8} < \left(\frac{1}{2}\right)^2 = \frac{1}{4}$

So, choice (B) is incorrect. When x is negative and x^2 is positive (a negative raised to an odd power is always negative and a negative raised to an even power is always positive), then $x^3 < x^2$ and choice (C) is therefore incorrect. Only when $x > 1$ will the inequality be true.

Choice A is incorrect because $x^3 > x^2$ is not true for all values of x. **Choice B** is incorrect because $x^3 > x^2$ is not always true when $x > 0$. **Choice C** is incorrect because $x^3 > x^2$ is true when $x > 1$ but not true when $x < -1$. **Choice D** is incorrect because $x^3 > x^2$ is not true when $x = 0$.

86 **Choice C is correct** because the loss percentage incurred is 7%.

Write the correct equation that reflects the data in the given question.

(Selling price + $351) represents 20% more than (Cost price less 3%)

$1,395 + $351 = (1+20%) × Cost price × (1–3%)

Cost price = $\frac{\$1746}{97\% \times 120\%} = \$1,500$

If we know the Cost price and the Selling price, we can now calculate the value of the loss incurred
= $1,500 – $1,395 = $105

Choice A is incorrect because 2% is less than the obtained percentage. **Choice B** is incorrect because 5% is less than the obtained percentage. **Choice D** is incorrect because 10% is greater than the obtained percentage. **Choice E** is incorrect because 12% is greater than the obtained percentage.

87 **Choice C is correct** because the obtained answer is 165 birch trees.

First determine how many trees are maple and birch by calculating 60% of 440, 0.6 × 440 = 264.

The ratio of maple to birch is 3:5, which means $\frac{3}{8}$ are maple and $\frac{5}{8}$ are birch. $\frac{5}{8} \times 264 = 165$. There are 165 birch trees.

Choice A is incorrect because 33 is less than the obtained number of birch trees. **Choice B** is incorrect because 99 is less than the obtained number of birch trees. **Choice D** is incorrect because 264 is greater than the obtained number of birch trees. **Choice E** is incorrect because 275 is greater than the obtained number of birch trees.

88 **Choice A is correct** because Quantity A is greater than Quantity B.

Since ∠AOB is a central angle, it equals the measure of AB, and since ∠AOB is outside the circle but connects to AB, it is less than half of AB. Therefore ∠AOB > ∠AOB.

Alternate method: The external ∠AOB must be larger than either of the remote interior angles.

Choice B is incorrect because Quantity B is less than Quantity A. **Choice C** is incorrect because Quantity A is not equal to Quantity A. **Choice D** is incorrect because it is possible to use the given information to make a comparison between Quantity A and Quantity B.

89 **Choice D is correct** because since the cylinders have the same height, you can keep h constant and use the radius to compare the surface areas. To find the radius of each cylinder, use the volume formula for cylinders $V = \pi r^2 h$. Since h and π are constant that means the volumes ratios are the ratios of the r^2 value of each volume. So Cylinder A must have a radius of 6 if the value of 36 from the ratio equals r^2. Cylinder B must have a radius of 7 if the value of 49 from the ratio equals r^2.

Now that you have the radius of each cylinder, use the surface area formula for cylinders $SA = 2\pi rh + 2\pi r^2$. For Cylinder A you would get a surface area of $2\pi(6)h + 2\pi(6)^2$ which would simplify to be $12\pi h + 72\pi$. Factoring out 12π would get you $12\pi(h + 6)$.

For Cylinder B's surface area, you would get the formula $2\pi(7)h + 2\pi(7)^2$ which simplifies to be $14\pi h + 98\pi$. Factoring out 14π would get you $14\pi(h + 7)$.

Chapter 3: Arithmetic

Making these two surface areas into a ratio would get you $\frac{12\Pi(h+6)}{14\Pi(h+7)}$ which would simplify to be $\frac{6(h+6)}{7(h+7)}$.

Choice A is incorrect because this would not properly account for the surface area formula. **Choice B** is incorrect because this does not use r^2 or the proper formula to solve. **Choice C** is incorrect because this is not the correct relationship between variables. **Choice E** is incorrect because this does not account for r^2.

90 **Choice D is correct** because the obtained answer is $220.

If $\frac{2}{5}$ of the prize ($\frac{2}{5}$ of $600 = $240) is distributed to $\frac{3}{5}$ of the winners ($\frac{3}{5}$ of 20 is 12 *winners*), this indicates that each of those 12 winners will receive a minimum of $20. That leaves $360 to be divided among 8 remaining winners. If 7 of those winners receive minimum $20 (total $140), then the eighth winner would receive all the remaining prize money, $360 – $140 = $220.

Choice A is incorrect because $20 is less than the obtained remaining price. **Choice B** is incorrect because $25 is less than the obtained remaining price. **Choice C** is incorrect because $200 is less than the obtained remaining price. **Choice E** is incorrect because $300 is greater than the obtained remaining price.

91 **Choice B is correct** because each letter repeats after every five vowels, divide 327 by 5, and the remainder will determine the vowel in that place of the pattern. Since $327 \div 5 = 65$ with a remainder of 2, indicates that the second vowel (E) will be the 327th letter.

Choice A is incorrect because a is the first vowel in the line and not the second. **Choice C** is incorrect because i is the third vowel in the line and not the second. **Choice D** is incorrect because o is the fourth vowel in the line and not the second. **Choice E** is incorrect because u is the fifth vowel in the line and not the second.

92 **Choice C is correct** because to find the sum of a geometric series, you can use the formula $S = \frac{a_1(1-r^n)}{1-r}$. You need to first find r in order to solve which can be done by using the explicit formula for geometric series $a_n = a_1 r^{n-1}$. Plugging in from what is given you would get the equation $768 = \frac{3}{4}r^{6-1}$ which would simplify to be $768 = \frac{3}{4}r^5$.

Divide both sides by $\frac{3}{4}$ to get $\frac{768}{\frac{3}{4}}$ which is 1024. Now use a root to solve $1024 = r^5$ by doing $\sqrt[5]{1024} = r$ making $r = 4$.

Now you can use the formula $S = \frac{a_1(1-r^n)}{1-r}$ by plugging in $\frac{\frac{3}{4}(1-4^6)}{1-4}$ which equals $\frac{4095}{4}$.

Choice A is incorrect because this would be the answer if you just added a_1 and a_6. **Choice B** is incorrect because this answer results from a math error. **Choice D** is incorrect because this answer results from a math error. **Choice E** is incorrect because this answer results from a math error.

93 **Choice A is correct** because setting up an expression and working backwards would get you $46,890 as the original amount of funds. Start with $9378 and use that to determine the funds given to Charity C was also $9378 since they received half of the remaining and the other half would have been given to Charity D. Add these two amounts together to get $18,756 as the amount left before Charity C received their funds.

This means that since Charity B received $\frac{2}{5}$ of what was left over $18,756 represents $\frac{3}{5}$ which is what Charity A received. Use the expression $18756 \div \left(\frac{3}{5}\right)$ to get $31,260 as the amount remaining after Charity A took their funds. This is $\frac{2}{3}$ of the total amount so divide $31,260 by $\frac{2}{3}$ to get $46,890 as the total amount of funds available.

Choice B is incorrect because this would be the amount if you multiplied by 3 at the end. **Choice C** is incorrect because this results from a math error. **Choice D** is incorrect because this results from a math error. **Choice E** is incorrect because this results from multiplying the amount Charity D received by the denominator of each fraction which is not the proper way to solve.

94 **Choice C is correct** because to get an even integer from $x(a + b)$, you can only multiply an even and an odd or an even and an even. Therefore x does not always have to be odd and the relationship between a and b does not have to be *a* > *b*. If *a* = *b* + 2 then that means *a* + *b* will always be even since a number and the number 2 digits later will always be both even or both odd. An odd plus an odd will always be an even and an even plus an even will always be an even. If *a* + *b* is always even then *x* can be even or odd and the result will always be even.

Choice A is incorrect because this does not always result in an even. **Choice B is incorrect** because this does not always result in an even. **Choice D is incorrect because I and II are not always true. Choice E is incorrect because I is not always true.

95 **Choice E is correct** because statements I and III are correct.

Evaluate each statement separately.

Statement I must be true: Raising an even number to a power will always result in an even number. Eliminate choices (B) and (C) since they do not include statement I.

Statement II is not always true: If $2n = 8$, $n = 4$. Since this statement isn't always true, eliminate choice (D).

Statement III must be true: $2n$ will always result in an even number (whether *n* is odd or even) and when you subtract 1 from any even number, the result will always be an odd number.

Therefore, choice (E) is correct.

Choice A is incorrect because statement I is not the only true statement. **Choice B is incorrect** because statement II is not always true. **Choice C is incorrect** because statement II is not the only true statement. **Choice D is incorrect** because statement II is not true. **Choice F is incorrect** because includes statement II which is not true.

96 **Choices B and D are correct** because the obtained students and percentage is 14 and 40% respectively.

Total drink drunk by 5th class students = $\left(\frac{3}{7}\right) \times 21 = 9$ liters

Remaining drink = 30 − 9 = 21 liters

As each student of 10th class is given $\frac{3}{2}$ liter of drink then 21 liters will be given to $\frac{21}{\frac{3}{2}} = 14$ students.

Percentage will be $\left(\frac{14}{35}\right) \times 100 = 40\%$

Choice A is incorrect because 12 students are less than the number of students that receives the drink. **Choice C is incorrect** because 16 students are greater than the number of students that receives the drink. **Choice E is incorrect** because 50% is not the obtained percentage. **Choice F is incorrect** because 60% is not the obtained percentage.

97 **Choices A, B and C are correct** because statements I, II and III are true.

Let the integers be $(x − 1)$, x, $(x + 1)$.

Then $M = \frac{x-1+x+x+1}{3} = \frac{3x}{3} = x$.

Choice D is incorrect because it does not include III which is also a true statement. **Choice E is incorrect** because it does not include II which is also a true statement. **Choice F is incorrect** because I, II and III are true statements.

98 **Choices A and E are correct** because if we subtract 25 pounds from the total 205, then in the remaining 180 pounds their weights are equal. So, Sarah's weight will be 90 + 25 = 115 pounds. In kilograms it will be 115 × 0.4535 = 52.15 kg, it comes to approximately 52 kg.

Weight of Tony will be 205−115=90 pounds = 90 × 0.4535 = 41 kg.

Choice B is incorrect because 45 is less than Sarah's weight but greater than Troy's weight. **Choice C is incorrect** because 48 is less than Sarah's weight but greater than Troy's weight. **Choice D is incorrect** because 50 is oy's weight and Sarah's weight.

99 **Choices A, B and D are correct.**

Choice A is correct because 1 is less than 2 so $\frac{2^1}{1^2}$ would be an integer since it equals 2. **Choice B is correct** because 2 would still allow for an integer with $\frac{2^2}{2^2}$ equaling 1.

Choice D is correct because plugging in $\frac{2^4}{4^2}$ would give you $\frac{16}{16}$ which equals 1.

For the expression to be an integer the value of the numerator must be greater than the denominator. Since the value on top would represent a power of 2 it would always be less than the denominator for all values of $x \leq 2$ with the exception of $x = 4$ in the range {1, 8}.

Choice C is incorrect because 3 is greater than 2 so the numerator would be smaller than the denominator which would not result in an integer. Plugging in $\frac{2^3}{3^2}$ would give

Chapter 3: Arithmetic

you $\frac{8}{9}$. **Choice E is incorrect** because plugging in $\frac{2^5}{5^2}$ would give you $\frac{32}{25}$.

100 **Choices C and E are correct.**

Choice C is correct because for the fraction to be between 0 and 1, either *y* or *z* has to be negative to make a positive value with *x*. If either term was negative *yz* would also be < 0.

Choice E is correct because for the value of $\frac{xy}{z}$ to be between 0 and 1, the numerator must be smaller than the denominator.

Choice A is incorrect because if *y* < 0 you would get a positive numerator, but that does not determine what *z* is which would impact if the number was positive or negative. **Choice B** is incorrect because *z* < 0 you could get a value between 0 and 1, but if *y* is greater than z the statement would not work. **Choice D** is incorrect because *y* < *x* you would get a negative *y* value, but *z* could also be negative which would not guarantee a value between 0 and 1.

101 **Choice A, B and C are correct** because the statements are proven true.

Let's analyze each statement.

Statement A: More than half of the fans at the games are Patriots fans. This statement is true because the ratio 6:5 means that there are 6 Patriots fans in 11 sports fans and 6 is more than half of 11.

Statement B: If there are 72 Patriots at the game, there are 132 total fans (for both teams) In attendance. This statement is true because ratio of 6 Patriots fans in 11 sports fan is proportional to 72 Patriots fans in 132 total fans.

Let *x* be the number of Jets fans.
$$\frac{6}{5} = \frac{72}{x}$$
$$6x = 72(5)$$
$$6x = 360$$
$$x = 60$$

The total fans is 72 + 60 = 132 fans.

Statement C: If there are 110 total fans at the game, there are 10 more Patriots fans than Jets fans in attendance.

Divide 110 by 11. The answer is 10.

Use the ratio to find the number of fans for Patriots and Jets.

6:5
6(10):5(10)
60:50

Hence, the statement is true.

Statement D: There are more Jets fans at the game than Patriots fans. This statement is false because the ratio is clear that there are more Patriots fans than the Jets fans.

Choice D is incorrect because the ratio is clear that there are more Patriots fans than the Jets fans.

102 **Choices A and B are correct.**

Choice A is correct because if the side length decreases by 40%, it would be 60% of its original amount. The area would also be 60% of the original since only one side length changed.

Choice B is correct because imagine that the rectangle was a square. The original perimeter if the side length is *x* would be 4*x* since the perimeter is found by adding up all the sides. If one pair of the sides was reduced by 40% its new length would be 0.60*x*. The new perimeter would be 0.6*x* + 0.6*x* + *x* + *x*, which simplifies to be 2.2*x*. To find percentage loss, use the formula $\frac{initial - final}{initial}$ and plug in $\frac{4x - 2.2x}{4x}$ to get 0.45. Multiply this by 100 to get a percent change of 45%.

Choice C is incorrect because 60% less means to take 60% off the original area. This would not work if the side length is reduced by 40% because the area would have 40% taken off, not 60%.

103 **Choices B and D are correct.**

Choice B is correct because plugging in *x* = 10 would get you $0.2 \times \frac{9(10)}{250}$ which equals 0.072. **Choice D is correct** because this is the simplified equation of what is given. You can simplify the given expression to be $\frac{18}{1000} \times \frac{2x}{5}$ which equals $\frac{9x}{1250}$ to compare across the simplified answers. You can also use *x* = 10 within the given equation to yield $0.018 \times \frac{2(10)}{5}$ which equals 0.072 and compare this to the results from the answer choices.

Choice A is incorrect because this does not keep the same relationship between the numbers. If you use

$x = 10$, the given equation would yield $0.09 \times \dfrac{4(10)}{5}$ which equals 0.72 not 0.072. **Choice C is incorrect because** this does not keep the same relationship between the numbers. If you use $x = 10$, the given equation would yield $0.18 \times 4(10)$ which equals 7.2 not 0.072.

104 **Choices A, B and C are correct.** To find the possible range of respondents who were of voting age and did not own a home, first find the number of respondents who are of voting age by finding 70% of 5000. Multiplying 0.70 by 5000 would give you 3500 respondents of voting age. The problem then states at least 35% own a home. That means at most 65% do not own a home (100 − 35 = 65). That means the highest number of respondents that are of voting age and do not own a home would be 2275.

Choice A is correct because this number is less than 2275. **Choice B is correct** because this number is less than 2275. **Choice C is correct** because this is the highest number of respondents of voting age who do not own a home.

Choice D is incorrect because this is outside the possible number of respondents who do not own a home.

105 **Choices B, D and E are correct.**

Choice B is correct because if there were 270 people who voted for Candidate B, the ratio would be 450:270. This would give a total of 720 people surveyed which fits the given range. **Choice D is correct** because if there were 540 people who voted for Candidate B, the ratio would be 900:540 which would give a total of 1440 people surveyed which can be split evenly. **Choice E is correct** because if there were 840 people who voted for Candidate B, the ratio would be 1400:840 which would give a total of 2240 people which can be split evenly.

The total number of people surveyed needs to be divisible by 8 since the ratio of 5:3 would mean dividing the number of people by 8 (5 + 3).

Choice A is incorrect because this would not result in over 720 respondents. **Choice C is incorrect** because if there were 460 people who voted for Candidate B, the ratio would be 766.66:460 which is not a whole number ratio.

106 **Choices B, C, D, and H are correct** because the number of 6-inch train cars should be an even number to be hooked in pairs.

The table gives the number of train cars that need to be hooked to get the train lengths.

Total train length	No. of 6-inch trains	No. of 7-inch trains
30 inches	5	
31 inches	4	1
40 inches	2	4
46 inches	3	4
38 inches	4	2
53 inches	3	5
51 inches	5	3
59 inches	4	5

It is given that 6-inch train cars come in pairs. Option A, E, F, and G require that an odd number of 6-inch train cars be hooked together. However, they can be hooked in pairs.

Choice A is incorrect because the 30 inches train has one 6-inch train that has no pair. **Choice E is incorrect** because the 46 inches train has one 6-inch train that has no pair. **Choice F is incorrect** because the 51 inches train has one 6-inch train that has no pair. **Choice G is incorrect** because the 53 inches train has one 6-inch train that has no pair.

107 **Choice C is correct** because 12 divided by 4 results in 3 which is prime. **Choice E is correct** because 20 divided by 4 results in 5 which is prime.

If a number line is divided into 5 tick marks, that means that there are 4 intervals between them where x is added. If the first number on the number line is a then the next spot would be $a + x$ and so on until the last spot which would be $a + 4x$. The range of the number line would be the largest minus the smallest number which would be $a + 4x - a$ which would equal $4x$. This means any number divisible by 4 that results in a prime number would work.

Choice A is incorrect because 4 divided by 4 results in 1 which is not prime. **Choice B is incorrect** because 5 is not divisible by 4. **Choice D is incorrect** because 16 divided by 4 results in 4 which is not prime.

108 **The correct answer is 17** because the smallest possible value of b would be 6 since there is a remainder of 5 when a is divided by b since b has to be greater than 5. The smallest number that is divisible by 6 and would leave a remainder of 5 is 6 + 5 = 11. This means $a = 11$ and $b = 6$, making the smallest possible value of $a + b = 11 + 6 = 17$.

Chapter 3: Arithmetic

109 The correct answer is 2%. Those who do not use Instagram nor Pinterest can be represented as $P(A \cup B)'$.
First, let's solve for $P(A \cup B) = P(A) + P(B) - P(A \cap B)$
Substituting the given values in decimal form,
$P(A \cup B) = 0.96 + 0.85 - 0.83 = 0.98$
$P(A \cup B)' = 1 - (A \cup B)$
$P(A \cup B)' = 1 - 0.98 = 0.02$
The percentage form of the answer is 2%.

110 The correct answer is 11 because if you simplify by using properties of exponents you will be able to solve for x. Multiply both sides by 216^8 to get $36^x < 216^8$. Rewrite both numbers with the same base of 6 so that it becomes $\left(6^2\right)^x < \left(6^3\right)^8$. Simplify to get $6^{2x} < 6^{24}$. Since the numbers have the same base, you can compare the exponents, $2x < 24$. Divide both sides by 2 to get $x < 12$. This means the greatest integer value of x would be 11.

111 The correct answer is $-\dfrac{13}{2}$ because you can simplify the expression to solve for n. First simplify the numerator and denominator of the first fraction by finding a common denominator. For the top of the fraction, you can multiply 2 by $\dfrac{n}{n}$ to get $\dfrac{2n}{n} + \dfrac{4}{n}$ which could combine to be $\dfrac{2n+4}{n}$. For the bottom of the fraction, multiply 4 by $\dfrac{n}{n}$ to get $\dfrac{4n}{n} + \dfrac{2}{n}$ which could combine to be $\dfrac{4n+2}{n}$.
Now you will have the statement $\dfrac{\frac{2n+4}{n}}{\frac{4n+2}{n}}$ which can be simplified by keeping the numerator and multiplying by the reciprocal of the denominator. This would get you $\dfrac{2n+4}{n} \times \dfrac{n}{4n+2}$. The n will cancel out to leave $\dfrac{2n+4}{4n+2}$.
The equation is now $\dfrac{2n+4}{4n+2} = \dfrac{3}{8}$. Cross multiply to get $8(2n+4) = 3(4n+2)$. Distribute to get $16n + 32 = 12n + 6$. Subtract 32 from both sides and $12n$ to get $-4n = 26$. Divide by -4 and simplify to get $-\dfrac{13}{2}$.

112 The correct answer is $\dfrac{1}{7}$.
Let the area of the square be in square units.
Let the area of C be represented as c square units and the area of D be represented as d square units.
It is given that area of C = $\dfrac{2}{5}$ area of D, hence, Area of D = $\dfrac{5}{2}$ area of C
We also know that, area of C + Area of D = $\dfrac{1}{2}$ area of the square
Therefore,
$$c + \dfrac{5}{2}c = \dfrac{1}{2}s$$
$$\dfrac{2c+5c}{2} = \dfrac{s}{2}$$
$$\dfrac{7c}{2} = \dfrac{s}{2}$$
$$\dfrac{c}{s} = \dfrac{1}{2}\left(\dfrac{2}{7}\right)$$
$$\dfrac{c}{s} = \dfrac{1}{7}$$

113 The correct answer is 23 which is found quickest through guess and check. 9177 is a little greater than 8000 which is $20 \times 20 \times 20$. Using this relationship, you can use the closest odd consecutive numbers and do $19 \times 21 \times 23$ which does yield 9177.

114 The correct answer to 100.8 because if you set-up the relationship between the variables, you can solve for a relationship between d and $3a$. If a is 70% of b, b is 60% of c, and c is 80% of d, the $a = 0.7b$, $b = 0.6c$, and $c = 0.8d$. Working backwards, you could get the statement $a = 0.7(0.6)(0.8)d$. Plugin this into $3a$ would get you $3(0.7)(0.6)(0.8)d$ which simplifies to be $1.008d$. This means d is 100.8% of a.

115 The correct answer is $\dfrac{24}{25}$ because if you simplify both statements and compare you will be able to solve for a. For $\dfrac{16x}{5} = \dfrac{5}{4y}$, cross-multiply to get $64xy = 25$. For $\dfrac{4x}{3} = \dfrac{a}{2y}$, cross-multiply to get $8xy = 3a$. Compare $8xy$ to $64xy$ to determine multiplying by 8 will get the terms to match. Therefore $8(3a) = 25$. Simplify and then divide by 24 to solve for the value of $a = \dfrac{24}{25}$.

64 | GRE Quantitative Practice Questions

Practice Set 3 (Hard): Answers & Explanations

116 **Choice E is correct** because you can write expressions to identify a and b using the information given. If a is divided by 3 and has a remainder of 2, the algebraic expression $a = 3k + 2$ can be created where k is an integer. If b is divided by 6 and has a remainder of 1, the algebraic expression $b = 6m + 1$ can be created. Plugging these statements into $a^2 + b^2$ will give you the new statement $(3k+2)^2 + (6m+1)^2$ which can be expanded to be $9k^2 + 12k + 4 + 36m^2 + 12m + 1$.

To determine the remainder, rearrange the terms to be $9k^2 + 36m^2 + 12k + 12m + 5$. The number on the end would indicate a remainder of 5.

Choice A is incorrect because this answer results from a math error. **Choice B** is incorrect because this answer results from a math error. **Choice C** is incorrect because this answer results from a math error. **Choice D** is incorrect because this answer results from a math error.

117 **Choice B is correct** because working backwards and through guess and check you can determine −2, −1, 0, and 1 would work to get you a sum of −2. This would also satisfy $x^{y+z} = w$ if you arrange the numbers at $(-1)^{-2+0} = 1$.

Choice A is incorrect because no 4 consecutive integers will get you a sum of −3. **Choice C** is incorrect because no 4 consecutive integers will get you a sum of 0. **Choice D** is incorrect because the numbers −1, 0, 1, and 2 would work for this, but it is not possible to rearrange these to satisfy the expression $x^{y+z} = w$. **Choice E** is incorrect because the numbers 0, 1, 2 and 3 would work for this, but it is not possible to rearrange these to satisfy the expression $x^{y+z} = w$.

118 **Choice C is correct** because to find the sum of the 1st 50 terms, first see if there is a pattern to the terms. The value of the first term would be $-\frac{1}{1+1} + \frac{1}{1}$ which would simplify to be $-\frac{1}{2} + 1$ which equals $\frac{1}{2}$. The second term would be $-\frac{1}{2+1} + \frac{1}{2}$ which would simplify to be $-\frac{1}{3} + \frac{1}{2}$ which would equal $\frac{1}{6}$.

If you start adding these terms together unsimplified you might notice terms will cancel out $-\frac{1}{2} + 1 + -\frac{1}{3} + \frac{1}{2}$ cancels out the $\frac{1}{2}$. This cancellation will be the case all the way to term 50. So the final equation might look something like $1 + \frac{1}{50}$ with all the middle terms canceling each other. This means the sum will be $\frac{51}{50}$.

Choice A is incorrect because this results from a math error. **Choice B** is incorrect because this results from a math error. **Choice D** is incorrect because this results from a math error. **Choice E** is incorrect because this results from a math error.

119 **Choice B is correct** because the obtained answer is $1 - \frac{\pi}{4}$.

The circumference of a circle is the product of radius and 2π. So, dividing the circumference by 2π gives the measure of a radius. Denote the length of a radius by r. Then

$$r = \frac{12\pi}{2\pi}$$

Reduce the fraction by 2π.

$$r = 6$$

Denoting by Q, find the area of one-quarter of the circle.

$$Q = \frac{1}{4}\pi(6^2)$$
$$= 9\pi$$

A side of the square is same as a radius of the square. Denoting by S, find the area of the square.

$$S = 6^2 = 36$$

The difference between S and Q is the area of the region bounded by the circle, CE, and DE.

$$S - Q = 36 - 9\pi = 9(4 - \pi)$$

We are asked to find the ratio of S − Q to S. To do so, replace the known values in $\frac{S-Q}{S}$

$$\frac{S-Q}{S} = \frac{9(4-\pi)}{36}$$

Reduce the right fraction by 9.

$$\frac{S-Q}{S} = \frac{(4-\pi)}{4}$$

Decompose the right fraction.

$$\frac{S-Q}{S} = \frac{4}{4} - \frac{\pi}{4}$$
$$\frac{S-Q}{S} = 1 - \frac{\pi}{4}$$

Chapter 3: Arithmetic

Choice A is incorrect because $4\pi - 1$ is not equivalent to the obtained expression. **Choice C is incorrect** because $\frac{\pi}{4} - 1$ is not equivalent to the obtained expression. **Choice D is incorrect** because $\frac{1}{4} + 1$ is not equivalent to the obtained expression. **Choice E is incorrect** because $4\pi + 1$ is not equivalent to the obtained expression.

120 **Choice D is correct** because finding the prime factorization of 80, 450, and 760 will allow you to find their least common multiple. The prime factorization of $80 = 2^4 \times 5$, $450 = 2 \times 3^2 \times 5^2$ and $735 = 3 \times 5 \times 7^2$. Using these prime factorizations, it can be concluded that A must have a prime factorization at minimum of $2^4 \times 3^2 \times 5^2 \times 7^2$. This would give us the value 176400. Check each of the answers to determine which one would not be a factor of 176400 by dividing. Only 1512 is not divisible by 176400.

Choice A is incorrect because 245 is a factor of 17640 since 17640 divided by 245 equals 72. **Choice B is incorrect** because 315 is a factor of 17640 since 17640 divided by 315 equals 56. **Choice C is incorrect** because 980 is a factor of 17640 since 17640 divided by 980 equals 18. **Choice E is incorrect** because 3528 is a factor of 17640 since 17640 divided by 3528 equals 5.

121 **Choice C is correct** because you can create a table to visualize what is happening to the population from 1990 to 2010.

Year	Population
1990	x
2000	$(1+\frac{a}{100})x$
2010	$1.75x = (1+\frac{a}{100})(1+\frac{b}{100})x$

You also know that the increase in 2010 was double the increase in 2000 so you can create the statement that $2[(1+\frac{a}{100})x - x] = 1.75x - (1+\frac{a}{100})x$.

Now use a value of x to solve through for a which can be used to solve through with b. If you use 1000 for x, you can find a: $2[(1+\frac{a}{100})(1000) - 1000] = 1.75(1000) - (1+\frac{a}{100})(1000)$. This would simplify to be $2000(1+\frac{a}{100}) - 2000 = 1750 - (1000 + 10a)$. Simplifying further would get you $20a = 750 - 10a$. Simplify and combine like terms to get $30a = 750$. Divide by 30 to find $a = 25$. This means the population increased by 25% from 1990 to 2000.

Now solve for b, using the relationship $1.75x = \left(1+\frac{a}{100}\right)\left(1+\frac{b}{100}\right)x$. Plug in the values of $x = 1000$ and $a = 25$ to get $1.75(1000) = \left(1+\frac{25}{100}\right)\left(1+\frac{b}{100}\right)(1000)$. This will simplify to be $1750 = (1.25)(1000)\left(1+\frac{b}{100}\right)$. Simplify and divide by 1250 to get $1.4 = 1 + \frac{b}{100}$. Subtract 1 and multiply by 100 to find $b = 40$.

Choice A is incorrect because this would result from a calculation error. **Choice B is incorrect** because this is the value of a. **Choice D is incorrect** because this would not result in an overall 75% increase. **Choice E is incorrect** because this would result from a calculation error.

122 **Choice C is correct** because you can create an algebraic expression to compare the change in price to the total to find the new price of compound A. Use x to represent the original price of compound A and compound B. Since compound A increased in price by 40%, its new price would be $1.4x$. Since compound B decreased in price by 15%, its new price would be $0.85x$. You also know that 5 total ounces is split evenly between A and B so $2.5A + 2.5B = \$22.50$. Plug-in the earlier expressions in terms of x to get $2.5(1.4x) + 2.5(0.85x) = \$22.50$. Simplify to get $3.5x + 2.125x = 22.50$. Combine to get $5.625x = 22.50$ and then divide to get $x = 4$.

This is the original price of compound A so multiply by 1.4 to get the new price of $5.60.

Choice A is incorrect because this is the price of compound A before the price change. **Choice B is incorrect** because this is the price if you divide $22.50 by 5. **Choice D is incorrect** because this price would be too high for the relationship to work. **Choice E is incorrect** because this price would be too high for the relationship to work.

123 **Choice B is correct** because input in a value of a and b that satisfies the given relationship in order to compare all values. For example if $a = -10$ and $b = \frac{1}{2}$, the lowest value comes from $\frac{a}{b^2}$ which would be $\frac{-10}{\left(\frac{1}{2}\right)^2}$ which equals -40.

Choice A is incorrect because using $a = -10$ and $b = \frac{1}{2}$, you would get -5 which is not as low as -40.

Choice C is incorrect because using $a = -10$ and $b = \frac{1}{2}$, you would get $-\frac{21}{2}$ which is not as low as -40.

Choice D is incorrect because using $a = -10$ and $b = \frac{1}{2}$, you would get -20 which is not as low as -40.

Choice E is incorrect because using $a = -10$ and $b = \frac{1}{2}$, you would get $\frac{20}{21}$ which is not as low as -40.

124 **Choices C, D and E are correct.**

Choice C is correct because to give an even product you have to multiply an even and an odd or an even and an even. The only pairings possible with a 7:8 ratio are an even and an odd or two evens. **Choice D is correct** because to get a ratio of 7:8, x must always be a multiple of 7 and y must be the corresponding multiple of 8 so x will never be greater than y. **Choice E is correct** because y is a multiple of 8 and all multiples of 8 are divisible by 4.

Choice A is incorrect because if x was 7 and y was 8 then $x + y$ would be 15 which would have the greatest prime factor of 5. That being said, x could be 77 and y could be 88 making the value of $x + y$ equal to 165 which has a prime factor of 11. **Choice B is incorrect** because to get an even number when adding two integers, they both need to be odd or they both need to be even. This is possible if you make $x = 14$ and $y = 16$ since the answer to $14 + 16$ would be 30 which is even.

125 **Choices A, B, D and F are correct** because these expressions are even integers.

Define the even integers m and n as follows, where a and b are some integers.

(1) $m = 2a$

(2) $n = 2b$

Examine all the answer choices using the definitions (1) and (2).

Choice (A): $3mn = [3(2a)(2b)]$: Replace m and n with their equivalents.

$= 12ab$: Multiply the numbers on the right.

This is an even integer.

Choice (B): $(3m + 2)(3n - 2) = [3(2a) + 2][3(2b) - 2]$: Replace m and n with their equivalents.

$= [2(3a + 1)][2(3b - 1)]$: Factor 2 out within each bracket.

The result is divisible by 4. So, the choice (B) is an even integer, as well.

Choice (C): Using (1) and (2), we have

$3(2m - 3)(3n - 1) = 3[2(2a) - 3][3(2b) - 1]$

$= 3(4a - 3)(6b - 1)$: Find the product inside each bracket.

$= 3[3(2a - 1)][3(2b - 1)]$: Factor 3 out within each parenthesis.

$= 27(2a - 1)(2b - 1)$: Multiply the factors 3.

Since one less than an even number is an odd number, $(2a - 1)$ and $(2b - 1)$ are odd integers for all integers a and b. So, the product $27(2a - 1)$ and $(2b - 1)$ is an odd integer as a result. Therefore, this expression produces an odd integer for the integers m and n defined in the problem.

Choice (D): Using (1) and (2), we have

$5(5m + 2)(5n - 6) = 5[(5(2a) + 2][5(2b) - 6]$

$= 5(10a + 2)(10b - 6)$: Find the product inside each bracket.

$= 20(5a + 1)(5b - 3)$: Factor 2 out of each parenthesis.

$(5a + 1)$ and $(5b - 3)$ are odd integers for all integers a and b. However, the product $20(2a - 1)(2b - 1)$ is an even integer due to the coefficient 20.

Choice (E): Using (1) and (2), we have

$\frac{1}{64}m^3n^3 = (2a)^3(2b)^3$: Replace m and n with their equivalents.

$= \frac{1}{64}(8a^3)(8b^3)$: Raise inside each parenthesis to its power.

$= a^3 b^3$: Multiply the coefficients.

Since a and b can be odd numbers, then $a^3 b^3$ is not divisible by 2.

Choice (F): Using (1) and (2), we have

$m^2 n^3 = (2a)^2 (2b)^3$: Replace m and n with their equivalents.

$= (4a^2)(8b^3)$: Raise inside each parenthesis to its power.

$= 32a^2 b^3$: Multiply the coefficients.

Since $32a^2 b^3$ is divisible by 2, $m^2 n^3$ is divisible by 2, and it is an even integer.

Choice C is incorrect because $3(2m - 3)(3n - 1)$ does not satisfy the given condition where it should be an even integer. **Choice E is incorrect** because $\frac{1}{64}m^3n^3$ it is not divisible by 2, thus not an even integer.

126 **Choices B and C are correct.**

Choice B is correct because the only way to get this result is if $a = 1$ and $b = 2$ so you would be able to determine the relationship between a and b. **Choice C is correct** because this would mean $a = 1$ and $b = 2$ which would give a relationship between the numbers.

Chapter 3: Arithmetic

Based on the first statement that the remainder when x is divided by 2 is a, the value of a can only by 1 or 0. Likewise, the value of b must be 0, 1, or 2. If you know something about one of the integers, you likely can determine its relationship to the other.

Choice A is incorrect because this would mean $a = 1$, but it does not tell us anything about b. **Choice D is incorrect** because this does not solve for anything you don't already know.

127 **Choices B, C and D are correct.**

Choice B is correct because 6 is not prime. **Choice C is correct** because 12 is not prime. **Choice D is correct** because 15 is not prime.

To determine if $(n - 1)!$ is a multiple of n, there must be a value below n that n is a multiple of. Therefore prime numbers would not work. All other numbers should satisfy the condition.

Choice A is incorrect because 2 is a prime number.
Choice E is incorrect because 23 is a prime number.

128 **Choices A and D are correct.**

Choice A is correct because $30(A + B)$ will be $30\left(\frac{1}{2} + \frac{2}{3}x + \frac{3}{10} + \frac{3}{5}y\right)$ which will give you $20x + 18y + 24$.

Choice D is correct because $24y(A + C) = 24y\left(\frac{1}{2} + \frac{2}{3}x + \frac{5x}{8y} + \frac{5}{8}\right)$ which simplifies to equal $16xy + 15x + 27y$.

Simplify each of the given values first to be able to compare to the answers quicker. A will become $\frac{1}{2} + \frac{2}{3}x$, B will become $\frac{3}{10} + \frac{3}{5}y$, and C will end up $\frac{5x}{8y} + \frac{5}{8}$.

Choice B is incorrect because this does not work with the simplified version of B and C. The statement $10(B + C)$ would become $10\left(\frac{3}{10} + \frac{3}{5}y + \frac{5x}{8y} + \frac{5}{8}\right)$ which simplifies to be $3 + 6y + \frac{25x}{4y} + \frac{25}{4}$. This does not equal $6y + 6xy + 6$. **Choice C is incorrect** because this does not work with the simplified version of A and B. The statement $(B + A)$ would be $\left(\frac{3}{10} + \frac{3}{5}y + \frac{1}{2} + \frac{2}{3}x\right)$ which simplified to be $\frac{4}{5} + \frac{3}{5}y + \frac{2}{3}x$ which is not equal to $4x + 4y + 5$.

129 **Choices B and D are correct.**

Choice B is correct because each discount can be represented by $\left(1 - \frac{x}{100}\right)$ so the final price can be found by multiplying the original price by the discount twice.

Choice D is correct because the total percentage decrease would be the difference between the original value and the final value which is expressed as the final percent off minus the original percent off. If the value of x was 10% and the original price of the book was $100, then 10% reduction followed by another 10% reduction would be $100(1 - 0.10)(1 - 0.10)$ which equals 81. The total percent decrease would be $\frac{100 - 81}{100}$ which is 19%. Plugging in 10 into the statement $2\left(\frac{1}{x}\right) - \frac{x}{100x}$ gives you $2\left(\frac{1}{10}\right) - \frac{10}{100(10)}$ which simplifies to be 19%.

Choice A is incorrect because this does not properly solve for the complete discount. **Choice C is incorrect** because this does not properly solve for the total percent decrease.

130 **The correct answer is 30** because using the current ratio to get to a 1:3 ratio will require a removal of 30 jelly beans. To identify this create the statement $\frac{25-a}{25-b} = \frac{1}{3}$. The constant a will be the number of red jelly beans to remove and the constant b will be the number of yellow jelly beans to remove with $a > b$. Cross multiplying you will get the relationship $75 - 3a = 25 - b$. Simplifying this will get you $50 - 3a = b$.

You also know that $a > b$ so $a > 50 - 3a$ which would simplify to be $4a > 50$ and dividing both sides by 4 gives you $a > 12.5$. This means the least number of jelly beans to remove from the red jelly beans would be 13 and therefore the most amount of yellow jelly beans would be 12. Plugging these ideas into the equation $\frac{25-13}{25-12}$ would get us $\frac{12}{13}$ which is not $\frac{1}{3}$.

This atleast gives you a starting point to evaluate the ratio. You cannot go lower than 13 jellybeans for yellow so find the nearest multiple of 3 that is greater than 13 to try out options. This would be 15 and the ratio would be $\frac{x}{15} = \frac{1}{3}$ which allows you to determine x must be 5. To get to 5 red jelly beans, you would need to remove 20. To get to 15 yellow jelly beans you would need to remove 10. That would be a total of 30 jelly beans removed.

Chapter 4
Algebra

Chapter 4: Algebra

Practice Set 1: Easy

$x < 0$, $a > 0$ and $y > 0$

Quantity A	Quantity B
xy	$-a$

- Ⓐ Quantity A is greater.
- Ⓑ Quantity B is greater.
- Ⓒ The two quantities are equal.
- Ⓓ The relationship cannot be determined from the information given.

It is given that $4x - 10 \geq x + 8$

Quantity A	Quantity B
x	5

- Ⓐ Quantity A is greater.
- Ⓑ Quantity B is greater.
- Ⓒ The two quantities are equal.
- Ⓓ The relationship cannot be determined from the information given.

$3 > p > 1$

Quantity A	Quantity B
$\dfrac{p}{2}$	$\dfrac{p+2}{4}$

- Ⓐ Quantity A is greater.
- Ⓑ Quantity B is greater.
- Ⓒ The two quantities are equal.
- Ⓓ The relationship cannot be determined from the information given.

Quantity A	Quantity B
The slope of the line defined by $2y + 3x - 5 = 0$	$\dfrac{3}{2}$

- Ⓐ Quantity A is greater.
- Ⓑ Quantity B is greater.
- Ⓒ The two quantities are equal.
- Ⓓ The relationship cannot be determined from the information given.

$2x + 3y = 22$

$4x - y = 16$

Consider the following system of linear equations shown above.

Quantity A	Quantity B
x	y

- Ⓐ Quantity A is greater.
- Ⓑ Quantity B is greater.
- Ⓒ The two quantities are equal.
- Ⓓ The relationship cannot be determined from the information given.

If $8y - 4x = 5$ and $y > 800$.

Quantity A	Quantity B
The least integer value of x	1600

- Ⓐ Quantity A is greater.
- Ⓑ Quantity B is greater.
- Ⓒ The two quantities are equal.
- Ⓓ The relationship cannot be determined from the information given.

Practice Set 1: Easy

7 There was a group of students going on the train for an excursion. When a co-passenger asked one of the students how many of them were going for the excursion, the student replied "If you add twice the number of us and half the number and half of the number of us and yourself it will be 100 people".

Quantity A	Quantity B
The number of students traveling	42

Ⓐ Quantity A is greater.
Ⓑ Quantity B is greater.
Ⓒ The two quantities are equal.
Ⓓ The relationship cannot be determined from the information given.

8 James and Alex together can complete a task in 4 hours. James, Alex, and Robert together can complete the same task in 2 hours.

Quantity A	Quantity B
The time Robert can complete the task alone	The time James can complete the task alone

Ⓐ Quantity A is greater.
Ⓑ Quantity B is greater.
Ⓒ The two quantities are equal.
Ⓓ The relationship cannot be determined from the information given.

9 The roots of the quadratic inequality $x^2 + 2x - 24 < 0$ are a and b., where $a > 0$ and $b < 0$.

Quantity A	Quantity B
$a - b^2$	$ab + 2b$

Ⓐ Quantity A is greater.
Ⓑ Quantity B is greater.
Ⓒ The two quantities are equal.
Ⓓ The relationship cannot be determined from the information given.

10

$$x > y$$
$$xy \neq 0$$

Quantity A	Quantity B
$\dfrac{x}{y}$	$\dfrac{y}{x}$

Ⓐ Quantity A is greater.
Ⓑ Quantity B is greater.
Ⓒ The two quantities are equal.
Ⓓ The relationship cannot be determined from the information given.

11 The price of an item on sale is greater than $100 and less than $250.

Quantity A	Quantity B
The price of the item after a 15%-off discount then a $30-off discount	The price of the item after a $20-off discount then a 20%-off discount

Ⓐ Quantity A is greater.
Ⓑ Quantity B is greater.
Ⓒ The two quantities are equal.
Ⓓ The relationship cannot be determined from the information given.

12 One root of the equation $2x^2-(3-k)x + 17(x-2) - 20 = 0$ is the other root squared.

Quantity A	Quantity B
The smallest root of the equation	k

Ⓐ Quantity A is greater.
Ⓑ Quantity B is greater.
Ⓒ The two quantities are equal.
Ⓓ The relationship cannot be determined from the information given.

Chapter 4: Algebra

13. Distance from A to B is 12 miles.
Distance from A to C is 10 miles.

Quantity A	**Quantity B**
Distance from A to B	Distance from B to C

Ⓐ Quantity A is greater.
Ⓑ Quantity B is greater.
Ⓒ The two quantities are equal.
Ⓓ The relationship cannot be determined from the information given.

14.

Solve for x : $4^{2x+6} = 8^{6x+12}$

Quantity A	**Quantity B**
x	-2

Ⓐ Quantity A is greater.
Ⓑ Quantity B is greater.
Ⓒ The two quantities are equal.
Ⓓ The relationship cannot be determined from the information given.

15. If $a > b$, and $ab > 0$, which of the following must be true?

I. $a > 0$
II. $b > 0$
III. $\dfrac{a}{b} > 0$

Ⓐ I only
Ⓑ II only
Ⓒ III only
Ⓓ I and II only
Ⓔ I and III only

16. If $5 \leq x \leq 9$ and $6 \leq y \leq 12$, which of the following represents all the possible values of xy?

Ⓐ $30 < xy < 108$
Ⓑ $30 = xy = 108$
Ⓒ $30 > xy > 108$
Ⓓ $30 \leq xy \leq 108$
Ⓔ $30 \geq xy \geq 108$

17. Which linear equation is **not** equivalent to $y = 5x + (8 - 2x) - 2(1 + x)$?

Ⓐ $y - x - 6 = 0$
Ⓑ $y = -x - 6$
Ⓒ $y = x + 6$
Ⓓ $y - x = 6$
Ⓔ $-x + y = 6$

18. On the first day of the month, the bakery had an inventory of 600 loaves of bread. It bakes 180 loaves of bread and sells 220 loaves of bread each day that it is open, and closes for a baking day when it runs out of loaves. How many days can it be open before it must close for a baking day?

Ⓐ 5
Ⓑ 10
Ⓒ 15
Ⓓ 20
Ⓔ 25

19. If $-5x + 2y = 9$ and $3x - 4y = -4$, then what is the value of $7x + 10y$?

Ⓐ -19
Ⓑ -17
Ⓒ -9
Ⓓ 9
Ⓔ 19

Practice Set 1: Easy

20. Bill has to type a paper that is *P* pages long, with each page containing *w* words. If Bill types an average of *x* words per *minute*, how many *hours* will it take him to finish the paper?

    (A) 60 *wps*
    (B) $\dfrac{wx}{60p}$
    (C) $\dfrac{60wp}{60x}$
    (D) $\dfrac{wpx}{60}$
    (E) $\dfrac{wp}{60x}$

21. Alex invested $52,000 for one month in bonds that pay simple annual interest at the rate of *r* percent. He earned $390 in interest for the month. What is the value of *r*?

    (A) 7.5
    (B) 8
    (C) 8.5
    (D) 9
    (E) 9.5

22. In the *xy*-coordinate plane, point S lies on the line *y* = 3. What is the *x*-coordinate of point S if it is located 3 units to the left of point (5,3)?

    (A) 1
    (B) 2
    (C) 3
    (D) 4
    (E) 5

23. $9x^2 - 16y^2$ is equivalent to which of the following?

    (A) $(3x-4y)(3x-4y)$
    (B) $(3x-3y)(4x+4y)$
    (C) $(4x-3y)(4x+3y)$
    (D) $(3x-4y)(3x+4y)$
    (E) $(3x+4y)(3x+4y)$

24. A car travels 140 miles in 4 hours, while the return trip takes $3\dfrac{1}{2}$ hours. What is the average speed in miles per hour for the entire trip?

    (A) 35
    (B) $37\dfrac{1}{3}$
    (C) $37\dfrac{1}{2}$
    (D) 40
    (E) 75

25. Variables *x* and *y* are all positive integers.

Quantity A	Quantity B
$\sqrt{\dfrac{x^{12}y^2}{9x^2y^{-4}}}$	$\sqrt[3]{27x^4x^{11}y^{-7}y^{16}}$

    (A) Quantity A is greater
    (B) Quantity B is greater
    (C) The quantities are equal.
    (D) The relationship cannot be determined from the information given.

26. Consider the function $f(x) = \dfrac{13}{-2-x}$. Which of the following input values renders the function undefined?

    (A) −4
    (B) −2
    (C) 2
    (D) 4
    (E) 6

27. Dave jogs at a constant speed of 5 miles per hour. How far will he travel in 45 minutes?

    (A) 2.25
    (B) 3.75
    (C) 4.50
    (D) 5.25
    (E) 6.75

Chapter 4: Algebra

28 Solve for $x: 4^{3x+6} = 8^{6x+12}$

- Ⓐ −4
- Ⓑ −2
- Ⓒ 2
- Ⓓ 4
- Ⓔ 6

29 Jared placed $15,000 into a savings account that paid simple annual interest at a rate of *r* percent. After 6 months, Jared made $300 in interest. What is the value of *r*?

- Ⓐ 2.00
- Ⓑ 4.00
- Ⓒ 6.00
- Ⓓ 8.00
- Ⓔ 10.00

30 When x ≠ 1, what is the sum of the roots of the equation?

$$x+5 = \frac{-4x-17}{x+1} - \frac{-x-2}{x+1}$$

- Ⓐ −9
- Ⓑ −7
- Ⓒ 7
- Ⓓ 9
- Ⓔ 11

31

If $\frac{(x^2 + 7x + 6)}{2} = 3$, then *x* could equal:

- Ⓐ −6
- Ⓑ −1
- Ⓒ 0
- Ⓓ 1
- Ⓔ 3

32 Sophia starts the summer with $800 in her savings account. She wants to have at least $300 left in the account by the end of the summer. She withdraws $50 each week for dining out, entertainment, and other expenses. How many weeks can she withdraw $50 before she needs to ensure she has at least $300 remaining?

Indicate all that apply.

- A 6
- B 7
- C 8
- D 9
- E 10
- F 12
- G 14

33 Which of the following points fall outside of the region defined by $4y \leq -3x + 24$?

Indicate all such points.

- A (2,4)
- B (3,7)
- C (0,0)
- D (5,5)
- E (1,3)
- F (2,8)
- G (4,2)

34 Which of the following equations have an even integer as the solution?

Indicate all such answers.

- A $3x - 5 = 5x + 1$
- B $5(2x - 3) = 3x - 1$
- C $2x + 7 = 5x - 8$
- D $7 + 3x = 7x - 9$
- E $2x - 7 = 5x + 2$
- F $-10x - 9 = 2x + 3$

35 If $y = 2x + 7$ and $y = 4x - 5$, then what is the value of $(x + y)^2$?

☐

36. Car A was traveling at a speed of 20mph for 15 hours to get to Destination A. If Car B was driving 10mph faster than Car A, how long would it take Car B to get to the same destination?

37. Given the functions $f(x) = 2x + 4$ and $g(x) = 3x - 6$, what is x if $f(g(x)) = 28$?

Practice Set 2: Medium

38.

It is given that $0 < p < 1$

Quantity A	Quantity B
$\dfrac{1}{p^2}$	$\dfrac{1}{(p+1)^2}$

- Ⓐ Quantity A is greater.
- Ⓑ Quantity B is greater.
- Ⓒ The two quantities are equal.
- Ⓓ The relationship cannot be determined from the information given.

39.

$x > 0$

$0 < x^2 < 1$

Quantity A	Quantity B
$1 - x^2$	$1 - x$

- Ⓐ Quantity A is greater.
- Ⓑ Quantity B is greater.
- Ⓒ The two quantities are equal.
- Ⓓ The relationship cannot be determined from the information given.

40.

Quantity A	Quantity B
The value of x where $2 - 3|x| < 4$	The value of y where $4y - 3 > 13$

- Ⓐ Quantity A is greater.
- Ⓑ Quantity B is greater.
- Ⓒ The two quantities are equal.
- Ⓓ The relationship cannot be determined from the information given.

41.

Let $x < 0$, $y > 0$ and $|x| > y$

Quantity A	Quantity B
$= \dfrac{2x^2 + y}{2y + x^3 + 3}$	$= \dfrac{x + 2y^2}{2y + x^2 + 3}$

- Ⓐ Quantity A is greater.
- Ⓑ Quantity B is greater.
- Ⓒ The two quantities are equal.
- Ⓓ The relationship cannot be determined from the information given.

42. There are x employees in Company A. The number of employees in Company B is 85% of 20 less than thrice the employees in company A.

Quantity A	Quantity B
Employees in company B	$0.85(3x - 20)$

- Ⓐ Quantity A is greater.
- Ⓑ Quantity B is greater.
- Ⓒ The two quantities are equal.
- Ⓓ The relationship cannot be determined from the information given.

Chapter 4: Algebra

43.

$$\frac{9-5x}{7} \geq -3$$

Quantity A	Quantity B
The minimum value $10-x$	The minimum value of $\frac{-3x}{5} + 4$

- Ⓐ Quantity A is greater.
- Ⓑ Quantity B is greater.
- Ⓒ The two quantities are equal.
- Ⓓ The relationship cannot be determined from the information given.

44.

$$4x + 5y = 35$$
$$2 \leq x \leq 5$$

Quantity A	Quantity B
x	y

- Ⓐ Quantity A is greater.
- Ⓑ Quantity B is greater.
- Ⓒ The two quantities are equal.
- Ⓓ The relationship cannot be determined from the information given.

45.

$$y = x^2 + 4$$
$$y = 2x + 7$$

Quantity A	Quantity B
x	y

- Ⓐ Quantity A is greater.
- Ⓑ Quantity B is greater.
- Ⓒ The two quantities are equal.
- Ⓓ The relationship cannot be determined from the information given.

46.

$$3x - 2y = 6$$
$$2x + 2y = 9$$

Quantity A	Quantity B
$x - y$	1.5

- Ⓐ Quantity A is greater.
- Ⓑ Quantity B is greater.
- Ⓒ The two quantities are equal.
- Ⓓ The relationship cannot be determined from the information given.

47.

$$a > 1$$
$$a - 1 = b$$

Quantity A	Quantity B
b^2	$a^2 - 1$

- Ⓐ Quantity A is greater.
- Ⓑ Quantity B is greater.
- Ⓒ The two quantities are equal.
- Ⓓ The relationship cannot be determined from the information given.

48.

$$x > y > 0$$

Quantity A	Quantity B
$y - x$	0

- Ⓐ Quantity A is greater.
- Ⓑ Quantity B is greater.
- Ⓒ The two quantities are equal.
- Ⓓ The relationship cannot be determined from the information given.

49

$$0 < r < 5$$

Quantity A	Quantity B
$30(r-2)$	$20r$

Ⓐ Quantity A is greater.
Ⓑ Quantity B is greater.
Ⓒ The two quantities are equal.
Ⓓ The relationship cannot be determined from the information given.

50 An airplane flew 400 km from point P due east to point Q, then 400 km due north to point R, then 100 km due west to the point S, and finally straight back to P from S. The average speed from R to P is 50% more than the average speed form P to R.

Quantity A	Quantity B
The ratio of time taken to fly from point P to R to the time taken to return to point P	2:1

Ⓐ Quantity A is greater.
Ⓑ Quantity B is greater.
Ⓒ The two quantities are equal.
Ⓓ The relationship cannot be determined from the information given.

51 For the integers a, b and c, the sum of a and b is 75% of c.

Quantity A	Quantity B
$(2/3)(a + b)$	$(3/4)(c)$

Ⓐ Quantity A is greater.
Ⓑ Quantity B is greater.
Ⓒ The two quantities are equal.
Ⓓ The relationship cannot be determined from the information given.

52

$$n > 0$$

Quantity A	Quantity B
$\dfrac{n^2 + 2}{n}$	$n + \dfrac{1}{n}$

Ⓐ Quantity A is greater.
Ⓑ Quantity B is greater.
Ⓒ The two quantities are equal.
Ⓓ The relationship cannot be determined from the information given.

53 The roots of the quadratic equation $x^2 - 5x + 6 = 0$ are a and b.

Quantity A	Quantity B
$2(a - b)$	$-ab$

Ⓐ Quantity A is greater.
Ⓑ Quantity B is greater.
Ⓒ The two quantities are equal.
Ⓓ The relationship cannot be determined from the information given.

54

$f(x) = x^2 + kx - 6$, where k is constant.

3 is a root of $f(x)$

Quantity A	Quantity B
The value of k	-1

Ⓐ Quantity A is greater.
Ⓑ Quantity B is greater.
Ⓒ The two quantities are equal.
Ⓓ The relationship cannot be determined from the information given.

Chapter 4: Algebra

55.

Equation 1: $4^x - 4^{3-x} = 12$

Equation 2: $25^{\sqrt{y}} - 6 \times 5^{\sqrt{y}} + 5^{\sqrt{1}} = 0$

Quantity A	Quantity B
x	y

(A) Quantity A is greater.
(B) Quantity B is greater.
(C) The two quantities are equal.
(D) The relationship cannot be determined from the information given.

56.

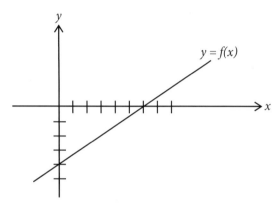

The figure shows the graph of function $f(x)$ with y intercept -4 and x intercept 6.

Quantity A	Quantity B
The slope of $f(x)$	The sum of the slopes of the following linear functions $g(x) = 3/4x - 2$, $h(x) = 4$ and $i(x) = x - 2$

(A) Quantity A is greater.
(B) Quantity B is greater.
(C) The two quantities are equal.
(D) The relationship cannot be determined from the information given.

57. Albert and Benjamin borrowed $8000 at 6% per annum simple interest and $6000 at 10% per annum simple interest respectively. If after N years their total debts are equal what is the value of N?

Quantity A	Quantity B
N	16

(A) Quantity A is greater.
(B) Quantity B is greater.
(C) The two quantities are equal.
(D) The relationship cannot be determined from the information given.

58. A bus left Dallas en route to Houston (195 miles away), traveling at an average speed of 39 mph. Later, a car left Houston for Dallas at an average speed of 65 mph. Both vehicles reached their destinations at the same time. They take the same route/ cover the same distance.

Quantity A	Quantity B
The distance covered by the bus before the car left Houston	The distance remaining for the bus to cover when the car was halfway the journey

(A) Quantity A is greater.
(B) Quantity B is greater.
(C) The two quantities are equal.
(D) The relationship cannot be determined from the information given.

59. A man buys 16 shirts. Some of them cost $13 each, while the remainder cost $10 each. The cost of all 16 shirts is $187.

Quantity A	Quantity B
The number of $13 shirts purchased	The number of $10 shirts purchased

(A) Quantity A is greater.
(B) Quantity B is greater.
(C) The two quantities are equal.
(D) The relationship cannot be determined from the information given.

Practice Set 2: Medium

60

$$y = 3x^2 + 8x - 10$$

Quantity A	Quantity B
x	$y - 10$

- (A) Quantity A is greater.
- (B) Quantity B is greater.
- (C) The two quantities are equal.
- (D) The relationship cannot be determined from the information given.

61 If $|x - y| = |x| + |y|$ and x and y are both nonzeroes, then which of the following must be true?

- (A) $xy = 0$
- (B) $xy > 0$
- (C) $x - y > 0$
- (D) $x + y \geq 0$
- (E) $x + y = 0$

62 For how many integer values of x, is $|2x + 3| + |x - 3| + |x| < 15$?

- (A) 4
- (B) 5
- (C) 6
- (D) 7
- (E) 8

63

$$4x - 3 \leq 5x + 2 < 3x + 12$$

Given the inequality above, which of the following is the range of possible values for x?

- (A) $x < 7$
- (B) $x \geq -6$
- (C) $-5 \leq x < 5$
- (D) $-6 \langle x \rangle 7$
- (E) $-7 \geq x > 5$

64 For which of the values of n is $27 < 3n < 243$ hold true?

- (A) 1
- (B) 2
- (C) 3
- (D) 4
- (E) 5

65 A grandmother was thirteen times the age of her granddaughter five years ago. The grandmother will be five times the age of her granddaughter 5 years hence. What is the sum of the present ages of the grandmother and the granddaughter?

- (A) 75
- (B) 80
- (C) 90
- (D) 95
- (E) 100

66 Jasmine and Alexa went shopping. Jasmine spent $120 on 3 pairs of shoes and 6 shirts. Alexa spent $90 on the same 2 pairs of shoes and 5 shirts. What is the cost of 1 pair of shoes?

- (A) $10.00
- (B) $12.00
- (C) $15.00
- (D) $20.00
- (E) $25.00

67 If $4|x + 3| - 7 \leq 5$, which of the following must be true about the value of x?

- (A) $4 \leq x \leq 6$
- (B) $-5 \leq x \leq 5$
- (C) $-6 \leq x \leq 6$
- (D) $-6 \leq x \leq 0$
- (E) $-2 \leq x \leq 4$

Chapter 4: Algebra

68. If $-10 < 2x < 12$ and $-9 < 3y < 27$, which of the following specifies all the possible values of xy?

- A) $-45 < xy < 54$
- B) $15 < xy < 54$
- C) $9 < xy < 36$
- D) $-9 < xy < 27$
- E) $-15 < xy < 42$

69.
$$3y - ax + 7 = 0$$
$$-8x + 16y - 10 = 0$$

In the linear system above, what is the value of a would give no solution?

- A) $-\dfrac{3}{2}$
- B) $\dfrac{1}{2}$
- C) 1
- D) $\dfrac{3}{2}$
- E) 2

70. After 4 years, Henry will be four times as many years old as Jacob is now. If Henry were thrice as old as he was 4 years ago, and if Jacob were twice as old as he was one year ago, the sum of their ages would be 30. What will be the sum of their ages after 5 years?

- A) 20
- B) 22
- C) 24
- D) 26
- E) 28

71.
$$ax - 3y = -7$$
$$4x + 6y = 5$$

In the linear system of equations above, what value of a would give no solution?

- A) -3
- B) -2
- C) 2
- D) 3
- E) 4

72. A taxi charges a base fare of d dollars for the first three miles and c cents per quarter mile for every mile after the first three. Which equation describes cost of a taxi ride of n miles in dollars.

- A) $dn - c/4$
- B) $cd + 4n - 3$
- C) $d - (3n)(1/4c)$
- D) $d + (n-3)(1/4c)$
- E) $d + (n+3)(1/4c)$

73. Find the slope of the linear inequality $3x - 4y \leq 12 - 2x + y$.

- A) 1
- B) 2
- C) 3
- D) 4
- E) 6

74. What is $x + y - z$ if $x + y = 8$, $x + z = 11$, $y + z = 7$?

- A) 3
- B) 6
- C) 12
- D) 13
- E) 23

Practice Set 2: Medium

75

Quantity A	Quantity B
The number of real roots in the quadratic equation $f(x) = 2x^2 - 3x + 1$	The number of real roots in the quadratic equation $f(x) = x^2 - 7x - 8$

(A) Quantity A is greater.
(B) Quantity B is greater.
(C) The two quantities are equal.
(D) The relationship cannot be determined from the information given.

76 If $x^2 - 6x - 27 = 0$ and $y^2 - 6y - 40 = 0$, what is the maximum value of $2(x - y)$?

(A) 17
(B) 18
(C) 19
(D) 21
(E) 26

77 If $f(x) = ax^4 - 5x^2 + ax - 5$, then $f(b) - f(-b)$ will equal:

(A) 0
(B) $2ab$
(C) $3ab^4 - 7b^2 - 8$
(D) $-3ab^4 + 7b^2 + 8$
(E) $3ab^4 - 4b^2 + 5ab - 6$

78 If $x > y$, $x < 9$, and $y > -4$, what is the largest prime number that could be equal to $x + y$?

(A) 5
(B) 7
(C) 11
(D) 13
(E) 17

79 If $x^2 - 6x - 27 = 0$ and $y^2 - 6y - 40 = 0$, what is the minimum value of $x + y$?

(A) -7
(B) -6
(C) -5
(D) -4
(E) -3

80 Carl leaves his house at 6:00 am and drives due west at a speed of 50 mph. Joseph leaves the same house at 7:30 pm and drives due west at a speed of 70 mph. At what time will Joseph have gone exactly 55 miles past Carl?

(A) 11:00 am
(B) 12:00 pm
(C) 1:00 pm
(D) 2:00 pm
(E) 3:00 pm

81 If $-5x + 2y = 9$ and $3x - 4y = -4$, then what is the value of $7x + 10y$?

(A) -19
(B) -17
(C) -9
(D) 9
(E) 19

82 If $y^2 - 12y = -27$ and $x^2 - 8x = 20$, what is the maximum value of $x + y$?

(A) 12
(B) 15
(C) 19
(D) 20
(E) 21

Chapter 4: Algebra

83 Which of the following equations is for the line that is perpendicular to $y = 1 - 2x$ and passes through the point $(0,3)$?

- A) $y = \dfrac{x}{2} + 3$
- B) $y = 2x + 8$
- C) $y = 4x + 1$
- D) $y = 3x - \dfrac{1}{2}$
- E) $y = 4x - 4$

84 Solve for x:

$$3^{x+2} + 3^{x-1} = \left(\dfrac{28}{9}\right)$$

- A) -2
- B) -1
- C) $-\dfrac{1}{2}$
- D) $\dfrac{1}{2}$
- E) 2

85 If $\dfrac{(3a+2b)}{(7a+4b)} = \dfrac{15}{32}$, then what is $\dfrac{(3a+b)}{7b}$?

- A) $\dfrac{1}{3}$
- B) $\dfrac{1}{2}$
- C) $\dfrac{2}{3}$
- D) $\dfrac{3}{4}$
- E) $\dfrac{4}{5}$

86 Three pipes take 24 minutes, 6 minutes and 12 minutes respectively to fill a tank. If these pipes are turned on at the same time, find the most accurate range of time within which the pipes will fill the tank.

- A) 7.1 to 9 minutes
- B) 1 to 3 minutes
- C) More than 9 minutes
- D) 5.1 to 7 minutes
- E) 3.1 to 5 minutes

87 Conglomerate Corp manufactures hubcaps in 3-different factories. How many days would it take to manufacture a million hubcaps if these factories produce hubcaps in the following ratios:

The first two factories can manufacture a hundred thousand hubcaps in 15 days while the third factory is thirty percent faster.

- A) 38
- B) 42
- C) 44
- D) 46
- E) 50

88

$$\dfrac{8^{2x} \times 4^{x+1}}{16^{x-2}}$$

What is the value of the expression above when $x = 2$?

- A) 128
- B) 512
- C) 2^{18}
- D) 12^8
- E) 8^{12}

89 If $m - n = 1$, where $m \neq -n$, which of the following statements could be true?

- A) $m(m - 1) = n(n + 1)$
- B) $m(m + 1) = n(n - 1)$
- C) $n(m + 1) = m(n - 1)$
- D) $n(m - 1) = m(n + 1)$
- E) $m(m + n) = n(m - n)$

90 In the xy coordinate plane $y = x\sqrt{5}$ is equation of a line. $P(x_1, y_1)$ is a point on the line

Quantity A	Quantity B
x_1	y_1

Ⓐ Quantity A is greater.
Ⓑ Quantity B is greater.
Ⓒ The two quantities are equal.
Ⓓ The relationship cannot be determined from the information given.

91 A principal amount becomes 4 times its original value in 20 years at simple interest. What is the rate of interest?

Ⓐ 5%
Ⓑ 10%
Ⓒ 12%
Ⓓ 15%
Ⓔ 20%

92 At the beginning of each year, an investment of $1500 is added to an account that earns simple interest at a rate of 6% per year. How much money will be in the account after 4 years?

Ⓐ $900
Ⓑ $4200
Ⓒ $5900
Ⓓ $6000
Ⓔ $6900

93

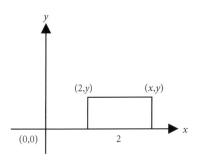

If the figure above is a rectangle, then what is the area of the figure, expressed in terms of x and y?

Ⓐ xy
Ⓑ 4x
Ⓒ 8x
Ⓓ y(x − 2)
Ⓔ x(y − 2)

94 Laura can paint a room in 12 hours, and Alex can paint the same room in 8 hours. How many hours will it take Laura and Alex, working together at their respective constant rates, to paint the room? (Assume that they can work on the same room without changing each other's work rate.)

Ⓐ 2.2
Ⓑ 3.8
Ⓒ 4.8
Ⓓ 5.2
Ⓔ 6.3

Chapter 4: Algebra

95

Points A, B, C, and D are on the number line above, $AB = CD = \frac{1}{2}(BC)$. What is the coordinate of C?

- A) $\frac{5}{24}$
- B) $\frac{6}{24}$
- C) $\frac{11}{24}$
- D) $\frac{15}{24}$
- E) $\frac{17}{24}$

96 If $|-2x+7| > 5$, select all possible values for x:

- A) -6
- B) 0
- C) 2
- D) 4
- E) 7

97 If $b < 2$ and $2x - 3b = 0$, then which of the following can be values of x?

Indicate all such answers.

- A) -4
- B) -3
- C) -2
- D) -1
- E) 0
- F) 1
- G) 2
- H) 3
- I) 4

98 The intersection of the following two equations is at (1,1). Find all possible values of t.

$$2x + 8y = 10$$
$$2tx - ty = t$$

- A) -4
- B) -3
- C) 1
- D) 2
- E) 5

99 The sum of the digits of two-digit number m is 12. The tens digit is 2 more than the units digit. Find the possible units digit of the number m.

- A) 1
- B) 2
- C) 3
- D) 4
- E) 5

100 Which of the following algebraic expressions are equivalent to $2x^2 - 2$?

Indicate all such answers.

- A) $4(x^2 - 2) - 2(x^2 - 3)$
- B) $2(x^2 - 2) - 4(x^2 + 3)$
- C) $2(x - 1)(x + 1)$
- D) $(x + 6)(x + 1) + (8 + x)(1 - x)$
- E) $2(x + 4)(x - 1) - 3(2x + 5)$

101 Which of the following are equivalent to $\dfrac{5x}{3y^2}$?

- A) $\dfrac{(15x^3)(x^{-2}y^3)^2}{\left(\frac{1}{3}xy^{-4}\right)^{-2}}$

- B) $\dfrac{(3x^3)(3x^2y^3)^2}{\left(\frac{1}{5}xy^{-4}\right)^2}$

- C) $\dfrac{(5x^2)^2(y^2)^2}{(15x^3)(y^2)^3}$

- D) $\dfrac{(3x^5y^2)^{-2}}{(5x^4y)^{-2}x^3}$

Practice Set 2: Medium

102 If x, y and z are three different non-negative integers, which of the following could be true?

i) $|x-y| = |x+y| = |y-z|$
ii) $x^y = y^z$
iii) $x^3 + y^3 = z^3$

- A) i only
- B) ii only
- C) iii only
- D) i and ii
- E) i and iii

103 If Kelly received $\frac{1}{3}$ more votes than Mike in a student election, which of the following could have been the total number of votes cast for the two candidates?

Indicate all such answers.

- A) 2
- B) 3
- C) 4
- D) 7
- E) 8
- F) 10
- G) 12
- H) 14
- I) 16
- J) 21

104 Select all of the following equations that are parallel and are 5 vertical units apart from $y = x - 5$

Indicate all such answers.

- A) $2x - 6y = 10$
- B) $3y - 9x = 12$
- C) $5x - 5y = 50$
- D) $10y = 10x$

105 In the xy-plane, triangular region R is bounded by the lines $x = 0$, $y = 0$ and $2x + 3y = 50$. Which of the following points lie inside region R?

Indicate all such points.

- A) (10,10)
- B) (6,5)
- C) (15,10)
- D) (5,15)
- E) (2,15)

106 If there is exactly one solution to the equation $4x2 - bx + 9 = 0$, where $b > 0$, what is the value of b?

107 Jane operates a coffee shop. Her monthly fixed costs amount to $660. It costs her $2 to make each cup of coffee. She sells each cup for $8. How many cups of coffee must Jane sell in order to break even?

108 A cricket player played 3 matches against team A with an average of 42 runs. Then he played 5 matches against team B with an average of 38 runs. What will be his average in all 8 matches? Write your answer in the answer box.

109 If $\frac{5x^2 + ax + b}{3x^2 + 7x + 5} = x$ and $3x^3 + 2x^2 - b = 0$, where $x \neq 0$, what is the value of a?

Chapter 4: Algebra

110. If $x^2 - 30x + 225 = 0$ then what the value of $(x + x^{-1})$?

111. If $0 < 5n < 500$, where n is a non-negative integer, what is the greatest value of $\frac{1}{2^n}$?

112. Max is traveling at 25 miles per hour during his trip. He travels for 14 hours to get to his destination. Gas costs $3.76 per gallon and his car averages 10 miles per gallon. If he starts off with $175.00, how much money does he have remaining when he reaches his destination?

113. Determine the positive value of y, where the graphs of $y = x^2 - 2$ and $y = 2x + 1$ intersect.

114. Find the rate of interest given that the money invested will triple in 25 years on simple interest.

115. Find the y-coordinates of the point that divides the directed line segment $\overline{AB}$ with the coordinates of endpoints at $A(-4, 0)$ and $B(0, 4)$ in the ratio 3:1.

Practice Set 3: Hard

116.

Inequality 1: $4(x+2) \leq 2(x+5) + 14$

Inequality 2: $\sqrt{16 - 8y + y^2} \leq 9$

Quantity A	Quantity B
x, where x is a solution of Inequality 1	y, where y is a solution of Inequality 2

- A) Quantity A is greater.
- B) Quantity B is greater.
- C) The two quantities are equal.
- D) The relationship cannot be determined from the information given.

117. Trapezoid JKLM in the x-y plane has coordinates $J = (-3, -4)$, $K = (-3, 1)$, $L = (4, 7)$, and $M = (4, -4)$.

Quantity A	Quantity B
Perimeter of Trapezoid JKLM	$23 + \sqrt{85}$

- A) Quantity A is greater.
- B) Quantity B is greater.
- C) The two quantities are equal.
- D) The relationship cannot be determined from the information given.

118
X is a 3-digit number and Y is a 4 digit number. All the digits of X are greater than 5, and all the digits of Y are less than 4.

Quantity A
The sum of the digits of X

Quantity B
The sum of the digits of Y

- Ⓐ Quantity A is greater.
- Ⓑ Quantity B is greater.
- Ⓒ The two quantities are equal.
- Ⓓ The relationship cannot be determined from the information given.

119
a and b are positive integers, and $a(a+3) - 153 = ab$.

Quantity A
The remainder when a is divided by 2

Quantity B
The remainder when b is divided by 2

- Ⓐ Quantity A is greater.
- Ⓑ Quantity B is greater.
- Ⓒ The two quantities are equal.
- Ⓓ The relationship cannot be determined from the information given.

120

$$f(x) = 7^x - 7^{x-2}$$
$$g(x) = 48(7^6)$$

Quantity A
x when $f(x) = g(x)$

Quantity B
10

- Ⓐ Quantity A is greater.
- Ⓑ Quantity B is greater.
- Ⓒ The two quantities are equal.
- Ⓓ The relationship cannot be determined from the information given.

121
Andrew can run 6 laps in x minutes. Ryan can run 11 laps in $2x$ minutes.

Quantity A
The number of minutes it takes Andrew to run 24 laps

Quantity B
The number of minutes it takes Ryan to run 22 laps

- Ⓐ Quantity A is greater.
- Ⓑ Quantity B is greater.
- Ⓒ The two quantities are equal.
- Ⓓ The relationship cannot be determined from the information given.

122
In the rectangular coordinate system shown, point A and E lie on the x-axis, and point B and D lie on the y-axis. Point C is the midpoint of the line AB, and point F is the midpoint of the line DE.

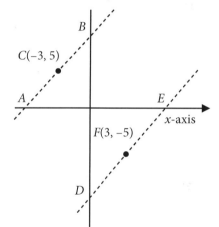

Quantity A
The slope of AB

Quantity B
The slope of DE

- Ⓐ Quantity A is greater.
- Ⓑ Quantity B is greater.
- Ⓒ The two quantities are equal.
- Ⓓ The relationship cannot be determined from the information given.

Chapter 4: Algebra

123

$$\frac{2x+7}{x-1} > 3$$

Given the inequality above, what are the possible values of *x*?

Indicate all such values.

- [A] −1
- [B] 0
- [C] 1
- [D] 3
- [E] 5
- [F] 7
- [G] 9
- [H] 11

124 Point *M*(3,2) lies on a line with slope 3/4. Point N lies on the same line and is 5 units from point M. Which of the following could be the y-coordinates of point N?

Indicate all such coordinates.

- [A] −1
- [B] 2
- [C] 3
- [D] 4
- [E] 5

125 A bakery receives a delivery of baked goods every day, 7 days per week. The delivery company charges *d* dollars per delivery plus *c* cents per item delivered. If in the first week, the bakery received an average of *x* items per day, what is the total cost, in *d* dollars, for the deliveries in that week?

Indicate all such answers.

- [A] $7x\left(\dfrac{c}{100}\right) + 7d$
- [B] $7d\left(\dfrac{x}{100}\right) + 7c$
- [C] $7c\left(\dfrac{d}{100}\right) + 7x$
- [D] $\dfrac{7c}{100} + 7xd$
- [E] $7\left(\dfrac{xc}{100} + d\right)$

126 Which of the following could be the units digit of $m = 87x$, where *x* is an integer greater than 1?

Indicate all such values.

- [A] 1
- [B] 2
- [C] 3
- [D] 4
- [E] 5
- [F] 6
- [G] 7
- [H] 8
- [I] 9

88 | GRE Quantitative Practice Questions

Practice Set 3: Hard

127 At 1:00 PM, a hose began draining water from a tank at a constant rate of 150 gallons per hour. At 3:00 PM, an additional hose started operating, increasing the total rate at which the water was being drained to 300 gallons per hour. The tank was empty before 5:00 PM the same day. Which of the following could have been the amount of water, in gallons, in the pool at 12:00 noon that day?

Indicate all such answers.

- [A] 600
- [B] 800
- [C] 1000
- [D] 1200
- [E] 1500

128 Which of the following conclusions are true of the graph $f(x) = 2x^2 - 7x + 3$?

Indicate all such answers.

- [A] The parabola opens down.
- [B] The parabola has a minimum of 3.
- [C] The roots can be calculated using factoring.
- [D] The axis of symmetry is located at the graph of the linear equation $x = \dfrac{7}{4}$.
- [E] The x–intercepts of the graph are located at $x = -3$ and $x = -\dfrac{1}{2}$.
- [F] The graph of the parabola intersects the y axis at $y = 3$.

129 Consider two lines in the coordinate plane: Line M with equation $y = mx + n$, and Line N with equation $y = px + q$. Which of the following could be the equations of M and N, respectively?

Indicate all that apply.

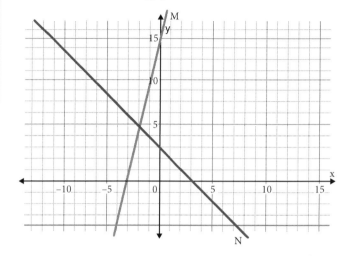

- [A] $y = -5x + 15$ and $y = 5x + 15$
- [B] $y = -5x + 10$ and $y = 3x + 1$
- [C] $y = 5x + 15$ and $y = -x + 3$
- [D] $y = 5x - 15$ and $y = -x - 3$
- [E] $y = 15x + 5$ and $y = 3x - 1$

130 Find the product of the integer values of x that satisfy the inequality.

$$(x^4 - 5x^2 + 4 < 0).$$

[ ]

Answer Key

Q. No.	Correct Answer	Your Answer	Q. No.	Correct Answer	Your Answer	Q. No.	Correct Answer	Your Answer	Q. No.	Correct Answer	Your Answer
1	D		34	B,D		68	A		100	A,C	
2	A		35	625		69	D		101	A,C	
3	D		36	10		70	D		102	D	
4	B		37	6		71	B		103	D,H,J	
5	A		38	A		72	D		104	C,D	
6	B		39	A		73	A		105	A,B,E	
7	B		40	D		74	A		106	12	
8	B		41	A		75	C		107	110	
9	A		42	C		76	E		108	39.5	
10	D		43	A		77	B		109	5	
11	B		44	D		78	E		110	$\frac{226}{15}$	
12	A		45	B		79	A		111	1	
13	D		46	C		80	D		112	43.40	
14	C		47	B		81	A		113	7	
15	C		48	B		82	C		114	8%	
16	D		49	B		83	A		115	3	
17	B		50	C		84	B		116	D	
18	C		51	B		85	A		117	C	
19	A		52	A		86	E		118	A	
20	E		53	D		87	D		119	C	
21	D		54	C		88	C		120	B	
22	B		55	A		89	A		121	C	
23	D		56	B		90	D		122	C	
24	B		57	A		91	D		123	D,E,F,G	
25	B		58	A		92	E		124	A,E	
26	A		59	A		93	D		125	A,E	
27	B		60	D		94	C		126	A,C,G,I	
28	B		61	C		95	C		127	A,B	
29	B		62	D		96	A,B,E		128	B,C,D,F	
30	A		63	C		97	A,B,C,D,E,F,G		129	C	
31	C		64	D		98	A,B,C,D,E		130	4	
32	A,B,C,D,E		65	B		99	E				
33	B,D,F		66	D							
			67	D							

Practice Set 1 (Easy): Answers & Explanations

1 **Choice D is correct.**

Since $x < 0$, x is less than zero, or a negative number

$y > 0$, y is greater than zero, or a positive number

Thus, xy is a product of a negative number and a positive number; hence it is a negative number of unknown value.

$a > 0$, a is greater than zero, or a positive number.

Thus, $-a$ makes the number negative; hence it is a negative number of unknown value.

Since both expressions are negative but have unknown values, a comparison cannot be made.

Choice A is incorrect. The explanation above shows that Quantity A is a negative number of unknown value. **Choice B** is incorrect. The explanation above shows that Quantity B is a negative number of unknown value. **Choice C** is incorrect. The quantities are not equal in any case.

2 **Choice A is correct.**

$$4x - 10 \geq x + 8$$
$$3x \geq 18$$
$$x \geq 6$$

Choice B is incorrect. Quantity B has 5 which is less than Quantity A. **Choice C** is incorrect. The two quantities have different values. **Choice D** is incorrect. There is enough data to determine the relationship between the two.

3 **Choice D is correct.**

Always be sure to plug in twice for Quantitative Comparison questions. You need to plug in numbers for p that are between 3 and 1. If $p = 2$, then Quantity A is 1 and Quantity B is 1. Since the quantities can be equal, you can cross out choices A and B. Now plug in a weird number. If $p = 1.5$ then Quantity A is .75 and Quantity B is .875. The quantities are no longer equal, so you can get more than one result. That means the answer must be D.

Choice A is incorrect. The example above shows that Quantity A is not always greater. **Choice B** is incorrect. The example above shows that Quantity B is not always greater. **Choice C** is incorrect. The quantities can be equal and not equal based on the number plug in.

4 **Choice B is correct.**

We know that if a line is represented as $y = mx + c$ then m defines the slope of the line.

Writing the given equation of the straight line in the similar format we get,

$$2y + 3x - 5 = 0$$
$$2y = -3x + 5$$
$$y = \left(-\frac{3}{2}\right)x + \frac{5}{2}$$

So, the slope of the given line is $-\frac{3}{2}$ which is smaller than $\frac{3}{2}$

The correct answer is Choice B.

Choice A is incorrect. Quantity A has a slope of $-\frac{3}{2}$ which is less than Quantity B. **Choice C** is incorrect. The two quantities have different values. **Choice D** is incorrect. There is enough data to determine the relationship between the two.

5 **Choice A is correct.** Apply the substitution method to solve the system of linear equations. Isolate y in the second equation first: $4x - 16 = y$ or $y = 4x - 16$. Now, substitute this expression of y into the first equation then solve for x.

$$2x + 3(4x - 16) = 22$$
$$2x + 12x - 48 = 22$$
$$14x = 70$$
$$x = 5$$

Solve for y by substituting $x = 5$ into the expression, $y = 4x - 16$. Hence, $y = 20 - 16 = 4$. This means that Quantity A is greater than Quantity B.

Choice B is incorrect $x = 5 > y = 4$. **Choice C** is incorrect because x and y have different values. **Choice D** is incorrect because it is possible to find the solution to the system of linear equations and then compare their quantities.

6 **Choice B is correct.**

Given $8y - 4x = 5$

$$8y = 4x + 5$$
$$y = \frac{4x + 5}{8}$$

Chapter 4: Algebra

Now $y > 800$

$$\therefore \frac{4x+5}{8} > 800$$

$$\therefore 4x + 5 > 6400$$

Hence $4x > 6395$

$$\therefore x > \frac{6395}{4}$$

$$\therefore x > 1598.75$$

So the least integer value of $x = 1599$

Choice A is incorrect. Quantity A has 1599 which is less than Quantity B. **Choice C** is incorrect. The two quantities have different numbers of values. **Choice D** is incorrect. There is enough data to determine the relationship between the two.

 Choice B is correct. Let x be the number of students traveling.

Then

By the given data

$$2x + \frac{1}{2}x + \frac{1}{2}\left(\frac{1}{2}\right)x + 1 = 100$$

$$2x + \frac{1}{2}x + \frac{1}{4}x = 99$$

$$2\frac{3}{4}x = 99$$

$$\frac{11}{4}x = 99$$

$$x = 99 \times \frac{4}{11} = 36$$

$\therefore 36$ students were traveling.

Choice A is incorrect. Quantity A has 36 which is less than Quantity B. **Choice C** is incorrect. The two quantities have different values. **Choice D** is incorrect. There is enough data to determine the relationship between the two.

8 **Choice B is correct** because the obtained values showed that Quantity B is greater than Quantity B. Write the equation using the combined rate of work formula $\frac{1}{t_1} + \frac{1}{t_2} = \frac{1}{t_b}$.

James and Alex working together $\frac{1}{J} + \frac{1}{A} = \frac{1}{4}$

James, Alex and Robert working together

$$\frac{1}{J} + \frac{1}{A} + \frac{1}{R} = \frac{1}{2}$$

Analyze the quantities.

Quantity A: The time Robert can complete the task alone

$$\frac{1}{J} + \frac{1}{A} + \frac{1}{R} = \frac{1}{2}$$

$$\left(\frac{1}{4}\right) + \frac{1}{R} = \frac{1}{2}$$

$$\frac{1}{R} = \frac{1}{2} - \frac{1}{4}$$

$$\frac{1}{R} = \frac{1}{4}$$

$$R = 4$$

Robert can do it alone in 4 hours.

Quantity B: The time James can complete the task alone

$$\frac{1}{J} + \frac{1}{A} = \frac{1}{4}$$

James and Alex together can complete the task in 4 hours. Hence, it can be assumed that James alone and Alex alone can complete the task in more than 4 hours.

Hence, Quantity B is greater than Quantity A.

Choice A is incorrect because Quantity A is not greater than Quantity B. **Choice C** is incorrect because Quantity A and Quantity B are not equal. **Choice D** is incorrect because a relation can be obtained from the given information.

9 **Choice A is correct** because the obtained values showed that Quantity A is greater than Quantity B.

Given: $x^2 + 2x - 24 < 0$

$a > 0$

$b < 0$

Find the roots of the quadratic inequality.

$$x^2 + 2x - 24 < 0$$

$$x^2 + 2x - 24 = 0$$

$$(x+6)(x-4) = 0$$

Roots are:

$(x+6) = 0 \qquad (x-4) = 0$

$x = -6 \qquad x = 4$

The roots are a and b, where $a > 0$ and $b < 0$. Hence, from the obtained value of the roots, $a = 4$ and $b = -6$.

Let's analyze the value of each quantity.

Practice Set 1 (Easy): Answers & Explanations

Quantity A	Quantity B
$a - b^2 = 4 - (-6)^2$	$ab + 2b = 4(-6) + 2(-6)$
$= 4 - 36$	$= -24 + (-12)$
$= -32$	$= -36$

Choice B is incorrect because Quantity B is less than Quantity A. **Choice C** is incorrect because Quantity A is not equal to Quantity B. **Choice D** is incorrect because a relation can be obtained from the given information.

10 **Choice D is correct.** Try values for the variables.

If $x = 2$ and $y = 1$, then 2 in Quantity A is greater than $\frac{1}{2}$ in Quantity B.

But, if $x = -1$ and $y = -2$, then $\frac{1}{2}$ in Quantity A is less than 2 in Quantity B.

Since more than one relationship is possible, choice D is correct.

Choice A is incorrect. The example above shows that Quantity A is not always greater. **Choice B** is incorrect. The example above shows that Quantity B is not always greater. **Choice C** is incorrect. The quantities are not equal in any case.

11 **Choice B is correct** because within the given range of the price, Quantity B is always greater than Quantity A.

Given: $\$100 < p < \$250$, where p is the price of the item
Apply the discounts for each quantity.

Quantity A:
Applying the 15% discount – $\quad p - 0.15p = 0.85p$
Applying the $30 less discount – $\quad 0.85p - 30$

Quantity B:
Applying the $20 discount – $\quad p - 20$
Applying the 20% discount – $0.8(p - 20) = 0.8p - 16$

Let's analyze the value of each quantity.
When $p = 101$
Quantity A:
$0.85p - 30$
$0.85(101) - 30$
$\$55.85$

Quantity B:
$0.8p - 16$
$0.8(101) - 16$
$\$64.80$

When $p = 245$
Quantity A:
$0.85p - 30$
$0.85(249) - 30$
$\$181.65$

Quantity B:
$0.8p - 16$
$0.8(249) - 16$
$\$183.2$

Choice A is incorrect because Quantity A is less than Quantity B. **Choice C** is incorrect because Quantity A is not equal to Quantity B. **Choice D** is incorrect because a relation can be obtained from the given information.

12 **Choice A is correct.**

$2x^2 - (3 - k)x + 17(x - 2) - 20 = 0$ is a quadratic equation, and any quadratic equation can be written as:

$x^2 - Sx + P = 0$ where S is the sum of the roots and P is the product of the roots. We need to bring it to this form.

$2x^2 - (3 - k)x + 17(x - 2) - 20$
$= 2x^2 - 3x + kx + 17x - 34 - 20$
$= 2x^2 + (14 + k)x - 54 = 0$

If we divide by 2, $x^2 + \frac{(14+k)x}{2} - 27 = 0$

We know that one root of the equation is the other root squared, we can express the roots as y and y^2

The product of the roots is -27
$y \times y^2 = -27$
$y^3 = -27$
$y = -3$

The roots of the equation are -3 and 9. The smallest root is -3.

The sum of the roots is $\frac{(14+k)}{2}$

$\frac{(14+k)}{2} = -(-3+9) = -6$

$14 + k = -12$
$k = -26$

-3 is greater than -26, hence Quantity A is greater.

Chapter 4: Algebra

Choice B is incorrect. Quantity B has −26 which is less than Quantity A. **Choice C** is incorrect. The two quantities have different values. **Choice D** is incorrect. There is enough data to determine the relationship between the two.

13 **Choice D is correct.** Since we know nothing about the placement of A, B, and C, we cannot determine anything about their distances.

Choice A is incorrect. The explanation shows that Quantity A cannot be determined as greater. **Choice B** is incorrect. The explanation shows that Quantity B cannot be determined as greater. **Choice C** is incorrect. The quantities cannot be determined as equal in any case.

14 **Choice C is correct.**

Given: $4^{3x+6} = 8^{6x+12}$

4^{3x+6} can be written as $2^{2\,(3x+6)} = 2^{18x+36}$

$\therefore 2^{6x+12} = 2^{18x+36}$

Since bases are the same exponents also will be the same.

Hence $6x+12 = 18x+36$

$\therefore 12x = -24$

$\therefore x = -2$

Choice A is incorrect. The two quantities are equal; therefore, neither quantity is greater. **Choice B** is incorrect. The two quantities are equal; therefore, neither quantity is greater. **Choice D** is incorrect. There is enough data to determine the relationship between the two.

15 **Choice C is correct.**

Because a and b must both be positive, or both be negative, choice C is the only answer that must be true.

Choice A is incorrect. If a and b are positive, then $a > 0$ must be true, but if both are negative, a could be negative, thus this is not valid. **Choice B** is incorrect. If a and b are positive, then $b > 0$ must be true, but if both are negative, b could be negative, thus this is not valid. **Choice D** is incorrect. Statement I and II are not valid. **Choice E** is incorrect. Only statement III is valid.

16 **Choice D is correct** because the obtained answer is $30 \leq xy \leq 108$.

Given:
$$5 \leq x \leq 9$$
$$6 \leq y \leq 12$$

Find the all the possible values of xy.
$$5(6) \leq xy \leq 9(12)$$
$$30 \leq xy \leq 108$$

Choice A is incorrect because the inequality symbol is < instead of ≤.

Choice B is incorrect because the symbol between the obtained range is not an equal sign but an inequality sign.

Choice C is incorrect because the inequality symbol is > instead of ≤.

Choice E is incorrect because the inequality symbol is ≥ instead of ≤.

17 **Choice B is correct** because the simplified form of given linear equation is not equivalent to $y = -x - 6$.

Simplify the linear equation.
$$y = 5x + (8-2x) - 2(1+x)$$
$$y = 5x + (8-2x) - 2 - 2x$$
$$y = 5x - 2x - 2x + 8 - 2$$
$$y = x + 6$$

The simplified form of the linear equation can be written in different ways such as:
$$y - x - 6 = 0$$
$$y = x + 6$$
$$y - x = 6$$
$$-x + y = 6$$

Choice A is incorrect because $y - x - 6 = 0$ is equivalent to the simplified form of the linear equation. **Choice C** is incorrect because $y = x + 6$ is equivalent to the simplified form of the linear equation. **Choice D** is incorrect because $y - x = 6$ is equivalent to the simplified form of the linear equation. **Choice E** is incorrect because $-x + y = 6$ is equivalent to the simplified form of the linear equation.

18 **Choice C is correct** because the obtained value of x is 15.

Given:

inventory of loaves	: 600 loaves
daily bake	: 180 loaves
# of loaves sold daily	: 220 loaves

Find the linear equation $y = mx + b$ that represents the problem.

Let y be the number of remaining loaves from the inventory.

Let x be the number of days that the bakery is open.

Let m be the net change in inventory per day.

Let b be the initial number of loaves.

Let's find the net change in inventory per day.

daily bake − # of loaves sold daily = # of loaves taken from the inventory

$m = -(220 - 180)$

$m = -40$

So the linear equation is

$y = -40x + 600$

To find the number of days that the bakery should be open before it closes for a baking day is when the number of remaining loaves from the inventory becomes zero. Hence, we find x when $y = 0$.

$y = -40x + 600$

$0 = -40x + 600$

$-600 = -40x$

$15 = x$

Choice A is incorrect because 5 is lesser than the obtained number of days before the bakery closes for a baking day. **Choice B** is incorrect because 10 is lesser than the obtained number of days before the bakery closes for a baking day. **Choice D** is incorrect because 20 is not the obtained number of days before the bakery closes for a baking day. **Choice E** is incorrect because 25 is greater than the obtained number of days before the bakery closes for a baking day.

19 **Choice A is correct.** To determine the value of $7x + 10y$, we need to solve the system of equations for x and y using the linear combination or elimination method.

$2(-5x + 2y = 9)$

$1(3x - 4y = -4)$

$-10x + 4y = 18$

$3x - 4y = -4$

$-7x = 14$

$x = -2$

Substituting $x = -2$ in the first equation, we get:

$-5(-2) + 2y = 9$

$-10 + 2y = 9$

$2y = -1$

$y = -\dfrac{1}{2}$

$\left(-2, -\dfrac{1}{2}\right)$

To solve for $7x + 10y$, plug the values of x and y into the equation.

$7(-2) + 10\left(-\dfrac{1}{2}\right)$

$-14 - 5$

-19

Choice B is incorrect. This may result if the given is $7x + 6y$ instead of $7x + 10y$. **Choice C** is incorrect. This may result if the given is $7x - 10y$ instead of $7x + 10y$. **Choice D** is incorrect. This may result if the given is $-7x + 10y$ instead of $7x + 10y$. **Choice E** is incorrect. This may result if the given is $-7x - 10y$ instead of $7x + 10y$.

20 **Choice E is correct.** Pick numbers for p, w, and x that work well in the problem. Let $p = 3$ and $w = 100$. So there are three pages with 100 words per page, or 300 words total. Say he types five words a minute, so $x = 5$. So he types 5 times 60, or 300 words an hour. Therefore it takes him one hour to type the paper. The only answer choice that equals 1 when $p = 3$, $w = 100$, and $x = 5$ is Choice E.

Choice A is incorrect. When substituted based on the example above, this expression equals 90,000 instead of 1. **Choice B** is incorrect. When substituted based on the example above, this expression equals 2.78 instead of 1. **Choice C** is incorrect. When substituted based on the example above, this expression equals 60 instead of 1. **Choice D** is incorrect. When substituted based on the example above, this expression equals 25 instead of 1.

21 **Choice D is correct.**

The formula for a simple interest rate is
S.I. = $(P.r.t)/100$.

We have P = 52000, $t = 1/12$, S.I. = 390, hence

$390 = (52000.r.1/12)/100 \rightarrow r = 9$.

Choice A is incorrect because a simple annual interest rate of 7.5% will give a profit of $325 in one month, which is less than $390. Hence, 7.5% is not enough. **Choice B** is incorrect because a simple annual interest rate of 8% will give a profit of $347, which is less than $390. Hence 8% is not enough. **Choice C** is incorrect because a simple annual interest rate of 8.5% will give a profit of $368. Hence, 8.5% is not enough. **Choice E** is incorrect because a simple interest rate of 9.5% will give a profit of $412, which is greater than $390. Hence, 9.5% is too much.

Chapter 4: Algebra

22 **Choice B is correct** because the obtained x-coordinate of point S is 2.
Given: point S lies on the line $y = 3$
point S lies 3 units to the left of (5,3).
Since point S lies on the line $y = 3$, its y-coordinate is at 3. It also lies 3 units to the left of (5,3), hence, its x-coordinate is 5−3 = 2.
Choice A is incorrect because 1 is 4 units to the left of (5,3). **Choice C** is incorrect because 3 is 2 units to the left of (5,3). **Choice D** is incorrect because 4 is 1 unit to the left of (5,3). **Choice E** is incorrect because 5 is 0 unit to the left of (5,3).

23 **Choice D is correct** because the obtained answer is equivalent to $(3x-4y)(3x+4y)$.
Given: $9x^2 - 16y^2$
Find the equivalent expression using the difference of squares formula $a^2 - b^2 = (a-b)(a+b)$.
$$9x^2 - 16y^2 = (3x)^2 - (4y)^2$$
$$9x^2 - 16y^2 = (3x-4y)(3x+4y)$$
Choice A is incorrect because $(3x-4y)(3x-4y)$ is not equivalent to $9x^2 - 16y^2$. **Choice B** is incorrect because $(3x-3y)(4x+4y)$ is not equivalent to $9x^2 - 16y^2$. **Choice C** is incorrect because $(4x-3y)(4x+3y)$ is not equivalent to $9x^2 - 16y^2$. **Choice E** is incorrect because $(3x+4y)(3x+4y)$ is not equivalent to $9x^2 - 16y^2$.

24 **Choice B is correct.** The car travels a total distance of 280 miles $7\frac{1}{2}$ hours for the road trip. Its average speed in miles per hour is
$$280 \div 7\frac{1}{2} = \frac{280}{1} \div \frac{15}{2}$$
$$= \frac{280}{1} \times \frac{2}{15} = \frac{560}{15} = \frac{112}{3} = 37\frac{1}{3}$$ here and simply divided 280 by 7.5, getting 37.333, or $37\frac{1}{3}$.
Choice A is incorrect. This may result if the car travels a total distance of 262.5 miles in $7\frac{1}{2}$ hours. **Choice C** is incorrect. This may result if the car travels a total distance of 281.25 miles in $7\frac{1}{2}$ hours. **Choice D** is incorrect. This may result if the car travels a total distance of 300 miles in $7\frac{1}{2}$ hours. **Choice E** is incorrect. This may result if the car travels a total distance of 562.5 miles in 712 hours.

25 **Choice B is correct.** Quantity A simplifies to $\frac{x^5 y^3}{3}$, while Quantity B simplifies to $3x^5 y^3$.
Therefore, Quantity B is greater because $x^5 y^3$ will be positive since both x and y are positive integers, and the coefficient is $9x$ the size of Quantity A's coefficient.
Choice A is incorrect. Quantity A simplifies to $\frac{x^5 y^3}{3}$ which is less than Quantity B. **Choice C** is incorrect. The two quantities have different numbers of values. **Choice D** is incorrect. There is enough data to determine the relationship between the two.

26 **Choice A is correct.** An input of −2 will have a denominator of zero, which is undefined.
Choice B is incorrect. This input will result in $f(x) = \frac{13}{-2}$.
Choice C is incorrect. This input will result in $f(x) = \frac{13}{-4}$.
Choice D is incorrect. This input will result in $f(x) = \frac{13}{-15}$. **Choice E** is incorrect. Choice A renders the function undefined.

27 **Choice B is correct.** Converting the time from minutes to hours yields
$$45\,minutes \times \frac{1\,hour}{60\,minutes} = 0.75\,hours.$$
Using the distance formula, $Distance = Speed \times Time$, substitute the given into the formula to get
$Distance = 5\,miles\,per\,hour \times 0.75\,hours = 3.75\,miles$.
Therefore, Dave will travel 3.75 miles in 45 minutes.
Choice A is incorrect. This may result if the speed is 3 miles per hour. **Choice C** is incorrect. This may result if the speed is 6 miles per hour. **Choice D** is incorrect. This may result if the speed is 7 miles per hour. **Choice E** is incorrect. This may result if the speed is 9 miles per hour.

28 **Choice B is correct.**
Given: $4^{3x+6} = 86^{x+12}$
4^{3x+6} can be written as $2^{2(3x+6)} = 2^{6x+12}$
and 8^{6x+12} can be written as $2^{3(6x+12)} = 2^{18x+36}$
$2^{6x+12} = 2^{18x+36}$
Since bases are the same exponents will also be the same.

Hence $6x + 12 = 18x + 36$

$12x = -24$

$x = -2$

Choice A is incorrect. This may result if the given is $4^6 x^{+6} = 8^6 x^{+12}$. **Choice C** is incorrect. This may result if the given is $4^3 x^{+30} = 8^6 x^{+12}$. **Choice D** is incorrect. This may result if the given is $4^3 x^{+9} = 8^3 x^{+2}$. **Choice E** is incorrect. This may result if the given is $4^7 x^{+18} = 8^6 x^{+4}$.

29 **Choice B is correct** because to find simple interest you can use the formula SI = P * R * T, where P is the principle, R is the rate expressed as a decimal, and T is the amount of years. P in this problem would be $15,000 and SI would be $300. Since he only put the money into the account for 6 months, T would equal half a year or 0.5. Plug all of these numbers into the equation and then solve for R, the rate. 300 = (15000)(R)(0.5) will give you R = 0.04 which when converted to a percent would be 4.00.

Choice A is incorrect because if you did not convert months to years and plugged in 1 for T, then you would have gotten Answer A. **Choice C** is incorrect because if the rate was 6.00%, the interest would be $450. **Choice D** is incorrect because if the rate was 8.00%, the interest would be $600. **Choice E** is incorrect because if the rate was 10.00%, the interest would be $750

30 **Choice A is correct.**

$x + 5 = \dfrac{-4x - 17}{x + 1} - \dfrac{-x - 2}{x + 1}$

$\therefore (x + 5)(x + 1) = \left[\dfrac{-4x - 17}{x + 1} - \dfrac{-x - 2}{x + 1}\right](x + 1)$

$\therefore x^2 + 6x + 5 = (-4x - 17) - (-x - 2)$

$\therefore x^2 + 6x + 5 = -3x - 15$

$\therefore x^2 + 9x + 20 = 0$

$\therefore x^2 + 5x + 4x + 20 = 0$

$\therefore x(x + 5) + 4(x + 5) = 0$

$\therefore (x + 4)(x + 5) = 0$

$\therefore (x + 4) = 0$ or $(x + 5) = 0$

$\therefore x = -4$ or $x = -5$

$\therefore$ Sum of the roots = $-5 - 4 = -9$

Choice B is incorrect. The roots are -4 and -5, thus the sum should be -9 instead of -7. **Choice C** is incorrect. The roots are both negative, thus the sum should be negative. **Choice D** is incorrect. The roots are both negative, thus the sum should be negative. **Choice E** is incorrect. The roots are both negative, thus the sum should be negative.

31 **Choice C is correct.** If we multiply both sides of the equation by 2, we get $x^2 + 7x + 6 = 6$, which can be rearranged into standard quadratic form:

$x^2 + 7x = 0$

This can be factored as: $(x)(x + 7) = 0$, so $x = 0$ or -7.

The correct answer is Choice C.

Choice A is incorrect. The value of x is 0 and -7 instead of -6.

Choice B is incorrect. The value of x is 0 and -7 instead of -1. **Choice D** is incorrect. The value of x is 0 and -7 instead of 1. **Choice E** is incorrect. The value of x is 0 and -7 instead of 3.

32 **Choice A, B, C, D and E are correct** because the values are equal to or less than 10.

Find the amount that she can withdraw from her account to make sure that she will leave $300.

$$\$800 - \$300 = \$500$$

Let w be the number of weeks she can withdraw leaving at least $300 in her account.

She should make sure not to withdraw more than $500 so that $300 will still remain in her account.

$$\$50w \leq \$500$$

$$w \leq \dfrac{\$500}{\$50}$$

$$w \leq 10$$

Hence, Sofia can withdraw in 10 weeks or less before she needs to ensure she has at least $300 remaining in her account.

Choice F is incorrect because the value is greater than 10. **Choice G** is incorrect because the value is greater than 10.

33 **Choice B, D, and F are correct** because the obtained analysis is false and that means that these points fall outside the inequality $4y \leq -3x + 24$.

To find the points that fall outside the given inequality, it means that when the value of x and y are substituted into the inequality, it makes the inequality false.

Chapter 4: Algebra

Analyze the given points.

Points	$4y \leq -3x + 24$
Choice A: (2, 4)	$4(4) \leq -3(2) + 24$ $16 \leq 18$ true
Choice B: (3, 7)	$4(7) \leq -3(3) + 24$ $28 \leq 15$ false
Choice C: (0, 0)	$4(0) \leq -3(3) + 24$ $0 \leq 15$ true
Choice D: (5, 5)	$4(5) \leq -3(3) + 24$ $20 \leq 15$ false
Choice E: (1, 3)	$4(3) \leq -3(1) + 24$ $12 \leq 21$ true
Choice F: (2, 8)	$4(8) \leq -3(2) + 24$ $24 \leq 18$ false
Choice G: (4, 2)	$4(2) \leq -3(4) + 24$ $8 \leq 10$ true

Choice A is incorrect because the point (2,4) falls within the given inequality. **Choice C** is incorrect because the point (0,0) falls within the given inequality. **Choice E** is incorrect because the point (1,3) falls within the given inequality. **Choice G** is incorrect because the point (4,2) falls within the given inequality.

34 **Choice B and Choice D are correct.** If we are looking for an even integer as the value of x, the value can either be negative or positive and an even number. We must solve each equation to determine if this requirement is met.

A) $3x - 5 = 5x + 1$
$-6 = 2x$ or $x = -3$

B) $5(2x - 3) = 3x - 1$
$10x - 15 = 3x - 1$
$7x = 14$ or $x = 2$

C) $2x + 7 = 5x - 8$
$15 = 3x$ or $x = 5$

D) $7 + 3x = 7x - 9$
$16 = 4x$ or $x = 4$

E) $2x - 7 = 5x + 2$
$-9 = 3x$ or $x = -3$

F) $-10x - 9 = 2x + 3$
$-12 = 12x$ or $x = -1$

Choice B and Choice D are the equations where x is an even integer.

Choice A is incorrect. This results in -3 which is odd.
Choice C is incorrect. This results in 5 which is odd.
Choice E is incorrect. This results in -3 which is odd.
Choice F is incorrect. This results in -1 which is odd.

35 **The correct answer is 625.**
Given:
$$y = 2x + 7$$
$$y = 4x - 5$$

Find x by setting the equations equal to each other.
$$2x + 7 = 4x - 5$$
$$2x - 4x = -5 - 7$$
$$-2x = -12$$
$$x = 6$$

Find y by substituting $x = 6$ into one of the equations.
$$y = 2x + 7$$
$$y = 2(6) + 7$$
$$y = 19$$

Solve for $(x + y)^2$.
$$(x + y)^2 = (6 + 19)^2$$
$$(x + y)^2 = (25)^2$$
$$(x + y)^2 = 625$$

36 **The correct answer is 10 hours.** If Car A was traveling at a speed of 20mph for 15 hours, using speed × time = distance, $20 \times 15 = 300$ miles. If Car B was driving 10mph faster than Car A, it was traveling at 20 + 10 = 30mph. If they went to the same destination, Car B traveled 300 miles. Plugging this into the speed × time = distance equation becomes $30 \times t = 300$, where t is the time. Dividing by 30 on both sides gives $t = 10$. This means it took Car B 10 hours to drive to the same destination.

37 The correct answer is 6.

Given:

$f(x) = 2x + 4$ and $g(x) = 3x - 6$

Find x when $f(g(x)) = 28$.

$$f(g(x)) = 2(3x - 6) + 4 = 28$$
$$6x - 12 + 4 = 28$$
$$6x - 8 = 28$$
$$6x = 28 + 8$$
$$6x = 36$$
$$x = 6$$

Practice Set 2 (Medium): Answers & Explanations

38 **Choice A is correct.** The best approach of solving such problems is picking a number. Since, p is a positive fraction less than 1 let's pick a value for it say $\frac{1}{9}$.

$\frac{1}{9^2} = \frac{1}{81}$ and $\frac{1}{(9+1)^2} = \frac{1}{10^2} = \frac{1}{100}$.

As, $\frac{1}{81}$ is greater than $\frac{1}{100}$ so clearly $\frac{1}{p^2}$ is greater than $\frac{1}{(p+1)^2}$.

Choice B is incorrect. Based on the explanation and example above, Quantity B is less than Quantity A. **Choice C** is incorrect. The two quantities have different values. **Choice D** is incorrect. There is enough data to determine the relationship between the two.

39 **Choice A is correct.** Since x^2 is a positive fraction less than 1, its positive square root, x, must also be a fraction less than 1, which you are told is positive. When a positive fraction less than 1 is squared, the result is positive fraction smaller than the original. Therefore, $x^2 < x$. For example, $\left(\frac{1}{2}\right)^2 < \frac{1}{2}$, since $\left(\frac{1}{2}\right)^2 = \frac{1}{4}$, so in Quantity A you are subtracting a positive value from 1, and in Quantity B you are subtracting a larger positive value from 1, so Quantity A must be greater.

Choice B is incorrect. Based on the explanation, in Quantity B you are subtracting a larger positive value from 1, thus Quantity A is greater. **Choice C** is incorrect. The two quantities have different values. **Choice D** is incorrect. There is enough data to determine the relationship between the two.

40 **Choice D is correct.** Quantity A is solved by first subtracting 2 from both sides to obtain $-3|x| < 2$, and then divide by -3 on both sides and switch the inequality. You then get $|x| > -2/3$. X can be any real number because any value's absolute value will give you a number greater than or equal to 0, which will always be greater than a negative value. Quantity B is solved by adding 3 to both sides to obtain $4y > 16$. Divide by 4 on both sides to get $y > 4$. Because we do not know the exact value of x or y, it is possible that either Quantity A or Quantity B could be larger, and therefore the solution is D. The relationship cannot be determined from the information given.

Choice A is incorrect. The example above shows that Quantity A is not always greater as the value of x and y is unknown. **Choice B** is incorrect. The example above shows that Quantity B is not always greater as the value of x and y is unknown. **Choice C** is incorrect. The quantities cannot be determined as equal.

41 **Choice A is correct.**

Since $x < 0$, $x^2 > 0$

Given that $|x| > y$, $x^2 > y^2$ and $2x^2 > 2y^2$

Since $x < 0$, $y > 0$, $x < y$ hence $2x^2 + y > 2y^2 + x$

$x < 0$ Implies that $x^3 < 0 < x^2$,

thus $2y + x^3 + 3 < 2y + x^2 + 3$

Choice B is incorrect. Quantity B has a value which is less than Quantity A. **Choice C** is incorrect. The two quantities have different values. **Choice D** is incorrect. There is enough data to determine the relationship between the two.

42 **Choice C is correct.** Try to write the information given in a mathematical statement.

Employees in Company A = x.

Thrice the employees in Company A = $3x$.

20 less than thrice the employees in Company A = $3x - 20$.

85% of 20 less than thrice the employees in Company A = $\left(\frac{85}{100}\right)(3x - 20) = 0.85(3x - 20)$

Therefore, employees in Company B = $0.85(3x - 20)$

Chapter 4: Algebra

Choice A is incorrect. The two quantities are equal; therefore, neither quantity is greater. **Choice B is incorrect.** The two quantities are equal; therefore, neither quantity is greater. **Choice D is incorrect.** There is enough data to determine the relationship between the two.

43 **Choice A is correct.** To solve here, first simplify the inequality given by multiplying 7 on both sides to get $9 - 5x \geq -21$. Then subtract 9 from both sides to get $-5x \geq -30$. Divide by -5, which flips the inequality sign to obtain $x \leq 6$. For Quantity A, the minimum value will be when $x = 6$, so $10 - 6 = 4$. Quantity A is 4. To find the minimum value for Quantity B, also choose 6, as this will give the largest negative value for the first term. Plugging in 6 turns the expression into $\frac{-3(6)}{5} + 4 = -3.6 + 4 = 0.4$ Therefore, $4 > 0.4$, and the answer is A, Quantity A is greater.

Choice B is incorrect. Based on the example, Quantity B has 0.4 which is less than Quantity A. **Choice C is incorrect.** The two quantities have different values. **Choice D is incorrect.** There is enough data to determine the relationship between the two.

44 **Choice D is correct** because within the given range of x, the value of y can be greater than, less than or even equal to x. Hence, a relationship cannot be determined from the information given.

Find the values of y for the given range of x.

when $x = 2$, $4x + 5y = 35$
$4(2) + 5y = 35$
$8 + 5y = 35$
$5y = 35 - 8$ $5y = 27$
$y = \frac{27}{5}$ or $y \approx 5.4$

when $x = 3$, $4x + 5y = 35$
$4(3) + 5y = 35$
$12 + 5y = 35$
$5y = 35 - 12$
$5y = 23$
$y = \frac{23}{5}$ or $y \approx 4.6$

when $x = 4$, $4x + 5y = 35$
$4(4) + 5y = 35$

$16 + 5y = 35$
$5y = 35 - 16$
$5y = 19$
$y = \frac{19}{5}$ or $y \approx 3.8$

when $x = 5$, $4x + 5y = 35$
$4(5) + 5y = 35$
$20 + 5y = 35$
$5y = 35 - 20$
$5y = 15$
$y = \frac{15}{5}$ or $y \approx 3$

Interpretation for each given range of x.

when $x = 2$, $y \approx 5.4$ hence, $x < y$
when $x = 3$, $y \approx 4.6$ hence, $x < y$
when $x = 4$, $y \approx 3.8$ hence, $x > y$
when $x = 5$, $y \approx 3$ hence, $x > y$

The value of x and y can also be equal at $\frac{35}{9}$ or ≈ 3.9

Choice A is incorrect because Quantity A is less than Quantity B when $x = 2$ and $x = 3$. **Choice B is incorrect** because Quantity B is less than Quantity A when $x = 4$ and $x = 5$. **Choice C is incorrect** because Quantity A is equal to Quantity B only when $x \approx 3.8$.

45 **Choice B is correct** because Quantity B is always greater than Quantity A.

Given:
$y = x^2 + 4$
$y = 2x + 7$

Find the intersection points of the given equations.
$x^2 + 4 = 2x + 7$
$x^2 - 2x + 4 - 7 = 0$
$x^2 - 2x - 3 = 0$
$(x - 3)(x + 1) = 0$
$(x - 3) = 0$ or $(x + 1) = 0$
$x = 3$ or $x = -1$

Find the value of y by substituting the obtained values of x into any of the original equations.

$y = 2x + 7$ $y = x^2 + 4$
$y = 2(3) + 7$ $y = 3^2 + 4$
$y = 13$ $y = 13$

100 | *GRE Quantitative Practice Questions*

Practice Set 2 (Medium): Answers & Explanations

$$y = 2x + 7 \qquad\qquad y = x^2 + 4$$
$$y = 2(-1) + 7 \qquad\qquad y = (-1)^2 + 4$$
$$y = 5 \qquad\qquad\qquad y = 5$$

Compare the quantities.

when $x = 3$, $y = 13$, hence, $x < y$

when $x = -1$, $y = 5$, hence, $x < y$

Choice B is correct because Quantity B is always greater than Quantity A.

Choice A is incorrect because Quantity A is less than Quantity B. **Choice C** is incorrect because Quantity A is not equal to Quantity B. **Choice D** is incorrect because a relation can be obtained from the given information.

46 **Choice C is correct** because the obtained values showed that Quantity A is equal to Quantity B.

Given:
$$3x - 2y = 6$$
$$2x + 2y = 9$$

Solve the system of equations by elimination.
$$(3x - 2y) + (2x + 2y) = 6 + 9$$
$$3x + 2x = 15$$
$$5x = 15$$
$$x = 3$$

Find y by substituting the obtained value of x into any of the original equation.
$$3x - 2y = 6$$
$$3(3) - 2y = 6$$
$$-2y = 6 - 9$$
$$y = \frac{3}{2} = 1.5$$

Compare the qualities.

Quantity A : $x - y = 3 - 1.5 = 1.5$

Quantity B : 1.5

Choice A is incorrect because Quantity A is not less than Quantity B. **Choice B** is incorrect because Quantity B is not equal to Quantity B. **Choice D** is incorrect because a relation can be obtained from the given information.

47 **Choice B is correct.** You are given $a - 1 = b$, so Quantity A can be rewritten as $(a - 1)^2$. Don't assume that the quantities are equal though. In fact, $(a - 1)^2$ is not equal to $a^2 - 1$.

$a^2 - 1$ factors to $(a + 1)(a - 1)$. Quantity A can be expressed as $(a - 1)(a - 1)$. Since you know that a $a > 1$, you can factor an $(a - 1)$ from each quantity. This gives you $(a - 1)$ in Quantity A and $(a + 1)$ in Quantity B, so Quantity B is greater.

Choice A is incorrect. Quantity A has $(a - 1)$ which is less than Quantity B. **Choice C** is incorrect. The two quantities have different values. **Choice D** is incorrect. There is enough data to determine the relationship between the two.

48 **Choice B is correct** because upon analysis Quantity B is always greater than Quantity B.

Given: $\qquad x > y > 0$

From the given, we can conclude that the values of x and y are positive where x is always greater than y.

Analyze the quantities.

Quantity A: $y - x$ is always negative because $x > y$.

Quantity B: 0

Hence, $y - x < 0$

Choice A is incorrect because Quantity A is less than Quantity B. **Choice C** is incorrect because Quantity A is not equal to Quantity B. **Choice D** is incorrect because a relation can be obtained from the given information.

49 **Choice B is correct** because from the obtained table, Quantity B is always greater than Quantity A.

Analyze the values of the quantities from the possible of values of r.

r	$30(r - 2)$	$20r$
1	−30	
2	0	
3	30	
4	60	
4.9	87	

Choice A is incorrect because Quantity A is less than Quantity B. **Choice C** is incorrect because Quantity A is not equal to Quantity B. **Choice D** is incorrect because a relation can be obtained from the given information.

Chapter 4: Algebra

50 Choice C is correct.

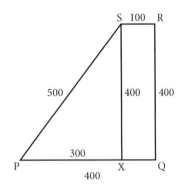

Let s be the speed from point P to point R. The distance is 800 km.

∴ Time taken from P to R $= \dfrac{800}{s}$

Draw SX ∥RQ.

By Pythagorean triplets, SP =500km.

∴ The distance from R to P is 600 km.

The speed is 1.5s

Time taken from R to P $= \dfrac{600}{1.5s}$

∴ The required ratio $= \dfrac{800}{s} : \dfrac{600}{1.5s} = 800 : \dfrac{600}{1.5} =$

$800 : 400 = 2 : 1$

Choice A is incorrect. The two quantities are equal; therefore, neither quantity is greater. **Choice B** is incorrect. The two quantities are equal; therefore, neither quantity is greater. **Choice D** is incorrect. There is enough data to determine the relationship between the two.

51 **Choice B is correct** because the obtained value of Quantity B is greater than Quantity A.

Given: $a + b = 0.75c$

Analyze the quantities.

Quantity A: $(2/3)(a+b) = (2/3)(0.75c) = 0.5c$

Quantity B: $(3/4)(c) = 0.75c$

Choice A is incorrect because Quantity A is less than Quantity B. **Choice C** is incorrect because Quantity A is not equal to Quantity B. **Choice D** is incorrect because a relation can be obtained from the given information.

52 **Choice A is correct.** Rewriting the entry in Quantity A, we obtain $\dfrac{n^2+2}{n} = n + \dfrac{1}{n}$ thus, the problem becomes a comparison between $\dfrac{2}{n}$ in Quantity A and $\dfrac{1}{n}$ in Quantity B. Since $n > 0$, the entry in Column A is greater.

Choice B is incorrect. Based on the explanation above, since $n > 0$, then $\dfrac{1}{n}$ in Quantity B is less than Quantity A. **Choice C** is incorrect. The two quantities have different values. **Choice D** is incorrect. There is enough data to determine the relationship between the two.

53 **Choice D is correct** because there are two possible values for both a and b that can either make Quantity A greater then Quantity B or the other way around.

Given: $x^2 - 5x + 6 = 0$.

Find the roots of the quadratic equation by factoring.

$$x^2 - 5x + 6 = 0$$
$$(x-3)(x-2) = 0$$

$(x-3) = 0$ $\quad\quad$ $(x-2) = 0$

$x = 3$ $\quad\quad\quad\quad$ $x = 2$

The roots are 3 and 2. The question did not specify if which of the root is a and b.

Analyze the quantities.

If $a = 3$ and $b = 2$

$\quad$Quantity A: $2(a-b)$ $\quad\quad$ Quantity B: $-ab$

$\quad\quad\quad\quad$ $2(3-2)$ $\quad\quad\quad\quad\quad\quad$ $-(3)(2)$

$\quad\quad\quad\quad\quad$ 2 $\quad\quad\quad\quad\quad\quad\quad\quad$ -6

If $a = 2$ and $b = 3$

$\quad$Quantity A: $2(a-b)$ $\quad\quad$ Quantity B: $-ab$

$\quad\quad\quad\quad$ $2(2-3)$ $\quad\quad\quad\quad\quad\quad$ $-(2)(3)$

$\quad\quad\quad\quad$ -2 $\quad\quad\quad\quad\quad\quad\quad\quad$ -6

Choice A is incorrect because Quantity A is less than Quantity B when $a = 2$ and $b = 3$. **Choice B** is incorrect because Quantity B is less than Quantity B when $a = 3$ and $b = 2$. **Choice C** is incorrect because Quantity A is not equal to Quantity B.

54 **Choice C is correct** because the obtained value of Quantity A is the same as Quantity B.

Given: $f(x) = x^2 + kx - 6$, where k is constant.

$\quad\quad\quad$ 3 is a root of $f(x)$

Find k.

Practice Set 2 (Medium): Answers & Explanations

If 3 is a root of $f(x)$, then $f(3) = 0$
$$f(x) = x^2 + kx - 6$$
$$f(3) = (3)^2 + k(3) - 6 = 0$$
$$9 + 3k - 6 = 0$$
$$3k = 6 - 9$$
$$3k = -3$$
$$k = -1$$

Choice A is incorrect because Quantity A is not greater than Quantity B. **Choice B** is incorrect because Quantity B is not greater than Quantity A. **Choice D** is incorrect because a relation can be obtained from the given information.

55 **Choice A is correct.**

First we solve Equation 1:
$$4^x - 4^{3-x} = 12$$
$$4^x - 4^3 \times 4^{-x} = 12$$
$$4^x - 4^3 \times \frac{1}{4^x} = 12$$
$$4^x \times 4^x - 4^3 = 12 \times 4^x$$
$$4^{2x} - 12 \times 4^x - 4^3 = 0$$

Let $4^x = t$

If we substitute in the equation, it becomes

$t^2 - 12t - 64 = 0$

This can be factorized into $(t+4)(t-16) = 0$

One solution is $t = -4$, but 4^x cannot be negative

$t = -4$ is not a valid solution

Second solution is $t = 16$

$4^x = 4^2$

$x = 2$

Now, we solve Equation 2:
$$25^{\sqrt{y}} - 6 \times 5^{\sqrt{y}} + 5^{\sqrt{1}} = 0$$
$$5^{2\sqrt{y}} - 6 \times 5^{\sqrt{y}} + 5 = 0$$

Let $5^{\sqrt{y}} = u$

If we substitute in the equation, it becomes

$u^2 - 6u + 5 = 0$

This can be factorized into $(u-1)(u-5) = 0$

One solution is $u = 1$
$$5^{\sqrt{y}} = 1 = 5^0$$
$$y = 0$$

Second solution is $u = 5$
$$5^{\sqrt{y}} = 5 = 5^1$$
$$y = 1$$

The unique solution of Equation 1 (i.e. $x = 2$) is greater than any of the solutions of Equation 2 (i.e. 0 and 1)

Choice B is incorrect. Quantity B has a solution of 0 and 1 which is less than Quantity A. **Choice C** is incorrect. The two quantities have different numbers of values. **Choice D** is incorrect. There is enough data to determine the relationship between the two.

56 **Choice B is correct.** To find the slopes we need to use the formula $m = \dfrac{x_1 - y_2}{x_1 - x_2}$ so we will need two points from each line.

We know two points on $f(x)$, as we were told the y and x intercepts – the points are $(0, -4)$ and $(6, 0)$

The slope of f is $\dfrac{-4-0}{0-6} = \dfrac{2}{3}$

For $h(x) = 4$ we can easily established that this is a horizontal line and all horizontal lines have a slope of 0. No need to calculate.

Pick two x's and solve for each the corresponding y to find the slope of $g(x)$.

If $x = 0$, $y = -2$ and if $x = 4$, $y = 1$

The slope of g is $\dfrac{-2-1}{0-4} = \dfrac{3}{4}$

Similarly for $i(x)$, if $x = 0$, $y = -2$ and if $x = 2$, $y = 0$, the slope of i is $\dfrac{-2-0}{0-2} = 1$

$i(x)$ has the greatest slope out of $g(x)$, $h(x)$ and $i(x)$ (i.e. 1) which is greater than the slope of $f(x)$ which is $\dfrac{2}{3}$

The right column is greater than the left column.

Choice A is incorrect. Quantity A has a slope of $\dfrac{2}{3}$ which is less than Quantity B. **Choice C** is incorrect. The two quantities have different values of slope. **Choice D** is incorrect. There is enough data to determine the relationship between the two.

57 **Choice A is correct.** We know that the total interest after N years is PNR/100 where P is the invested amount, N is the number of years and R is the rate of interest per annum.

Chapter 4: Algebra

Also total debt after N years = P + PNR/100.

So, according to the data

$$8000 + \frac{(8000 \times N \times 6)}{100} = 6000 + \frac{6000 \times N \times 10}{100}$$

$$\therefore 8000 + 480N = 6000 + 600N$$

$$\therefore 120N = 2000$$

$$N = 16\frac{2}{3} \text{ years}$$

Choice B is incorrect. Quantity B has 16 which is less than Quantity A. **Choice C** is incorrect. The two quantities have different numbers of years. **Choice D** is incorrect. There is enough data to determine the relationship between the two.

58 **Choice A is correct.** We must first determine the time it takes each vehicle to reach their destinations:

Travel time for bus = $\frac{195}{39}$ = 5 hours

Travel time for car = $\frac{195}{65}$ = 3 hours

Quantity A: Bus travel time before the car departed is 5 − 3 = 2 hours.

In 2 hours, travels 39 × 2 = 78 miles.

Quantity B: Time passed when car was halfway to destination is 2hrs + $\frac{3 \text{ hrs}}{2}$ = 3.5 hours

Since the bus takes 5 hours to complete the journey, 5 − 3.5 = 1.5 hours are remaining.

39 × 1.5 = 58.5 miles.

Choice B is incorrect. Quantity B has 58.5 miles which is less than Quantity A. **Choice C** is incorrect. The two distances have different values. **Choice D** is incorrect. There is enough data to determine the relationship between the two.

59 **Choice A is correct.** The problem can be worked out using simultaneous equations, but that is not the most efficient way of solving it. For that reason, we will set up the equation (for the "aficionados"), but we will not actually solve for x and y. Let x be the number of shirts costing $13 and y the number costing $10.

$x + y = 16$

$13x + 10y = 187$

Final solution: $x = 9$ and $y = 7$

We have omitted the detailed calculations because there is a simpler method. Let us assume, for the sake of argument, that the two quantities are equal–that is, that the man bought equal numbers of both types of shirts. If we are correct in assuming that he bought eight $13 shirts and eight $10 shirts, then (8 × 13) + (8 × 10) ought to equal $187. When we do the multiplication, we get the result $184. That tells us our original assumption of equal numbers was incorrect and, further, that the answer to the question is not (C). We should then make a second assumption, but should we assume that he bought more expensive shirts than we first guessed, or fewer? A moment of reflection will show that we should adjust our initial assumption to include a greater number of expensive shirts, for only by increasing that number will we add to the $184 which was the result of our original assumption. So, we would next assume–again for the purposes of argument–that the man bought nine $13 shirts and only seven $10 shirts. But at this point we have already solved the problem! We do not need to know the precise ratio, e.g., whether 9:7, 10:6, 11:5, 12:4, 13:3, 14:4, or 15:1; we have already determined that the ratio is one of those listed, and so it must be the case that Quantity A is greater.

Choice B is incorrect. Quantity B has 7 which is less than Quantity A. **Choice C** is incorrect. The two quantities have different values. **Choice D** is incorrect. There is enough data to determine the relationship between the two.

60 **Choice D is correct.** Select choices for x and determine the value of $y − 10$ and compare. $y = 3x^2 + 8x − 10$

When $x = 0$, $y = 3(0)^2 + 8(0) − 10 = −10$ and $y − 10 = −10 − 10 = −20$.

In this case Quantity A is greater.

When $x = 1$, $y = 3(1)^2 + 8(1) − 10 = 3 + 8 − 10 = 1$ and $y − 10 = 1 − 10 = −9$.

In this case Quantity A is greater.

When $x = 2$, $y = 3(2)^2 + 8(2) − 10 = 12 + 16 − 10 = 18$ and $y − 10 = 18 − 10 = 8$.

In this case Quantity B is greater.

Since different results were obtained the correct answer is D, the relationship cannot be determined based on the information given.

Choice A is incorrect. The example above shows that Quantity A is not always greater. **Choice B** is incorrect. The example above shows that Quantity B is not always greater. **Choice C** is incorrect. The quantities are not equal in any case.

Practice Set 2 (Medium): Answers & Explanations

61 **Choice C is correct** because for $|x-y| = |x| + |y|$ to be true, x must be positive and y must be negative. This would mean that $x - y \geq 0$ must also be true since a positive minus a negative would always be greater than or equal to 0.

Choice A is incorrect because this would mean either x or y or both values equal 0. This could be true since $|0-0| = |0| + |0|$, but it is not a situation that must be true. **Choice B** is incorrect because this would indicate that x and y are both positive or both negative and this is not the case. **Choice D** is incorrect because the absolute value of y can be greater than the absolute value of x and if y is negative this statement would not be true. **Choice E** is incorrect because while x and y can equal each other, this must not always be true.

62 **Choice D is correct** because through identifying the possible intervals the solutions are –3, –2, –1, 0, 1, 2, and 3.

To solve, identify the critical points of the formula by setting each absolute value equal to 0. This would get you $2x + 3 = 0$, $x - 3 = 0$, and $x = 0$. Solving $2x + 3 = 0$ would yield $-\frac{3}{2}$ and the other value $x - 3 = 0$ would yield $x = 3$. The critical points exist at $-\frac{3}{2}$, 3, and 0.

For the interval $x < -\frac{3}{2}$, the equation would become all negatives so you would solve $|2x+3| + |x-3| + |x| < 15$ as $-(2x + 3) - (x - 3) - x < 15$. Combining like terms will yield $-4x < 15$. Divide by –4 to get the range $x > \frac{-15}{4}$. This would complete the interval as $\frac{-15}{4} < x < -\frac{3}{2}$. The integers in this interval are –3 and –2.

For the interval $-\frac{3}{2} < x < 0$, so you would solve $(2x + 3) - (x - 3) - x < 15$. Combining like terms will yield $3 < 15$. So any integer in this range would work which would be –1.

For the interval $0 < x < 3$, you would solve the expression $(2x + 3) - (x - 3) + x < 15$. Combining like terms will yield $2x < 9$. Divide by 2 to get the range $x < \frac{9}{2}$. This would complete the interval as $0 < x < \frac{9}{2}$. The integers in this interval are 0, 1, 2, and 3.

Finally, for the scenario that $x > 3$, you would solve the expression as $(2x + 3) + (x - 3) + x < 15$. Simplifying would give you $4x < 15$. Dividing by 4 would give you $x < \frac{15}{4}$, yielding an integer value of 3.

Choice A is incorrect because there are more than 4 integer values possible. **Choice B** is incorrect because there are more than 5 integer values possible. **Choice C** is incorrect because there are more than 6 integer values possible. **Choice E** is incorrect because there are not 8 possible options.

63 **Choice C is correct.** Breaking down the compound inequality yields (1) $4x - 3 \leq 5x + 2$ and (2) $5x + 2 < 3x + 12$. Solving the first inequality $4x - 3 \leq 5x + 2$, subtract $4x$ from both sides to get $-3 \leq x + 2$. Subtracting 2 from both sides yields $-5 \leq x$.

Solving the second inequality $5x + 2 < 3x + 12$, subtract $3x$ from both sides to get $2x + 2 < 12$. Subtracting 2 from both sides yields $2x < 10$. Dividing both sides by 2 yields $x < 5$. Combining the two results in $-5 \leq x < 5$. Therefore, the correct answer is C.

Choice A is incorrect. The range of x is more limited than just $x < 7$ and must be greater than or equal to -5. **Choice B** is incorrect. The value of x must be at least -5 and not -6. **Choice D** is incorrect. This value of x is not a valid range notation. **Choice E** is incorrect. This value of x suggests that x is both less than or equal to -7 and greater than 5, which is impossible and does not match the solutions derived.

64 **Choice D is correct** because among the assigned values of n, it satisfies the given inequality.

Given: $27 < 3^n < 243$

Let's assign values to 3^n.

Let $n = 1$, $3^1 = 3$ which falls outside the given inequality.

Let $n = 2$, $3^2 = 9$ which falls outside the given inequality.

Let $n = 3$, $3^3 = 27$ which falls outside the given inequality.

Let $n = 4$, $3^4 = 81$ which falls within the given inequality.

Let $n = 5$, $3^4 = 243$ which falls outside the given inequality.

Choice A is incorrect because when $n = 1$, the obtained value falls outside the given inequality. **Choice B** is incorrect because when $n = 2$, the obtained value falls outside the given inequality. **Choice C** is incorrect because when $n = 3$, the obtained value falls outside the given inequality. **Choice E** is incorrect because when $n = 5$, the obtained value falls outside the given inequality.

Chapter 4: Algebra

65 **Choice B is correct.** Let the ages of grandmother and granddaughter be x and y.

Five years ago the ages would have been $x-5$ and $y-5$.

As per data $x-5 = 13(y-5)$

i.e. $x-13y = -60$ -----(1)

Five years hence

$x+5 = 5(y+5)$

i.e. $x-5y = 20$ -------(2)

Subtracting (1) from (2) we get

$8y = 80$

$y = 10$

Substituting in (2)

$x-50 = 20$

$x = 70$

$x+y = 80$

Choice A is incorrect. The sum of their ages is 80 not 75.
Choice C is incorrect. The sum of their ages is 80 not 90.
Choice D is incorrect. The sum of their ages is 80 not 95.
Choice E is incorrect. The sum of their ages is 80 not 100.

66 **Choice D is correct** because the obtained cost of 1-pair of shoes is $20.00.

Let p be the pair of shoes and s be the shirt.

Write the equation for Jasmine and Alexa's purchase.

Jasmine spent $120 on 3 pairs of shoes and 6 shirts. Hence, equation is $3p+6s = \$120$ (1)

Alexa spent $90 on 2 pairs of shoes and 5 shirts. Hence, equation is $2p+5s = \$90$ (2)

Find the cost of 1 pair of shoes p using the equation (1).

$$|x|$$

$$6s = \$120 - 3p$$

$$s = \frac{\$120}{6} - \frac{3p}{6}$$

$$s = \$20 - \frac{1}{2}p$$

Substitute the obtained equation of s into equation 2 to find p.

$$2p+5s = \$90$$

$$2p+5\left(\$20 - \frac{1}{2}p\right) = \$90$$

$$2p+\$100 - \frac{5}{2}p = \$90$$

$$\frac{4p-5p}{2} = \$90 - \$100$$

$$\frac{4p-5p}{2} = -\$10$$

$$-p = -\$20$$

$$p = \$20$$

Choice A is incorrect because $10.00 is below the obtained cost of 1-pair of shoes. **Choice B** is incorrect because $12.00 is below the obtained cost of 1-pair of shoes. **Choice C** is incorrect because $15.00 is below the obtained cost of 1-pair of shoes. **Choice E** is incorrect because $25.00 is above the obtained cost of 1-pair of shoes.

67 **Choice D is correct** because the obtained value is $-6 \leq x \leq 0$.

Given: $4|x+3|-7 \leq 5$

Find x.

$$4|x+3|-7 \leq 5$$

$$4|x+3| \leq 5+7$$

$$4|x+3| \leq 12$$

$$|x+3| \leq 3$$

Apply the theorem and rewrite the absolute value inequality as a compound inequality.

$$-3 \leq x+3 \leq 3$$

$$-3-3 \leq x+3-3 \leq 3-3$$

$$-6 \leq x \leq 0$$

Choice A is incorrect because $4 \leq x \leq 6$ is not the obtained value of x. **Choice B** is incorrect because $-5 \leq x \leq 5$ is not the obtained value of x. **Choice C** is incorrect because $-6 \leq x \leq 6$ is not the obtained value of x. **Choice E** is incorrect because $-2 \leq x \leq 4$ is not the obtained value of x.

68 **Choice A is correct** because the obtained value is $-45 < xy < 54$.

Given: $-10 < 2x < 12$

$-9 < 3y < 27$

Simplify the inequalities.

$$-10 < 2x < 12$$

$$\frac{-10}{2} < \frac{2x}{2} < \frac{12}{2}$$

$$-5 < x < 6$$

$$-9 < 3y < 27$$

$$\frac{-9}{3} < \frac{3y}{3} < \frac{27}{3}$$

Practice Set 2 (Medium): Answers & Explanations

$-3 < y < 9$

The extreme values of x and y.

$x = -5, x = 6$

$y = -3, y = 9$

Compute for xy for all possible combinations of the extreme bounds.

when $x = -5$ and $y = -3$, $xy = 15$

when $x = -5$ and $y = 9$, $xy = -45$

when $x = 6$ and $y = -3$, $xy = -18$

when $x = 6$ and $y = 9$, $xy = 54$

Hence, the range value of xy is $-45 < xy < 54$.

Choice B is incorrect because $15 < xy < 54$ is not the possible range of xy. **Choice C** is incorrect because $9 < xy < 36$ is not the possible range of xy. **Choice D** is incorrect because $-9 < xy < 27$ is not the possible range of xy. **Choice E** is incorrect because $-15 < xy < 42$ is not the possible range of xy.

69 **Choice D is correct** because the obtained answer is $\frac{3}{2}$.

Given: $3y - ax + 7 = 0$

$-8x + 16y - 10 = 0$

Rewrite the equations in slope intercept form.

$3y - ax + 7 = 0$

$3y = ax - 7$

$y = \frac{a}{3}x - \frac{7}{3} = 0$

$-8x + 16y - 10 = 0$

$16y = 8x + 10$

$y = \frac{8}{16}x + \frac{10}{16}$

$y = \frac{1}{2}x + \frac{5}{8}$

Find the value of a, where the system of euqation has no solution.

For the system to have no solution, the slope of both euations should be equal.

Hence, $\frac{a}{3} = \frac{1}{2}$

$2a = 3$

$a = \frac{3}{2}$

Choice A is incorrect because $-\frac{3}{2}$ will not give a no solution to the given system of equations. **Choice B** is incorrect because $\frac{1}{2}$ will not give a no solution to the given system of equations. **Choice C** is incorrect because 1 will not give a no solution to the given system of equations. **Choice E** is incorrect because 2 will not give a no solution to the given system of equations.

70 **Choice D is correct.** Let the present ages of Jacob and Henry be j and h.

$h + 4 = 4j$ ----(1)

Four years ago, Henry was $h - 4$ years old.

One year ago, Jacob was $j - 1$ years old

By the given data

$3(h - 4) + 2(j - 1) = 30$ ----(2)

$3h - 12 + 2j - 2 = 30$ -----(3)

$3h + 2j = 44$ ---------(4)

Multiplying (4) by 2 we get

$6h + 4j = 88$ ---------(5)

Substituting (1) in (4)

$6h + h + 4 = 88$ --------(6)

$7h = 84$

$h = 12$

$12 + 4 = 4j$

$J = 4$

Five years after, the sum of their ages $= 12 + 5 + 4 + 5 = 26$

Choice A is incorrect. This is the sum of their ages after 2 years. **Choice B** is incorrect. This is the sum of their ages after 3 years. **Choice C** is incorrect. This is the sum of their ages after 4 years. **Choice E** is incorrect. This is the sum of their ages after 6 years.

71 **Choice B is correct** because the obtained value of a is -2.

Given:

$ax - 3y = -7$ (1)

$4x + 6y = 5$ (2)

For the system of equations to have no solution, the slope of each equation should be equal.

Rewrite the equations in the form $y = mx + b$.

Chapter 4: Algebra

$$ax - 3y = -7$$
$$-3y = -ax - 7$$
$$y = \frac{ax}{3} + \frac{7}{3}$$
$$4x + 6y = 5$$
$$6y = -4x + 5$$
$$y = -\frac{4x}{6} + \frac{5}{6}$$

Find a when the slopes are equal.
$$\frac{a}{3} = -\frac{4}{6}$$
$$6a = -12$$
$$a = -2$$

Choice A is incorrect because –3 is not the obtained value of a. **Choice C** is incorrect because 2 is not the obtained value of a. **Choice D** is incorrect because 3 is not the obtained value of a. **Choice E** is incorrect because 4 is not the obtained value of a.

72 **Choice D is correct** because the obtained answer is Cost $= d + (n-3)(1/4c)$.

Given: Let d be the base fare for first 3 miles – d

Let $1/4c$ be the Fare per quarter mile after the first 3 miles

Let n be the number of miles

Cost = Base fare for the first 3 miles + (number of miles after 3 miles)(cost per quarter mile)

Cost $= d + (n-3)(1/4c)$

Choice A is incorrect because $dn - c/4$ does not represent the given conditions. **Choice B** is incorrect because $cd + 4n - 3$ does not represent the given conditions. **Choice C** is incorrect because $d - (3n)(1/4c)$ does not represent the given conditions. **Choice E** is incorrect because $d + (n+3)(1/4c)$ does not represent the given conditions.

73 **Choice A is correct** because the slope of the linear inequality is 1.

Given: $3x - 4y \leq 12 - 2x + y$

Rewrite the given linear inequality in slope–intercept form.
$$-4y - y \leq 12 - 2x - 3x$$
$$-5y \leq 12 - 5x$$
$$-5y \leq -5x + 12$$
$$y \geq x - \frac{12}{5}$$

The slope of the inequality is the coefficient of variable x, hence, slope is 1.

Choice B is incorrect because 2 is not the obtained slope of the given linear inequality. **Choice C** is incorrect because 3 is greater than the obtained slope. **Choice D** is incorrect because 4 not the coefficient of the variable $\underline{x}$. **Choice E** is incorrect because 6 is greater than the obtained slope.

74 **Choice A is correct.**

$x + y = 8$ and $x + z = 11$. Therefore, $x + y - (x + z) = 8 - 11 = -3$ or $z -y = 3$

$z - y = 3$ and $y + z = 7$. Therefore, $z - y + (y + z) = 3 + 7$ or, $2z = 10$ or $z = 5$.

Checking $z - y = 3$ and $z = 5$. Therefore, $y = 2$.

$x + y = 8$ and $y = 2$. Therefore, $x = 6$.

So, $x + y - z = 6 + 2 - 5 = 3$.

Choice B is incorrect. This is the value of x. **Choice C** is incorrect. This may result if the required is $2x$. **Choice D** is incorrect. This may result if the required is $x+y+z$. **Choice E** is incorrect. This may result if the required is $x+y+3z$.

75 **Choice C is correct.** To determine the number of roots in the equation, set $f(x)=0$ and use the determinant ($b^2 - 4ac$) to determine the number of roots. If the determinant is negative, there are no real roots. If the determinant is zero, then there is exactly one real root, and if the determinant is positive, there are two real roots.

Quantity A:
$$0 = 2x^2 - 3x + 1$$
$$a = 2, b = -3, c = 1$$

Determinant $= b^2 - 4ac = (-3)^2 - 4(2)(1) = 1$

2 real roots

Quantity B:
$$0 = x^2 - 7x - 8$$
$$a = 1, b = -7, c = -8$$

Determinant $= b^2 - 4ac = (-7)^2 - 4(1)(-8) = 81$

2 real roots

Both have two real roots, so the answer is C.

Choice A is incorrect. The two quantities have 2 real roots; therefore, neither quantity is greater. **Choice B** is incorrect. The two quantities have 2 real roots; therefore, neither quantity is greater. **Choice D** is incorrect. There is enough data to determine the relationship between the two.

76 **Choice E is correct.**

$x^2 - 6x - 27 = 0 \to (x + 3)(x - 9) = 0 \to x = -3$ or $x = 9$.

$y^2 - 6y - 40 = 0 \to (y + 4)(y - 10) = 0 \to y = -4$ or $y = 10$.

Therefore, the maximum value of $x - y = 9 - (-4) = 13$ and hence, maximum value of $2(x - y) = 2 \times 13 = 26$.

Choice A is incorrect. Based on the explanation, the maximum value is 26 and not 17. **Choice B** is incorrect. Based on the explanation, the maximum value is 26 and not 18. **Choice C** is incorrect. Based on the explanation, the maximum value is 26 and not 19. **Choice D** is incorrect. Based on the explanation, the maximum value is 26 and not 21.

77 **Choice B is correct.**

Since $f(x) = ax^4 - 5x^2 + ax - 5$,

$f(b) = ax^4 - 5x^2 + ax - 5$

$= ab^4 - 5b^2 + ab - 5$

$f(-b) = ax^4 - 5x^2 + ax - 5$

$= a(-b)^4 - 5(-b)^2 + a(-b) - 5$

$= ab^4 - 5b^2 - ab - 5$

Therefore, $f(b) - f(-b) = ab^4 - 5b^2 + ab - 5 - (ab^4 - 5b^2 - ab - 5) = 2ab$

Alternatively, we could have recognized that the only term of the function that will be different for $f(b)$ than for $f(-b)$ is "ax." The other three terms are all unaffected by the sign of the variable. More succinctly, $f(b)-f(-b)$ must equal $ab-(-ab) = 2ab$.

Choice A is incorrect. The answer is $2ab$ instead of 0. **Choice C** is incorrect. The answer is 2ab instead of $3ab^4 - 7b^2 - 8$. **Choice D** is incorrect. The answer is 2ab instead of $-3ab^4 + 7b^2 + 8$. **Choice E** is incorrect. The answer is 2ab instead of $3ab^4 - 4b^2 + 5ab - 6$.

78 **Choice E is correct.** Simplify the inequalities, so that all the inequality symbols point in the same direction. Then, line up the inequalities as shown. Finally, combine the inequalities.

$y < x$, $x < 7$, and $-4 < y$ can be written together as $-4 < y < x < 9$.

Now as x and y each cannot be equal to 9 and so the maximum value of $x + y < 18$. The largest prime number smaller than 18 is 17. Hence, the largest prime number that can be equal to $x + y$ is 17.

Choice A is incorrect. The largest prime number is 17 instead of 5. **Choice B** is incorrect. The largest prime number is 17 instead of 7. **Choice C** is incorrect. The largest prime number is 17 instead of 11. **Choice D** is incorrect. The largest prime number is 17 instead of 13.

79 **Choice A is correct.**

$x^2 - 6x - 27 = 0 \to (x + 3)(x - 9) = 0 \to x = -3$ or $x = 9$.

$y^2 - 6y - 40 = 0 \to (y + 4)(y - 10) = 0 \to y = -4$ or $y = 10$.

Therefore, the minimum value of $x + y = (-3) + (-4) = -7$.

Choice B is incorrect. Based on the explanation, the minimum value is -7 and not -6. **Choice C** is incorrect. Based on the explanation, the minimum value is -7 and not -5. **Choice D** is incorrect. Based on the explanation, the minimum value is -7 and not -4. **Choice E** is incorrect. Based on the explanation, the minimum value is -7 and not -3.

80 **Choice D is correct.** To solve this equation, we need to use the formula $d = rt$ (distance = rate × time). We need to write an equation to represent Carl's and Joseph's distance driven. If we assume that Carl drove for time t, then Joseph drove for $t - 1.5$, since he left an hour and a half after Carl left.

Carl: $d_c = (50mph)(t)$

Joseph: $d_J = (70mph)(t - 1.5)$

We want to know when Joseph will be 55 miles beyond Carl, so the difference between their distances will be 55 miles. We then solve the equation for t.

$$d_J - d_c = 55$$
$$70(t-1.5) - 50t = 55$$
$$70t - 105 - 50t = 55$$
$$20t - 105 = 55$$
$$20t = 160$$
$$t = 8 \text{ hours}$$

If Carl started at 6:00am and he drove 8 hours, Joseph will be 55 miles beyond him at 2:00pm.

Choice A is incorrect. This is the time Carl is exactly 5 miles beyond Joseph. **Choice B** is incorrect. This is the time Joseph has gone exactly 15 miles past Carl. **Choice C** is incorrect. This is the time Joseph has gone exactly 35 miles past Carl. **Choice E** is incorrect. This is the time Joseph has gone exactly 75 miles past Carl.

Chapter 4: Algebra

81 **Choice A is correct.** To determine the value of $7x + 10y$, we need to solve the system of equations for x and y using the linear combination or elimination method.

$$2(-5x + 2y = 9)$$
$$1(3x - 4y = -4)$$
$$-10x + 4y = 18$$
$$3x - 4y = -4$$
$$-7x = 14$$
$$x = -2$$

Substituting $x = -2$ in the first equation i.e. $-5x + 2y = 9$, we get:

$$-5(-2) + 2y = 9$$
$$10 + 2y = 9$$
$$2y = -1$$
$$y = -\frac{1}{2}$$

Therefore, $(x, y) = \left(-2, -\frac{1}{2}\right)$

To solve for $7x + 10y$, plug the values of x and y into the equation.

$$7(-2) + 10\left(-\frac{1}{2}\right)$$
$$= -14 - 5$$
$$= -19$$

The answer is Choice A.

Choice B is incorrect. This may result if the required is $6x + 10y$. **Choice C is incorrect.** This may result if the required is $2x + 10y$. **Choice D is incorrect.** This may result if the required is $-2x - 10y$. **Choice E is incorrect.** This may result if the required is $-7x - 10y$.

82 **Choice C is correct** because the obtained maximum value of $x + y$ is 19.

Given: $y^2 - 12y = -27$
$x^2 - 8x = 20$

Solve for the values of x and y by factoring.

$$x^2 - 8x = 20$$
$$x^2 - 8x - 20 = 0$$
$$(x + 2)(x - 10) = 0$$
$$(x + 2) = 0 \quad (x - 10) = 0$$
$$x = -2 \quad x = 10$$
$$y^2 - 12y = -27$$

$$y^2 - 12y + 27 = 0$$
$$(y - 9)(y - 3) = 0$$
$$(y - 9) = 0 \quad (y - 3) = 0$$
$$y = 9 \quad y = 3$$

Find the maximum value of $x + y$. To do this, use the greatest values of x and y.

$$x + y = 10 + 9 = 19$$

Choice A is incorrect because 12 is less than the obtained maximum value of $x + y$. **Choice B is incorrect** because 15 is less than the obtained maximum value of $x + y$. **Choice D is incorrect** because 20 is more than the obtained maximum value of $x + y$. **Choice E is incorrect** because 21 is not the obtained maximum value of $x + y$.

83 **Choice A is correct.** The equation of the first line can be rewritten as $y = -2x + 1$. Therefore, the first line's slope is -2. Use the rule that perpendicular lines have opposite reciprocal slopes and just flip -2 and change the sign to get $\frac{1}{2}$.

Use slope intercept form from here. Now we know the slope of the perpendicular line, which is $\frac{1}{2}$. Because it passes through (0.3), we also know the y intercept. Using $y = mx + b$ and plugging in $\frac{1}{2}$ for m and 3 for b, we obtain $y = \frac{1}{2}x + 3$.

Choice B is incorrect. This option has a slope of 2 instead of 12. **Choice C is incorrect.** This option has a slope of 4 instead of 12. **Choice D is incorrect.** This option has a slope of 3 instead of 12. **Choice E is incorrect.** This option has a slope of 4 instead of 12.

84 **Choice B is correct.**

Given $3^{x+2} + 3^{x-1} = \left(\frac{28}{9}\right)$

$$\Rightarrow 3^x\left(3^2 + 3^{-1}\right) = \left(\frac{28}{9}\right)$$

$$\Rightarrow 3^x\left(9 + \frac{1}{3}\right) = \left(\frac{28}{9}\right)$$

$$\Rightarrow 3^x\left(\frac{28}{3}\right) = \left(\frac{28}{9}\right) \Rightarrow 3^x\left(\frac{28}{3}\right) = \left(\frac{28}{3}\right)\left(\frac{1}{3}\right)$$

Practice Set 2 (Medium): Answers & Explanations

Because $\dfrac{28}{3}$ appears on both sides of the equation, you can cancel it out.

$\Rightarrow 3^x = \dfrac{1}{3}$

$\Rightarrow 3^x = 3^{-1}$

$\Rightarrow x = -1$

Choice A is incorrect. If substituted to the given equation yields $\dfrac{28}{27}$ which is not equal to $\dfrac{28}{9}$. **Choice C** is incorrect. If substituted to the given equation yields 5.388 which is not equal to $\dfrac{28}{9}$. **Choice D** is incorrect. If substituted to the given equation yields 16.165 which is not equal to $\dfrac{28}{9}$. **Choice E** is incorrect. If substituted to the given equation yields 84 which is not equal to $\dfrac{28}{9}$.

85 **Choice A is correct.** First, we solve the first equation for a in terms of *b*:

$\dfrac{(3a+2b)}{(7a+4b)} = \dfrac{15}{32}$; $(3a+2b) \times 32 = 15 \times (7a+4b)$ or $96a + 64b = 105a + 60b$ or $4b = 9a$; $a = \dfrac{4b}{9}$

Now substitute the expression for a into the second equation:

$\dfrac{(3a+b)}{7b} = \left(\dfrac{\dfrac{3 \times 4b}{9} + b}{7b}\right) = \left(\dfrac{\dfrac{4b}{3} + b}{7b}\right) = \dfrac{7b}{(3 \times 7b)} = \dfrac{1}{3}$

Choice B is incorrect. The correct value is $\dfrac{1}{3}$ instead of $\dfrac{1}{2}$.
Choice C is incorrect. The correct value is $\dfrac{1}{3}$ instead of $\dfrac{2}{3}$.
Choice D is incorrect. The correct value is $\dfrac{1}{3}$ instead of $\dfrac{3}{4}$. **Choice E** is incorrect. The correct value is $\dfrac{1}{3}$ instead of $\dfrac{4}{5}$.

86 **Choice E is correct.**

The pipes can fill $\dfrac{1}{24}, \dfrac{1}{6}$ and $\dfrac{1}{12}$ of the tank individually, per minute.

If they are turned on at the same time, they take fill $\dfrac{1}{24} + \dfrac{1}{6} + \dfrac{1}{12} = \dfrac{1}{24}$ of the tank in one minute.

To be full, it takes $\dfrac{24}{7} = 3.43$ minutes, which falls within the range of 3.1 to 5 minutes.

Choice A is incorrect. The tank takes 3.43 minutes to be full which does not fall within the range of 7.1 to 9 minutes. **Choice B** is incorrect. The tank takes 3.43 minutes to be full which does not fall within the range of 1 to 3 minutes. **Choice C** is incorrect. The tank takes 3.43 minutes to be full which does not fall within the range of more than 9 minutes. **Choice D** is incorrect. The tank takes 3.43 minutes to be full which does not fall within the range of 5.1 to 7 minutes.

87 **Choice D is correct.** First, calculate the rates of production per day. Two of the factories each make $100{,}000/15 \cong 6667$ hubcaps per day. The third plant makes $1.3 \times 6667 \cong 8667$ hubcaps per day. The total production rate is $8667 + 2(6667) = 22{,}001$ hubcaps per day. At that rate, it would take 45.5 days to produce a million hubcaps.

Choice A is incorrect. This is the number of days to produce 836,000 hubcaps. **Choice B** is incorrect. This is the number of days to produce 924,000 hubcaps. **Choice C** is incorrect. This is the number of days to produce 968,000 hubcaps. **Choice E** is incorrect. This is the number of days to produce 1,100,000 hubcaps.

88 **Choice C is correct.** Rewrite the expression to come up with common bases. Rewriting each base as a power of 2 yields $\dfrac{(2^3)^{2x} \times (2^2)^{x+1}}{(2^4)^{x-2}}$. Simplifying yields $\dfrac{2^{6x} \times 2^{2x+2}}{2^{4x-8}}$.

Applying the laws of exponents by combining the exponents in the numerator yields $\dfrac{2^{8x+2}}{2^{4x-8}}$. Subtracting the exponents yields $2^{(8x+2)-(4x-8)}$ or 2^{4x+10}.

Substituting $x = 2$ result in $2^{4(2)+10}$ or 2^{18}. Therefore, the correct answer is C.

Choice A is incorrect. This is 2^7, which is not equal to 2^{18}. **Choice B** is incorrect. This is 2^9, which is not equal to 2^{18}. **Choice D** is incorrect. This value is not equal to 2^{18}. **Choice E** is incorrect. This is 2^{36}, which is not equal to 2^{18}.

89 **Choice A is correct.** Multiply each side of the given equation by $(m + n)$.

$(m + n)(m - n) = (m+n)$

Find the product on the left using conjugate identity $a^2 - b^2 = (a + b)(a - b)$.

Chapter 4: Algebra

$m^2 - n^2 = m + n$

Subtract m from and add n^2 to each side.

$m^2 - n^2 - m + n^2 = m + n - m + n^2$

Combine the like terms.

$m^2 - m = n + n^2$

Factor each side.

$m(m - 1) = n(n + 1)$

Thus, Choice A is the correct answer.

Choice B is incorrect because the correct answer based on the explanation is $m(m - 1) = n(n + 1)$. **Choice C** is incorrect because the correct answer based on the explanation is $m(m - 1) = n(n + 1)$. **Choice D** is incorrect because the correct answer based on the explanation is $m(m - 1) = n(n + 1)$. **Choice E** is incorrect because the correct answer based on the explanation is $m(m - 1) = n(n + 1)$.

90 **Choice D is correct.**

When $x_1 = 0$, $y_1 = 0$. So $x_1 = y_1$
When $x_1 = 1$, $y_1 = \sqrt{5}$. So $x_1 < y_1$
When $x_1 = -1$, $y_1 = -\sqrt{5}$. So $x_1 > y_1$

So the relationship cannot be determined from the information given.

Choice A is incorrect. The example above shows that Quantity A is not always greater. **Choice B** is incorrect. The example above shows that Quantity B is not always greater. **Choice C** is incorrect. The quantities can be equal and not equal in some cases.

91 **Choice D is correct** because the obtained value of the rate is 15%.

Given: $t = 20$

$A = 4P$

Let P be the principal amount.

Let A be the amount after t years

Find r using the formula for simple interest.

$A = P(1 + rt)$
$4P = P(1 + 20r)$
$4 = (1 + 20r)$
$4 - 1 = 20r$
$3 = 20r$
$\dfrac{3}{20} = r$ or $r = 0.15$ or $r = 15\%$

Choice A is incorrect because at 5% interest for 20 years, the amount becomes only **double** the principal, not quadruple. **Choice B** is incorrect because at 10% interest for 20 years, the amount becomes **3 times** the principal, not 4 times. **Choice C** is incorrect because at 12% interest for 20 years, the amount becomes **3.4 times** the principal, not 4 times. **Choice E** is incorrect because at 20% interest for 20 years, the amount becomes **5 times** the principal, not 4 times.

92 **Choice E is correct** because the obtained total amount is $6900.

Each deposit will earn interest for a different number of years depending on when it was deposited. Specifically:

At year 1, an investment of $1500 will earn an interest for 4 years.

At year 2, an investment of $1500 will earn an interest for 3 years.

At year 3, an investment of $1500 will earn an interest for 2 years.

At year 4, an investment of $1500 will earn an interest for 1 year.

Find the amount earned on each deposit using the simple interest formula $A = P(1 + rt)$.

At year 1: $A_1 = \$1500(1 + 0.06(4)) = \$1860$
At year 2: $A_2 = \$1500(1 + 0.06(3)) = \$1770$
At year 3: $A_3 = \$1500(1 + 0.06(2)) = \$1680$
At year 4: $A_4 = \$1500(1 + 0.06(1)) = \$1590$

Total Amount Earned $= A_1 + A_2 + A_3 + A_4$
$= \$1860 + \$1770 + \$1680 + \$1590$
$= \$6900$

Choice A is incorrect because $900 is lesser than the obtained total amount. **Choice B** is incorrect because $4200 is not the obtained total amount. **Choice C** is incorrect because $5900 is not the obtained total amount. **Choice D** is incorrect because $6000 is lesser than the obtained total amount.

93 **Choice D is correct.** Here is question testing your understanding of the coordinate graph. To find the area of the rectangle, we must express the dimensions using x and y. The width of the rectangle is simply y, because the point (x, y) is located y units above the x-axis. The length of the rectangle is $x-2$ because it runs from point 2 to point x, parallel to the x-axis. Since width is y and length is $x-2$, the area is $y(x-2)$.

Practice Set 2 (Medium): Answers & Explanations

Choice A is incorrect because the length of the rectangle is $x-2$ as it runs from point 2 to x. **Choice B is incorrect** because the area is $y(x-2)$ and not $4x$. **Choice C is incorrect** because the area is $y(x-2)$ and not $8x$. **Choice E is incorrect** because the x and y are swapped.

94 **Choice C is correct** because the calculated time for Laura and Alex to paint the room together is 4.8 hours.

Given: Laura's rate = $\dfrac{1}{12}$

Alex's rate = $\dfrac{1}{8}$

Find the time it takes for Laura and Alex to work together.

$$\frac{1}{t} = \frac{1}{12} + \frac{1}{8}$$

$$\frac{1}{t} = \frac{2}{24} + \frac{3}{24}$$

$$\frac{1}{t} = \frac{5}{24}$$

$$t = \frac{24}{5} \text{ or } t = 4.8 \text{ hours}$$

Choice A is incorrect because 2.2 less than the obtained value of the time. **Choice B is incorrect** because 3.8 less than the obtained value of the time. **Choice D is incorrect** because 5.2 greater than the obtained value of the time. **Choice E is incorrect** because 6.3 greater than the obtained value of the time.

95 **Choice C is correct** because the obtained value is $\dfrac{11}{24}$.

Given: $AB = CD = \dfrac{1}{2}(BC)$

Find the distance between A & D.

$$\left| \frac{1}{3} - \frac{1}{2} \right|$$

$$\left| \frac{2-3}{6} \right|$$

$$\left| -\frac{1}{6} \right|$$

$$\frac{1}{6}$$

From the given, C is $\dfrac{3}{4}$ from A or $\dfrac{1}{4}$ from D.

Find the location of C from A.

$$\frac{1}{3} + \left(\frac{1}{6}\right)\left(\frac{3}{4}\right) = \frac{1}{3} + \frac{3}{24} = \frac{11}{24}$$

Choice A is incorrect because $\dfrac{5}{24}$ is less than the obtained location of C. **Choice B is incorrect** because $\dfrac{6}{24}$ is less than the obtained location of C. **Choice D is incorrect** because $\dfrac{15}{24}$ is greater than the obtained location of C. **Choice E is incorrect** because $\dfrac{17}{24}$ is greater than the obtained location of C.

96 **Choice A, Choice B and Choice E are correct.** To solve this absolute value inequality, separate the inequality into $-2x + 7 > 5$ and $-2x + 7 < -5$. For both inequalities, subtract 7 from both sides and then divide by -2 (make sure to switch the inequality sign when dividing by a negative). The first inequality then becomes $x < 1$ and the second becomes $x > 6$. Therefore, 7, -6, and 0 work. This makes the solutions A, D, and E.

Choice C is incorrect. 2 is not within the solution set of the inequality $1 > x > 6$. **Choice D is incorrect.** 4 is not within the solution set of the inequality $1 > x > 6$.

97 **Choice A, Choice B, Choice C, Choice D, Choice E, Choice F and Choice G are correct.** First solve the equation for b.

$$2x - 3b = 0$$
$$2x = 3b$$
$$\frac{2x}{3} = b$$

Then by substitution, the inequality $b < 2$ becomes

$$\frac{2x}{3} < 2$$

$$x < \left(\frac{3}{2}\right)(2)$$

$$x < 3$$

So, x is valid for all values less than 3.

Choice H is incorrect. x should be less than 3, thus 3 is therefore not valid. **Choice I is incorrect.** 4 is greater than 3 and is therefore not valid.

Chapter 4: Algebra

98 **Choice A, B, C, D and E are correct** because all values are possible value of t at which it will insect $2x + 8y = 10$ at point $(1,1)$

Given:
$$2x + 8y = 10$$
$$2tx - ty = t$$

The intersection of the two lines is at $(1,1)$. Hence, when $x = 1$ and $y = 1$, satisfies the given equations.

$$2(1) + 8(1) = 10$$
$$2 + 8 = 10$$
$$10 = 10$$
$$2tx - ty = t$$
$$2t(1) - t(1) = t$$
$$t = t$$

Hence, any value of t will satisfy the equation.

99 **Choice E is correct** the only possible units digit of number m is 5.

Let t be the tens digit.
Let u be the units digit.
Given : $t + u = 12$
number $m = 10t + u$
$t = u + 2$

Find u.
$$t + u = 12$$
$$(u + 2) + u = 12$$
$$2u + 2 = 12$$
$$2u = 12 - 2$$
$$u = 5$$

Find t.
$$t + u = 12$$
$$t + 5 = 12$$
$$t = 12 - 5$$
$$t = 7$$

Choice A is incorrect because 1 is not a possible unit digit for number m. **Choice B** is incorrect because 2 is not a possible unit digit for number m. **Choice C** is incorrect because 3 is not a possible unit digit for number m. **Choice D** is incorrect because 4 is not a possible unit digit for number m.

100 **Choice A and Choice C are correct.** We need to simplify each expression to determine if it is equivalent to $2x^2 - 2$ using the distributive property and FOIL method.

A. $4(x^2 - 2) - 2(x^2 - 3) = 4x^2 - 8 - 2x^2 + 6$
$= 2x^2 - 2$

B. $2(x^2 - 2) - 4(x^2 + 3) = 2x^2 - 4 - 4x^2 - 12$
$= -2x^2 - 16$

C. $2(x - 1)(x + 1) = 2(x^2 - x + x - 1) = 2(x^2 - 1)$
$= 2x^2 - 2$

D. $(x + 6)(x + 1) + (8 + x)(1 - x)$
$= x^2 + x + 6x + 6 + 8 - 8x + x - x^2 = 14$

E. $2(x + 4)(x - 1) - 3(2x + 5)$
$= 2(x^2 - x + 4x - 4) - 6x - 15$
$= 2(x^2 + 3x - 4) - 6x - 15$
$= 2x^2 + 6x - 8 - 6x - 15$
$= 2x^2 - 23$

The only answers that simplify to $2x^2 - 2$ are Choice A and Choice C.

Choice B is incorrect. This results in $-2x^2 - 16$ which is not equivalent to $2x^2 - 2$. **Choice D** is incorrect. This results in 14 which is not equivalent to $2x^2 - 2$. **Choice E** is incorrect. This results in $2x^2 - 23$ which is not equivalent to $2x^2 - 2$.

101 **Choice A and Choice C are correct.**
Simplify each expression using the properties of exponents to see if it is equivalent to $\dfrac{5x}{3y^2}$.

A. $\dfrac{(15x^3)(x^{-2}y^3)^2}{\left(\dfrac{1}{3}xy^{-4}\right)^{-2}} = \dfrac{15x^3 x^{-4} y^6}{\dfrac{1}{3^{-2}} x^2 y^8} = \dfrac{15x^{-1} y^6}{9x^{-2} y^8} = \dfrac{5x^2}{3xy^2} = \dfrac{5x}{3y^2}$

B. $\dfrac{(3x^3)(3x^{-2}y^3)^2}{\left(\dfrac{1}{5}xy^{-4}\right)^2} = \dfrac{3x^3 \cdot 9x^{-4} y^6}{\dfrac{1}{25} x^2 y^{-8}} = \dfrac{25 \cdot 27 x^{-1} y^6}{x^2 y^{-8}} = \dfrac{675 y^{14}}{x^3}$

C. $\dfrac{(5x^2)^2 (y^2)^2}{(15x^3)(y^2)^3} = \dfrac{25 x^4 y^4}{15 x^3 \cdot y^6} = \dfrac{25x}{15 y^2} = \dfrac{5x}{3y^2}$

D. $\dfrac{(3x^5 y^2)^{-2}}{(5x^4 y)^{-2} x^3} = \dfrac{3^{-2} x^{-10} y^{-4}}{5^{-2} x^{-8} y^{-2} x^3} = \dfrac{5^2 x^5 y^2}{3^2 x^{10} y^4} = \dfrac{25}{9 x^5 y^2}$

A and C are equivalent to $\frac{5x}{3y^2}$.

Choice B is incorrect. This results in $\frac{675y^{14}}{x^3}$, which is not equivalent to $\frac{5x}{3y^2}$. **Choice D is incorrect.** This results in $\frac{25}{9x^5y^2}$, which is not equivalent to $\frac{5x}{3y^2}$.

102 **Choice D is correct** because both i and ii can be true for specific values of
$$x, y \text{ and } z.$$
Analyze the given equations. We can make counter example to prove the expressions.

For i) $|x-y| = |x+y| = |y-z|$.

Let $x = 1$, $y = 0$ and $z = 1$.
$$|1-0| = |1+0| = |0-1|$$
$$|1| = |1| = |-1|$$
$$1 = 1 = 1.$$

Can be true for specific values of x, y and z.

For ii) $x^y = y^z$

Let $x = 2$, $y = 4$ and $z = 2$.
$$2^4 = 4^2$$
$$16 = 16$$

Can be true for specific values of x, y and z.

For iii) $x^3 + y^3 = z^3$

This is reminiscent of Fermat's Last Theorem for $n = 3$, which states that there are no positive

Let $x = 1$, $y = 2$ and $z = 3$
$$1^3 + 2^3 = 3^3$$
$$1 + 8 = 27$$
$$9 \neq 27$$

Can't be true to any for specific values of x, y and z

Choice A is incorrect because ii is also true for specific values of x, y and z. **Choice B is incorrect** because i is also true for specific values of x, y and z. **Choice C is incorrect** because iii is not true for specific values of x, y and z. **Choice E is incorrect** because iii is not true for specific values of x, y and z.

103 **Choice D, Choice H, and Choice J are correct.**

Let M be the number of votes cast for Mike. Then Kelly received $M + \left(\frac{1}{3}\right)M$, or $\left(\frac{4}{3}\right)M$ votes. The total number of votes cast was therefore "votes for Mike" + "votes for Kelly" or $M + \left(\frac{4}{3}\right)M = \frac{7M}{3}$.

Because M is number of votes, it cannot be a fraction – specifically, not a fraction with a 7 in the denominator. Therefore, the 7 in the expression $\frac{7M}{3}$ cannot be cancelled out. As a result, the total number of votes cast must be a multiple of 7. Among these answer choices, the multiples of 7 are D, H, J.

Choice A is incorrect. 2 is not a multiple of 7. **Choice B is incorrect.** 3 is not a multiple of 7. **Choice C is incorrect.** 4 is not a multiple of 7. **Choice E is incorrect.** 8 is not a multiple of 7. **Choice F is incorrect.** 10 is not a multiple of 7. **Choice G is incorrect.** 12 is not a multiple of 7. **Choice I is incorrect.** 16 is not a multiple of 7.

104 **Choice C and Choice D are correct.** To be 5 vertical units apart, the y intercepts must be 5 units apart on the y axis.

Choice C: Putting Choice C into slope-intercept form becomes $y = x - 10$. This y intercept of –10 is 5 away from the original y intercept of –5, and the slopes are both 1, so these lines are parallel with a distance of 5 vertical units. Choice C is correct.

Choice D: Putting Choice D into slope-intercept form becomes $y = x$. This y intercept of 0 is 5 away from the original y intercept of –5, and the slopes are both 1, so these lines are parallel with a distance of 5 vertical units. Choice D is correct.

The solutions are then both Choice C and D.

Choice A is incorrect. The y-intercept of –53 is not 5 away from the original y-intercept of –5, and the slopes are not the same so these are not parallel lines. **Choice B is incorrect.** The y-intercept of 4 is not 5 away from the original y intercept of –5, and the slopes are not the same.

105 **Choice A, B, and E are correct** because the points satisfy the conditions.

For the points to be within the triangular region, it should satisfy the following conditions, $x \geq 0$, $y \geq 0$ and $2x + 3y \leq 50$.

Test the points if it satisfies the conditions.

At point $(10,10)$
$$x \geq 0, y \geq 0,$$
$$2(10) + 3(10) \leq 50$$

Chapter 4: Algebra

$$50 \leq 50 \quad \text{true}$$

At point $(6,5)$

$$x \geq 0, \, y \geq 0,$$
$$2(6)+3(5) \leq 50$$
$$27 \leq 50 \quad \text{true}$$

At point $(15,10)$

$$x \geq 0, \, y \geq 0,$$
$$2(15)+3(10) \leq 50$$
$$60 \leq 50 \quad \text{false}$$

At point $(5,15)$

$$x \geq 0, \, y \geq 0,$$
$$2(5)+3(15) \leq 50$$
$$55 \leq 50 \quad \text{false}$$

At point $(2,15)$

$$x \geq 0, \, y \geq 0,$$
$$2(2)+3(15) \leq 50$$
$$49 \leq 50 \quad \text{true}$$

Choice C is incorrect because $(15,10)$ is not within the region R. **Choice D** is incorrect because $(5,15)$ is not within the region R.

106 The correct answer is 12.

Given: $4x^2 - bx + 9 = 0$

A quadratic equation $ax^2 + bx + c = 0$ has exactly one solution when its discriminant is zero. The discriminant is given by: $b^2 - 4ac = 0$.

Find b using the discriminant formula.

$$4x^2 - bx + 9 = 0$$
$$a = 4, b = -b, c = 9$$
$$(-b)^2 - 4(4)(9) = 0$$
$$b^2 - 144 = 0$$
$$b^2 = 144$$
$$b = \pm 12$$

Since $b > 0$, the value of b is 12.

107 The correct answer is 110.

Let x be the number of cups sold.

Given: Fixed cost = $660

Cost for each cup = $2

Price of the cup = $8

Find the break-even point.

The break-even point is where total revenue equals total costs.

Total Revenue = Price of the cup (The number of cups sold)

$$= \$8x$$

Total Cost = Cost for each cup (The number of cups sold) + fixed cost

$$= \$2x + 660$$

Total Revenue = Total Cost

$$\$8x = \$2x + \$600$$
$$\$8x - \$2x = \$660$$
$$\$6x = \$660$$
$$x = 110$$

108 The correct answer is 39.5.

Total score in 3 matches against team A = $3 \times 42 = 126$ runs

Total score in 5 matches against team B = $5 \times 38 = 190$ runs

Total scores in 8 matches = 316 runs

$$\text{Average} = \frac{316}{8} = 39.5$$

109 The correct answer is 5. Place x over 1 to form a fraction on the right side.

$$\frac{5x^2 + ax + b}{3x^2 + 7x + 5} = \frac{x}{1}$$

Cross multiply and simplify.

$x(3x^2 + 7x + 5) = 5x^2 + ax + b$

$3x^3 + 7x^2 + 5x = 5x^2 + ax + b$

Subtract $5x^2$, ax, and b from each side, and factor.

$3x^3 + 7x^2 + 5x - 5x^2 - ax - b = 5x^2 + ax + b - 5x^2 - ax - b$

$3x^3 + 2x^2 + 5x - ax - b = 0$

$3x^3 + 2x^2 + (5-a)x - b = 0$

$3x^3 + 2x^2 - b = 0$ (given in the problem)

$(5 - a)x = 0$

Divide each side by x knowing that we are given $x \neq 0$.

$5 - a = 0$

$a = 5$

110 The correct answer is $\dfrac{226}{15}$.

Find the roots using factoring.

$$x^2 - 30x + 225 = 0$$
$$(x-15)(x-15) = 0$$
$$(x-15) = 0 \qquad (x-15) = 0$$
$$x = 15 \qquad x = 15$$

Find $(x + x^{-1})$ using the negative exponent rule.

$$(x + x^{-1}) = (15 + 15^{-1}) = \left(15 + \frac{1}{15}\right) = \frac{225 + 1}{15} = \frac{226}{15}$$

111 The correct answer is 1.

Find the possible range for n.

$$0 < 5^n < 500$$

Let $n = 0$ $\qquad 5^0 = 1$
Let $n = 1$ $\qquad 5^1 = 5$
Let $n = 2$ $\qquad 5^2 = 25$
Let $n = 3$ $\qquad 5^3 = 125$
Let $n = 4$ $\qquad 5^4 = 625$

Since $n = 4$, the range of 5^4 is greater than 500. Hence, possible range of n is from 0 to 3.

Find the greatest value of $\frac{1}{2^n}$ using $n = 0, 1, 2, 3$.

Let $n = 0$ $\qquad \frac{1}{2^0} = 1$
Let $n = 1$ $\qquad \frac{1}{2^1} = 0.5$
Let $n = 2$ $\qquad \frac{1}{2^2} = 0.25$
Let $n = 3$ $\qquad \frac{1}{2^3} = 0.125$

Hence, the greatest value of $\frac{1}{2^n}$ is 1 at $n = 0$.

112 The correct answer is 43.40. If Max travels 25 mph for 14 hours, he travels $25 \times 14 = 350$ miles in total. If his car averages 10 miles per gallon, he must use $350 / 10 = 35$ gallons to get to his destination. Gas costs $3.76 per gallon, so the total he will spend on gas is $35 \times 3.76 = 131.60$. To find the amount he has remaining, you must subtract the total he spent on gas from the original amount he had. Therefore, 175 − 131.6 = 43.40.

113 The correct answer is 7.

Math procedure	Strategy/Explanation
$x^2 - 2 = 2x + 1$	When two curves intersect, they will have a common value of y.
$x^2 - 2x - 3 = 0$	Therefore, set the right sides of the two equations equal, and simplify.
$(x - 3)(x + 1) = 0$ $x = 3, x = -1$	Factorize and solve to obtain $x = 3, x = -1$.
$y(3) = 2(3) + 1 = 7$ $y(-1) = 2(-1) + 1 = -1$	Use the simpler equation to compute y-values for $x = 2$, and for $x = -1$.
	The positive value of $y = 7$

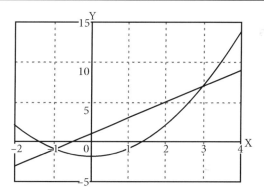

114 The correct answer is 8%

Given:
$$t = 25$$
$$A = 3P$$

Let P be the principal amount.

Let A be the amount after t years

Find r using the formula for simple interest.

$$A = P(1 + rt)$$
$$3P = P(1 + 25r)$$
$$3 = (1 + 25r)$$
$$3 - 1 = 25r$$
$$2 = 25r$$
$$\frac{2}{25} = r \quad \text{or} \quad r = 0.08 \quad \text{or} \quad r = 8\%$$

The value of the rate is 8%.

Chapter 4: Algebra

115 The correct answer is 3

Given: $A(-4,0)$
$B(0,4)$
ratio $m:n = 3:1$

Use the section formula to find the point.

$$\left(\frac{mx_2 + nx_1}{m+n}, \frac{my_2 + ny_1}{m+n}\right)$$

$$\left(\frac{3(0)+1(-4)}{3+1}, \frac{3(4)+1(0)}{3+1}\right)$$

$$\left(\frac{-4}{4}, \frac{12}{4}\right)$$

$$(-1, 3)$$

Hence, the y-coordinates of the point is 3.

Practice Set 3 (Hard): Answers & Explanations

116 **Choice D is correct.** First, we solve Inequality 1:

$4(x + 2) \leq 2(x + 5) + 14 \rightarrow 4x + 8 \leq 2x + 10 + 14 \rightarrow 2x \leq 16$
$\rightarrow x \leq 8$

Then we solve Inequality 2:

$$\sqrt{16 - 8y + y^2} \leq 9 \rightarrow \sqrt{(4-y)^2} \leq 9$$

The square root of a square expression will always be a positive number, so we can write this inequality as:

$$|4 - y| \leq 9 \rightarrow -9 \leq 4 - y \leq 9 \rightarrow -13 \leq -y \leq 5$$

We multiply with (−1) so the inequality sign changes:

$$13 \geq y \geq -5$$

Any number equal to, or less than, 8 is a solution of the first inequality, while for the second inequality the solutions are numbers equal to, or greater than, −5 and less than, or equal to, 13.

This means that 13 for instance is a solution for Inequality 2 which is greater than any solution of Inequality 1. However, in another example, 6 is a solution of Inequality 2 which is less than some solutions of Inequality 1 (8 for instance)

The relationship cannot be determined without further information and Choice D is the correct answer.

Choice A is incorrect. The example above shows that Quantity A is not always greater. **Choice B** is incorrect. The example above shows that Quantity B is not always greater. **Choice C** is incorrect. The quantities cannot be determined as equal in any case.

117 **Choice C is correct** because Quantity A is equal to Quantity B.

Analyze the quantities.

Quantity A: The perimeter of Trapezoid JKLM

The perimeter of Trapezoid JKLM is the sum of its side lengths. JK, KL, LM and MJ.

Use the distance formula to find the distance between points J (−3,−4) and K (−3,1).

$$d = \sqrt{(x_2 - x_1)^2 + (y_2 - y_1)^2}$$
$$d = \sqrt{(-3-(-3))^2 + (1-(-4))^2}$$
$$d = \sqrt{(0)^2 + (5)^2}$$
$$d = \sqrt{0 + 25}$$
$$d = \sqrt{25}$$
$$d = 5$$

Use the distance formula to find the distance between points K(−3,1) and L(4,7).

$$d = \sqrt{(x_2 - x_1)^2 + (y_2 - y_1)^2}$$
$$d = \sqrt{(4-(-3))^2 + (7-1)^2}$$
$$d = \sqrt{(7)^2 + (6)^2}$$
$$d = \sqrt{49 + 36}$$
$$d = \sqrt{85}$$

Use the distance formula to find the distance between points L(4,7) and M(4,−4).

$$d = \sqrt{(x_2 - x_1)^2 + (y_2 - y_1)^2}$$
$$d = \sqrt{(4-4)^2 + (-4-7)^2}$$
$$d = \sqrt{(0)^2 + (11)^2}$$
$$d = \sqrt{121}$$
$$d = 11$$

Use the distance formula to find the distance between points M(4,−4) and J(−3,−4).

$$d = \sqrt{(x_2 - x_1)^2 + (y_2 - y_1)^2}$$
$$d = \sqrt{(-3-4)^2 + (-4-(-4))^2}$$
$$d = \sqrt{(-7)^2 + (0)^2}$$

$$d = \sqrt{49 + 0}$$
$$d = 7$$

The perimeter of Trapezoid JKLM is
$$P = JK + KL + LM + MJ$$
$$P = 5 + \sqrt{85} + 11 + 7$$
$$P = 23 + \sqrt{85}$$

Quantity B: $23 + \sqrt{85}$

Choice A is incorrect because Quantity A is not greater than Quantity B. **Choice B** is incorrect because Quantity B is not greater than Quantity B. **Choice D** is incorrect because a relation can be obtained from the given information.

118 **Choice A is correct** because the sum of digits of X is always greater than the sum of the digits of Y.

Identify the possible digits for X and Y.

For X – 3–digit number where digits are greater than 5. Possible digits are 6, 7, 8 and 9.

For Y – 4–digit number where digits are less than 4. Possible digits are 0, 1, 2 and 3.

Find the possible sum of the digits.

For X with minimum digit 6, minimum sum is 6+6+6 =18.

For X with maximum digit 9, maximum sum is 9+9+9 =27.

Hence, the sum of the digits of X ranges from 18 to 27.

For Y with minimum digit 0, minimum sum is 0+0+0+0 =0.

For Y with maximum digit 3, maximum sum is 3+3+3+3 =12.

Hence, the sum of the digits of Y ranges from 0 to 12.

Choice B is incorrect because Quantity B is less than Quantity A. **Choice C** is incorrect because Quantity A is not equal to Quantity B. **Choice D** is incorrect because a relation can be obtained from the given information.

119 **Choice C is correct** because Quantity A is equal to Quantity B.

Rewrite the given expression.
$$a(a+3) - 153 = ab$$
$$a^2 + 3a - 153 = ab$$

$$a^2 + 3a - ab = 153$$
$$a(a + 3 - b) = 153$$

Analyze the quantities.

153 is an odd integer. An odd integer is a product of two odd integers, hence, a is an odd integer and $(a+3-b)$ is also an odd integer.

Quantity A: The remainder when a is divided by 2.

An odd integer divided by 2 yields to a remainder of 1.

Note that a is an odd integer hence, the remainder when a is divided by 2 is 1.

Quantity B: The remainder when b is divided by 2.

An odd integer divided by 2 yields to a remainder of 1.

Note that $(a+3-b)$ is an odd integer hence, the value of b is also an odd integer. The remainder when b is divided by 2 is 1.

Choice A is incorrect because Quantity A is not greater than Quantity B. **Choice B** is incorrect because Quantity B is not greater than Quantity B. **Choice D** is incorrect because a relation can be obtained from the given information.

120 **Choice B is correct** because Quantity B is greater than Quantity A.

Analyze the quantities.

Quantity A: x when $f(x) = g(x)$

$$f(x) = g(x)$$
$$7^x - 7^{x-2} = 48(7^6)$$
$$7^x - \frac{7^x}{7^2} = 48(7^6)$$
$$7^x\left(1 - \frac{1}{7^2}\right) = 48(7^6)$$
$$7^x\left(1 - \frac{1}{49}\right) = 48(7^6)$$
$$7^x\left(\frac{48}{49}\right) = 48(7^6)$$
$$7^x = 48(7^6)\left(\frac{49}{48}\right)$$
$$7^x = (7^6)(49)$$
$$7^x = (7^6)(7^2)$$

Chapter 4: Algebra

$$7^x = 7^8$$
$$x = 8$$

Quantity B: 10

Choice A is incorrect because Quantity A is less than Quantity B. **Choice C** is incorrect because Quantity A is not equal to Quantity B. **Choice D** is incorrect because a relation can be obtained from the given information.

121 **Choice C is correct** because Quantity A is equal to Quantity B.

Analyze the quantities.

Quantity A: The number of minutes it takes Andrew to run 24 laps.

Time per lap = $\dfrac{x}{6}$ minutes per lap

Time for 24 laps = $\dfrac{x}{6}(24) = 4x$ minutes per lap

Quantity A: The number of minutes it takes Andrew to run 24 laps.

Time per lap = $\dfrac{2x}{11}$ minutes per lap

Time for 22 laps = $\dfrac{2x}{11}(22) = 4x$ minutes per lap

Choice A is incorrect because Quantity A is not greater than Quantity B. **Choice B** is incorrect because Quantity B is not greater than Quantity A. **Choice D** is incorrect because a relation can be obtained from the given information.

122 **Choice C is correct** because Quantity A is equal to Quantity B.

Analyze the quantities.

Quantity A: The slope of AB

Given: midpoint $(-3, 5)$

A $(x, 0)$, B $(0, y)$

Midpoint formula: $\left(\dfrac{x-0}{2}, \dfrac{y-0}{2}\right) = (-3, 5)$

$\left(\dfrac{x}{2}, \dfrac{y}{2}\right) = (-3, 5)$

$\dfrac{x}{2} = -3 \quad \dfrac{y}{2} = 5$

$x = -6 \quad y = 10$

Point A is $(-6, 0)$

B is $(0, 10)$

Slope of AB is $\dfrac{y_2 - y_1}{x_2 - x_1} = \dfrac{10 - 0}{0 - (-6)} = \dfrac{10}{6} = \dfrac{5}{3}$

Quantity B: The slope of DE

Given: midpoint $(3, -5)$

E $(x, 0)$, D $(0, y)$

Midpoint formula: $\left(\dfrac{x-0}{2}, \dfrac{y-0}{2}\right) = (3, -5)$

$\left(\dfrac{x}{2}, \dfrac{y}{2}\right) = (3, -5)$

$\dfrac{x}{2} = 3 \quad \dfrac{y}{2} = -5$

$x = 6 \quad y = -10$

Point E is $(6, 0)$

D is $(0, -10)$

Slope of AB is $\dfrac{y_2 - y_1}{x_2 - x_1} = \dfrac{-10 - 0}{0 - (6)} = \dfrac{10}{6} = \dfrac{5}{3}$

Choice A is incorrect because Quantity A is not greater than Quantity B. **Choice B** is incorrect because Quantity B is not greater than Quantity A. **Choice D** is incorrect because a relation can be obtained from the given information.

123 **Choices D, E, F, and G are correct.** To solve the given inequality $\dfrac{2x+7}{x-1} > 3$, isolate x and determine the values that satisfy the inequality.

Subtracting 3 from both sides yields $\dfrac{2x+7}{x-1} - 3 > 0$.

Combining the fractions yields $\dfrac{2x+7-3(x-1)}{x-1} > 0$ or $\dfrac{-x+10}{x-1} > 0$.

Finding the critical points yields the numerator $= -x + 10 = 0$ or $x = 10$ and the denominator $= x - 1 = 0$ or $x = 1$.

Testing each interval, for $x < 1$, substitute $x = 0$ into $\dfrac{-x+10}{x-1}$ to get -10, which is negative.

For $1 < x < 10$, substitute $x = 5$ into $\dfrac{-x+10}{x-1}$ to get $\dfrac{5}{4}$, which is positive.

For $x > 10$, substitute $x = 11$ into $\dfrac{-x+10}{x-1}$ to get $-\dfrac{1}{10}$, which is negative.

Practice Set 3 (Hard): Answers & Explanations

Thus, the expression is positive in the interval $1 < x < 10$.
Therefore, the values of x are 2, 3, 4, 5, 6, 7, 8, and 9, from the choices, D, E, F, and G are correct.

Choice A is incorrect. -1 does not satisfy $1 < x < 10$.
Choice B is incorrect. 0 does not satisfy $1 < x < 10$.
Choice C is incorrect. 1 is the boundary point and does not satisfy $1 < x < 10$. **Choice H is incorrect.** 11 does not satisfy $1 < x < 10$.

124 **Choice A and E are correct** because the obtained possible y coordinates of point N are -1 and 5.
Find the equation of the line using the point–intercept formula.

$$y - y_1 = m(x - x_1)$$
$$y - 2 = \frac{3}{4}(x - 3)$$
$$4y - 8 = 3x - 9$$
$$3x = 1 + 4y$$
$$x = \frac{1 + 4y}{3}$$

Find the possible y–coordinates of point N.
Let (x, y) be the coordinates of point N. Use the distance formula of MN.

$$d^2 = (x - x_1)^2 + (y - y_1)^2$$
$$5^2 = (x - 3)^2 + (y - 2)^2$$
$$25 = (x - 3)^2 + (y - 2)^2$$
$$25 = x^2 - 6x + 9 + y^2 - 4y + 4$$
$$25 = x^2 - 6x + y^2 - 4y + 13$$

Substitute $x = \frac{1 + 4y}{3}$

$$\left(\frac{1+4y}{3}\right)^2 - 6\left(\frac{1+4y}{3}\right) + y^2 - 4y + 13 = 25$$
$$\frac{(16y^2 + 8y + 1)}{9} - \frac{6 + 24y}{3} + y^2 - 4y + 13 - 25 = 0$$
$$\frac{(16y^2 + 8y + 1)}{9} - 2 - 8y + y^2 - 4y + 13 - 25 = 0$$
$$16y^2 + 8y + 1 - 18 - 72y + 9y^2 - 36y + 117 - 225 = 0$$
$$(16y^2 + 9y^2) + (8y - 72y - 36y) + (1 - 18 + 117 - 225) = 0$$
$$25y^2 - 100y - 125 = 0$$
$$y^2 - 4y - 5 = 0$$
$$(y + 1)(y - 5) = 0$$
$$(y + 1) = 0 \qquad (y - 5) = 0$$
$$y = -1 \qquad y = 5$$

Choice B is incorrect because 2 is not a possible y-coordinates of point N. **Choice C is incorrect** because 3 is not a possible y-coordinates of point N. **Choice D is incorrect** because 4 is not a possible y-coordinates of point N.

125 **Choice A and E are correct** because it represents the given problem.

Give: Items per week = $7x$
Charge per delivery = d
Charge per item in dollars = $\frac{c}{100}$
Write the equation.
Total cost in a week = Items per week (charge per item in dollar) + 7(charge per delivery)

$$= 7x\left(\frac{c}{100}\right) + 7d$$

It can also be expressed as:

$$= 7\left(\frac{xc}{100} + d\right)$$

Choice B is incorrect because $7x\left(\frac{c}{100}\right) + 7d$ does not represent the given problem. **Choice C is incorrect** because $7d\left(\frac{x}{100}\right) + 7c$ does not represent the given problem. **Choice D is incorrect** because $\frac{7c}{100} + 7xd$ does not represent the given problem.

126 **Choice A, C, G and I are correct** because the obtained unit digits from the given value of m is 1, 3, 7 and 9.
Find the units digit of $m = 87^x$. For the unit digits, we can consider the expression 7^x because the units digit represent teh successive powers of 7.

Units digit when $x = 1$	$7^1 = 7$	7
Units digit when $x = 2$	$7^2 = 49$	9
Units digit when $x = 3$	$7^3 = 343$	3
Units digit when $x = 4$	$7^4 = 2401$	1
Units digit when $x = 5$	$7^5 = 16807$	7

Choice B is incorrect because 2 is not a unit digit in a successive power of 87. **Choice D is incorrect** because 4 is not a unit digit in a successive power of 87. **Choice E is incorrect** because 5 is not a unit digit in a successive power of 87. **Choice F is incorrect** because 6 is not a unit

Chapter 4: Algebra

digit in a successive power of 87. **Choice H is incorrect** because 8 is not a unit digit in a successive power of 87.

127 **Choice A and B are correct** because the values are less than 900.

Find the amount of water in each time.

1:00 PM –3:00 PM , 2hours water drained at a rate 150 gallons per hour.

Amount of water = 150(2) = 300

3:00 PM –5:00 PM , 2hours water drained at a rate 300 gallons per hour.

Amount of water = 300(2) = 600

The tank is empty at 5:00 PM

Possibe amount of water is 300+600 =900.

Since the water is empty before 5:00 pm, the amount of water must be all possible values less than 900.

Choice C is incorrect because 1000 is more than the obtained value 900. **Choice D is incorrect** because 1200 is more than the obtained value 900. **Choice E is incorrect** because 1500 is more than the obtained value 900.

128 **Choice C, Choice D and Choice F are correct.**

In the equation $f(x) = 2x^2 - 7x + 3$, we can determine the following without any calculation. The value of "a", the leading coefficient, is 2. Since it is positive the parabola opens up, so A is false. Find the vertex of the polynomial by calculating.

$$x = -\frac{b}{2a}$$

$$a = 2, b = -7$$

$$x = -\frac{(-7)}{2(2)} = \frac{7}{4}$$

$$f\left(\frac{7}{4}\right) = 2\left(\frac{7}{4}\right)^2 - 7\left(\frac{7}{4}\right) + 3$$

$$= 2\left(\frac{49}{16}\right) - \frac{49}{4} + 3$$

$$= \frac{49}{8} - \frac{49}{4} + 3$$

$$= \frac{49}{8} - \frac{98}{8} + \frac{24}{8} = -\frac{25}{8}$$

Therefore we know that the axis of symmetry is $x = \frac{7}{4}$,

with a minimum of $-\frac{25}{8}$. Therefore B is false but D is true.

To find the y–intersect of the graph we can set x equal to 0, and calculate the value of y or $f(x)$.

Therefore F is true.

Next we can set $f(x)$ equal to 0 and see whether the polynomial can be factored.

The factored form is $(2x-1)(x-3)$

The roots of the equation are $\frac{1}{2}$ and 3.

Therefore, the roots can be calculated using factoring but the roots are not -3 and $-\frac{1}{2}$. C is true, E is false.

Choice A is incorrect. The value of coefficient "a" is positive thus, the parabola opens up instead of down.

Choice B is incorrect. The parabola has a minimum of $-\frac{25}{8}$ and not 3.

Choice E is incorrect. The x-intercepts of the graph are located at $x = 3$ and $x = \frac{1}{2}$ instead of $x = -3$ and $x = -\frac{1}{2}$.

129 **Choice C is correct.**

Looking at the graph, the slope of M is positive and the slope of N is negative.

Let's analyze the equations from the choices.

Choice C : $y = 5x + 15$ and $y = -x + 3$

Slope of M is positive and slope of N is negative, hence, a possible answer.

Find the intersection between the lines.

$$5x + 15 = -x + 3$$
$$5x + x = 3 - 15$$
$$6x = -12$$
$$x = -2$$
$$y = -x + 3$$
$$y = -(-2) + 3$$
$$y = 5$$

The intersection is at $(-2, 5)$ which satisfies the graph.

Choice A is incorrect because $y = -5x + 15$ and $y = 5x + 15$ does not satisfy the equations for line M and line N. **Choice B is incorrect because** $y = -5x + 10$ and $y = 3x + 1$ does not satisfy the equations for line M and line N. **Choice D** is incorrect because $y = 5x - 15$ and $y = -x - 3$ does not satisfy the equations for line M and line N. **Choice E** is incorrect because $y = 15x + 5$ and $y = 3x - 1$ does not satisfy the equations for line M and line N.

130 **The correct answer is 4.**

Find the roots of $x^4 - 5x^2 + 4 < 0$.

Rewrite as $x^4 - 5x^2 + 4 = 0$.

$$x^4 - 4x^2 - x^2 + 4 = 0$$
$$(x^2 - 1)(x^2 - 4) = 0$$
$$(x - 1)(x + 1)(x - 2)(x + 2) = 0$$

The roots are $x = 1, -1, 2, -2$.

Hence, the product of the roots is $1(-1)(2)(-2) = 4$.

This page is intentionally left blank

Chapter 5
Geometry

Chapter 5: Geometry

Practice Set 1: Easy

1. The longer leg of a right-angled triangle is fourteen yards more than the shorter leg. The shorter leg is three yards less than the shorter leg. The shorter leg is three yards less than half of the hypotenuse.

Quantity A	Quantity B
The length of the hypotenuse.	28

- Ⓐ Quantity A is greater.
- Ⓑ Quantity B is greater.
- Ⓒ The two quantities are equal.
- Ⓓ The relationship cannot be determined from the information given.

2.

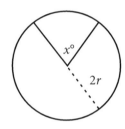 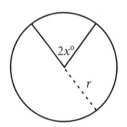

Quantity A	Quantity B
The area of the sector in the left circle	The area of the sector in the right circle

- Ⓐ Quantity A is greater.
- Ⓑ Quantity B is greater.
- Ⓒ The two quantities are equal.
- Ⓓ The relationship cannot be determined from the information given.

3.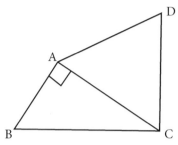

In $\triangle ABC$, $m\angle BAC = 90°$ and $m\angle ACB = 30°$. $\triangle ADC$ is equilateral. (figure not to scale)

Quantity A	Quantity B
Area of $\triangle ABC$	Area of $\triangle ADC$

- Ⓐ Quantity A is greater.
- Ⓑ Quantity B is greater.
- Ⓒ The two quantities are equal.
- Ⓓ The relationship cannot be determined from the information given.

4.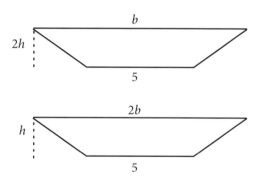

Quantity A	Quantity B
The area of the top trapezoid	The area of the bottom trapezoid

- Ⓐ Quantity A is greater.
- Ⓑ Quantity B is greater.
- Ⓒ The two quantities are equal.
- Ⓓ The relationship cannot be determined from the information given.

Practice Set 1: Easy

5 The variable r is a positive whole number.

Quantity A	Quantity B
The area formed from a circle with $\frac{2}{3}r$ radius.	The circumference of a circle formed with $\frac{1}{5}r$ radius.

A) Quantity A is greater.
B) Quantity B is greater.
C) The two quantities are equal.
D) The relationship cannot be determined from the information given.

6

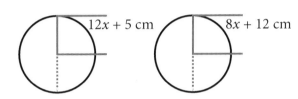

Quantity A	Quantity B
Circumference of the left circle if $x = 2$	Circumference of the right circle if $x = 2$

A) Quantity A is greater.
B) Quantity B is greater.
C) The two quantities are equal.
D) The relationship cannot be determined from the information given.

7

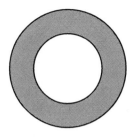

The radius of the inner circle is r, and the distance from the inner circle to the outer circle is also r.

Quantity A	Quantity B
The area of the unshaded portion	The area of the shaded portion

A) Quantity A is greater.
B) Quantity B is greater.
C) The two quantities are equal.
D) The relationship cannot be determined from the information given.

8

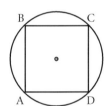

In the figure above, the diameter of the circle is 7.

Quantity A	Quantity B
The area of square ABCD	25

A) Quantity A is greater.
B) Quantity B is greater.
C) The two quantities are equal.
D) The relationship cannot be determined from the information given.

Chapter 5: Geometry

9.

Quantity A	Quantity B
The sum of the interior angles of a convex pentagon	500°

Ⓐ Quantity A is greater.
Ⓑ Quantity B is greater.
Ⓒ The two quantities are equal.
Ⓓ The relationship cannot be determined from the information given

10. The perimeter of a square is 25% less than the perimeter of a rectangle.

Quantity A	Quantity B
The side length of the square	The length of the rectangle's longest side

Ⓐ Quantity A is greater.
Ⓑ Quantity B is greater.
Ⓒ The two quantities are equal.
Ⓓ The relationship cannot be determined from the information given.

11. Within a circle with a radius of 15, a sector has an area of 75π.

Quantity A	Quantity B
The measure of the sector in degrees	120

Ⓐ Quantity A is greater.
Ⓑ Quantity B is greater.
Ⓒ The two quantities are equal.
Ⓓ The relationship cannot be determined from the information given.

12.

B 8 C   F   G
                  8
A   D E 10 H

Quantity A	Quantity B
The area of square ABCD	The area of trapezoid EFGH

Ⓐ Quantity A is greater.
Ⓑ Quantity B is greater.
Ⓒ The two quantities are equal.
Ⓓ The relationship cannot be determined from the information given.

13. The diagonal of one TV is 50 inches. Another TV has a diagonal of 75 inches.

Quantity A	Quantity B
The longest side length of the first TV.	The shortest side length of the second TV.

Ⓐ Quantity A is greater.
Ⓑ Quantity B is greater.
Ⓒ The two quantities are equal.
Ⓓ The relationship cannot be determined from the information given.

14. What is the value of the length of the height in an equilateral triangle with a length of $2\sqrt{3}$?

Ⓐ $\dfrac{\sqrt{3}}{3}$
Ⓑ $\sqrt{3}$
Ⓒ $2\sqrt{3}$
Ⓓ 3
Ⓔ $3\sqrt{3}$

15

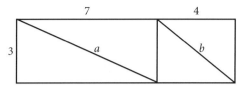

In the above diagram, the sum $a + b$ is equal to:

Ⓐ $5 + \sqrt{58}$
Ⓑ $16 + \sqrt{2}$
Ⓒ 14
Ⓓ $\dfrac{25}{3}$
Ⓔ $17 + 3\sqrt{6}$

16

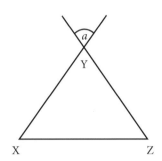

In $\triangle XYZ$, $XY = 10$, $YZ = 10$, and $\angle a = 84°$. What is the degree measure of $\angle Z$?

Ⓐ $24°$
Ⓑ $42°$
Ⓒ $48°$
Ⓓ $84°$
Ⓔ $96°$

17

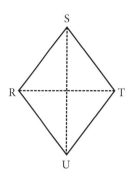

The diagram above shows rhombus RSTU. If $\angle RST = 5x - 14$ and $\angle UST = 2x + 4$, what is the value of x?

Ⓐ 2.5
Ⓑ 4
Ⓒ $5\dfrac{1}{3}$
Ⓓ 18
Ⓔ 22

18 How many different pentagons can be drawn inside a hexagon?

Ⓐ 3
Ⓑ 4
Ⓒ 5
Ⓓ 6
Ⓔ 7

19 Which of the following is the equation describing a circle that has as center $C(3, 4)$ and it is tangent to the y-axis?

Ⓐ $x^2 + y^2 + 10 = 0$
Ⓑ $x^2 + y^2 - 2(3x + 4y) + 9 = 0$
Ⓒ $x^2 + y^2 + 4(x + y) + 16 = 0$
Ⓓ $(x - 3)^2 + (y - 1)(y - 7) = 0$
Ⓔ $x^2 + y^2 + 2(3x + y) - 7 = 0$

Chapter 5: Geometry

20 The center of a circle in the *xy*-plane is (5, 4). If the circle passes through (5, 14), what is the equation of the circle?

- A. $(x - 5)^2 + (y - 4)^2 = 100$
- B. $(x + 5)^2 + (y + 4)^2 = 100$
- C. $(x - 5)^2 + (y - 4)^2 = 10$
- D. $(x + 5)^2 + (y + 4)^2 = 10$
- E. $(x + 5)^2 + (y - 4)^2 = 10$

21

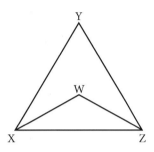

WX and WZ are angle bisectors of the base angles of isosceles △XYZ above. If ∠Y = 80°, what is the degree measure of ∠XWZ ?

- A. 65
- B. 80
- C. 100
- D. 130
- E. 160

22 Length of a rectangle is 3cm less than the double of its width. If the perimeter of the rectangle is 96cm, then what will be its width and length?

- A. 16cm & 29cm
- B. 15cm & 27cm
- C. 14cm & 25cm
- D. 13cm & 23cm
- E. 17cm & 31cm

23

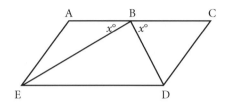

Note: Figure not drawn to scale.

In the figure above, AC ∥ ED. If the length of BD = 3, what is the length of BE?

- A. 3
- B. 4
- C. 5
- D. $3\sqrt{3}$
- E. It cannot be determined from the information given.

24

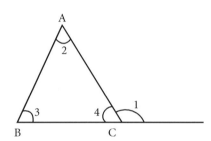

If ABC is a triangle, the measure of angle 1 is 124°, and the measure of angle 2 is 46°, then what is the measure of angle 3?

- A. 46°
- B. 56°
- C. 78°
- D. 124°
- E. 132°

25. A parallelogram has a base of 15m and a height that is $\frac{3}{5}$ the base. What is the area of the parallelogram?

   A) 9m²
   B) 25m²
   C) 135m²
   D) 375m²
   E) 485m²

26. A pool has dimensions of 15 feet wide and 35 feet long. A tile border is built around it that adds 2.5 feet to each side of the pool. What is the area of the pool and tile border?

   A) 656.25
   B) 700.00
   C) 750.00
   D) 800.00
   E) 855.75

27.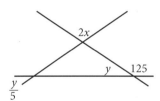

   What is the value of x?

   A) 11
   B) 55
   C) 57
   D) 66
   E) 114

28. In a regular polygon, the exterior angle has a measure of 12°. What type of polygon is it?

   A) Dodecagon
   B) 15-gon
   C) 20-gon
   D) 25-gon
   E) 30-gon

29.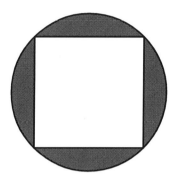

   The square inscribed in the circle above has side length s. What is the area of the shaded portion?

   A) πs^2
   B) $\frac{\pi s - \pi}{2}$
   C) $\left(\frac{\pi}{2}\right)s^2 - s^2$
   D) $\pi^2 s$
   E) $\frac{s^2}{\pi}$

30. If the diagonal of a square is 16, what is its area?

   A) 64
   B) $32 + 16\sqrt{2}$
   C) 128
   D) 256
   E) 512

Chapter 5: Geometry

31

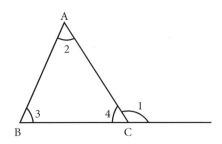

ABC is a triangle and ∠1 is 124° and ∠2 is 46° then ∠3 & ∠4 will be?

Indicate all such values.

- [A] 46°
- [B] 56°
- [C] 78°
- [D] 124°
- [E] 132°
- [F] 136°

32 Square ABCD has a perimeter of 28. Circle X has less area than the square. Which of the following can be a value of the radius of Circle X?

Indicate all such values.

- [A] 5
- [B] 6
- [C] 7
- [D] 8
- [E] 9

33 A field is of a square shape. The total expense of building fence around it is $1600 at rate of $5 per meter. What will be the perimeter and length of one side of the field?

Indicate all such values.

- [A] 40m
- [B] 80m
- [C] 100m
- [D] 320m
- [E] 350m
- [F] 370m

34

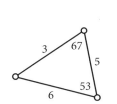 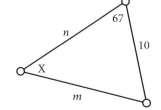

What is the value of $2x + m + 2n$ if the triangles are similar?

[ ]

35

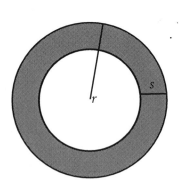

If $r = 15$ and $s = 7$, then what is the area of the shaded portion? Round to the nearest tenth.

[ ]

36

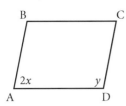

For the parallelogram ABCD, $y = 110°$, what is the value of x?

37

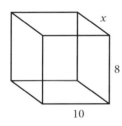

In the figure above, the surface area of the rectangular prism equals 412. What is its volume?

Practice Set 2: Medium

38 Given the segments MN, NP, and PD, only points M, D, and N are collinear.

D is the midpoint of MN.

Quantity A	Quantity B
DN − PN	PD

- Ⓐ Quantity A is greater.
- Ⓑ Quantity B is greater.
- Ⓒ The two quantities are equal.
- Ⓓ The relationship cannot be determined from the information given.

39

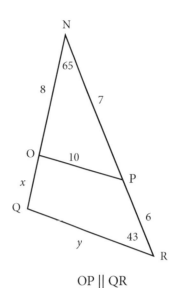

OP ∥ QR

Quantity A	Quantity B
Length of QR	Length of NQ

- Ⓐ Quantity A is greater.
- Ⓑ Quantity B is greater.
- Ⓒ The two quantities are equal.
- Ⓓ The relationship cannot be determined from the information given.

Chapter 5: Geometry

40

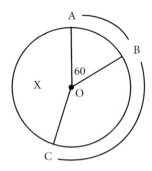

Note: Figure not drawn to scale

In this figure, the radius of the circle is 4, the length of arc *BC* is 3π

Quantity A	Quantity B
Area X	$\dfrac{21\pi}{3}$

- Ⓐ Quantity A is greater.
- Ⓑ Quantity B is greater.
- Ⓒ The two quantities are equal.
- Ⓓ The relationship cannot be determined from the information given.

41

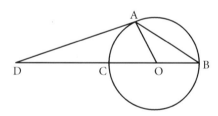

Quantity A	Quantity B
∠AOB	∠ADB

- Ⓐ Quantity A is greater.
- Ⓑ Quantity B is greater.
- Ⓒ The two quantities are equal.
- Ⓓ The relationship cannot be determined from the information given.

42

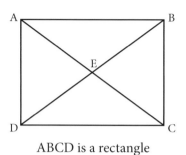

ABCD is a rectangle

Quantity A	Quantity B
The perimeter of ABCD	The sum of the diagonals

- Ⓐ Quantity A is greater.
- Ⓑ Quantity B is greater.
- Ⓒ The two quantities are equal.
- Ⓓ The relationship cannot be determined from the information given.

43 If the diameter of a circle P is 40 percent of the diameter of circle Q, then the area of circle P is what percentage of the area of circle Q?

- Ⓐ 16
- Ⓑ 20
- Ⓒ 40
- Ⓓ 80
- Ⓔ It cannot be determined from the information given.

44

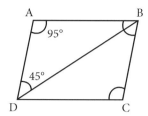

Quantity A	Quantity B
Angle B	Angle C

Ⓐ Quantity A is greater.
Ⓑ Quantity B is greater.
Ⓒ The two quantities are equal.
Ⓓ The relationship cannot be determined from the information given.

45

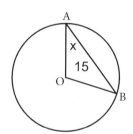

$90 < x < 180$

Quantity A	Quantity B
The perimeter of AOB	45

Ⓐ Quantity A is greater.
Ⓑ Quantity B is greater.
Ⓒ The two quantities are equal.
Ⓓ The relationship cannot be determined from the information given.

46

R is the radius of the large circle, and r the radius of the smaller circles.

Quantity A	Quantity B
The area of the unshaded portion	The area of the shaded portion

Ⓐ Quantity A is greater.
Ⓑ Quantity B is greater.
Ⓒ The two quantities are equal.
Ⓓ The relationship cannot be determined from the information given.

47

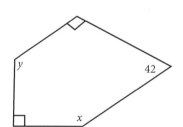

Quantity A	Quantity B
$2x$	$2y$

Ⓐ Quantity A is greater.
Ⓑ Quantity B is greater.
Ⓒ The two quantities are equal.
Ⓓ The relationship cannot be determined from the information given.

48

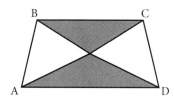

AC and BD are the diagonals of the trapezoid ABCD.

Quantity A
The area of the shaded region

Quantity B
The area of the unshaded region

Ⓐ Quantity A is greater.
Ⓑ Quantity B is greater.
Ⓒ The two quantities are equal.
Ⓓ The relationship cannot be determined from the information given.

49

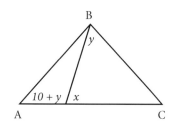

Angle ABC is a right angle.

Quantity A
x

Quantity B
80 + y

Ⓐ Quantity A is greater.
Ⓑ Quantity B is greater.
Ⓒ The two quantities are equal.
Ⓓ The relationship cannot be determined from the information given.

50

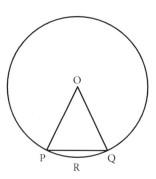

In the above figure O is the centre of the circle with area 81π and angle $\angle POQ = 40°$

Quantity A
Perimeter of the Sector OPRQO

Quantity B
$3\pi + 18$

Ⓐ Quantity A is greater.
Ⓑ Quantity B is greater.
Ⓒ The two quantities are equal.
Ⓓ The relationship cannot be determined from the information given.

51

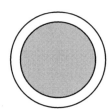

The area of the outer ring of the circle is 45Π and the large circle has a radius that is $\frac{3}{2}$ as large as the inner circle.

Quantity A
The area of the shaded region

Quantity B
36Π

Ⓐ Quantity A is greater.
Ⓑ Quantity B is greater.
Ⓒ The two quantities are equal.
Ⓓ The relationship cannot be determined from the information given.

52

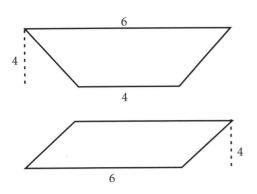

Quantity A
The area of the trapezoid

Quantity B
The area of the parallelogram

Ⓐ Quantity A is greater.
Ⓑ Quantity B is greater.
Ⓒ The two quantities are equal.
Ⓓ The relationship cannot be determined from the information given.

53

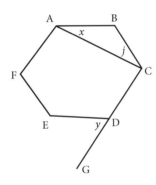

Hexagon ABCDEF is a regular hexagon.

Quantity A
$x + j$

Quantity B
y

Ⓐ Quantity A is greater.
Ⓑ Quantity B is greater.
Ⓒ The two quantities are equal.
Ⓓ The relationship cannot be determined from the information given.

54

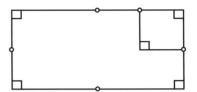

Length of the rectangle is twice as its width, and the measure of one side of the square is one half as the width of the rectangle. The perimeter of the square is 8.

Quantity A
Area of Rectangle

Quantity B
32

Ⓐ Quantity A is greater.
Ⓑ Quantity B is greater.
Ⓒ The two quantities are equal.
Ⓓ The relationship cannot be determined from the information given.

55

Quantity A
Volume of cube with side 6

Quantity B
Volume of rectangular prism with two dimensions less than 6

Ⓐ Quantity A is greater.
Ⓑ Quantity B is greater.
Ⓒ The two quantities are equal.
Ⓓ The relationship cannot be determined from the information given.

56

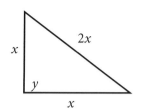

Quantity A	Quantity B
90	y

Ⓐ Quantity A is greater.
Ⓑ Quantity B is greater.
Ⓒ The two quantities are equal.
Ⓓ The relationship cannot be determined from the information given.

57 Circle A has a radius of 5 and a sector of 45°. Circle B has a radius of 9 and a sector of 30°.

Quantity A	Quantity B
The area of the sector in Circle A.	The area of the sector in Circle B.

Ⓐ Quantity A is greater.
Ⓑ Quantity B is greater.
Ⓒ The two quantities are equal.
Ⓓ The relationship cannot be determined from the information given.

58

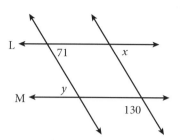

Lines L and M are parallel.

Quantity A	Quantity B
x	y

Ⓐ Quantity A is greater.
Ⓑ Quantity B is greater.
Ⓒ The two quantities are equal.
Ⓓ The relationship cannot be determined from the information given.

59 Rectangle A and Square B have the same perimeter.

Quantity A	Quantity B
The area of Rectangle A	The area of Square B

Ⓐ Quantity A is greater.
Ⓑ Quantity B is greater.
Ⓒ The two quantities are equal.
Ⓓ The relationship cannot be determined from the information given.

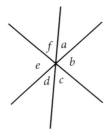

$f + a = b + c$

Quantity A	**Quantity B**
f	$e - d$

Ⓐ Quantity A is greater.
Ⓑ Quantity B is greater.
Ⓒ The two quantities are equal.
Ⓓ The relationship cannot be determined from the information given.

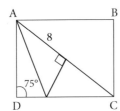

ABCD is a square

Quantity A	**Quantity B**
The length of the diagonal AC	16

Ⓐ Quantity A is greater.
Ⓑ Quantity B is greater.
Ⓒ The two quantities are equal.
Ⓓ The relationship cannot be determined from the information given.

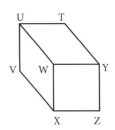

Note: Figure not drawn to scale

Each dimension of the rectangular solid above is an even number. The area of face TUWY is 20, and the area of face WXZY is 8

Quantity A	**Quantity B**
Total surface area of the rectangular solid	Volume of the rectangular solid

Ⓐ Quantity A is greater.
Ⓑ Quantity B is greater.
Ⓒ The two quantities are equal.
Ⓓ The relationship cannot be determined from the information given.

63. Quadrilateral ABCD has two right angles. The other angles are x and $2x$.

Quantity A	**Quantity B**
x	90

Ⓐ Quantity A is greater.
Ⓑ Quantity B is greater.
Ⓒ The two quantities are equal.
Ⓓ The relationship cannot be determined from the information given.

64

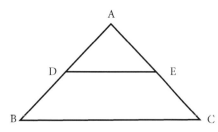

ABC is an isosceles triangle with the perimeter equal to 128 inches. DE is parallel to BC and it is crossing line segments AB and AC through the middle (i.e. AD = DB and AE = EC). If DE = 24 inches, what is the area of △ABC?

- (A) 656 square inches
- (B) 693 square inches
- (C) 768 square inches
- (D) 812 square inches
- (E) 848 square inches

65

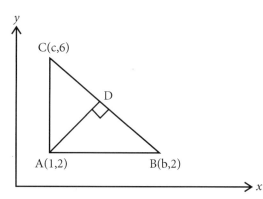

△ABC is an isosceles right triangle with hypotenuse BC. AD is perpendicular to BC. Points A, B and C are defined by their coordinates. What is the length of AD?

- (A) 2
- (B) $2\sqrt{2}$
- (C) 3
- (D) $3\sqrt{2}$
- (E) $4\sqrt{2}$

66

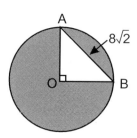

In the diagram above, if the hypotenuse of the right triangle is $8\sqrt{2}$, what is the area of the shaded region?

- (A) $16\pi - 32$
- (B) $16\pi - 32\sqrt{2}$
- (C) 32π
- (D) $64\pi - 32$
- (E) $64\pi - 32\sqrt{2}$

67

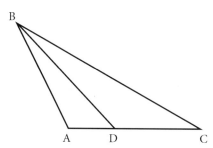

Note: Figure not drawn to scale.

In the preceding figure, AB = AD and BD = CD. If ∠C measures 19°, what is the measure of ∠A in degrees?

- (A) 75
- (B) 94
- (C) 104
- (D) 114
- (E) 142

68 What is the area (in square meters) of an isosceles triangle with equal sides of 3 meters and base angles of 30°?

- A) $\dfrac{3}{2}\sqrt{3}$
- B) $\dfrac{9\sqrt{3}}{4}$
- C) $\dfrac{9\sqrt{3}}{2}$
- D) $\dfrac{3\sqrt{3}}{4}$
- E) $\dfrac{2\sqrt{3}}{9}$

69 What is the area of rhombus with a perimeter of 40 and a diagonal of 10?

- A) $50\sqrt{3}$
- B) 100
- C) $100\sqrt{3}$
- D) 200
- E) 400

70 In △MNP, ∠M is 65° and ∠P is 40°. Q is a point on side MP such that NQ ⊥ MP. Of the following line segments, which one is the shortest?

- A) MN
- B) NP
- C) PQ
- D) NQ
- E) MQ

71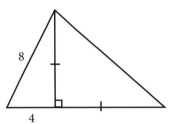

What is the area of the above triangle?

- A) 16 units²
- B) 22.5 units²
- C) 30 units²
- D) $8\sqrt{3}$ + 24 units²
- E) $8\sqrt{3}$ + 6 units²

72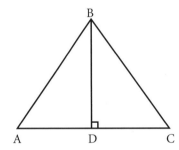

Note: Figure not drawn to scale

In the preceding figure, BD ⊥ AC, AB = 34, BD = 30, and BC = 34. What is the length of AC?

- A) 8
- B) 18
- C) 30
- D) 32
- E) 34

73

Which of the following are true of an isosceles trapezoid inside a circle if the radius of the circle is 10 cm, the bases are 7cm and 5cm, and height of the isosceles trapezoid is 2π cm?

- A) The area of the trapezoid is 12π cm².
- B) The area of the trapezoid is 12 cm².
- C) The area of the circle is 10π cm².
- D) The shaded area is 2π cm².
- E) The area of the trapezoid is 6% the area of the circle.

74

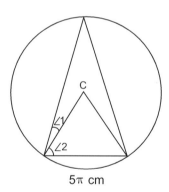

5π cm

What is the ratio of ∠1 to ∠2 if C is the center of the circle, the larger triangle is isosceles, and the radius is 15cm?

- A) $\frac{1}{4}$
- B) $\frac{3}{4}$
- C) $\frac{4}{5}$
- D) $\frac{5}{4}$
- E) $\frac{4}{1}$

75

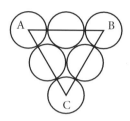

Triangle ABC is an equilateral triangle that runs through the six circles with each points A, B, and C at the center of each circle. The perimeter of triangle ABC is 18. What is the circumference of all six circles combined?

- A) 6π
- B) 12π
- C) 18π
- D) 24π
- E) 36π

76 Which of the following is the circumference of a circle $x^2 - 16x + y^2 + 12y + 75 = 0$?

- A) 5π
- B) 6π
- C) 10π
- D) 25π
- E) 75π

77

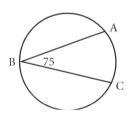

If the diameter of the circle is 21, what is the length of arc ABC?

- A) 4.375π
- B) 10.125π
- C) 16.625π
- D) 18.025π
- E) 21.075π

78

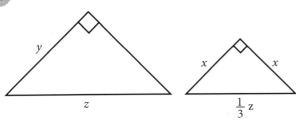

Note: Figure not drawn to scale.

In the figures above, what is the value of y in terms of x?

(A) $\sqrt{2}x$ (approximately 1.41x)
(B) $2x$
(C) $2\sqrt{2}x$ (approximately 2.83x)
(D) $3x$
(E) $3\sqrt{2}x$ (approximately 4.24x)

79

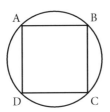

Inscribed square ABCD has a perimeter of 52. What is the area of the circle?

(A) 13π
(B) 55.5π
(C) 62.5π
(D) 84.5π
(E) 169π

80 Circle A has an area of πx^2. If the radius of Circle B is triple of Circle A, which expression would be the circumference of Circle B?

(A) $3\pi x$
(B) $6\pi x$
(C) $9\pi x$
(D) $12\pi x$
(E) $324\pi x$

81

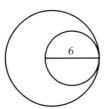

The radius of the larger circle is equal to the diameter of the smaller circle. Which of the following is the ratio of the area of the smaller circle compared to the area of the larger circle?

(A) $\dfrac{1}{12}$
(B) $\dfrac{1}{9}$
(C) $\dfrac{1}{6}$
(D) $\dfrac{1}{4}$
(E) $\dfrac{1}{3}$

82

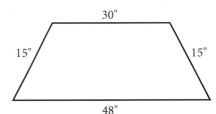

What is the area of the preceding trapezoid in square inches?

(A) 108
(B) 234
(C) 368
(D) 468
(E) 585

Chapter 5: Geometry

83.

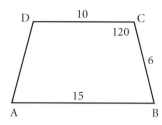

If AB ∥ DC, what is the area of figure ABCD?

(A) $\dfrac{15\sqrt{3}}{2}$

(B) $\dfrac{25\sqrt{2}}{2}$

(C) $\dfrac{35\sqrt{3}}{2}$

(D) $\dfrac{75\sqrt{3}}{2}$

(E) $150\sqrt{3}$

84. A circle has a diameter of $\dfrac{3x}{4}$. What is the area of a sector with an angle of 120° within this circle?

(A) $\dfrac{3x^2}{64}\pi$

(B) $\dfrac{x^2}{21}\pi$

(C) $\dfrac{27x^2}{8}\pi$

(D) $\dfrac{3x^2}{4}\pi$

(E) $\dfrac{3x^2}{7}\pi$

85. What is the maximum possible area of parallelogram with a side length of 4 meters and a perimeter of 50 meters?

(A) 8
(B) 24
(C) 84
(D) 100
(E) 128

86. Line A passes through the points (0, –2) and (1, 0). Line B passes through the points (1, b) and (2, 1). Line C passes through the points (c, –4) and (–b, –2). For which values of b and c are the three lines parallel?

(A) b = 0, c = –2
(B) b = 1, c = –1
(C) b = –1, c = 2
(D) b = 2, c = 0
(E) b = –1, c = 0

87. A square with an area of x has one side length doubled and the other reduced by a length of 3. What would be the area of the resulting rectangle?

(A) $6\sqrt{x} - 2x$
(B) $2x - 6\sqrt{x}$
(C) $2x - x\sqrt{3}$
(D) $x^2 + 3x$
(E) $x^2 - 3x$

88.

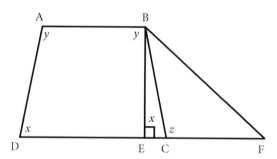

Quadrilateral ABCD is a trapezoid and BEF is a right triangle. For the figure, which of the following must be true?

(A) x = y
(B) z < x
(C) y > z
(D) y < x
(E) z = y

89

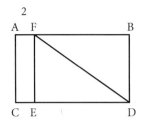

In the figure, triangle DEF is congruent to triangle FBD. If the area of rectangle ABCD is equal to $y(x + 2)$, what is the area of triangle DEF?

(A) xy
(B) $\dfrac{xy}{2}$
(C) $\dfrac{y(x+2)}{2}$
(D) $2y(x + 2)$
(E) $2xy + 2$

90 In trapezoid ABCD, AB||CD and AC = BD. If the area of the trapezium is 60 and the height of the trapezoid is 4 units, what is the length of the diagonal AC?

(A) $\sqrt{241}$
(B) $4\sqrt{15}$
(C) $\sqrt{173}$
(D) 16
(E) $8\sqrt{110}$

91 There are three cubes with volumes of 27 cubic feet, 1 cubic feet, and 1/27 cubic feet respectively. The second cube is placed on the first cube and the third cube is placed on the second cube. What is the height in inches of the stacked cubes?

(A) 44
(B) 48
(C) 52
(D) 56
(E) 60

92

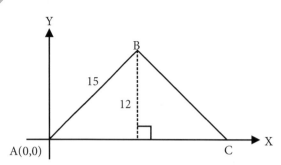

In the figure above, side AB of △ABC contains which of the following points?

(A) (3, 2)
(B) (3, 5)
(C) (4, 6)
(D) (4, 10)
(E) (6, 8)

93 In a regular polygon with n sides, the ratio of each interior angle to each exterior angle is 3:2, the polygon is

(A) Square
(B) Pentagon
(C) Hexagon
(D) Heptagon
(E) Octagon

94

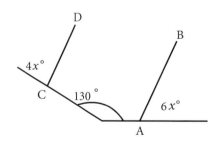

In the above figure given that AB || CD, x is,

(A) 8.33
(B) 12.5
(C) 13
(D) 26
(E) 50

Chapter 5: Geometry

95

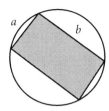

If $a = \frac{1}{2}b$ and the area of the circle is 1225Π, what is the area of the shaded region?

- A) 490
- B) 575
- C) 980
- D) 1960
- E) 3500

96 A metallic sheet of paper whose shape is a sector of 60° is extracted from a circle of diameter 18 inches. If the sector is used to make a cone, what would be the approximate volume of the cone?

- A) 21 cubic inches
- B) 50 cubic inches
- C) 95 cubic inches
- D) 185 cubic inches
- E) 191 cubic inches

97 What is the area of a square inscribed in a circle whose circumference is 16π?

- A) 32
- B) 64
- C) 128
- D) 256
- E) 512

98 A circle has the same area as a square with side of length $\frac{1}{\pi}$. What is the diameter of the circle?

- A) $\frac{1}{\sqrt{\pi}}$
- B) $\frac{2}{\sqrt{\pi}}$
- C) $\frac{1}{\pi\sqrt{\pi}}$
- D) $\frac{2}{\pi\sqrt{\pi}}$
- E) $\frac{1}{\pi^3}$

99

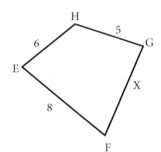

What is the value of x in the figure above?

- A) 4
- B) $3\sqrt{3}$
- C) $3\sqrt{5}$
- D) $5\sqrt{3}$
- E) 9

100

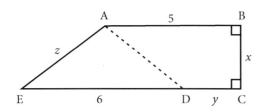

Which of the following statements could be true for the figure shown above?

Area of △AED = 12

y = 2

Indicate all such values.

- [A] x = 4.5
- [B] x = 4
- [C] z = 5
- [D] z = 6

101 The points A(0, 0), B(0, 5p − 2), and C(2p + 2, 4p + 6) form a triangle. If ∠ABC = 90°, what is the area of △ABC?

Indicate all such statements.

- [A] Area of △ABC is < 250
- [B] Area of △ABC is < 300
- [C] Area of △ABC is > 300
- [D] Area of △ABC is < 350
- [E] Area of △ABC is > 380
- [F] Area of △ABC is > 420

102

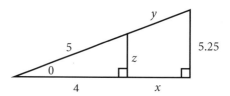

Which of the following statements could be true for the figure shown above?

Indicate all that apply.

- [A] x + y < 7
- [B] x > 3
- [C] y < 4
- [D] x and y cannot be determined
- [E] The correct answers are (A), and (C)

103

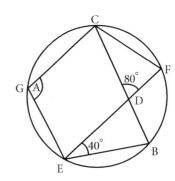

Select all the statements that best give the measure of ∠A.

Indicate all such statements.

- [A] between 80° and 100°
- [B] between 100° and 130°
- [C] between 50° and 80°
- [D] between 90° and 125°
- [E] between 130° and 150°
- [F] between 70° and 100°
- [G] between 91° and 115°

Chapter 5: Geometry

104 Five disks have circumferences $\pi, 10\pi, 12\pi, 20\pi$, and 50π. Label the disks A, B, C, D, E, respectively. Which disk(s) would fit into a hoop with area 470 units^2?

Indicate all that apply.

- [A] A
- [B] B
- [C] C
- [D] D
- [E] E
- [F] A, D and E

105

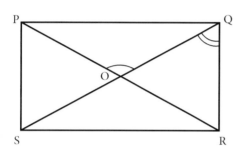

The above figure PQRS is a quadrilateral. What could be the degree measures of the marked angles?

Indicate all such answers.

- [A] 100°, 40°
- [B] 110°, 55°
- [C] 120°, 60°
- [D] 130°, 60°
- [E] 140°, 75°
- [F] 150°, 75°

106 Length of a rectangle is 3cm less than the double of the width. If perimeter of the rectangle is 96cm then what will be its width and length?

Indicate all such answers.

- [A] 15cm
- [B] 17cm
- [C] 27cm
- [D] 31cm
- [E] 34cm
- [F] 37cm

107 If area and perimeter of a rectangular region are $24cm^2$ and $20cm$ respectively. Then length and width in cm will be?

Indicate all such values.

- [A] 2 cm
- [B] 3 cm
- [C] 4 cm
- [D] 6 cm
- [E] 8 cm
- [F] 12 cm

108

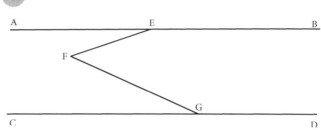

In the above figure line AB is parallel to line CD. Also, $\angle BEF = x$, $\angle EFG = y$, $\angle FGD = z$.

Which of the following statements could be true?

Indicate all such answers.

- [A] $x + y + z = 270°$
- [B] $x + y + z = 360°$
- [C] $x + z = 150°$
- [D] $x + z = 170°$
- [E] $x + z = 180°$
- [F] $x + z = 270°$
- [G] $x + z = 300°$
- [H] $x + z = 360°$

109) If the diagonal of the face of a cube is between 4√3 and 4√15, which of the following can be the volume of the cube?

Indicate all such values.

- [A] 95
- [B] 115
- [C] 254
- [D] 1120
- [E] 1350

110)

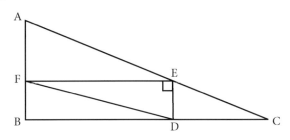

Area of the right triangle ABC is 18. If $BF = \frac{1}{3}(AB)$ and $EF = \frac{2}{3}(BC)$, what is the area of the right △ DEF?

111) The diameter of a circle is $2\sqrt{2m}$. The diameter of another circle having 8 times the area of the first circle is:

☐ m

112)

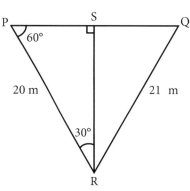

Study the figure shown above.

What is the length of the segment PQ to the nearest tenth of a meter?

☐ meters

113)

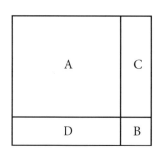

In the given figure areas A and B are squares. The side of the square A is 10 units more than the side of the square B. Sum of the areas of these squares is 625 square units. What is the the sum of the areas of the remaining rectangles C and D?

Chapter 5: Geometry

114

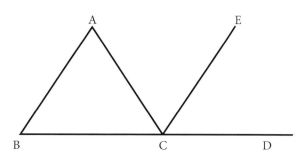

In the above figure AB is parallel to EC. CE is the bisector of external ∠ACD and ∠ACD =140°

What is the value of ∠BAC? (Omit the degree symbol)

☐

115 A can has a diameter that is $\frac{1}{3}$ the height. If the volume of the can is 48π, what is the radius of the can?

☐

Practice Set 3: Hard

116

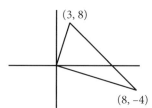

What is the area of the triangle in the figure above?

- A) 38
- B) 45
- C) 60
- D) 65
- E) 96

117

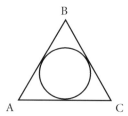

If triangle ABC is an equilateral triangle and the area of the circle is $\frac{9}{16}\pi$, what is the length of AB?

- A) $\frac{9}{16}$
- B) $\frac{9\sqrt{3}}{16}$
- C) $\frac{3\sqrt{3}}{4}$
- D) $\frac{3\sqrt{3}}{2}$
- E) $\frac{\sqrt{3}}{2}$

118

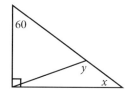

Based on the figure above, what is the value of y?

- A) 35
- B) 115
- C) 140
- D) 150
- E) 160

119

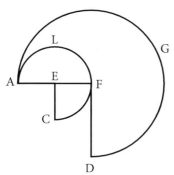

In the figure above, E and F are the centers of the circular curves (portions of circles). ALF is a semicircle, and EFC is a quadrant of a circle. Also, quadrant AFD is cut-out of the larger circle. If the arc CF measures 3π, what is the perimeter of the figure AGDFLA?

Ⓐ $20\pi + 8$
Ⓑ $12\pi + 8$
Ⓒ $16\pi + 6$
Ⓓ $22\pi + 12$
Ⓔ $24\pi + 12$

120 A circle is circumscribed about a regular polygon with each exterior angle measuring 60 degrees. The radius of the circle is 4cm. What is the area between the circle and the polygon?

Ⓐ $16\pi - 2\sqrt{3}$
Ⓑ 16π
Ⓒ $32\sqrt{3}\pi$
Ⓓ $16\pi - 12\sqrt{3}$
Ⓔ $2\sqrt{3}$

121

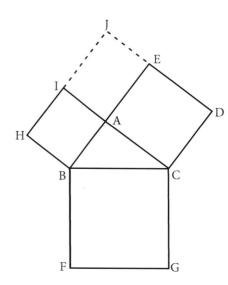

ABC is a triangle with $m\angle BAC = 90°$ and $m\angle ACB = 30°$. Three squares (ACDE, BCGF and ABHI) were built using the sides of $\triangle ABC$ as basis. HIJ and DEJ are line segments.

What is the area of quadrilateral AEJI?

Ⓐ Area $AEJI = (\text{Area } BCGF - \text{Area } ABHI) \times \sqrt{3}$

Ⓑ Area $AEJI = \dfrac{(\text{Area } BCGF - \text{Area } ABHI)}{\sqrt{3}}$

Ⓒ Area $AEJI = \dfrac{(\text{Area } BCGF - \text{Area } ACDE)}{\sqrt{3}}$

Ⓓ Area $AEJI = \dfrac{\sqrt{(\text{Area } ACDE)}}{2}$

Ⓔ Area $AEJI = \text{Area } ACDE \times \sqrt{3}$

Chapter 5: Geometry

122

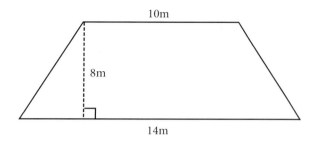

The sandpit in a park is in the shape of a trapezoid. The parallel sides of the section measure 10 m and 14 m. The distance between the parallel sides is 8 m.

The section was remodeled to have an area that was *96 square meters* more than the original area. What change in the dimensions of the trapezoid was made to create the remodeled section?

- A The length of the parallel sides and the height were doubled.
- B The height was doubled.
- C The length of the parallel sides and the height were multiplied by four.
- D The height was multiplied by four.
- E The lengths of the parallel sides were increased by *5 m*.

123

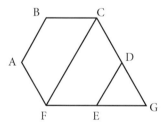

In the figure above, ABCDEF is a regular hexagon. If the area of equilateral triangle CFG is $81\sqrt{3}$, what is the area of the hexagon?

- A $81\sqrt{3}$
- B $\dfrac{243\sqrt{3}}{2}$
- C $486\sqrt{3}$
- D $\dfrac{486\sqrt{3}}{3}$
- E $972\sqrt{3}$

124 A 16-inch by 36-inch piece of material is to be cut into equal circles, with the least amount of material left over. What is the amount of material that remains if the largest possible circles are cut from the material?

- A $576(\pi - 1)$
- B $4(144 - \pi)$
- C 144π
- D $144 - \pi$
- E $144(4 - \pi)$

125 Using the regular hexagon with a side length of 4cm intersecting isosceles right triangle as a mid segment, which of the following statements could be true?

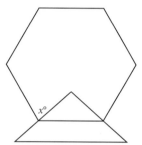

Indicate all such statements.

- A The area of the smaller triangle formed is 1 square cm.
- B The area of the larger triangle formed is 4 square cm.
- C The area of the hexagon is $24\sqrt{3}$ square cm.
- D The area of the hexagon is $4\sqrt{3}$ square cm
- E The value of *x* is 75.
- F None of the above

Practice Set 3: Hard

 Point A is located at (5,5) and Circle B has a center at (5, -4) and sits below Point A. If the radius of Circle B is an integer value, which of the following could be the distance between Point A and the closest point on Circle B?

Indicate all such values.

- [A] 0
- [B] 4
- [C] 10
- [D] 15
- [E] 18
- [F] 25

127

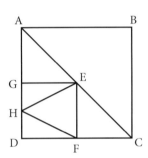

If E is the midpoint of AC, which of the following must be true?

Indicate *all* such statements.

- [A] ABCD is a square
- [B] Triangle GHE is congruent to Triangle DHF
- [C] Triangle AGE is congruent to Triangle EFC
- [D] Triangle HEF is an equilateral triangle

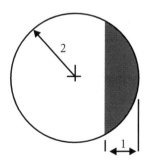

Determine the area of the shaded portion of the circle, with 1 decimal place accuracy.

129 Circle A and Circle B intersect so that the intersecting points are a distance of 18 apart. If the radius of Circle A is 16 and the radius of Circle B 21, what is the distance between the centers of the two circles rounded to the nearest whole number?

130

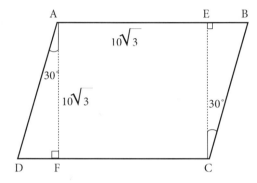

What is the total area of the figure above? (Round to the nearest hundredths)

Answer Key

Q. No.	Correct Answer	Your Answer	Q. No.	Correct Answer	Your Answer	Q. No.	Correct Answer	Your Answer	Q. No.	Correct Answer	Your Answer
1	B		34	144		67	C		100	B,C	
2	A		35	505.8		68	B		101	C,D	
3	B		36	35		69	A		102	A,C	
4	A		37	560		70	E		103	B,D	
5	A		38	B		71	D		104	A,B,C,D	
6	A		39	A		72	D		105	B,C,F	
7	B		40	A		73	A,E		106	B,D	
8	B		41	A		74	A		107	C,D	
9	A		42	A		75	C		108	B,F,G	
10	B		43	A		76	C		109	C,D	
11	C		44	B		77	C		110	4	
12	C		45	A		78	D		111	8	
13	D		46	C		79	D		112	21.9	
14	D		47	D		80	B		113	525	
15	A		48	D		81	D		114	70	
16	C		49	D		82	D		115	2	
17	E		50	B		83	D		116	A	
18	C		51	C		84	A		117	D	
19	D		52	B		85	C		118	C	
20	A		53	C		86	E		119	E	
21	D		54	C		87	B		120	D	
22	E		55	D		88	E		121	B	
23	A		56	D		89	B		122	B	
24	C		57	B		90	A		123	B	
25	C		58	B		91	C		124	E	
26	D		59	D		92	E		125	A,C,E	
27	C		60	A		93	B		126	B,C,D	
28	E		61	B		94	C		127	A,C	
29	C		62	A		95	D		128	0.4	
30	C		63	B		96	A		129	32	
31	B,C		64	C		97	C		130	473.21	
32	A,B,C		65	B		98	D				
33	B,D		66	D		99	D				

Practice Set 1 (Easy): Answers & Explanations

1 **Choice B is correct** because Quantity B is greater than Quantity A.

Let the shorter leg be x yards.

The longer leg is $x + 14$ yards.

If h is the hypotenuse then $x = h/2 - 3$

$$h/2 = x + 3$$
$$h = 2(x + 3)$$
$$h = 2x + 6$$

By Pythagorean theorem, the quare of the hypotenuse is equal to the sum of the squares of the legs.

$$(2x+6)^2 = x^2 + (x+14)^2$$
$$4x^2 + 24x + 36 = x^2 + x^2 + 28x + 196$$
$$2x^2 - 4x - 160 = 0$$
$$x^2 - 2x - 80 = 0$$
$$x^2 - 10x + 8x - 80 = 0$$
$$x(x-10) + 8(x-10) = 0$$
$$(x-10)(x+8) = 0$$
$$x = 10 \text{ or } x = -8$$

Hence we get $x = 10$, eliminating the negative value.

Therefore $h = 2x + 6 = 20 + 6 = 26$

Choice A is incorrect because Quantity A is not greater than B. **Choice C** is incorrect because it is not possible for the two quantities to be equal. **Choice D** is incorrect because it is possible to use the given information to make a comparison between Quantity A and Quantity B.

2 **Choice A is correct** because Quantity A is greater than Quantity B.

The area of the left sector is $\left(\dfrac{x}{2}\right)(2r)^2 = 2r^2 x$.

The area of the right one is $\left(\dfrac{2x}{2}\right)r^2 = r^2 x$.

Choice B is incorrect because Quantity B is less than Quantity A. **Choice C** is incorrect because it is not possible for the two quantities to be equal. **Choice D** is incorrect because it is possible to use the given information to make a comparison between Quantity A and Quantity B.

3 **Choice B is correct** because Quantity B is greater than Quantity A.

In $\triangle ABC$, $m\angle BAC = 90°$ and $m\angle ACB = 30°$

$$\sin(\angle ACB) = \frac{AB}{BC}$$
$$\sin(30°) = \frac{1}{2} = \frac{AB}{BC}$$
$$\cos(\angle ACB) = \frac{AC}{BC}$$
$$\cos(30°) = \frac{\sqrt{3}}{2} = \frac{AC}{BC}$$

Let $BC = s$

$AB = s/2$ and $AC = \left(s\sqrt{3}\right)/2$

As per the formula for the area of an equilateral triangle, the area of $ADC = 4$

$$\text{Area} \triangle ABC = \frac{\left(\dfrac{s\sqrt{3}}{2}\right)^2 \times \sqrt{3}}{4} = \frac{s^2 3\sqrt{3}}{16}$$

(If you do not remember the formula for the area of an equilateral, you can still arrive at the correct result by drawing a height in $\triangle ADC$ and using Pythagoras' theorem)

$$\text{Area} \triangle ABC = \frac{(AB \times AC)}{2}$$

$$\text{Area} \triangle ABC = \frac{\dfrac{s}{2} \times \dfrac{s\sqrt{3}}{2}}{2} = \frac{s^2\sqrt{3}}{8}$$

which can also be written as $\dfrac{s^2 2\sqrt{3}}{16}$. $\dfrac{s^2 3\sqrt{3}}{16}$ is greater than $\dfrac{s^2 2\sqrt{3}}{16}$, so Area ADC is greater than Area ABC.

Choice A is incorrect because Quantity A is not greater than B. **Choice C** is incorrect because it is not possible for the two quantities to be equal. **Choice D** is incorrect because it is possible to use the given information to make a comparison between Quantity A and Quantity B.

4 **Choice A is correct** because Quantity A is greater than Quantity B.

The area of the top figure is $\dfrac{2h(b+5)}{2} = hb + 5h$.

The area of the bottom figure is $\dfrac{h(2b+5)}{2} = hb + \left(\dfrac{5}{2}\right)h$.

So, the correct answer is (A).

Chapter 5: Geometry

Choice B is incorrect because Quantity B is not greater than A. **Choice C** is incorrect because it is not possible for the two quantities to be equal. **Choice D** is incorrect because it is possible to use the given information to make a comparison between Quantity A and Quantity B.

5   **Choice A is correct** because Quantity A is greater than Quantity B.

To find the Quantity A, use the area formula for a circle, $A = \pi r^2$, where $r = \frac{2}{3}r$.

Plugging this in gives $A = \pi \left(\frac{2}{3}r\right)^2 = \frac{4\pi}{9}r^2$. Now find Quantity B using the circumference formula for a circle, $C = 2\pi r$, where $r = \frac{1}{5}r$. Plugging this in gives $C = 2\pi\left(\frac{1}{5}r\right) = \frac{2\pi}{5}r$. Because r is a positive whole number, the quantity $\frac{4\pi}{9}r^2$ will be larger than $\frac{2\pi}{5}r$ and therefore the answer is A.

Choice B is incorrect because Quantity B is less than Quantity A. **Choice C** is incorrect because it is not possible for the two quantities to be equal. **Choice D** is incorrect because it is possible to use the given information to make a comparison between Quantity A and Quantity B.

6   **Choice A is correct** because Quantity A is greater than Quantity B.

It is given that the radius of Quantity A is $12x + 5$. Calculating the circumference of Quantity A using the formula $C = 2\pi r$ yields $C = 2\pi(12x + 5) = (24x + 10)\pi cm$. Substituting $x = 2$ yields $C = (24(2) + 10)\pi cm$ or $C = 58\pi cm$.

The radius of Quantity B is $8x + 12$. Calculating the circumference of Quantity B using the formula $C = 2\pi r$ yields $C = 2\pi(8x + 12) = (16x + 24)\pi cm$. Substituting $x = 2$ yields $C = (16(2) + 24)\pi cm$ or $C = 56\pi cm$.

Therefore, Quantity A has a greater circumference than Quantity B.

Choice B is incorrect. Quantity B has $56\pi cm$ circumference that is less than Quantity A. **Choice C** is incorrect. The two circumferences have different quantities. **Choice D** is incorrect. There is enough data to determine the relationship between the two.

7   **Choice B is correct** because Quantity B is greater than Quantity A.

The unshaded area is πr^2.

The area of the shaded portion is $\pi(2r)^2 - \pi r^2 = 4\pi r^2 - \pi r^2 = 3\pi r^2$

Choice A is incorrect because Quantity A is not greater than B. **Choice C** is incorrect because it is not possible for the two quantities to be equal. **Choice D** is incorrect because it is possible to use the given information to make a comparison between Quantity A and Quantity B.

8   **Choice B is correct** because to find the area of square ABCD, use the diameter of circle and the 45–45–90 triangle ratios of $x\sqrt{2}$, x, and x to solve.

If the diameter of the circle is 7, then that means the side lengths of the square can be found by using the diameter as the hypotenuse of a triangle with the same side lengths at the square. Using the rules of 45–45–90 triangle ratios, $7 = x\sqrt{2}$. Dividing both sides by $\sqrt{2}$ would yield $\frac{7}{\sqrt{2}}$ which would rationalize to be $\frac{7\sqrt{2}}{2}$.

This means each side of the square is $\frac{7\sqrt{2}}{2}$. To find the area of the square, multiply $\frac{7\sqrt{2}}{2}$ by $\frac{7\sqrt{2}}{2}$ to get $\frac{49}{2}$ which equals 24.5. This is less than 25 so Quantity B is greater.

Choice A is incorrect because 24.5 is less than 25. **Choice C** is incorrect because the area does not equal 25. **Choice D** is incorrect because it is possible to solve for the area of square ABCD.

9   **Choice A is correct** because Quantity A is greater than Quantity B.

To find the sum of the interior angles of a convex pentagon, use the formula $180 \times (n - 2)$, where n is the number of sides. Therefore, $180 \times (5 - 2) = 180 \times 3 = 540°$

$540° > 500°$

Another method would be to draw the pentagon and break it into triangles connecting verticals (lines cannot cross), as shown here.

Practice Set 1 (Easy): Answers & Explanations

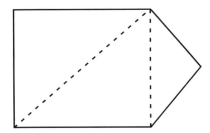

Multiplying the number of triangles (3) by 180° (degrees in a triangle) gives the same result, 540°.

Choice B is incorrect because Quantity B is less than Quantity A. **Choice C** is incorrect because it is not possible for the two quantities to be equal. **Choice D** is incorrect because it is possible to use the given information to make a comparison between Quantity A and Quantity B.

10 **Choice B is correct** because there are many different scenarios for the side length of the rectangle but no matter the case, the rectangle's longest side will always be greater than the square's. Let's take the perimeter of a square to be 4x, where x is its side length. This would mean the perimeter of the rectangle would be (0.75)P = 4x, since 25% less means the same as 75% of a number. Simplifying this expression would give you the perimeter of the rectangle, $\frac{4x}{0.75}$ which simplifies to be $\frac{16x}{3}$. It is possible for the rectangle to have a variety of different combinations of side lengths based on the perimeter. In any case, the longest side length would be greater than x. If the sides of the rectangle were even, which would make it a square, its side lengths would be $\frac{\frac{16x}{3}}{4}$ equal $\frac{4x}{3}$.

This is the shortest side length of the longest side of the rectangle which is still greater than x.

Choice A is incorrect because Quantity A cannot be greater than Quantity B. **Choice C** is incorrect because Quantity A and Quantity B cannot equal each other. **Choice D** is incorrect because it is possible to compare the two values.

11 **Choice C is correct** because to find the measure of the sector in degrees, use the area of a sector equation of A = $\frac{x}{360}\Pi r^2$. Plugging into this expression would yield 75Π = $\frac{x}{360}\Pi(15)^2$. Simplifying this expression would result in 75Π = $\frac{5x}{8}\Pi$. Dividing both sides by $\frac{5}{8}\Pi$ would give you 120 = x.

Choice A is incorrect because the measure in degrees is 120. **Choice B** is incorrect because the measure in degrees is 120. **Choice D** is incorrect because it is possible to compare the two quantities.

12 **Choice C is correct** because both Quantity Are equal, the area of both figures is 64. To find the area of square ABCD, use the formula A = s^2 by plugging in 8 for s to get 8^2 = 64. To find the area of the trapezoid, use the area formula A = $(\frac{b_1+b_2}{2})h$ and plugging in to get A = $(\frac{6+10}{2})(8)$ which also equals 64.

Choice A is incorrect because the two areas are equal. **Choice B** is incorrect because the two areas are equal. **Choice D** is incorrect because it is possible to solve for each area.

13 **Choice D is correct** because despite having the length of the diagonals of the rectangles, there are many combinations of side lengths possible that would not allow for the comparison to be made.

For example, the TV with a diagonal of 50 could have side lengths of 30 and 40 and the TV with a diagonal of 75 could have side lengths of 45 and 60. The longest side of the first TV would be 40 and the smallest side of the second TV would be 45. This would make Quantity B larger.

In another instance, where the TV with a diagonal still has side lengths of 30 and 40, but the TV with a diagonal of 75 has side lengths of 25 and 70, the first TV would have a longer side length compared to the other TV's shortest side length since 30 > 25.

Choice A is incorrect because Quantity A is not always greater than Quantity B. **Choice B** is incorrect because Quantity B is not always greater than Quantity A. **Choice C** is incorrect because it is not possible for the two side lengths to equal each other.

14 **Choice D is correct** because the obtained height is 3.

If you split the equilateral triangle into two parts, the vertical part represents the height, which is the value we are solving for. This then creates a 30-60-90 triangle ratio, with the value across from 30 being $\sqrt{3}$, which we will call x. Because 30-60-90 triangles have a x, $x\sqrt{3}$, 2x length pattern, respectively, the value across from 60 is going to be $x\sqrt{3}$, where x is $\sqrt{3}$, making the length across from 60 (the height) equal to $\sqrt{3}\sqrt{3} = 3$.

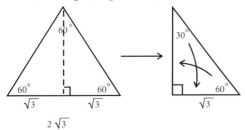

$\sqrt{3} = x$
$\sqrt{3}\sqrt{3} = x\sqrt{3}$
$3 = x\sqrt{3}$ length opp. 60°

Choice A is incorrect because $\dfrac{\sqrt{3}}{3}$ is less than the obtained height of the triangle. **Choice B is incorrect** because $\sqrt{3}$ is the value of x only. **Choice C is incorrect** because $2\sqrt{3}$ is less than the height of the triangle. **Choice E is incorrect** because $3\sqrt{3}$ is greater than the obtained value.

15 **Choice A is correct** because the sum of $a + b$ is $5 + \sqrt{58}$.
$b = \sqrt{4^2 + 3^2} = \sqrt{25} = 5$
$a = \sqrt{7^2 + 3^2} = \sqrt{58}$
Hence $a + b = 5 + \sqrt{58}$

Choice B is incorrect because $16 + \sqrt{2}$ overestimates the value of $a + b$. **Choice C is incorrect** because 14 is greater than the obtained value of $a + b$. **Choice D is incorrect** because $\dfrac{25}{3}$ is less than the obtained value of $a + b$. **Choice E is incorrect** because $17 + 3\sqrt{6}$ overestimates the value of $a + b$.

16 **Choice C is correct** because the measure of Z is 48°.

Since $XY = YZ = 10$, ΔXYZ is an isosceles triangle and $\angle X = \angle Z$.

$\angle Y = 84°$ because it forms a vertically opposite angle with the given angle

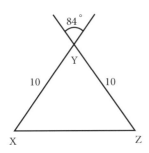

$\angle X + \angle Y + \angle Z = 180°$
$\angle X + 84° + \angle Z = 180°$
$2(\angle Z) + 84° = 180°$
$2(\angle Z) = 96°$
$\angle Z = 48°$

Therefore, the measure of $\angle Z = 48°$

Choice A is incorrect because 24° is less than the obtained value of Z. **Choice B is incorrect** because 42° is close but not accurate value of Z. **Choice D is incorrect** because 84° overestimates the value of Z. **Choice E is incorrect** because 96° is greater than the obtained value of Z.

17 **Choice E is correct.** The diagonals of the rhombus bisect the angles. The measure of $\angle RST$ is thus twice the measure of $\angle UST$. Use this relationship to create an equation and solve for x.
$\angle RST = 2(\angle UST)$
$5x - 14 = 2(2x + 4)$
$5x - 14 = 4x + 8$
$x - 14 = 8$
$x = 22$

Choice A is incorrect because 2.5 is lower than the obtained value of x. **Choice B is incorrect** because 4 is less than the obtained value of x. **Choice C is incorrect** because $5\dfrac{1}{3}$ is less than the obtained value of x. **Choice D is incorrect** because 18 is close to the obtained value of x but not accurate.

18 **Choice C is correct** because 5 different pentagons can be made out of a hexagon.

Draw a hexagon and see how many pentagons can be drawn inside the hexagon.

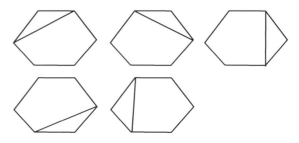

5 different pentagons can be made out of a hexagon.

Choice A is incorrect because 3 is less than the obtained number of pentagons. **Choice B is incorrect** because 4 is less than the obtained number of pentagons. **Choice D is incorrect** because 6 is greater than the obtained number of pentagons. **Choice E is incorrect** because 7 is greater than the obtained number of pentagons.

Practice Set 1 (Easy): Answers & Explanations

19 Choice D is correct because the obtained equation of the circle is $(x - 3)^2 + (y - 1)(y - 7) = 0$

The circle is tangent to the Y axis. The radius must be the distance between the center $C(3, 4)$ and the Y axis, i.e. the distance between point $C(3, 4)$ and a point of coordinates $(0, 4)$ which describes a perpendicular from $C(3, 4)$ to Y axis

The radius $r = \sqrt{(3-0)^2 + (4-4)^2} = 3$

The standard form for the equation of a circle is $(x - a)^2 + (y - b)^2 = r^2$ where (a, b) are the coordinates of the center and r is the radius. If we substitute the values we find:

$(x - 3)^2 + (y - 4)^2 = 3^2$

$(x - 3)^2 + y^2 - 8y + 16 = 9$

$(x - 3)^2 + y^2 - 8y + 16 - 9 = 0$

$(x - 3)^2 + y^2 - 8y + 7 = 0$

$(x - 3)^2 + (y-1)(y-7) = 0$

Choice A is incorrect because $x^2 + y^2 + 10 = 0$ is not equivalent to the obtained equation of the circle.
Choice B is incorrect because $x^2 + y^2 - 2(3x + 4y) + 9 = 0$ is not equivalent to the obtained equation of the circle.
Choice C is incorrect because $x^2 + y^2 + 4(x + y) + 16 = 0$ is not equivalent to the obtained equation of the circle.
Choice E is incorrect because $x^2 + y^2 + 2(3x + y) - 7 = 0$ is not equivalent to the obtained equation of the circle.

20 Choice A is correct because the obtained equation of the circle is $(x - 5)^2 + (y - 4)^2 = 100$.

If (h, k) is the center and r is the radius of the circle then the equation of the circle is $(x - h)^2 + (y - k)^2 = r^2$.

Hence the equation of the circle is $(x - 5)^2 + (y - 4)^2 = r^2$

Since the circle passes through $(5,14)$ it will satisfy the equation.

Hence

$(5 - 5)^2 + (14 - 4)^2 = r^2$

$0 + 10^2 = r^2$

hence $100 = r^2$

Hence the equation is $(x - 5)^2 + (y - 4)^2 = 100$

Choice B is incorrect because $(x + 5)^2 + (y + 4)^2 = 100$ is not equivalent to the obtained equation of the circle.
Choice C is incorrect because $(x - 5)^2 + (y - 4)^2 = 10$ is not equivalent to the obtained equation of the circle.
Choice D is incorrect because $(x + 5)^2 + (y + 4)^2 = 10$ is not equivalent to the obtained equation of the circle.

21 Choice D is correct because the degree measure of $\angle XWZ$ is 130.

In isosceles $\triangle XYZ$, $\angle X = \angle Z$.

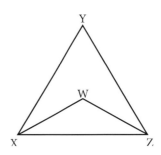

$\angle X + \angle Y + \angle Z = 180°$

$\angle X + 80° + \angle Z = 180°$

$\angle X + \angle Z = 100°$

$\angle X = \angle Z = 50°$

Since WX bisects $\angle YXZ$ and $\angle WZ$ bisects $\angle YZX$,

$\angle YXW = \angle WXZ = \angle XYZ = \angle WZX = 25°$

Therefore, on $\triangle XWZ$,

$\angle XWZ + \angle WXZ + \angle WZX = 180°$

$\angle XWZ + 25° + 25° = 180°$

$\angle XWZ + 50° = 180°$

$\angle XWZ = 130°$

Choice A is incorrect because 65 is less than the obtained value of $\angle XWZ$. **Choice B is incorrect** because 80 is less than the obtained value of $\angle XWZ$. **Choice C is incorrect** because 100 is greater than the obtained value of $\angle XWZ$.
Choice E is incorrect because 160 is greater than the obtained value of $\angle XWZ$.

22 Choice E is correct because the obtained values are Width = 17cm and length = 31cm.

Let width = x

Then length = $2x - 3$

Perimeter = $2(x + 2x - 3) = 6x - 6$

According to the condition

$6x - 6 = 96$

$x = 17$cm

width = 17cm and length = 31cm

Choice A is incorrect because 16cm & 29cm is not equal to the obtained values of the width and the length.
Choice B is incorrect because 15cm & 27cm is not equal to the obtained values of the width and the length.
Choice C is incorrect because 14cm & 25cm is not

Chapter 5: Geometry

equal to the obtained values of the width and the length. **Choice D is incorrect** because 13cm & 23cm is not equal to the obtained values of the width and the length.

23 **Choice A is correct** because the obtained length of BE is 3.

Keep in mind that this figure is not drawn to scale. Since AC ∥ ED, we know that the following angles are equal:

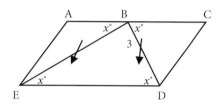

Since ∆EBD has equal angles, the opposing sides are also equal. Therefore, BE = BD = 3.

Choice B is incorrect because 4 is greater than the obtained length of BE. **Choice C is incorrect** because 5 is greater than the obtained length of BE. **Choice D is incorrect** because $3\sqrt{3}$ is greater than the obtained length of BE. **Choice E is incorrect** because it can be determined from the information given.

24 **Choice C is correct** because the obtained measure of angle 3 is 78°.

Angle 1 and ∠ACB are supplementary angles then ∠ACB will be 180° − 124° = 56°.

As sum of all three angle of a triangle is 180° then angle 3 will be 180° − (56° + 46°) = 78°.

Choice A is incorrect because 46° is less than the obtained value of angle 3. **Choice B is incorrect** because 56° is less than the obtained value of angle 3. **Choice D is incorrect** because 124° overestimates the obtained value of angle 3. **Choice E is incorrect** because 132° overestimates the obtained value of angle 3.

25 **Choice C is correct** because The formula for the area of a parallelogram is:

$A = base \times height$

$A = 15 \times \dfrac{3}{5}(15)$

$A = 15(9)$

$A = 135$

Choice A is incorrect because it gives the height, not the area. **Choice B is incorrect** because it results from a miscalculation unrelated to the area formula. **Choice D is incorrect** because it uses the reciprocal of the height

fraction, leading to an inflated area. **Choice E is incorrect** because it is a random, unrelated value with no basis in the given dimensions.

26 **Choice D is correct** because each side of the pool gets an additional 5 feet added to it. Create a diagram to visualize this:

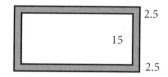

This would mean the new dimensions would be 15 + 5 = 20 and 35 + 5 = 40. Multiply 20 and 40 to get a new area of 800.

Choice A is incorrect because this would be the result if you only added 2.5 once to each side. **Choice B is incorrect** because this would result from a math error. **Choice C is incorrect** because this would result from a math error. **Choice E is incorrect** because this is larger than the new area of the pool.

27 **Choice C is correct** because you can use the diagram to evaluate the value of y and then use the triangle to find the value of x.

Since 125 is the supplementary angle to y, you can subtract the value 180 − 125 = 55 to get y = 55. This would mean $\dfrac{y}{5} = \dfrac{55}{5} = 11$.

Therefore you will have 2 of the 3 angles in the middle triangle needed. Subtract 180 − (55 + 11) = 114 for the value of the missing angle in the triangle.

Since this angle and $2x$ are vertical angles, then $2x$ = 114. Divide by 2 to get x = 57.

Choice A is incorrect because this is the value of one of the angles in the triangle, but it is not equal to x. **Choice B is incorrect** because this is the value of y. **Choice D is incorrect** because this is the value of the two angles of the triangle not including $2x$. **Choice E is incorrect** because this is the value of $2x$.

28 **Choice E is correct** because the obtained value of N is 30.

The sum of the exterior angles of a polygon is 360°. N represents the number of sides in the polygon. A represents the angle measure of one exterior angle.

AN = 360

(12)(N) = 360

N = 30

Therefore, the polygon is a 30-gon.

The answer is E.

Choice A is incorrect because it is not equivalent to the obtained value of N. **Choice B** is incorrect because it is not equivalent to the obtained value of N. **Choice C** is incorrect because t is not equivalent to the obtained value of N. **Choice D** is incorrect because t is not equivalent to the obtained value of N.

29 **Choice C is correct** because the area of the shaded region is $\left(\frac{\pi}{2}\right)s^2 - s^2$

By using the diameter as the hypotenuse of the square, you can apply the Pythagorean Theorem. The Pythagorean Theorem will have the two sides as the legs and the diameter as the hypotenuse. This is plugged in as follows; $s^2 + s^2 = D^2$. Combine the s^2 terms to get $2s^2 = D^2$. Call the diameter of the circle D. $D^2 = 2s^2$ by the Pythagorean theorem, and so $r = \left(\frac{s}{2}\right)\sqrt{2}$. The area of the circle is $\pi r^2 = \left(\frac{\pi}{2}\right)s^2$. The area of the unshaded square is s^2, and so the area of the shaded portion is $\left(\frac{\pi}{2}\right)s^2 - s^2$.

Choice A is incorrect because πs^2 is not equivalent to the obtained area of the shaded portion. **Choice B** is incorrect because $\frac{\pi s - \pi}{2}$ is not equivalent to the obtained area of the shaded portion. **Choice D** is incorrect because $\pi^2 s$ is not equivalent to the obtained area of the shaded portion. **Choice E** is incorrect because $\frac{s^2}{\pi}$ is not equivalent to the obtained area of the shaded portion.

30 **Choice C is correct** because to find the area of a square, use the diagonal and 45–45–90 relationships of leg lengths $x-x-x\sqrt{2}$.

Since the diagonal is 16, this would mean $x\sqrt{2} = 16$. Divide both sides by $\sqrt{2}$ would yield $\frac{16}{\sqrt{2}}$. Multiply by $\frac{\sqrt{2}}{\sqrt{2}}$ to rationalize the denominator and get each side length to be $\frac{16\sqrt{2}}{2}$ which is the value $8\sqrt{2}$. To find the area, use the formula $A = s^2$. Plugging in $8\sqrt{2}$ would yield $\left(8\sqrt{2}\right)^2$ which is 128.

Practice Set 1 (Easy): Answers & Explanations

Choice A is incorrect because this uses 8 as the incorrect side length. **Choice B** is incorrect because this is the perimeter of the square. **Choice D** is incorrect because this uses 16 as the side length. **Choice E** is incorrect because this uses $16\sqrt{2}$ as the side length.

31 **Choices B and C are correct** because the obtained answers are 56° and 78°.

∠1 and ∠4 are supplementary angles then ∠4 will be 180° − 124° = 56°.

As sum of all three angle of a triangle is 180° then ∠3 will be 180° − (56° + 46°) = 78°

Choice A is incorrect because 46° is less than the obtained values. **Choice D** is incorrect because 124° is greater than the obtained values. **Choice E** is incorrect because 132° is greater than the obtained values. **Choice F** is incorrect because 136° is greater than the obtained values.

32 **Choices A, B and C are correct.** The area of the circle will be less than the area of the square whenever the value of the radius of the circle is equal to or lower than the value of the diameter of the square. This is seen in the diagram below:

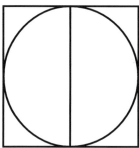

The side length of the square can be found by dividing the perimeter by 4 since the perimeter is the sum of all sides. If you divide 28 by 4, you will get a side length of 7. This means 7 or below would work for the radius of the circle.

Choice A is correct because 5 falls within the possible values for the radius. **Choice B** is correct because 6 falls within the possible values for the radius. **Choice C** is correct because 7 falls within the possible values for the radius.

Choice D is incorrect because this is larger than the radius can be for the circle to have a smaller area compared to the square. **Choice E** is incorrect because this is larger than the radius can be for the circle to have a smaller area compared to the square.

33 **Choices B and D are correct** because the obtained perimeter is 320 meters and 80 meters for the length of one side.

Total length of the fence will be $\frac{1600}{5} = 320$ meters.

This will equal to the perimeter of the square field, so length of one side will be $\frac{320}{4} = 80$ meters.

Choice A is incorrect because 40 m is less than the obtained values. **Choice C** is incorrect because 100 m is not one of the obtained values. **Choice E** is incorrect because 350 m is greater than the obtained values. **Choice F** is incorrect because 370 m is greater than the obtained values.

34 The correct answer is **144**. In this problem, we are using properties of similar triangles. The sides of the smaller triangle are proportional to the sides of the larger triangle.

Smaller Triangle 3 : 5 : 6

Larger Triangle n : 10 : m

Based on the middle side, the sides of the smaller triangle are multiplied by two to get the sides of the larger triangle. Therefore, the $n = 3 \times 2 = 6$ and $m = 6 \times 2 = 12$

All three interior angles of a triangle have a sum of 180°. We can use this property to solve for *x*.

$x + 67 + 53 = 180$

$x + 120 = 180$ or $x = 60°$

We know $x = 60$, $m = 6$, and $n = 12$

Substitute these values into the expression.

$2x + m + 2n$

$2(60) + 12 + 2(6)$; $120 + 12 + 12$;

$120 + 24 = 144$

35 The correct answer is **505.8**. The area of the entire figure is πr^2, and the area of the unshaded portion is $\pi(r^2 - (r - s)^2)$.

Therefore, $\pi(15^2 - (15 - 7)^2) = 161\pi$ which is approximately 505.8.

36 The correct answer is **35** because the angles in a parallelogram must add to 360 degrees. If y = 110° then 110 + 110 = 220. This means the final two congruent angles must be added to 360 – 220 = 140. Divide 140 by 2 to get a value of 70 for the bottom left corner angle. Since 70 = 2x, divide by 2 to get x = 35.

37 The correct answer is **560** because if the surface area equals 412, then you can find the missing value of *x* using the formula SA = 2lh + 2lw + 2wh.

Since the length equals 10 and the height equals 8, you can plug in to get 412 = 2(10)(8) + 2(10)(x) + 2(8)x. Simplify this statement to get 412 = 160 + 36x. Subtract 160 to get 252 = 36x. Divide by 36 to find the value of x = 7.

Now to find the volume use the formula V = lwh. This would give you 10(8)(7) = 560.

Practice Set 2 (Medium): Answers & Explanations

38 **Choice B is correct** because Quantity B is greater than Quantity A.

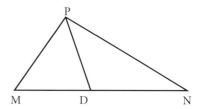

Since *M*, *D*, and *N* are collinear due to the statement (1) and *D* is the midpoint of *MN* by statement (2), then the segment *MN* is a straight line segment, where *D* is an internal point between *M* and *N*, as shown in the graph below. Since only *M*, *N*, and *D* are given collinear in (1), therefore *P* is not on *MN*. Draw *PM* and *PN*. We know that in a triangle, the sum of two sides is greater than the third side. Hence, in △*PDM*,

(1) *PD* + *PM* > *MD*

Statement (2) indicates that

(2) *DN* = *MD*

Replacing *DN* for *MD* from (2) in (1), we get

DN < *PD* + *PM* or *PD* > *DN* – *PM*

Therefore, the proper answer choice is (B).

Choice A is incorrect because Quantity A is not greater than B. **Choice C** is incorrect because it is not possible for the two quantities to be equal. **Choice D** is incorrect because it is possible to use the given information to make a comparison between Quantity A and Quantity B.

39 **Choice A is correct** because Quantity A is greater than Quantity B.

Because OP ∥ QR, we know △NQR ~ △NOP. Therefore, we can conclude the following segments are proportional.

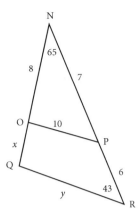

Choice B is incorrect because Quantity B is less than Quantity A. Choice C is incorrect because it is not possible for the two quantities to be equal. Choice D is incorrect because it is possible to use the given information to make a comparison between Quantity A and Quantity B.

40 Choice A is correct because Quantity A is greater than Quantity B.

To solve this question, we need to know how to find the angle given the arc length and how to calculate area given the angle. Since the radius is 4, the diameter is 8 and the circumference of the circle is 8π. Therefore, ratio of arc $\frac{BOC}{Cir} = \frac{3\pi}{8\pi} = \frac{3}{8}$, which means $\frac{\angle BOC}{360°} = \frac{3}{8} \times 360 = 135°$. Therefore, $\angle AOB + \angle BOC = 135 + 60 = 195$, and $\angle AOC = 360 - 195 = 165°$. The ratio of X to the total area of the circle is $\frac{165}{360}$ or $\frac{11}{24}$. The total area of the circle is $A = r^2\pi = 4^2\pi = 16\pi$ and the area of $X = \frac{11}{24} \times 16\pi = \frac{22\pi}{3}$, which is larger than $\frac{21\pi}{3}$. Therefore, the correct answer is A.

Choice B is incorrect because Quantity B is less than Quantity A. Choice C is incorrect because it is not possible for the two quantities to be equal. Choice D is incorrect because it is possible to use the given information to make a comparison between Quantity A and Quantity B.

41 Choice A is correct because Quantity A is greater than Quantity B.
Since $\angle AOB$ is a central angle, it equals the measure of AB, and since $\angle ABC$ is outside the circle but connects to AB, it is less than half of AB. Therefore, $\angle AOB > \angle ADC$
Alternate method: The external $\angle AOB$ must be larger than either of the remote interior angles.

Practice Set 2 (Medium): Answers & Explanations

Choice B is incorrect because Quantity B is less than Quantity A. Choice C is incorrect because it is not possible for the two quantities to be equal. Choice D is incorrect because it is possible to use the given information to make a comparison between Quantity A and Quantity B.

42 Choice A is correct because Quantity A is greater than Quantity B.

Consider the Triangle Inequality Theorem, which states that the sum of two sides of a triangle must be greater than the third side. In the rectangle above, Triangle ABC is made up of two sides of Rectangle ABCD ($\overline{AB}$, $\overline{BC}$) and one of the diagonals $\angle(\overline{AC})$. The Triangle Inequality Theorem tells us that $\overline{AB} + \overline{BC} > (\overline{AC}.)$ Since a rectangle has two pairs of opposite sides that are congruent, you can determine that $2(\overline{AB} + \overline{BC}) > 2(\overline{AC})$.

Choice B is incorrect because Quantity B is less than Quantity A. Choice C is incorrect because it is not possible for the two quantities to be equal. Choice D is incorrect because it is possible to use the given information to make a comparison between Quantity A and Quantity B.

43 Choice A is correct because Quantity A is greater than Quantity B.

The radius of circle P will also be 40% of the radius of circle Q. Because the area of any circle is πr^2, the radius will be used to compare the area of the two circles. Since $40\% = 0.40 = 0.4$ and $(0.4)^2 = (0.16) = 16\%$
Thus, area of circle P will be 16% of the area of circle Q.
Choice B is incorrect because Quantity B is less than Quantity A. Choice C is incorrect because it is not possible for the two quantities to be equal. Choice D is incorrect because it is possible to use the given information to make a comparison between Quantity A and Quantity B.

44 Choice B is correct. The properties of a parallelogram state that opposite angles are equal to each other, then $\angle A = \angle C$ and $\angle B = \angle D$. Since $\angle A = 95°$, then $\angle C = 95°$.

Diagonal BD is dividing the parallelogram ABCD into two triangles. The sum of two adjacent angles is equal to 180°, thus $\angle B = 180 - 95 = 85°$.

Therefore, $\angle C = 95°$ is greater than $\angle B = 85°$.

Chapter 5: Geometry

Choice A is incorrect. Quantity A has 85° which is less than Quantity B. **Choice C** is incorrect. The two angles have different quantities. **Choice D** is incorrect. There is enough data to determine the relationship between the two.

45 **Choice A is correct** because if the value of the angle is greater than 90 degrees, the perimeter will be greater than the perimeter of a 45–45–90 triangle.

The side ratios of a 45–45–90 triangle are x–x–$x\sqrt{2}$. One of the legs of the triangle is 15 so the hypotenuse has to be at least $15\sqrt{2}$. This would make the perimeter of the triangle $15 + 15 + 15\sqrt{2}$ which would be greater than 45.

Choice B is incorrect because the perimeter of the triangle is greater than 45. **Choice C** is incorrect because if the angle is more than 90 degrees, the perimeter cannot equal 45. **Choice D** is incorrect because it is possible to make a comparison.

46 **Choice C is correct** because Quantity A and Quantity B are equal.

The two smaller circles are the same size, and so each has a diameter equal to R, and so a radius $r = \dfrac{R}{2}$.

The combined area of the two smaller circles is $2\pi\left(\dfrac{R}{2}\right)^2 = \dfrac{\pi R^2}{2}$.

The area of the large circle is πR^2, so the shaded portion has area $\pi R^2 - \dfrac{\pi R^2}{2} = \dfrac{\pi R^2}{2}$. The answer is C.

Choice A is incorrect because Quantity A is not greater than B. **Choice B** is incorrect because Quantity B is not greater than Quantity A. **Choice D** is incorrect because it is possible to use the given information to make a comparison between Quantity A and Quantity B.

47 **Choice D is correct** because it is not possible to use the given information to make a comparison between Quantity A and Quantity B.

First, we need to determine the sum of the interior angles in the pentagon. The sum of the interior angles in a polygon is dictated by the following equation.
$(S = (n - 2)180°)$

Number of sides in a Pentagon = 5

Sum of interior angles = $(5 - 2)180 = 3(180) = 540°$

We know all interior angles of the polygon should sum to 540°. Now we can find the measure of x and y.

$x + y + 90 + 90 + 42 = 540°$

$x + y + 222 = 540°$

$x + y = 318°$

We know that the sum of the angles is 318°, but we are unable to calculate the measure of each individual angle. The answer is D, cannot be determined.

Choice A is incorrect because Quantity A is not greater than Quantity B. **Choice B** is incorrect because Quantity B is not greater than Quantity A. **Choice C** is incorrect because it is not possible for the two quantities to be equal.

48 **Choice D is correct** because the diagonals of a trapezoid sometimes divide a trapezoid into four equal triangles. This can be proven by the properties of trapezoids. Since the shaded region is two of the four triangles, its area would be half of the trapezoid. The unshaded region will also be equal to half of the area.

In other cases, the diagonals of the trapezoid do not create equal areas so it is not possible to determine the scenario for this trapezoid without further information.

Choice A is incorrect because it is not possible to compare the quantities **Choice B** is incorrect because it is not possible to compare the quantities. **Choice C** is incorrect because the areas are not always equal.

49 **Choice D is correct** because it is possible for x to equal 80 + y, but there are other options possible as well. Use the rule that the angles in triangles add to 180 degrees to assist in solving.

If $x = y + 80$, then you could solve for y by substituting in $y + 80$ into the expression $y + y + 10 + y + 80 = 180$. This would simplify to be $3y + 90 = 180$. Subtracting 90 from both sides and dividing by 3 would yield $y = 30$. Plugging this back in to solve for x would yield $80 + 30 = 110$. This would make the expressions equivalent.

Other options would work for the values of x and y, however, such as y = 10. This would make x equal to 150 ($y + y + 10 + x = 180$) which is greater than $y + 80$.

Choice A is incorrect because it is not possible to determine the relationship. **Choice B** is incorrect because it is not possible to determine the relationship. **Choice C** is incorrect because it is not possible to compare the two values.

50 **Choice B is correct** because Quantity B is greater than Quantity A.

Area of the circle $= 81\pi$

If r is the radius, then $\pi r^2 = 81\pi \Rightarrow r = 9$

Length of arc PRQ $= \dfrac{40}{360} \times 2\pi \times r = \dfrac{40}{360} \times 2\pi \times 9 = 2\pi$

Perimeter of the Sector OPRQO $= 2\pi + 9 + 9 = 2\pi + 18$

Choice A is incorrect because Quantity A is not greater than B. **Choice C is incorrect** because it is not possible for the two quantities to be equal. **Choice D is incorrect** because it is possible to use the given information to make a comparison between Quantity A and Quantity B.

51 **Choice C is correct** because the inner circle can be found to have an area of 36Π based on the information given.

To determine the area of the shaded region, it is important to find its radius first. If the larger circle had a radius $\dfrac{3}{2}$ as larger as the smaller circle, the area of the outer ring can be found by subtracting the two areas with this radius plugged in.

The area of a circle equals Πr^2. If the inner radius equals x, the larger circle's radius would be $\dfrac{3}{2}x$. Subtracting the areas with these radii plugged in would yield

$\Pi\left(\dfrac{3}{2}x\right)^2 - \Pi x^2 = 45\Pi$. Simplifying this expression would get $\Pi\dfrac{9}{4}x^2 - \Pi x^2 = 45\Pi$, which simplifies further to yield

$\dfrac{5}{4}x^2\Pi = 45\Pi$. Divide both sides by $\dfrac{5}{4}\Pi$ to get $x^2 = 36$. Square root both sides to find $x = 6$.

Now that you have the radius of the smaller circle, you can plug it back into the area formula to get $A = \Pi r^2 = 36\Pi$.

Choice A is incorrect because the quantities are equal. **Choice B is incorrect** because the quantities are equal. **Choice D is incorrect** because it is possible to solve for the area.

52 **Choice B is correct** because Quantity B is greater than Quantity A.

The area of the trapezoid $= \dfrac{4(4+6)}{2} = 20$.

The area of the parallelogram $= 4 \times 6 = 24$.

Choice A is incorrect because Quantity A is not greater than B. **Choice C is incorrect** because it is not possible for the two quantities to be equal. **Choice D is incorrect** because it is possible to use the given information to make a comparison between Quantity A and Quantity B.

53 **Choice C is correct** because the two quantities are equal.

If Hexagon ABCDEF is a regular hexagon, all sides and angles are congruent. First, we need to determine the sum of the interior angles in the hexagon. The sum of the interior angles in a polygon is $(S = (n-2)180)$

Number of sides in a Hexagon = 6

Sum of interior angles = $(6-2)180 = 4(180) = 720°$

The measure of $\angle B$ can be calculated by dividing the sum of the interior angles by the total number of angles.

$\angle B = \dfrac{720°}{6} = 120°$

Now we can calculate the measure of x and j. They are both equal since the sides opposite them are equal.

The degrees in the three angles of a triangle sum to 180°.

$x + j + 120 = 180°$

$x + x + 120 = 180°$

$2x + 120 = 180°$

$2x = 60°$

$x = 30°, j = 30°$

Therefore, Quantity A is 60°.

For Quantity B, the interior angle is 120° just like all interior angles of a regular hexagon. A straight line has an angle measure of 180°. The measure of y is 180 − 120, so y is 60°.

The question can also be evaluated conceptually without calculations by using the knowledge that the interior angles B and D are equal, $x + j$ will be supplementary to B, and y will be supplementary to D. Therefore, $x + j$ must equal y.

Both quantities are 60°; therefore, the answer is C.

Choice A is incorrect because Quantity A is not greater than B. **Choice B is incorrect** because Quantity B is less than Quantity A. **Choice D is incorrect** because it is possible to use the given information to make a comparison between Quantity A and Quantity B.

54 **Choice C is correct** because the two quantities are equal.

Use the following notation in solution process:

m = Length of the rectangle

n = Width of the rectangle

a = Side of the square

P = Perimeter of the square

Q = Perimeter of the rectangle

Chapter 5: Geometry

Translate the given facts in the same order listed above.

(1) $m = 2n$

(2) $n = 2a$

(3) $P = 8$

Also, using the formulas of perimeters of square and rectangle, we have

(4) $P = 4a = 2(2a)$

(5) $Q = 2(m + n)$

Replace (2) and (3) in (4)

(6) $8 = 2n$

Divide each side by 4.

(7) $n = 4$

Apply (7) in (1) and simplify.

$m = 2(4) = 8$

Having measures of a length and a width of the rectangle, calculate its area.

$A_{rectangle} = mn = (4)(8) = 32$

The two quantities are equal.

Choice A is incorrect because Quantity A is not greater than B. **Choice B** is incorrect because Quantity B is less than Quantity A. **Choice D** is incorrect because it is possible to use the given information to make a comparison between Quantity A and Quantity B.

55 **Choice D is correct** because it is not possible to use the given information to make a comparison between Quantity A and Quantity B.

Volume of cube with side 6 is $6 \times 6 \times 6 = 216$. Volume of rectangular prism with two dimensions less than 6 is not determinable because the third dimension is needed. Therefore, no comparison can be made.

Choice A is incorrect because Quantity A is not greater than B. **Choice B** is incorrect because Quantity B is less than Quantity A. **Choice C** is incorrect because it is not possible for the two quantities to be equal.

56 **Choice D is correct** because it is possible to determine that y is not equal to 90, but it is not possible to evaluate if it is greater than or less than 90.

To determine if y equals 90, use the Pythagorean theorem to evaluate if there is a right angle present. The equation $a^2 + b^2 = c^2$ can be filled in with the two side lengths of x, x, and the hypotenuse of 2x. This will yield $x^2 + x^2 = (2x)^2$ which simplifies to be $2x^2 = 4x^2$. The solution to this equation is an infinite number of answers so it is not possible that this is a right angle.

It is not possible to determine the value of y with the given side lengths so Choice D is the best option.

Choice A is incorrect because it is not possible to solve for y. **Choice B** is incorrect because it is not possible to solve for y. **Choice C** is incorrect because y does not equal 90.

57 **Choice B is correct** because to find the area of a sector use the formula $\frac{x}{360} \Pi r^2$.

For the sector in Circle A, plugging into the formula will yield $\frac{45}{360} \Pi (5)^2$ which simplifies to be $\frac{25\Pi}{8}$.

For the sector in Circle B, plugging into the formula will yield $\frac{30}{360} \Pi (9)^2$ which simplifies to be $\frac{27\Pi}{4}$.

Since $\frac{27\Pi}{4} > \frac{25\Pi}{8}$, then Quantity B is greater.

Choice A is incorrect because Quantity A is less than Quantity B. **Choice C** is incorrect because the two quantities do not equal each other. **Choice D** is incorrect because it is possible to solve for the areas.

58 **Choice B is correct** because it can be determined that y equals 71 degrees and x equals 70 degrees.

To solve for y, you can use the parallel lines to determine that y and the 71-degree angle are opposite interior angles which makes them congruent.

To solve for x, it can be determined based on the parallel lines that x equals the supplementary angle of 130 using opposite interior angles. The supplementary angle to 130 is $180 - 130 = 50$.

Choice A is incorrect because x is less than y. **Choice C** is incorrect because the two values are not equal. **Choice D** is incorrect because it is possible to compare the two values.

59 **Choice D is correct** because the rectangle could have an area the same or less than the area of the square.

For example, if the square and rectangle had a perimeter of 16, then that means the side lengths of the square would be 4. This would make its area 16 since $A = s^2 = 4^2$. The rectangle could have a variety of options for side lengths with its largest area resulting from having a length of 4 and a width of 4. This would make its area also 16 since $A = lw$.

Practice Set 2 (Medium): Answers & Explanations

The rectangle could have a smaller area if its dimensions were 6 by 2. This would yield an area of 12 which would be less than the square's area of 16.

Choice A is incorrect because it is not possible for the rectangle to have a larger area. **Choice B** is incorrect because only in some situations is the area of the square greater. **Choice C** is incorrect because the areas can be equal, but there are other solutions.

60 **Choice A is correct** because there are infinite possibilities for the value of f, but it can be found that $e - d = 0$ making any value of f still greater.

It can be found based on the image given that $e + f + a = 180$ and $c + b + d = 180$ since all of these values lie on a straight line. Therefore, $e + f + a = c + b + d$. Since $f + a = b + c$, these can be canceled in the equation which leaves $e = d$. This means $e - d = 0$. Since f had to be a nonzero value, Quantity A is greater than Quantity B.

Choice B is incorrect because Quantity A is greater than Quantity B. **Choice C** is incorrect because the two quantities are not equal. **Choice D** is incorrect because it is possible to compare the two values.

61 **Choice B is correct** because the length of the diagonal can be found to be less than 16. If ABCD is a square, that means ∠DCA is 45 degrees. This would then make the smaller triangle a 45–45–90 triangle with side proportions of x–x–$x\sqrt{2}$.

Based on the 45–45–90 triangle and the 75–degree angle, the triangle with a leg of 8 can be determined to be a 30–60–90 triangle. This is because the angles that make up line DC must equal 180 so 180 − 45 − 75 = 60. This would make the ratio of this triangle to be x–$x\sqrt{3}$ –$2x$ with $8 = x\sqrt{3}$. Dividing both sides by $\sqrt{3}$ and rationalizing the denominator would make the shortest leg equal to $\frac{8\sqrt{3}}{3}$.

This means the 45–45–90 triangle would have side lengths of $\frac{8\sqrt{3}}{3}$, $\frac{8\sqrt{3}}{3}$, and $\frac{8\sqrt{6}}{3}$. The diagonal of the square will then be $\frac{8\sqrt{6}}{3} + 8$ which equals approximately 14.53.

Choice A is incorrect because the length of the diagonal is less than 16. **Choice C** is incorrect because the length of the diagonal is not 16. **Choice D** is incorrect because it is possible to solve for the length of the diagonal.

62 **Choice A is correct** because Quantity A is greater than Quantity B.

Since the area of face TUWY is 20, the dimensions must be 2 × 10.

Remember, each dimension must be an even number. The dimension of face WXZY must therefore be 2 × 4. Since edge WY is common in both faces, the dimensions of face UVXW are 10 × 4.

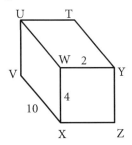

The surface of the rectangular solid is

2 × 10 = 20 (doubled) = 40

+ 2 × 4 = 8 (doubled) =16

+ 10 × 4 = 40 (doubled) = 80 = 136

Volume equals 2 ×10 × 4 = 80

Therefore, the surface area is greater.

Choice B is incorrect because Quantity B is less than Quantity A. **Choice C** is incorrect because it is not possible for the two quantities to be equal. **Choice D** is incorrect because it is possible to use the given information to make a comparison between Quantity A and Quantity B.

63 **Choice B is correct** because it is possible to solve and determine that $x = 60$. A quadrilateral has four angles that add up to 360 degrees. If the quadrilateral has two right angles and the other angles are x and $2x$, the equation to solve for x would be $90 + 90 + x + 2x = 360$.

Simplify to get $180 + 3x = 360$. Subtract 180 to get $3x = 180$ and then divide to find $x = 60$.

Choice A is incorrect because 60 is not greater than 90. **Choice C** is incorrect because the two quantities are not equal. **Choice D** is incorrect because it is possible to solve.

64 **Choice C is correct** because the obtained answer is 768 square inches.

DE is parallel to BC. So, the Δs ADE and ABC are similar. Therefore, the ratio of any side or height of one triangle to the corresponding side or height of the second triangle is constant.

Chapter 5: Geometry

$\dfrac{AD}{AB} = \dfrac{DE}{BC}$

We know AD = DB

$\dfrac{AD}{AB} = \dfrac{1}{2}$

$\dfrac{1}{2} = \dfrac{24}{BC}$

BC = 48 inches

Perimeter ΔABC = 128 inches

AB + AC + BC = 128 inches

AB + AC = 128 − 48 inches

ΔABC is isosceles

$AB = AC = \dfrac{80}{2} = 40$ inches

In order to find the area of ΔABC we need to know one of its heights.

First, we draw a height by drawing line segment AF as a perpendicular to BC.

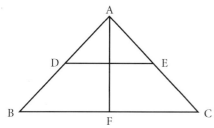

As ΔABC is isosceles

BF = FC = BC/2 = 24 inches

We can apply Pythagoras' theorem in either of the Δs ABF or ACF. Let's apply it in ΔACF:

$AC^2 = AF^2 + FC^2$

$AF^2 = AC^2 - FC^2$

$AF^2 = 40^2 - 24^2 = 1600 - 576 = 1024$

$AF = \sqrt{1024} = 32$ inches

Area $\Delta ABC \dfrac{(AF \times BC)}{2} = \dfrac{(32 \times 48)}{2} = 768$ square inches

Choice A is incorrect because 656 square inches is less than the obtained area. **Choice B** is incorrect because 693 square inches is less than the obtained area. **Choice D** is incorrect because 812 square inches is greater than the obtained area. **Choice E** is incorrect because 848 square inches is greater than the obtained area.

65 **Choice B is correct** because the obtained answer is $2\sqrt{2}$.

ΔABC is an isosceles right triangle with hypotenuse BC.

AC and AB are perpendicular

AB has a slope of 0 $\left(slope = \dfrac{(2-2)}{(b-1)} = \dfrac{0}{(b-1)} = 0 \right)$

AB is parallel to x-axis.

AC must be parallel to y-axis.

C(c, 6) = C(1,6) because c must be 1 to match with A(1,2)

ΔABC is isosceles with hypotenuse BC

AC = AB

We use the coordinates of the points and the definition of the distance between the points, to rewrite the above as:

$\sqrt{(1-c)^2 + (2-6)^2} = \sqrt{(b-1)^2 + (2-2)^2}$

$\sqrt{(1-1)^2 + 16} = \sqrt{(b-1)^2}$

$b - 1 = 4$

$b = 5$

$AC = AB = 4$

Using the same the definition of the distance between the points:

$BC = \sqrt{(b-c)^2 + (2-6)^2} = \sqrt{(5-1)^2 + 16} = \sqrt{2 \times 16} = 4\sqrt{2}$

AD is perpendicular to BC. Area of ΔABC can be calculated as $\dfrac{(AD \times BC)}{2}$ but because the triangle is also a right triangle the area is also equal to $\dfrac{(AB \times AC)}{2}$

$AD = \dfrac{(AB \times AC)}{BC}$

$AD = \dfrac{(4 \times 4)}{4\sqrt{2}} = \dfrac{4}{\sqrt{2}} = 2\sqrt{2}$

Choice A is incorrect because 2 is less than the obtained value of AD. **Choice C** is incorrect because 3 is close but not accurately equal to the obtained value of AD. **Choice D** is incorrect because $3\sqrt{2}$ is greater than the obtained value of AD. **Choice E** is incorrect because $4\sqrt{2}$ is greater than the obtained value of AD.

66 **Choice D is correct** because the area of the shaded region is $64\pi - 32$.

Find the area of the triangle and subtract it from the area of the circle to find the area of the shaded region.

Area of the triangle:

Since leg OB and OA are also radii we know they are equal. An isosceles right triangle is a 45° – 45° – 90° triangle. The ratio of the sides of an isosceles triangle is $1:1:\sqrt{2}$, thus we know the length of the OB and OA are 8.

$A(\Delta AOB) = \dfrac{bh}{2} = \dfrac{(8)(8)}{2} = \dfrac{64}{2} = 32$

The radius of the circle is the length of OB and OA: $r = 8$

Area of circle $= \pi r^2 = \pi \times 8^2 = 64\pi$

Area of shaded region: $64\pi - 32$

Choice A is incorrect because $16\pi - 32$ is less than the obtained area of the shaded region. **Choice B is incorrect** because $16\pi - 32\sqrt{2}$ is less than the obtained area of the shaded region. **Choice C is incorrect** because 32π overestimates the obtained area of the shaded region. **Choice E is incorrect** because $64\pi - 32\sqrt{2}$ is less than the obtained area of the shaded region.

67 **Choice C is correct** because 104 is the measure of $\angle$ A in degrees.

BD = CD, $\angle$CBD = $\angle$C = 19°

Therefore, $\angle$BDC = 180° – ($\angle$CBD + $\angle$C)

= 180° – (19° + 19°)

= 180° – 38° = 142°

Then $\angle$BDA = 180° – $\angle$BDC = 180° – 142° = 38°

Since AB = AD, $\angle$ABD = $\angle$BDA = 38°

Therefore, $\angle$A = 180° – ($\angle$BDA + $\angle$ABD)

= 180° – (38° + 38°)

= 180° – 76° = 104°

The correct answer is C.

Choice A is incorrect because 75 is less than the measure of $\angle$ A in degrees. **Choice B is incorrect** because 94 is less than the measure of $\angle$ A in degrees. **Choice D is incorrect** because 114 is greater than the measure of $\angle$ A in degrees. **Choice E is incorrect** because 142 is greater than the measure of $\angle$ A in degrees.

68 **Choice B is correct** because the obtained area is $\dfrac{9\sqrt{3}}{4}$.

To find the height and base, split the triangle up into two 30, 60, 90 triangles. Then use the 30, 60, 90 relationship to find the missing height and base, and then multiply the base by 2 to get the original triangle's base. Then use the area formula of a triangle ($A = b*h/2$) to find the area.

Practice Set 2 (Medium): Answers & Explanations

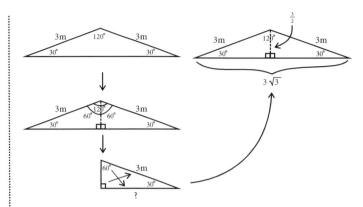

$x \to 30^0 \to \dfrac{3}{2}$

$x\sqrt{3} \to 60^0 \to \dfrac{3\sqrt{3}}{2}$

$2x \to 90^0 \to \dfrac{2x}{2} = \dfrac{3}{2} \to x = \dfrac{3}{2}$

$A = \dfrac{b \cdot h}{2}$

$A = \dfrac{\dfrac{3}{2} \cdot 3\sqrt{3}}{2}$

$A = \dfrac{9\sqrt{3}}{4} m^2$

Choice A is incorrect because $\dfrac{3}{2}\sqrt{3}$ is not equivalent to the obtained area. **Choice C is incorrect** because $\dfrac{9\sqrt{3}}{2}$ is not equivalent to the obtained area. **Choice D is incorrect** because $\dfrac{3\sqrt{3}}{4}$ is not equivalent to the obtained area. **Choice E is incorrect** because $\dfrac{2\sqrt{3}}{9}$ is not equivalent to the obtained area.

69 **Choice A is correct** because the obtained area is $50\sqrt{3}$.

Because the perimeter of the rhombus is 40, each side has length 10. Because the diagonals of a rhombus are perpendicular and bisect each other.

$x^2 + 5^2 = 10^2$

$x^2 + 25 = 100$

$x^2 = 75$

$x = \sqrt{75}$, $x = 5\sqrt{3}$.

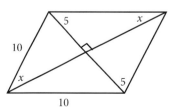

Chapter 5: **Geometry**

The area of a quadrilateral with perpendicular diagonals d_1 and d_2 is

$= \frac{1}{2} d_1 \cdot d_2$

$= \frac{1}{2}(10)(10\sqrt{3})$

$= 50\sqrt{3}$

Choice B is incorrect because 100 is greater than the obtained area of the rhombus. **Choice C** is incorrect because $100\sqrt{3}$ is greater than the obtained area of the rhombus. **Choice D** is incorrect because 200 is greater than the obtained area of the rhombus. **Choice E** is incorrect because 400 is greater than the obtained area of the rhombus.

70 **Choice E is correct.** Draw a quick sketch. Label the important information.

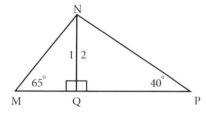

MN and NP are the hypotenuses of ΔQNM and ΔQNP. Therefore, these are greater than MQ, NQ, and QP (the hypotenuse is the longest side of a right triangle). So, eliminate MN and NP. NQ > MQ, since ∠QMN(65°) > ∠MNQ(25°) (the longest side is opposite the greatest angle in a triangle).

Eliminate NQ, Similarly, since ∠QNP(50°) > ∠NPQ(50°) > NPQ(40), QP > NQ. Eliminate QP.

Therefore, the answer is MQ, the only remaining line.

The answer is (E).

Choice A is incorrect because MN is the hypotenuse and thus longer than other sides. **Choice B** is incorrect because NP is the hypotenuse and therefore not the shortest. **Choice C** is incorrect because PQ is longer than NQ, which is longer than MQ. **Choice D** is incorrect because NQ is longer than MQ based on triangle angle properties.

71 **Choice D is correct** because the obtained area is $8\sqrt{3} + 24$ $units^2$

In the figure we are going to use the ratios of the sides of a 30°– 60°– 90° triangle, which is $x : x\sqrt{3} : 2x$

The smaller triangle has a side length of 4 and a hypotenuse of 8.

4 : h : 8

$x : x\sqrt{3} : 2x$

The value of x is 4 in this triangle. Therefore, the height of the triangle is $4\sqrt{3}$. The length of the base is $4 + 4\sqrt{3}$

If we use the formula for the area of triangle, we can calculate the area of the triangle.

$A = \frac{1}{2} bh = \frac{1}{2}(4 + 4\sqrt{3})(4\sqrt{3})$

$A = \frac{1}{2}(16\sqrt{3} + 16\sqrt{9}) = \frac{1}{2}(16\sqrt{3} + 48)$

$A = 8\sqrt{3} + 24$

Choice A is incorrect because 16 $units^2$ is less than the obtained area. **Choice B** is incorrect because 22.5 $units^2$ is less than the obtained area. **Choice C** is incorrect because 30 $units^2$ is less than the obtained area. **Choice E** is incorrect because $8\sqrt{3} + 6$ $units^2$ is less than the obtained area.

72 **Choice D is correct** because 32 is the obtained length of AC.

Since AB = BC = 34, ΔABC is an isosceles triangle and altitude BD will bisect AC. Since ΔBDC is right triangle, use the Pythagorean Theorem, which says

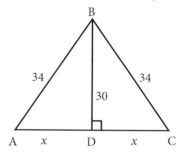

$(BC)^2 = (BD)^2 + (CD)^2$

$(34)^2 = (30)^2 + x^2$

$1{,}156 = 900 + x^2$

$x^2 = 1{,}156 - 900$

$x^2 = 256$

$x = \sqrt{256} = 16$

Therefore, CD = 16 = AD

AC = AD + DC

= 16 + 16

= 32

Choice A is incorrect because 8 is less than the obtained length of AC. **Choice B** is incorrect because 18 is less than the obtained length of AC. **Choice C** is incorrect because 30 is less than the obtained length of AC. **Choice E** is incorrect because 34 is greater than the obtained length of AC.

Practice Set 2 (Medium): Answers & Explanations

73 **Choices A and E are correct** because the area of the trapezoid is 12π cm²

The area of the circle is found by using the formula $A = \pi r^2$, where $r = 10$cm.

Therefore, the area of the circle is found by using the formula $A = \pi 10^2 = 100\pi$ cm². Hence, **Choice C is not correct.**

The Area of the trapezoid is found using the formula $A = \dfrac{b_1 + b_2}{2} \times h$, where b_1 and b_2 are the bases and h is the height. Plugging in the given values, $A = \dfrac{7+5}{2} \times 2\pi = 12\pi$ cm². This 12% means that answer **Choice E is incorrect.**

The yellow area is the area of the circle subtracted by the area of the trapezoid. This is therefore $100\pi - 12\pi = 88$ cm². **Choice D is incorrect.** The area of the trapezoid represents $\dfrac{12\pi}{100\pi}$, or 6% the area of the circle. **Choice E is correct.**

Choice B is incorrect because the statement does not satisfy the given conditions. **Choice C is incorrect** because the statement does not satisfy the given conditions. **Choice D is incorrect** because the statement does not satisfy the given conditions.

74 **Choice A is correct** because the obtained ratio is $\dfrac{1}{4}$. Because we are given the radius and the arc measure, we can find the central angle and the inscribed angle using the arc length equation Arc length $= 2\pi r \times \dfrac{x}{360°}$, where x is the central angle. Plugging in the given values, we obtain $5\pi = 2\pi \times 15 \times \dfrac{x}{360°}$. Solving for x we get $x = 60$, meaning the central angle is 60°. The inscribed angle is therefore 30°. The smaller triangle is therefore an equiangular and equilateral triangle, as the base angles must both be 60°, making $\angle 2 = 60°$. Because the larger triangle is isosceles, the two base angles must be the same, so let's call them y. Then, $y + y + 30 = 180$, and $y = 75$. Therefore, $\angle 1 + \angle 2 = 75$. Since $\angle 2 = 60°$, $\angle 1 = 15°$, and the ratio is therefore $\dfrac{15}{60} = \dfrac{1}{4}$.

Choice B is incorrect because $\dfrac{3}{4}$ is not equivalent to the obtained ratio. **Choice C is incorrect** because $\dfrac{4}{5}$ is greater than the obtained ratio. **Choice D is incorrect** because $\dfrac{5}{4}$ is not the obtained ratio. **Choice E is incorrect** because $\dfrac{4}{1}$ is greater than the obtained ratio.

75 **Choice C is correct** because if triangle ABC is equilateral that means each side length is $\dfrac{1}{3}$ of the total perimeter. Multiply 18 by $\dfrac{1}{3}$ to get a side length of 6. This would then be used to determine the radius of each circle. Since each point is the center of the circle, the length of one side of the triangle is made up of two radiuses and a diameter. Divide 6 in half to get a diameter of 3 for each circle.

The formula for circumference is $C = 2\Pi r$ and since there are six circles, the circumference for all six can be expressed as $6(2\Pi r)$. Plugging in 3/2 for the radius will yield a total circumference of $6(2\Pi(3/2))$ which simplifies to be 18Π.

Choice A is incorrect because this would be incorrectly solving with a radius of 1. **Choice B is incorrect because** this is the circumference of just one of the circles. **Choice D is incorrect** because this results from a math error. **Choice E is incorrect** because this results when the diameter is mistaken for a radius.

76 **Choice C is correct** because the circle equation needs to be put into a standard form to evaluate its radius and then its circumference. To rearrange the equation, first, subtract the 75 to the other side to get $x^2 - 16x + y^2 + 12y = -75$. Then, complete the square by taking the value in front of the variable raised to the first power, dividing it by 2, and then squaring it.

For the x values, this would be -16 divided by 2 and then squared, which yields $\left(\dfrac{-16}{2}\right)^2 = 64$. For the y values, this would be 12 divided by 2 and then squared, which yields $\left(\dfrac{12}{2}\right)^2 = 36$.

Add these values to both sides of the expression: $x^2 - 16x + 64 + y^2 + 12y + 36 = 36 + 64 - 75$. This would simplify to be $x^2 - 16x + 64 + y^2 + 12y + 36 = 25$. This can be further factored to get the standard form of the circle as $(x-h)^2 + (y-h)^2 = r^2$ which would look like $(x-8)^2 + (y+6)^2 = 25$. This means that $r^2 = 25$ and $r = 5$.

Plug this into the circumference formula to get $C = 2\pi r$ to get $C = 10\pi$.

Choice A is incorrect because this uses the radius and not the diameter. **Choice B is incorrect** because this is using the wrong radius. **Choice D is incorrect** because this is the area, not the circumference. **Choice E is incorrect** because this answer results from a math error.

For more practice, visit www.vibrantpublishers.com

Chapter 5: Geometry

77 **Choice C is correct** because to find the arc length, use the arc length formula $\frac{x}{360} 2\pi r$. Using the information given, you can solve for the measure of arc ABC by subtracting 360 − 75 to get 285.

Now use the arc length formula to get $\frac{285}{360}(21\pi)$ which simplifies to be 16.625π.

Choice A is incorrect because this is the length of minor arc AC. **Choice B is incorrect** because this results from a math error. **Choice D is incorrect** because this results from a math error. **Choice E is incorrect** because this results from a math error.

78 **Choice D is correct** because 3x is the value of y. Both figures are isosceles right triangles, so they are similar. Corresponding lengths of figures are proportional. Since the ratio of the hypotenuses z and $\frac{1}{3}z$ is 3:1, the ratio of the legs must also be 1:3. Therefore, leg y of the larger triangles must be 3 times as great as leg x of the smaller triangle, and $y = 3x$.

Choice A is incorrect because it is not the correct representation of y. **Choice B is incorrect** because it is not the correct representation of y. **Choice C is incorrect** because it is not the correct representation of y. **Choice E is incorrect** because it is not the correct representation of y.

79 **Choice D is correct** because if the perimeter of the square is 52, that means each side length is 13 since $\frac{52}{4} = 13$.

To find the area of a circle, you need to first find its radius. The radius can be found by identifying the diameter of the circle, which is also the diagonal of the square. The diagonal of a square follows the ratio x–x–$x\sqrt{2}$. Since $x = 13$, the diagonal is $13\sqrt{2}$.

The diameter is double the radius so the radius would be $\frac{13\sqrt{2}}{2}$. Plug this into the area formula of $A = \pi r^2$ to get $A = \pi \left(\frac{13\sqrt{2}}{2}\right)^2$ which would become 84.5π.

Choice A is incorrect because this would be using the side length of 13 and not correctly solving for the diameter. **Choice B is incorrect** because this results from a math error. **Choice C is incorrect** because this results from a math error. **Choice E is incorrect** because this would be the result if you plug in 13 into the area formula as the radius of the circle.

80 **Choice B is correct** because to find the circumference of Circle B, first identify the radius of Circle B. This can be found by breaking down the area formula of Circle A and determining the radius of Circle A must be x since $A = \pi r^2$ meaning $\pi r^2 = \pi x^2$.

If the radius of Circle B is triple Circle A, then the radius of Circle B would be $3x$. Plugging this into the circumference formula of $C = 2\pi r$ would yield $2\pi(3x)$ which simplifies to $6\pi x$.

Choice A is incorrect because this answer uses the wrong radius to solve. **Choice C is incorrect** because this answer uses the wrong radius to solve. **Choice D is incorrect** because this answer uses the wrong radius to solve. **Choice E is incorrect** because this answer uses the wrong radius to solve.

81 **Choice D is correct** because the areas are a $\frac{1}{4}$ ratio based on using the formula $A = \pi r^2$. The radius of the larger circle is 6 so its area would be 36π. The area of the smaller circle with a radius of 3 would be 9π. Creating a ratio of these two areas would be $\frac{9\pi}{36\pi}$ which simplifies to be $\frac{1}{4}$.

Choice A is incorrect because this would be the answer if the diameter of the larger circle was somehow used in the solving process. **Choice B is incorrect** because this simplifies the ratio incorrectly. **Choice C is incorrect** because this incorrectly uses the given diameter in the ratio. **Choice E is incorrect** because this is larger than the actual ratio.

82 **Choice D is correct** because the obtained area is 468 square inches.

Since the area of a trapezoid $= \frac{1}{2} \times h \times (b_1 + b_2)$, we need to find the altitude, h. Draw altitudes in figures as follows:

Since the triangles formed are right triangles, use the Pythagorean Theorem, which says

$c^2 = a^2 + b^2$

$15^2 = 9^2 + h^2$

$225 = 81 + h^2$

$h^2 = 225 - 81$

$h^2 = 144$
$h = \sqrt{144} = 12$ inches
Hence the area of the trapezoid will be
$\frac{1}{2} \times h \times (b_1 + b_2) = \frac{1}{2} \times 12 \times (30 + 48)$
$= 6(78)$
$= 468$ square inches.

Choice A is incorrect because 108 is less than the obtained area of the trapezoid. **Choice B** is incorrect because 234 is less than the obtained area of the trapezoid. **Choice C** is incorrect because 368 is less than the obtained area of the trapezoid. **Choice E** is incorrect because 585 is greater than the obtained area of the trapezoid.

83 **Choice D is correct** because to find the area of a trapezoid, use the equation $A = (\frac{b_1 + b_2}{2})h$. The base values are given, but the height will be found by finding the right triangle as seen in the diagram below.

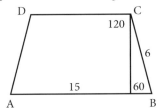

Angle B can be found to be 60 because the adjacent angles of a trapezoid add up to 180. Since angle C is 120, then angle B would be $180 - 120 = 60$.

To find the height use the $x - x\sqrt{3} - 2x$ ratios of 30–60–90 triangles. Since the hypotenuse $6 = 2x$, then $x = 3$. This means the height is $3\sqrt{3}$ since it represents the $x\sqrt{3}$ side of the triangle.

Plugging in the known values into the formula yields $A = (\frac{10+15}{2})(3\sqrt{3})$ which simplifies to be $\frac{75\sqrt{3}}{2}$.

Choice A is incorrect because it uses an improper form of the area formula. **Choice B** is incorrect because it does not multiply by 3. **Choice C** is incorrect because this results from a math error. **Choice E** is incorrect because this does not divide the area by 2.

84 **Choice A is correct** because the radius of the circle and the area of a sector formula must be used to solve.

To find the radius, divide the diameter of $\frac{3x}{4}$ in half to get $\frac{3x}{8}$. Then plug this in to find the area of the circle using the formula $A = \pi r^2$. This would result in an area of $\pi \left(\frac{3x}{8}\right)^2$ which simplifies to be $\frac{9x^2}{64}\pi$.

This should then be multiplied by the fraction of the circle that the sector takes up which is $\frac{120}{360}$ or $\frac{1}{3}$. The result of $\frac{9x^2}{64}\pi \times \frac{1}{3} = \frac{9x^2}{192}\pi$ which simplifies to be $\frac{3x^2}{64}\pi$.

Choice B is incorrect because this does not use all parts of the problem to evaluate. **Choice C** is incorrect because this results from a math error. **Choice D** is incorrect because this misidentifies the radius. **Choice E** is incorrect because this results from a math error.

85 **Choice C is correct** because the largest area of a parallelogram occurs when it is a rectangle since the area of a parallelogram equals its length times its height. To find the area if the parallelogram was a rectangle, the height needs to be identified. If one side length is 4, that means two of the sides would add up to 8. Subtract 8 from 50 and divide by two to find the other side lengths of $\frac{50-8}{2} = 21$. Now multiply the side lengths to get $4 \times 21 = 84$.

Choice A is incorrect because this area is too small. **Choice B** is incorrect because this area is too small. **Choice D** is incorrect because it is not possible to get an area this large. **Choice E** is incorrect because it is not possible to get an area this large.

86 **Choice E is correct** because the obtained values are $b = -1$ and $c = 0$.

For lines A, B and C to be parallel, their slopes must be equal.

To find the slopes we need to use the slope formula $m = \frac{y_1 - y_2}{x_1 - x_2}$

Slope of $A = \frac{-2-0}{0-1} = 2$

Slope of $B = \frac{b-1}{1-2} = 1 - b$

Slope of $C = \frac{-4+2}{c+b} = \frac{-2}{c+b}$

Slope of A = Slope of B = Slope of C

$2 = 1 - b = \frac{-1}{c+b}$

Chapter 5: Geometry

Choice A is incorrect because it is not the obtained value of b and c. **Choice B** is incorrect because it is not the obtained value of b and c. **Choice C** is incorrect because it is not the obtained value of b and c. **Choice D** is incorrect because it is not the obtained value of b and c.

87 **Choice B is correct** because the sides of the square can be manipulated based on the given information and then multiplied to find the new area. If the square had an area of x, it can be concluded that each side is equal to $\sqrt{x}$ since the area of a square formula is $A = x^2$.

If one side is doubled, its new length would be $2\sqrt{x}$. If the other side is reduced by 3, its new length would be $\sqrt{x} - 3$. Multiplying these two together yields $2\sqrt{x}(\sqrt{x} - 3)$.

Distribute to get $2x - 6\sqrt{x}$ as the new area of the rectangle.

Choice A is incorrect because it results from a math error.
Choice C is incorrect because it results from a math error.
Choice D is incorrect because it results from a math error.
Choice E is incorrect because it results from a math error.

88 **Choice E is correct** because based on the figure it can be concluded that y and z are equal in measure.

In the trapezoid, $x + x + y + y = 360$ since the sum of the angles of a quadrilateral add to 360. Simplifying this would give the expression $2x + 2y = 360$ which simplifies again to be $x + y = 180$. It can also be concluded that $x + z = 180$ since they are adjacent angles.

Setting these two statements equal to each other would yield $x + y = x + z$. Through elimination, it can be concluded that $y = z$.

Choice A is incorrect because, in a trapezoid, opposite angles are not equal. **Choice B** is incorrect because z is an obtuse angle and x is acute. **Choice C** is incorrect because y and z are equal. **Choice D** is incorrect because y is obtuse and x is acute.

89 **Choice B is correct** because since the area of rectangle ABCD is $y(x + 2)$, this must mean that FB is length x. This would give the dimensions of the triangle as having a length of x and a height of y. Plugging this into the area expression for triangles $A = \dfrac{bh}{2}$ would yield $\dfrac{xy}{2}$.

Choice A is incorrect because this would be the area of BDEF. **Choice C** is incorrect because this uses the wrong side lengths. **Choice D** is incorrect because this uses the wrong relationship between the sides. **Choice E** is incorrect because this does not properly relate the values of x and y.

90 **Choice A is correct** because a diagram can be drawn to represent the scenario in order to solve for the diagonal.

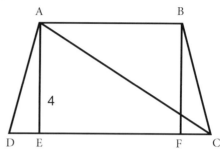

If the area of the trapezoid equals 60, the area formula can be used to evaluate the length of the two bases. The area of a trapezoid equals $A = \left(\dfrac{b_1 + b_2}{2}\right)h$ which means $60 = \left(\dfrac{b_1 + b_2}{2}\right)4$. Simplifying this would give you $30 = b_1 + b_2$.

In the figure, AB and EF would be similar, so let's name them x. This means that DE and FC would $\dfrac{30 - 2x}{2}$ since AB + EF + DE + FC = 30 and DE = FC.

This would simplify to be $15 - x$ as the length of DE and FC. Therefore EC = $x + 15 - x$ which equals 15.

Now using the Pythagorean theorem $a^2 + b^2 = c^2$, you can plug in 4 and 15 to find the diagonal. This would yield $4^2 + 10^2 = c^2$ which equals $241 = c^2$. This means the length of the diagonal is $\sqrt{241}$.

Choice B is incorrect because it results from a math error.
Choice C is incorrect because it results from a math error.
Choice D is incorrect because it results from a math error.
Choice E is incorrect because it results from a math error.

91 **Choice C is correct** because the height of the stacked cubes is 52.

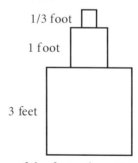

The volume of the first cube = 27 cubic feet
∴ Height of the first cube = 3 feet

The volume of the second cube = 1 cubic foot
∴ Height of the second cube = 1 feet

Practice Set 2 (Medium): Answers & Explanations

The volume of the third cube $\frac{1}{27}$ cubic foot

∴ Height of the third cube = $\frac{1}{3}$ feet

∴ Total height of the stack = 3 + 1 + $\frac{1}{3}$ feet = $4\frac{1}{3}$ feet = 52 inches

Choice A is incorrect because 44 is less than the obtained height of the stacked cubes. **Choice B is incorrect** because 48 is less than the obtained height of the stacked cubes. **Choice D is incorrect** because 56 is greater than the obtained height of the stacked cubes. **Choice E is incorrect** because 60 is greater than the obtained height of the stacked cubes.

92 **Choice E is correct** because (6,8) is on the side AB.

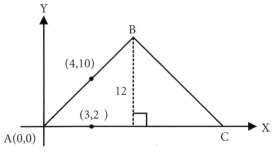

To solve this problem, you need to figure out the ratio between the *x* and *y* values in line segment AB. If you look at the figure, AB is the hypotenuse of a right triangle with a side of 12. Without even using the Pythagorean Theorem, you can tell that this triangle is one of the favorite right triangles: a 3: 4: 5. So this has to be a 9: 12: 15 triangle, and the coordinates of point B are (9, 12). All the points on line segment AB are in a ratio of 9 and 12 (which is the same as 3 to 4). The only answer with that ratio is E(6, 8).

Choice A is incorrect because (3,2) is not on the side AB.
Choice B is incorrect because (3,5) is not on the side AB.
Choice C is incorrect because (4,6) is not on the side AB.
Choice D is incorrect because (4,10) is not on the side AB.

93 **Choice B is correct** because the obtained polygon is a pentagon.
We know that the sum of the interior angles of an n–sided polygon is given by $(n-2) \times 180°$

∴ Each interior angle = $\frac{[(n-2) \times 180°]}{n}$.

Also, we know that the sum of the interior angles of an n–sided polygon is given by $360°$, Irrespective of n.

∴ Each exterior angle = $\frac{360°}{n}$

∴ $\dfrac{\left[\dfrac{(n-2) \times 180°}{n}\right]}{\dfrac{360°}{n}} = \dfrac{3}{2}$

∴ $\dfrac{[(n-2) \times 180°]}{360°} = \dfrac{3}{2}$

∴ $\dfrac{(n-2)}{2} = \dfrac{3}{2}$

∴ $n - 2 = 3$

∴ $n = 5$

Hence the regular polygon is a pentagon.

Choice A is incorrect because Square does not have 5 sides. **Choice C is incorrect** because Hexagon does not have 5 sides. **Choice D is incorrect** because Heptagon does not have 5 sides. **Choice E is incorrect** because Octagon does not have 5 sides.

94 **Choice C is correct** because *x* = 13.

As a rule, for all geometry questions it may be necessary to either redraw the diagram/ add lines/labels etc. We are aware of rules for parallel & transverse lines. Thus, we will have to create a similar situation. This is achieved by drawing a line EF which is parallel to both AB & CD as shown. Now ∠CEF = 4*x*°(Corresponding angles, CD ∥ EF, CE is the transverse) and ∠AEF = 6*x*°. Thus 130°= 10*x*° and *x* = 13

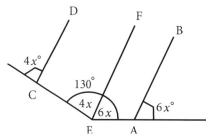

Note: If we do not pay close attention to the fact that AEC is NOT a straight line we may be tempted to say 6*x*° = 180 – 130, and *x* = 8.33 OR 4*x*° = 180 – 130, and *x* = 12.5. Once again it always helps to redraw the diagram provided to you. Remember it may not be the best representation of what you need.

Choice A is incorrect because 8.33 is less than the obtained value of *x*. **Choice B is incorrect** because 12.5 is close but not accurate value of *x*. **Choice D is incorrect** because 26 is greater than the obtained value of *x*. **Choice E is incorrect** because 50 is an overestimation of the obtained value of *x*.

Chapter 5: Geometry

95 **Choice D is correct** because to find the area of the shaded region, you must first find the length of a and b. The diagonal of the rectangle can be found first as it is the diameter of the circle.

If the area of the circle is 1225π, then the radius can be found using $A = \pi r^2$. If $1225\pi = \pi r^2$ then the radius can be found to be 35 since the square root of 1225 is 35. Now create a triangle using the diagonal of the rectangle as the hypotenuse and a and b as the legs. If $b = x$, then $a = \dfrac{x}{2}$. Plugging this into the Pythagorean theorem of $a^2 + b^2 = c^2$ would give you $x^2 + (\dfrac{x}{2})^2 = 70^2$. Simplifying will yield $\dfrac{5x^2}{4} = 4900$. To solve for x, multiply by $\dfrac{4}{5}$ and then square root on both sides to get $x = \sqrt{3920}$.

Thus the sides of the rectangle are $\sqrt{3920}$ and $\dfrac{\sqrt{3920}}{2}$.

To find the area, use the formula $A = bh$ to get $A = \sqrt{3920} \left(\dfrac{\sqrt{3920}}{2}\right) = 1960$.

Choice A is incorrect because it results from a math error.
Choice B is incorrect because it results from a math error.
Choice C is incorrect because it results from a math error.
Choice E is incorrect because it results from a math error.

96 **Choice A is correct** because the obtained volume is 21 cubic inches.

Length of the arc of the sector = the circumference of the base of the cone

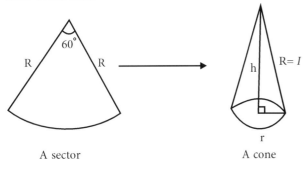

A sector   A cone

Taking R to be the radius of the circle where the sector is extracted and r to be the radius of the base of the cone, we have

Length of the arc of the sector = the circumference of the base of the cone

That is,

$\dfrac{60}{360} \times \pi \times 2R = \pi \times 2r$

Dividing both sides by 2π, we have

$r = \dfrac{60}{360}$ $R = \dfrac{60}{360} \times 9 = \dfrac{3}{2}$ inches

The radius of the sector = the slant height of the cone

The perpendicular height h, slant height l, and the radius of the cone r forms a right-angle triangle where the slant height is the hypotenuse.

Using the Pythagorean Theorem, perpendicular height = $\sqrt{9^2 - 1.5^2} = \sqrt{78.75} = 8.874$

Volume = $\left(\dfrac{1}{3}\right) \times \pi \times \left(\dfrac{3}{2}\right)^2 \times 8.874 = 20.909 \approx 21$ cubic inches

Choice B is incorrect because 50 cubic inches is greater than the obtained volume. **Choice C is incorrect** because 95 cubic inches is greater than the obtained volume. **Choice D is incorrect** because 185 cubic inches is an overestimation of the volume. **Choice E is incorrect** because 191 cubic inches is an overestimation of the volume.

97 **Choice C is correct** because the obtained area is 128. Circumference = πd.

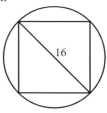

$16\pi = \pi d$

$d = 16$

Diameter of circle = diagonal of square

Area of square = $\dfrac{1}{2}$ (product of diagonals)

$= \dfrac{1}{2} d_1 \times d_2$

$= \dfrac{1}{2}(16)(16) = 128$

Therefore, the area of the square is 128.

Alternate method: assume x for side of square.

Using Pythagorean Theorem for isosceles right triangles gives $x^2 + x^2 = 16^2$, $2x^2 = 256$, and $x^2 = 128$, which is the area of the square.

Choice A is incorrect because 32 is less than the obtained area of the square. **Choice B is incorrect** because 64 is less than the obtained area of the square. **Choice D is incorrect** because 256 an overestimation of the obtained are of the square. **Choice E is incorrect** because 512 an overestimation of the obtained are of the square.

Practice Set 2 (Medium): Answers & Explanations

98 **Choice D is correct** because $\dfrac{1}{\pi\sqrt{\pi}}$ is the obtained expression for the diameter of the circle.

The formulas to use in this problem are:

Divide both sides by π^3.

Area of a square = s^2

Area of a circle = πr^2

Diameter = $2r$

Area of square of side $\left(\dfrac{1}{\pi}\right) = \left(\dfrac{1}{\pi}\right)^2 = \dfrac{1}{\pi^2}$

We want to find radius of circle whose area equals $\dfrac{1}{\pi^2}$

Substitute πr^2 for the area of the circle.

Area of circle = Area of square

$\pi r^2 = \dfrac{1}{\pi^2}$ Solve for r. Multiply both side by π^2

$\pi^2(\pi r^2) = \pi^2\left(\dfrac{1}{\pi^2}\right) = \pi^3 r^2 = 1$

$r^2 = \dfrac{1}{\pi^3}$

$\sqrt{r^2} = \sqrt{\dfrac{1}{\pi^3}}$ Take square root on both the sides

$r = \dfrac{\sqrt{1}}{\sqrt{\pi^3}} = \dfrac{1}{\sqrt{\pi^2 \cdot \pi}} = \dfrac{1}{\pi\sqrt{\pi}}$ Simplify the radical

$d = 2r; d = \dfrac{2}{\pi\sqrt{\pi}}$

The answer is (D).

Choice A is incorrect because $\dfrac{1}{\sqrt{\pi}}$ is not equivalent to the obtained expression. **Choice B** is incorrect because $\dfrac{2}{\sqrt{\pi}}$ is not equivalent to the obtained expression. **Choice C** is incorrect because $\dfrac{1}{\pi\sqrt{\pi}}$ is not equivalent to the obtained expression. **Choice E** is incorrect because $\dfrac{1}{\pi^3}$ is not equivalent to the obtained expression.

99 **Choice D is correct** because $x = 5\sqrt{3}$.

Draw a straight line from point H to point F, to divide the figure into two right triangles.

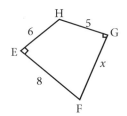

ΔEFH is a $3 - 4 - 5$ right triangle with a hypotenuse of length 10.

Use the Pythagorean Theorem in ΔFGH to find x:

$x^2 + 5^2 = 10^2$

$x^2 + 5^2 = 100$

$x^2 = 75$

$x = \sqrt{75}$

$x = \sqrt{25}\sqrt{3}$

$x = 5\sqrt{3}$

Choice A is incorrect because 4 is less than the obtained value of x. **Choice B** is incorrect because $3\sqrt{3}$ is less than the obtained value of x. **Choice C** is incorrect because $3\sqrt{5}$ is less than the obtained value of x. **Choice E** is incorrect because 9 is greater than the obtained value of x.

100 **Choices B and C are correct** because it is a true statement.

Area of $\Delta AED = 12 = \dfrac{1}{2}(6)(x) \rightarrow x = 4$

$z^2 = 3^2 + 4^2 \rightarrow z = 5$

Choice A is incorrect because it is a false statement when x = 4.5. **Choice D** is incorrect because z is not equal to 6.

101 **Choices C and D are correct** because Area of ΔABC is >300 and Area of ΔABC is <350.

Let us plot all the points on the coordinate plane.

The point A is the origin on the coordinate plane.

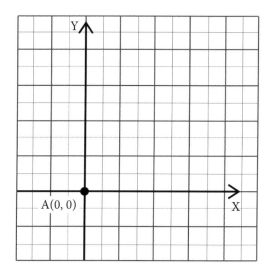

Chapter 5: Geometry

The point B has its *x* coordinate = 0, that shows it lies somewhere on the *y*–axis.

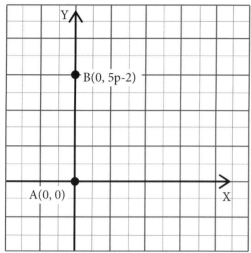

∠ABC = 90°, then △ABC will look like:

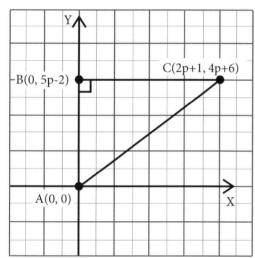

Since line BC is horizontal, the *y* coordinates of point B and C will be equal.

$5p - 2 = 4p + 6$

$5p - 4p = 6 + 2$

$p = 8$

Substituting the value of p to find the coordinates of B and C:

B $(0, 5p - 2)$

y coordinate of B = $5 \times 8 - 2 = 40 - 2 = 38$

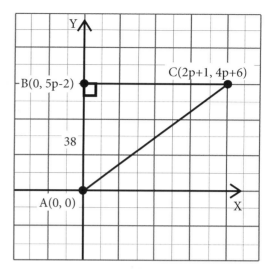

Similarly, C $(2p + 2, 4p + 6)$

x coordinate of C = $2 \times 8 + 2 = 16 + 2 = 18$

y coordinate of C = $4 \times 8 + 6 = 32 + 6 = 38$

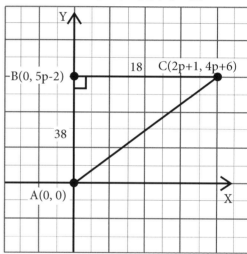

Area of Triangle = $\dfrac{base \times height}{2}$

Area of ∠ABC = $\dfrac{18 \times 38}{2} = 9 \times 38 = 342$

Options C and D are correct.

Choice A is incorrect because the area is not within the obtained range. **Choice B** is incorrect because the area is not within the obtained range. **Choice E** is incorrect because the area is not within the obtained range. **Choice F** is incorrect because the area is not within the obtained range.

Practice Set 2 (Medium): Answers & Explanations

102 **Choices A and C are correct** because $x + y < 7$ and $y < 4$ are true statements based on the given figure.

From the Pythagorean Theorem $z = \sqrt{5^2 - 4^2} = 3$

Since the triangles are similar, we can calculate the variables using ratios:

$\dfrac{5.25}{4+x} = \dfrac{3}{4} \rightarrow 3(4+x) = (4)(5.25) \rightarrow x = 3$

$\dfrac{5.25}{5+x} = \dfrac{3}{5} \rightarrow 3(5+y) = (5)(5.25) \rightarrow y = 3.75$

Answers: (A), (C)

Choice B is incorrect because it is not true for the given figure. **Choice D is incorrect** because it is not true for the given figure. **Choice E is incorrect** because it is not true for the given figure.

103 **Choices B and D are correct** because the measure of $\angle A$ is within the given range.

In the figure, $\angle CDF$ and $\angle EDB$ are vertically opposite angles. Therefore, they are of equal measure.

$\angle CDF = \angle EDB = 80°$

Consider ΔDEB.

$\angle EDB = 80°$ and $\angle DEB = 40°$

Since the three angles of a triangle add to give 180°,

$\angle DBE = 180° - 40° - 80°$
$= 180° - 120°$
$= 60°$

Consider the cyclic quadrilateral GEBC. Opposite angles of a quadrilateral add to 180°.

$\angle CGE + \angle CBE = 180°$
$\angle A + \angle CBE = 180°$
$\angle A = 180° - 60° = 120°$

Among the options, statements B and D give the measure of $\angle A$ correctly.

Choice A is incorrect because the measure of $\angle A$ does not fall within the given range. **Choice C is incorrect** because the measure of $\angle A$ does not fall within the given range. **Choice E is incorrect** because the measure of $\angle A$ does not fall within the given range.

104 **Choices A, B, C and D are correct** because it fits into the hoop.

Find the radius of each disc using the formula: $C = 2\pi r$

A: $\pi = 2\pi r \rightarrow r = \dfrac{1}{2}$

B: $10\pi = 2\pi r \rightarrow r = 5$

C: $12\pi = 2\pi r \rightarrow r = 6$

D: $20\pi = 2\pi r \rightarrow r = 10$

E: $50\pi = 2\pi r \rightarrow r = 25$

Find the area of each disc using the formula: $A = \pi r^2$

A: $A = \pi \left(\dfrac{1}{2}\right)^2 = \pi/4 \approx 0.79$

B: $A = \pi(5)^2 = 25\pi \approx 78.54$

C: $A = \pi(6)^2 = 36\pi \approx 113.1$

D: $A = \pi(10)^2 = 100\pi \approx 314.16$

E: $A = \pi(25)^2 = 625\pi \approx 1,963.46$

To save time, you can alternatively start with finding the area of disc C, since the options will increase. If C is too high to fit, D and E will be too high as well, and you only need to check A and B. Since C is small enough to fit, so are A and B, so you just need to check D and E.

The answers are A, B, C, D.

Choice E is incorrect because it does not fit into the hoop. **Choice F is incorrect** because disc C fits into the hoop and disc D does not.

105 **Choices B, C and F is correct** because they are possible degree measures of the marked angles.

Take $\angle POQ = 100°$

Then $\angle QOR = 80°$ (Linear Pair)

But $\angle OQR = \angle ORQ$ (Since the (half) diagonals of a rectangle are equal. i. e $\angle OQ = OR$)

By angle sum property $\angle QOR + 2\angle OQR = 180°$

$80° + 2\angle OQR = 180°$

$2\angle OQR = 180° - 80°$

$\angle OQR = 50°$

But it is given as, 40° in the answer choice. Hence Option (A) is not correct.

Similarly, we can arrive at the angle pairs as
110°, 55°; 120°, 60°; 130°, 65°; 140°, 70°; 150°, 75°

So the answer choices B, C, and F are correct.

Choice A is incorrect because it is not a possible degree measure of the marked angles. **Choice D is incorrect** because it is not a possible degree measure of the marked angles. **Choice E is incorrect** because it is not a possible degree measure of the marked angles.

106 **Choices B and D are correct** because 17cm and 31cm are the obtained length and width.

Let width $= x$

Then length $= 2x - 3$

Perimeter = 2(x + 2x − 3) = 6x − 6

According to the condition,

6x − 6 = 96

x = 17cm

Width = 17cm and length = 31cm

Choice A is incorrect because 15 is not a possible value of either the length or the width of the rectangle. **Choice C is incorrect** because 27 is not a possible value of either the length or the width of the rectangle. **Choice E is incorrect** because 34 is not a possible value of either the length or the width of the rectangle. **Choice F is incorrect** because 37 is not a possible value of either the length or the width of the rectangle.

107 **Choices C and D are correct** because length will be 6 cm and width will be 4 cm.

Let x be the width and y be the length

Perimeter = $2x + 2y = 20$

$x = 10 − y$

Area = $xy = 24$

Putting the value of x

$y(10 − y) = 24$

$10y − y^2 = 24$

$y^2 − 10y + 24 = 0$

$(y − 6)(y − 4) = 0$

Length will be 6 cm and width will be 4 cm.

Choice A is incorrect because it is not a possible value for the length or width of the rectangle. **Choice B is incorrect** because it is not a possible value for the length or width of the rectangle. **Choice E is incorrect** because it is not a possible value for the length or width of the rectangle. **Choice F is incorrect** because it is not a possible value for the length or width of the rectangle.

108 **Choices B, F and G are correct** because these statements are true based on the figure.

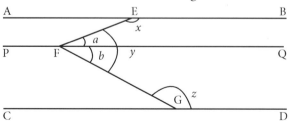

Given AB||CD

Draw a line PFQ parallel to both AB and CD.

Now let EFQ = a and $\angle GFQ = b$

$x + a = 180°$ (co-interior angles)

$b + z = 180°$ (co-interior angles)

$\angle x + a + b + z = 360°$

But $a + b = y$

Hence $x + y + z = 360°$

Choice B is correct because $x + y + z$ together complete a full rotation around point F, so their sum can be 360°.

But y is less than 180° (since EFG is not a straight line)

$\angle x + z < 180°$

Also, $x + z < 360°$ since $y > 0$

Therefore, $x + z$ must lie between 180° and 360°

Hence (C),(D), and (E) are not correct as each value is less than or equal to 180°

Also, Choices F and G are correct since the values lie between 180° and 360°.

Choice A is incorrect because $x + y + z = 270°$ is not consistent with the full angle formed around point F. **Choice C is incorrect** because $x + z = 150°$ does not align with standard relationships in this parallel-line setup. **Choice D is incorrect** because $x + z = 170°$ is not geometrically supported by the parallel lines and transversal structure. **Choice G is incorrect** because $x + z = 300°$ exceeds possible combinations based on interior and exterior angle rules. **Choice H is incorrect** because $x + z = 360°$ would imply a full circle without including angle y, which contradicts the structure of the diagram.

109 **Choices C and D are correct.** The diagonal of a cube can be represented as $s\sqrt{2}$. If the diagonal is between $4\sqrt{3}$ and $4\sqrt{15}$, then the possible side lengths would be $s\sqrt{2} = 4\sqrt{3}$ and $s\sqrt{2} = 4\sqrt{15}$. Simplifying both these expressions will yield the range for side length as $\dfrac{4\sqrt{3}}{\sqrt{2}}$ and $\dfrac{4\sqrt{15}}{\sqrt{2}}$ which is $2\sqrt{6} \leq s \leq 2\sqrt{30}$. Volume of a cube is equal to s^3 so using this range of side lengths would yield a range for volume of $(2\sqrt{6})^3 \leq V \leq (2\sqrt{30})^3$. This is approximately $117 \leq V \leq 1315$

Choice C is correct because it falls within the range for the volume. Choice D is correct because it falls within the range for the volume.

Practice Set 2 (Medium): Answers & Explanations

Choice A is incorrect because it falls outside the range for the volume. **Choice B is correct** because it falls outside the range for the volume. **Choice E is incorrect** because it falls outside the range for the volume.

110 **The correct answer is 4.**

We are given

(1)   Area of triangle $ABC = 18$

(2)   Area of triangle $ABC = 1/2 (AB)(BC)$

Replace the value of the area from (1) in (2).

$1/2(AB)(BC) = 18$

Multiply each side by 2.

(3) $(AB)(BC) = 36$

We are given

(4) $BF = 1/3(AB)$

(5) $EF = 2/3(BC)$

The area of the right triangle $DEF = (EF)(BF)$

Replace equivalents of BF and EF from (4) and (5) in this equation.

Area of triangle $DEF = 1/2 [1/3 (AB)][2/3 (BC)] = 1/9(AB)(BC)$

Replace the known value from (3) in this equation, and then simplify.

Area of the triangle $DEF = 1/9(36) = 4$

111 **The correct answer is 8m.** The area of a circle is πr^2. Area varies as the square of the radius. If the area becomes 8 times, the radius, and thus the diameter, becomes $\sqrt{8}$ times or $2\sqrt{2}$ times. The diameter of another circle having 8 times the area of the first circle becomes $2\sqrt{2} \times 2\sqrt{2} = 8m$.

112 **The correct answer is 21.9 meters.**

Consider the ΔPSR.

The segments PS, SR and PR will be in the ratio $1:\sqrt{3}:2$ respectively, considering that the angles of the triangle are $30°$, $60°$ and $90°$

It is given that PR measures 20 meters.

$\dfrac{SR}{PR} = \dfrac{\sqrt{3}}{2}$

$SR = \dfrac{\sqrt{3}}{2} \times 20 = 17.32$ meters

Similarly,

$\dfrac{PS}{PR} = \dfrac{1}{2}$

$PS = \dfrac{1}{2} \times 20 = 10$ meters

Now, consider the ΔQSR.

By Pythagoras theorem, $QR^2 = SR^2 + SQ^2$

$21^2 = 17.32^2 + SQ^2$

$SQ^2 = 21^2 - 17.32^2$

$= 441 - 299.98$

$= 141.02$

$= \sqrt{141.02}$

$= 11.88$ meters

From the figure, it can be seen that $PQ = PS + SQ$.

$PQ = 10 + 11.88 = 21.88$ meters or 21.9 meters

113 **The correct answer is 525 square units.** Let the side of the small square be x units. Then the side of the larger square A will be $(x+10)$ units.

Now the sum of the areas of A and B = 625 square units (Given)

$(x + 10)(x + 10) + x(x) = 625$

$x^2 + 20x + 100 + x^2 = 625$

$2x^2 + 20x = 525$

Now length of each rectangle = $(x + 10)$

Width of each rectangle = x

Area of one rectangle = $(x + 10)x = x^2 + 10x$

Sum of the areas of the two rectangles C and D = $2(x^2 + 10x) = 2x^2 + 20x = 525$ from (1)

114 **The correct answer is 70°.**

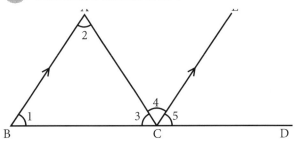

Name the angles, 1,2,3,4, and 5 as in the figure.

CE is the bisector

$\angle 4 = \angle 5 = 70°$

AB||CE (Given)

BCD is a transversal

$\angle 1 = \angle 5$ (Corresponding angles)

AC is a transversal

Chapter 5: Geometry

∠2 = ∠4 (Alternate interior angles)

Hence, ∠1 = ∠2 = ∠4 = ∠5 = 70°

∠BAC = 70°

115 **The correct answer is 2** because the volume formula $V = \pi r^2 h$ can be used to find the radius. First, use x as the diameter of the can and $3x$ as the height. Since the radius is half of the diameter it can be expressed as $\frac{x}{2}$.

Plug in the known values to solve for x: $48\pi = \pi\left(\frac{x}{2}\right)^2 (3x)$. This simplifies to be $48\pi = \frac{3\pi x^3}{4}$. Multiply both sides by 4 to get $192\pi = 3\pi x^3$. Divide by 3π and take the cube root of both sides to find $x = 4$. Since the x is the diameter, divide by 2 to get the radius of 2.

Practice Set 3 (Hard): Answers & Explanations

116 **Choice A is correct** because a rectangle can be drawn around the triangle and then the outer triangles can be subtracted from the area of the rectangle to get the area of the triangle. Here are all of the dimensions of these shapes:

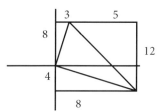

The area of the rectangle would be equal to its base of 8 times its height of 12 which equals 96. All of the triangle areas can be found to be 12, 30, and 16 using the area of a triangle formula of $A = \frac{bh}{2}$. Adding these up and subtracting from 96 yields the area of the triangle which would be 96 − (12 + 30 + 16) = 38.

Choice B is incorrect because this results from a miscalculation. **Choice C is incorrect** because this is the wrong area. **Choice D is incorrect** because this results from a miscalculation. **Choice E is incorrect** because this is the area of the rectangle that can be drawn to encompass the triangle.

117 **Choice D is correct** because the length of the radius of the circle can be used to evaluate the length of the triangle using the relationship drawn out below:

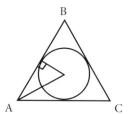

Since the area of the circle is $\frac{9}{16}\pi$, the radius can be found using the area formula $A = \pi r^2$. This would mean $\frac{9}{16}\pi = \pi r^2$. Dividing by π and taking the square root would give a radius of $\frac{3}{4}$. This means the shortest side of the 30-60-90 triangle in the diagram would be $\frac{3}{4}$. Using the ratio of x–$x\sqrt{3}$ –$2x$, this would mean the longest leg of the 30-60-90 triangle would be $\frac{3\sqrt{3}}{4}$. This makes up half the side length AB so doubling it would result in an answer of $\frac{3\sqrt{3}}{2}$.

Choice A is incorrect because this results from a miscalculation. **Choice B is incorrect** because this results from a miscalculation. **Choice C is incorrect** because this results from a miscalculation. **Choice E is incorrect** because this results from a miscalculation.

118 **Choice C is correct** because using the process of elimination can help to identify the correct value for y. It can be determined that x equals 30 degrees since the angles of a triangle must add up to 180. The given angles of 90 and 60 would result in 180 − 90 − 60 = 30 for the value of angle x.

Using the process of elimination, if y was 140, then the supplementary angle to y would be 40 since 180 − 140 = 40. This would mean the 90-degree angle was split to be 80 and 10 which would work for all angles.

Choice A is incorrect because y needs to be greater than 90. **Choice B is incorrect** because this would result in the smaller triangle having more than 180 degrees. **Choice D is incorrect** because this would not complete the correct angle measurements for each of the triangles. **Choice E is incorrect** because this would make the smaller triangle have more than 180 degrees.

119 **Choice E is correct** because the obtained answer is $24\pi + 12$.

From the figure, we realize that CF is an arc from a circle whose diameter is AF and whose center is at E. The circumference of the circle E is four times the length of the arc CF according to the given fact. If we multiply the length of arc CF by 4, it gives us the circumference of the circle E.

Circumference of Circle E = 4[Length of arc (CF)]

= 4(3π)

= 12π

If we divide the circumference of the circle E by π, the result is the diameter of the circle.

Diameter of Circle E = $\frac{12\pi}{\pi}$ = 12

Now, we have a diameter of the circle E, then we can calculate the length of the semicircle ALF.

Length of Semicircle ALF = $\frac{\text{Circumference of Circle E}}{2}$

= $\frac{\pi(12)}{2}$

= 6π

The radius of the circle F is equal to the diameter of the circle E. Thus, Radius of Circle F = AF

Doubling AF gives a diameter of the circle F.

Diameter of Circle F = 2(AF)

= 2(12)

= 24

Having a diameter of the circle F, calculate its circumference.

Circumference of Circle F = π(24) = 24π

Length of the arc AGD is $\frac{3}{4}$ the circumference of the circle F.

Therefore, Length of arc AGD = $\frac{3}{4}$ (24π) = 18π

From the given figure, Perimeter of the figure AGDFLA = Length of arc AGD + DF + Length of Semicircle ALF

Replace the measure of each arc in the equation above, knowing that DF is a radius of the circle F and is found to be 12.

Perimeter of the figure AGDFLA = 18π + 12 + 6π

= 24π + 12

Choice A is incorrect because 20π + 8 is not the obtained perimeter of the figure. **Choice B is incorrect because** 12π + 8 is less than the obtained perimeter of the figure. **Choice C is incorrect** because 16π + 6 is not equivalent to the obtained perimeter of the figure. **Choice D is** incorrect because 22π + 12 is less than the obtained perimeter of the figure.

120 **Choice D is correct** because the area between the circle and the polygon is $16\pi - 12\sqrt{3}$.

If you have a regular polygon with exterior angles measuring 60 degrees, this means you have 6 angles and therefore 6 sides, making it a hexagon. This is because every polygon's exterior angles add up to 360, so if each exterior angle is 60°, then 360/60 = 6 and there are 6 angles. Therefore, a hexagon is inscribed in the circle. The diagram will then look as follows:

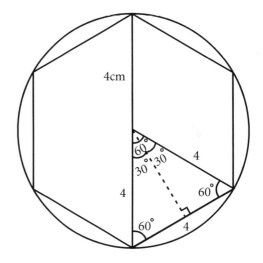

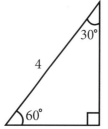

$4 = 2x \leftarrow 90°$

$2 = x \leftarrow 30°$

$2\sqrt{3} = x\sqrt{3} \leftarrow 60°$

By using the triangles formed inside the hexagon, and the 30–60–90 relationship, we find the height of one of the triangles to be $2\sqrt{3}$, and the base to be 2. The area of just one of the triangles is then $A = \frac{2\sqrt{3} + 2}{2} = 2\sqrt{3}$. Multiply this by 6 to form the entire hexagon to them obtain $12\sqrt{3}$. The area of the circle is $A = \pi r^2$, where r is 4. This becomes 16π. We then subtract the area of the hexagon from the area of the circle to get $16\pi - 12\sqrt{3}$, which is Choice D.

Choice A is incorrect because $16\pi - 2\sqrt{3}$ is greater than the obtained area between the circle and the polygon. **Choice B is incorrect** because 16π is greater than the obtained area between the circle and the polygon. **Choice C is incorrect** because $32\sqrt{3}\pi$ is greater than the obtained area between the circle and the polygon.

Chapter 5: Geometry

Choice E is incorrect because $2\sqrt{3}$ is less than the obtained area between the circle and the polygon.

121 **Choice B is correct** because the area of quadrilaterals is represented by $AEJI = \dfrac{(Area\ BCGF\ -\ Area\ ABHI)}{\sqrt{3}}$.

$m\angle BAC = 90°$ So, ABC is a right angle triangle

$m\angle ACB = 30°$, sine of $m\angle ACB = \sin 30° = \dfrac{1}{2}$,

$\dfrac{AB}{BC} = \dfrac{1}{2}$, if $BC = s$, then $AB = \dfrac{s}{2}$

We can apply Pythagoras' theorem in $\triangle ABC$.

$BC^2 = AB^2 + AC^2$

$AC^2 = s^2 - \dfrac{s^2}{4}$

$AC = s\dfrac{\sqrt{3}}{2}$

We can now calculate the area of each of the squares:

Area $BCGF = BC^2 = s^2$

Area $ABHI = AB^2 = \dfrac{s^2}{4}$

Area $ACDE = AC^2 = \dfrac{3s^2}{4}$

Choice A is incorrect because it does not represent the area of the given quadrilateral. **Choice C is incorrect** because it does not represent the area of the given quadrilateral. **Choice D is incorrect** because it does not represent the Area of the given quadrilateral. **Choice E is incorrect** because it does not represent the Area of the given quadrilateral.

122 **Choice B is correct.**

Area of a trapezium is calculated using the formula $\dfrac{1}{2} \times h \times (a+b)$, where h is the height and a and b are the dimensions of the sides.

Area of the original trapezium

$A = \dfrac{1}{2} \times 8 \times (10+14) = 96$ square units.

Area of the remodeled toddler section = 96 + 96 = 192 square units

The change represents a scaling by a factor of 2. Therefore, we want to look for an answer choice that doubles just one dimension.

Option B: The height was doubled.

Height after remodeling = 2 × 8 = 16 units

Area after remodeling

$\dfrac{1}{2} \times 16 \times (10+14) = 192$ square units

Choice A is incorrect because only the height was doubled. **Choice C is incorrect** because length of the parallel sides and the height were not multiplied by four. **Choice D is incorrect** because the height was doubled and not multiplied by four. **Choice E is incorrect** because lengths of the parallel sides were not increased by 5 m.

123 **Choice B is correct** because using the equilateral triangle's area can help identify the length of each side of the hexagon.

The formula for the area of an equilateral triangle is $A = \dfrac{\sqrt{3}}{4}s^2$. Setting this equal to the known area would give you $81\sqrt{3} = \dfrac{\sqrt{3}}{4}s^2$. Multiply both sides by $\dfrac{4}{\sqrt{3}}$ and take the square root to find the side length of the equilateral triangle to be 18.

Based on the orientation of the equilateral triangle inside the hexagon, it can be concluded that the hexagon's side length is half the length of the equilateral triangle's side length. This means the side length of the hexagon is $\dfrac{18}{2} = 9$.

The formula for the area of a hexagon is $A = \dfrac{3\sqrt{3}}{2}s^2$ which yields $A = \dfrac{3\sqrt{3}}{2}(9)^2 = \dfrac{243\sqrt{3}}{2}$.

Choice A is incorrect because this is the area of the triangle. **Choice C is incorrect** because this results from a math error. **Choice D is incorrect** because this results from a math error. **Choice E is incorrect** because this results from a math error.

124 **Choice E is correct** because the obtained answer is $144(4 - \pi)$.

The amount of material that will remain after the circles are cut out is the area of the entire piece of material, minus the total area of the circles that were cut out. The area of the circles that were cut out will be equal to the area of one of the circles times the total number of circle.

To minimize the amount of wasted material, the diameter of the circle cut out should divide evenly into both the length and width of the cloth. Therefore, what you're really looking for is the greatest common factor of the length and width. To find the greatest common factor of 16 and 36, break down each number to its prime factorization and then multiply together all the prime factors that the two have in common. In this case, 16 and 36 share 2 prime factors of 2, so their greatest common factor is 4. Since 4 goes into 16 and 36 nine times, a total of (4)(9) = 36 circles with diameter of each circle is 4, its radius is 2 and the area of each circle is π r². Since the diameter of each circle is 4, its radius is 2 and the area of each circle is π × (2)² = 4π. So, the material that will be left over is (36)(16) − 36(4π) = 26(16 − 4π) = 144(4 − π).

Choice A is incorrect because 576 (π − 1) is not equivalent to the obtained answer. **Choice B is incorrect** because 4 (144 − π) is not equivalent to the obtained answer. **Choice C is incorrect** because 144π is not equivalent to the obtained answer. **Choice D is incorrect** because 144 − π is not equivalent to the obtained answer.

125 **Choice A, C and E are correct.** The area of the small triangle is found by using 45–45–90 side relationships to get a height of $\sqrt{2}$ and a base of $\sqrt{2}$. The area of the small triangle is therefore $A = \frac{b \times h}{2} = \frac{\sqrt{2}\sqrt{2}}{2} = 1$ square cm. Choice A is correct. The area of the larger triangle is also found using 45–45–90, and the length of the hypotenuse is 8 using the midsegment properties. The base is therefore $4\sqrt{2}$ and the height is therefore $4\sqrt{2}$. The area is therefore $A = \frac{b \times h}{2} = \frac{4\sqrt{2} \times 4\sqrt{2}}{2} = 16$ square cm, not 4 square cm. B is incorrect. The area of the hexagon is found by creating 6 equilateral triangles, and using 30–60–90 relationships, you can find the heigh to be $2\sqrt{3}$ and the base is the length of the side of the hexagon, 4cm. The area of the triangle is then $A = \frac{b \times h}{2} = \frac{4 \times 2\sqrt{3}}{2} = 4\sqrt{3}$ Multiply this by 6 to get the total area of the hexagon, which is $24\sqrt{3}$ square cm. Choice C is therefore correct. Because the hexagon is regular, the value of each angle is Angle = $\frac{180 \times (n-2)}{n} = \frac{180 \times (6-2)}{6}$. The total angle is 120, made up of x and 45. Therefore, x = 75 and E is correct.

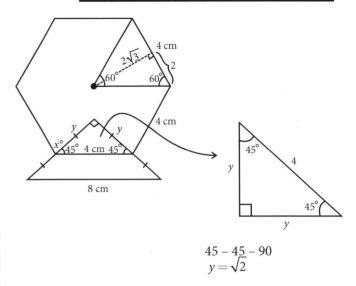

$$45 - 45 - 90$$
$$y = \sqrt{2}$$

Choice B is incorrect because the statement does not satisfy the conditions of the problem. **Choice D is incorrect** because the statement does not satisfy the conditions of the problem. **Choice F is incorrect** because the statement does not satisfy the conditions of the problem.

126 **Choices B, C and D are correct.** The maximum and minimum distance would occur when the circle has the largest radius. Since the circle's center sits 9 below the point, its largest radius could be 8. This would leave a distance of 1 between the circle and the point. This would mean the maximum value would be from (5,5) to (5,−12) which would be a distance of 17. Any values between 1 and 17 would work.

Choice B is correct because it falls within the possible range. Choice C is correct because it falls within the possible range. Choice D is correct because it falls within the possible range.

Choice A is incorrect because this would mean the point falls on the circle, which is not true. **Choice E is incorrect** because this falls outside the possible range. **Choice F is incorrect** because this falls outside the possible range.

127 **Choices A and C are correct.**

Choice A is correct because if E is the midpoint of the diagonal AC, then it is likely that the shape is a square.

Choice C is correct because using the side, angle, side theorem of triangles, this statement can be proven to be correct. Since E is the midpoint, that would make AE and EC congruent. Angle G and angle F are right angles so they are congruent. Finally, side AG and EF are also congruent.

Choice B is incorrect because there is not enough information to prove Triangle GHE is congruent to Triangle DHF. Choice D is incorrect because there is not enough information to prove Triangle HEF is an equilateral triangle.

128 The correct answer is 0.4. From the geometry, we can determine that $\sin(\theta) = \frac{1}{2}$, or $\theta = 30°$.

The area of the triangle = $(\sqrt{3})(1) = \sqrt{3}$

Area of entire circle (with 360° angle about the center) = $\pi(2^2) = 4\pi$

Area of arc of circle (with 300° angle about the center) = $\frac{300°}{360°}(4\pi) = \frac{10}{3}\pi$

Area of shaded portion of circle = (Area of entire circle) − (Area of arc, shaded grey) − (Area of triangle, shaded white)

$= 4\pi - \frac{10}{3}\pi - \sqrt{3} = 0.3623 \approx 0.4$ (with 1 decimal place accuracy)

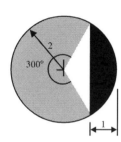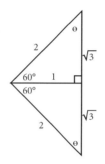

The correct answer is 0.4.

129 The correct answer is 32 because using a diagram to evaluate the circles can help with solving.

By drawing out and connecting the radius and centers, two triangles form. The Pythagorean theorem can be used to evaluate the missing leg of each triangle to determine the distance between the two centers.

For the first triangle, using the Pythagorean theorem $a^2 + b^2 = c^2$ would yield $9^2 + b^2 = 16^2$ means b = 13.23.

For the second triangle, using the Pythagorean theorem $a^2 + b^2 = c^2$ would yield $9^2 + b^2 = 21^2$ means b = 18.97.

Add these two lengths together to get 13.23 + 18.97 = 32.2 which rounds to 32.

130 The correct answer is 473.21 square units. To solve the area of the figure, break down the figure, then solve for their areas. The figure is a combination of a square and two right triangles.

The area of a square is given by the formula $A_{square} = a^2$. Substituting $a = 10\sqrt{3}$ into the formula yields $A_{square} = (10\sqrt{3})^2 = 300\,squared\,units$.

The area of a triangle is given by the formula $A_{triangle} = \frac{1}{2}bh$. The triangles ADF and CEB is a 90–60–30 right triangles with the same dimensions. AF and EC are the longer sides that is the square root of 3 times the shorter sides DF and EB. Thus, $DF = EB = 10$. Substituting the values into the formula $A_{triangle} = \frac{1}{2}(10)(10\sqrt{3}) = 50\sqrt{3}\,squared\,units$. Multiplying the result by 2 since there are two triangles yields $A_{triangles} = 2(50\sqrt{3}) = 100\sqrt{3}\,squared\,units$.

Adding the areas together results in

$A_{total} = A_{square} + A_{triangles} = 300 + 100\sqrt{3} = 473.21\,square\,units$.

Chapter 6
Data Analysis

Chapter 6: Data Analysis

Practice Set 1: Easy

1. There are 500 employees in an organization. For a charity they donated a total of $9000. If 300 employees donated at least $15 and 180 employees donated at least $20, and x is the maximum average amount the remaining 20 employees could have donated.

Quantity A	Quantity B
x	$40

   Ⓐ Quantity A is greater.
   Ⓑ Quantity B is greater.
   Ⓒ The two quantities are equal.
   Ⓓ The relationship cannot be determined from the information given.

2. The average (arithmetic mean) of 55 consecutive numbers is 672.

Quantity A	Quantity B
Median of the 55 numbers	672

   Ⓐ Quantity A is greater.
   Ⓑ Quantity B is greater.
   Ⓒ The two quantities are equal.
   Ⓓ The relationship cannot be determined from the information given.

3. Data Set A consists of the values 4, 5, 6, and a and has a mean of 5.

Quantity A	Quantity B
The mode of Data Set A	a

   Ⓐ Quantity A is greater.
   Ⓑ Quantity B is greater.
   Ⓒ The two quantities are equal.
   Ⓓ The relationship cannot be determined from the information given.

4. The median of a data set of heights was 66 inches. The tallest person in the data set was 75 inches and the shortest person in the data set was 60 inches.

Quantity A	Quantity B
The average height of the data set	66

   Ⓐ Quantity A is greater.
   Ⓑ Quantity B is greater.
   Ⓒ The two quantities are equal.
   Ⓓ The relationship cannot be determined from the information given.

5. A pack of candies contains 5 yellow, 3 pink and 7 white candies. Two candies are taken from the pack without replacement.

Quantity A	Quantity B
Probability of drawing a yellow candy, followed by a 1 pink candy	Probability of drawing 2 white candies

   Ⓐ Quantity A is greater.
   Ⓑ Quantity B is greater.
   Ⓒ The two quantities are equal.
   Ⓓ The relationship cannot be determined from the information given.

6. There are two options for the field trip that students can choose from. If they choose Option A, they will have 3 different meal choices and 2 different transportation methods. If they choose Option B they will have 2 different meal choices and 2 different transportation methods.

Quantity A	Quantity B
The total combination of choices of field trips, meals, and transportation	20

   Ⓐ Quantity A is greater.
   Ⓑ Quantity B is greater.
   Ⓒ The two quantities are equal.
   Ⓓ The relationship cannot be determined from the information given.

Practice Set 1: Easy

7 A design contains a variety of polygons. Of the polygons, 45% are quadrilaterals. Of the quadrilaterals, 75% are squares.

Quantity A	Quantity B
Percent of polygons that are not square quadrilaterals	30%

- A) Quantity A is greater.
- B) Quantity B is greater.
- C) The two quantities are equal.
- D) The relationship cannot be determined from the information given.

8

Region	Sales Amount (USD) 2015	Sales Amount (USD) 2020
North America	25,090	36,050
Europe	18,520	23,170
Asia	15,000	13,950
South America	9,030	10,520
Africa	6,510	7,270

Sales Percentages in North America by Subregion in 2015

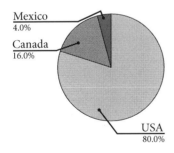

For sales in 2020, which of the following is closest to the ratio of sales in Asia compared to the sales in Africa?

- A) 1 to 2
- B) 2 to 3
- C) 5 to 3
- D) 3 to 2
- E) 2 to 1

Questions 9 and 10 are based on the following graph.

Class Size	Frequency
10-15	10
16-20	12
21-25	22
26-30	21

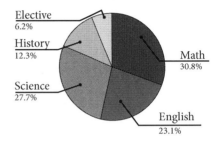

9 Based on the data, what is the median class size?

Indicate all such answers.

- A) 12
- B) 20
- C) 22
- D) 24
- E) 26
- F) 31

10 The class sizes come from all of the course offerings. Of the math courses offered, at least 20% will be taught by a student teacher. How many math courses are taught by a student teacher?

Indicate all such answers.

- A) 2
- B) 4
- C) 8
- D) 10
- E) 12
- F) 21

Chapter 6: Data Analysis

Questions 11 to 13 are based on the following graph.

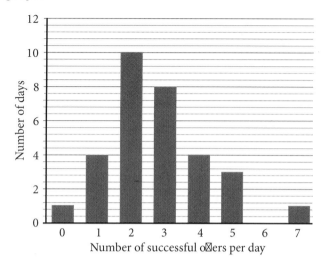

11. What is the probability that Michael will make 7 successful offers in any given day? (Round off to 3 decimal places)

    A) 0.032
    B) 0.100
    C) 0.125
    D) 0.143
    E) 0.169

12. What is the probability that Michael will make 2 or 3 successful offers on a given day? (Round off to 3 decimal places)

    A) 0.083
    B) 0.323
    C) 0.581
    D) 0.600
    E) 0.815

13. Find the probability that Michael makes at least 1 successful offer on a given day. (Round off to 3 decimal places)

    A) 0.017
    B) 0.032
    C) 0.419
    D) 0.677
    E) 0.968

14. James weighs 236 lb now and his wife's weight was 210lb a week ago. Since then she lost 2 lb per day. The weight average of their four children is 60 lb. What is the average weight of this family?

    A) 110 lb
    B) 112 lb
    C) 112.5 lb
    D) 131 lb
    E) 132 lb

15. If the mean of a data set of 10 integers is 16 and the range is n, what is the least possible value for n?

    A) 0
    B) 1
    C) 2
    D) 3
    E) 4

16. The mean of the numbers 13, 18, 17, and x is an integer less than 17. What could be the value of x?

    Indicate all such values.

    A) 0
    B) 8
    C) 10
    D) 20
    E) 22
    F) 28

17

Store Location	Revenue ($)	Number of customers
Princeton Street	31,144	458
St Agnes Road	58,320	720
Hayat Street	34,336	592

The table above shows the revenue generated and the number of customers in three different store locations of a certain business over the last week.

What is the average of the revenues generated per customer at the three locations?

A) 55
B) 58
C) 68
D) 69
E) 81

18 A road test was conducted, and results showed that cars fail the test for two reasons: bad brakes or defective lights. The probability of a car failing due to bad brakes is 0.30, while the probability of a car failing due to defective lights is 0.15. Also, the probability of failure due to having defective lights and bad brakes is 0.10. If any random car is tested, what is the probability that it will fail the road test?

A) 0.25
B) 0.35
C) 0.45
D) 0.55
E) 0.65

19 If 200 inches of rainfall were expected to fall during all of 1998, what percent of the expected yearly rainfall was reached during this 30-day period?

A) 7%
B) 14%
C) 28%
D) 42%
E) 56%

20 Adam's grandmother wants to display photos of her grandchildren on her mantel. She has one photo of each of her 12 grandchildren, but she can fit only five photos on the mantel. Adam requests her to keep his photo center. How many different arrangements of photos are possible?

A) 330
B) 495
C) 7,920
D) 11,880
E) 95,040

21 Maria plans to make sandwiches for a picnic. She has three types of bread from which to choose (rye, sourdough, and white), four types of meat from which to choose (salami, bologna, ham, and pastrami), and three types of cheese from which to choose (Swiss, cheddar, and jack). If Maria will use only one type of bread, one type of meat, and one type of cheese on each sandwich, how many different kinds of sandwiches can Maria make?

A) 3
B) 4
C) 10
D) 17
E) 36

22 Gasoline varies in cost from $0.96 to $1.12 per gallon. If a car's mileage varies from 16 to 24 miles per gallon, what is the difference between the most and the least that the gasoline for a 480-mile trip will cost?

A) $5.12
B) $7.04
C) $11.52
D) $14.40
E) $52.80

Chapter 6: Data Analysis

23. Rob and Tom drive independently but take the same route every day. The probability that Rob arrives late for work is 0.12, while the probability that Tom arrives late for work is 0.16. Find the probability that at least one of them arrives on time for work on any given day.

    Ⓐ 0.0192
    Ⓑ 0.2416
    Ⓒ 0.7392
    Ⓓ 0.9808
    Ⓔ 0.9982

24. The average (arithmetic mean) of six numbers is 16. If five of the numbers are 15, 37, 16, 9, and 23, what is the sixth number?

    Ⓐ −20
    Ⓑ −4
    Ⓒ 0
    Ⓓ 6
    Ⓔ 16

25. The average (arithmetic mean) of five numbers is 8. If the average of two of these numbers is −6, what is the sum of the other three numbers?

    Ⓐ 28
    Ⓑ 34
    Ⓒ 46
    Ⓓ 52
    Ⓔ 60

26. In a class of 30 students, 12 students like Mathematics, 15 students like Science, and 5 students like both Mathematics and Science. If a student is chosen at random, what is the probability that the student likes either Mathematics or Science?

    Ⓐ $\frac{1}{6}$
    Ⓑ $\frac{2}{5}$
    Ⓒ $\frac{1}{2}$
    Ⓓ $\frac{11}{15}$

27.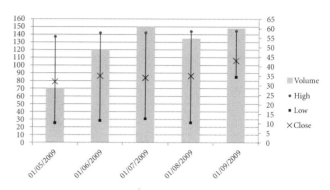

    On which dates were the closing price of the share same?

    Indicate all such answers.

    A 01-05-2009
    B 01-06-2009
    C 01-07-2009
    D 01-08-2009
    E 01-09-2009

28. ### Sales Record of a Retail Shop

    Units Sold for Different Types of Electronics Gadgets

Product Type	Units Sold
Smartphones	120
Laptops	180
Tablets	150
Headphones	250
Smartwatches	100

    Percentage of Total Revenue Contributed by Each Gadget

    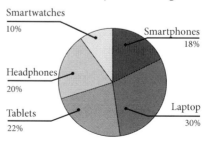

Which of the five gadgets has the highest ratio of products sold to the revenue generated?

- Ⓐ Smartphones
- Ⓑ Laptops
- Ⓒ Tablets
- Ⓓ Headphones
- Ⓔ Smartwatches

Questions 29 and 30 are based on the following graph.

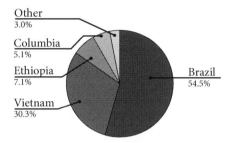

Country	Average Annual Export Quantity (Millions of Metric Tons)
Brazil	2.6
Columbia	1.5
Ethiopia	1.4
Vietnam	2.3
Kenya	0.8
Peru	0.4

㉙ Which countries exported less than the average number of millions of metric tons from the table?

Indicate all such countries.

- Ⓐ Brazil
- Ⓑ Columbia
- Ⓒ Ethiopia
- Ⓓ Vietnam
- Ⓔ Kenya
- Ⓕ Peru

㉚ The amount of coffee beans produced in Brazil was equal to or greater than the annual export quantity for Brazil during the year referenced in the table and graph. What is the total possible amount of coffee beans produced worldwide that same year in millions of metric tons?

Indicate all such values.

- Ⓐ 3.8
- Ⓑ 4.2
- Ⓒ 4.7
- Ⓓ 5.6
- Ⓔ 6.8
- Ⓕ 7.9

Questions 31 and 32 are based on the following table.

Destination	North America	Europe	Asia
Number of males	55	72	23
Number of females	48	60	17

㉛ A traveler is chosen at random. What is the probability that this traveler is going to Asia? (Answer in fraction)

☐
☐

㉜ A traveler is selected at random. Find the probability that the traveler is a female going to Europe. (Answer in fraction)

☐
☐

Chapter 6: Data Analysis

33 The product of two numbers is 90. What could be the average (arithmetic mean) of the two numbers?

Indicate all such answers.

- [A] −45.5
- [B] −15
- [C] 9.5
- [D] 10
- [E] 11.5

34 A traveler is selected at random. What is the probability that this traveler is a male, given that he is going to North America? (Answer in fraction)

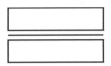

Questions 35 and 36 are based on the following graph.

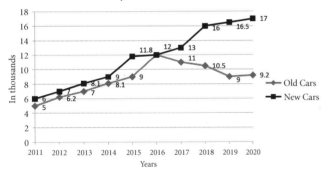

35 In which two years total cars sold are equal?

- (A) 2012, 2013
- (B) 2018, 2019
- (C) 2016, 2017
- (D) 2015, 2019
- (E) 2019, 2020

36 In how many years the old car sales was less than the previous year but the new car sales were more than the previous year?

- (A) 1
- (B) 2
- (C) 3
- (D) 4
- (E) 5

37 A six-sided die is rolled. What is the probability of rolling a number greater than 4?

Practice Set 2: Medium

38 The mean of a group of 10 numbers is 83. A different group of 20 numbers has a mean of 65. When k is added to the first 10 numbers, the new mean is 82.

Quantity A	Quantity B
The mean of the 30 numbers	k

- (A) Quantity A is greater.
- (B) Quantity B is greater.
- (C) The two quantities are equal.
- (D) The relationship cannot be determined from the information given.

39

Set A: {2, −1, 7, −4, 11, 3}

Set B: {10, 5, −3, 4, 7, −8}

Quantity A	Quantity B
The median of set A	The average (arithmetic mean) of Set B

- (A) Quantity A is greater.
- (B) Quantity B is greater.
- (C) The two quantities are equal.
- (D) The relationship cannot be determined from the information given.

Practice Set 2: Medium

40 Last week, Rachael sold 110 tickets to a concert at $26 each, 140 tickets to a play at $30 each, and 200 tickets to a movie at $23 each. She sold no other tickets.

Quantity A	Quantity B
The average (arithmetic mean) price per ticket that Rachael got for all of the tickets she sold last week.	$26

- (A) Quantity A is greater.
- (B) Quantity B is greater.
- (C) The two quantities are equal.
- (D) The relationship cannot be determined from the information given.

41 For her shift on Monday, Mandy made $15 per hour and worked 5 hours. On Tuesday, she made $12 per hour and worked 6 hours. On Wednesday, she made $16 per hour and worked 8 hours.

Quantity A	Quantity B
The average (arithmetic mean) amount Mandy made per hour from Monday to Wednesday	$14.50

- (A) Quantity A is greater.
- (B) Quantity B is greater.
- (C) The two quantities are equal.
- (D) The relationship cannot be determined from the information given.

42 Sarah and John are comparing their test scores. Sarah's test scores are 88, 92, and 93. After the fourth test, her average test score is 91. John's test scores are 85, 90, and 95. After the fourth test, his average test score is 90.

Quantity A	Quantity B
Sarah's fourth test score.	John's fourth test score.

- (A) Quantity A is greater.
- (B) Quantity B is greater.
- (C) The two quantities are equal.
- (D) The relationship cannot be determined from the information given.

43

Set A: 2, 5, 7, 10, x	Set B: 3, 4, 8, 9, y
mean = 6	mean = 6

Quantity A	Quantity B
x	y

- (A) Quantity A is greater.
- (B) Quantity B is greater.
- (C) The two quantities are equal.
- (D) The relationship cannot be determined from the information given.

44 Set A contains all positive integers between 1 and x.

Quantity A	Quantity B
The standard deviation of Set A.	The standard deviation of Set A if all numbers were multiplied by 10.

- (A) Quantity A is greater.
- (B) Quantity B is greater.
- (C) The two quantities are equal.
- (D) The relationship cannot be determined from the information given.

Chapter 6: Data Analysis

45 The values x, y, z, and w are all positive integers. The average of x and y is 32. The average of x, y, z, and w is 48.

Quantity A	Quantity B
The greatest possible value of w	128

- Ⓐ Quantity A is greater.
- Ⓑ Quantity B is greater.
- Ⓒ The two quantities are equal.
- Ⓓ The relationship cannot be determined from the information given.

Quantity A	Quantity B
The probability of picking a perfect cube when choosing any two digit positive integer	The probability that by choosing any positive integer less than 100, that is a perfect square or it is divisible by 25

- Ⓐ Quantity A is greater.
- Ⓑ Quantity B is greater.
- Ⓒ The two quantities are equal.
- Ⓓ The relationship cannot be determined from the information given.

47 A box of chocolates has 3 with mint cream filling, 5 with strawberry cream filling, and 9 with an almond center. Three pieces of chocolate were taken, and the first 2 chocolates were both almond–centered.

Quantity A	Quantity B
Probability that the 3rd chocolate has either mint cream or strawberry cream filling	Probability that the 3rd chocolate is almond centered

- Ⓐ Quantity A is greater.
- Ⓑ Quantity B is greater.
- Ⓒ The two quantities are equal.
- Ⓓ The relationship cannot be determined from the information given.

48 A six-sided number cube is rolled two times.

Quantity A	Quantity B
The probability of rolling a number greater than 1 on the first roll and a prime number on the second roll	The probability of rolling an even number on the first roll and a factor of six on the second roll

- Ⓐ Quantity A is greater.
- Ⓑ Quantity B is greater.
- Ⓒ The two quantities are equal.
- Ⓓ The relationship cannot be determined from the information given.

Questions 49 and 50 are based on the following graph.

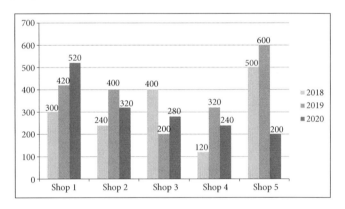

49 What is the ratio between the number of laptops sold by shop 1 in all the years together and the total number of laptops sold in 2019 in all the shops together?

- Ⓐ 12:11
- Ⓑ 87:62
- Ⓒ 62:97
- Ⓓ 61:62
- Ⓔ 87:88

196 | GRE Quantitative Practice Questions

50
The total number of laptops sold by shop 3 in all the years together is approximately what percentage of the total number of laptops sold by shop 4 in all the years together?

- Ⓐ 110.7%
- Ⓑ 129.4%
- Ⓒ 145.2%
- Ⓓ 180.8%
- Ⓔ 185.6%

Questions 51 and 52 are based on the following graph.

The graphs below show the variation of price of a particular brand of smart watch for a store and revenues generated from the sale of all watches by the store during the period 2011 – 2020.

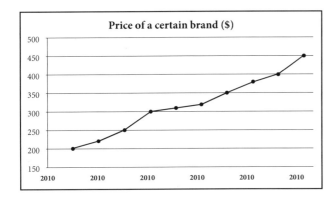

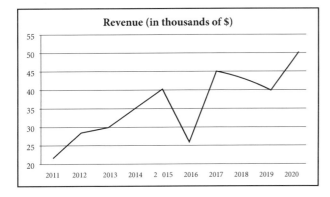

51
During which of the following periods was the percentage increase in the price between 60% and 100%, inclusive?

Indicate *all* such options.

- A 2012 to 2014
- B 2011 to 2016
- C 2013 to 2018
- D 2011 to 2019
- E 2012 to 2020
- F 2015 to 2019

52
If it is known that the revenue generated from the sale of this brand of smart watches was more than 50% of the total revenue generated by the store in 2019, which of the following could be the number of watches of the given brand sold by the store in that year?

Indicate *all* such numbers.

- A 38
- B 45
- C 50
- D 62
- E 88
- F 100
- G 105
- H 110

Chapter 6: Data Analysis

53

Distribution of Employees in a Office

Department	Full Time	Part Time
Accounting	50	20
Sales	100	30
Marketing	120	50
Human Resources	30	10
Management	50	40

Healthcare Enrollment by Department

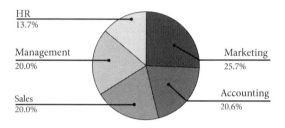

If only full time employees can be enrolled in healthcare, what percent of all employees are enrolled in healthcare rounded to the next nearest percent?

Questions 54 to 57 are based on the following graph.

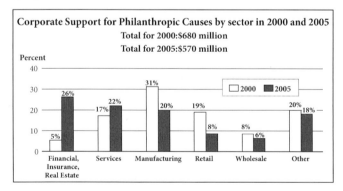

54 What was the total contribution in 2005(approx. in million dollars) by the corporate sectors that decreased their support for Philanthropic causes from 2000 to 2005?

- (A) 150 million dollars
- (B) 200 million dollars
- (C) 250 million dollars
- (D) 300 million dollars
- (E) 350 million dollars

55 What is the average amount contributed by those sectors who contributed more than $100 million each to the Philanthropic Causes in both 2000 and 2005?

- (A) $114 million
- (B) $238.6 million
- (C) $268.13 million
- (D) $324.8 million
- (E) $342.6 million

56 Of the Financial, Insurance and Real Estate Sector's 2005 contribution to Philanthropic Causes, one-third went for rebuilding homes lost due to Hurricane Katrina and one fourth of the remainder went to providing medical aid to the injured. Approximately how many million dollars more did the Financial, Insurance and Real Estate Sector contribute towards rebuilding homes that year than to providing medical aid?

- (A) $20 million
- (B) $25 million
- (C) $30 million
- (D) $35 million
- (E) $40 million

57 Financial, Insurance and Real Estate Sector showed a steep increase in contribution for philanthropic causes between 2000 and 2005. If the government excluded this industry and calculated, what would be the average change in contribution of all the other industries, calculated to the nearest integer?

(A) −34%
(B) −33%
(C) −32%
(D) −31%
(E) −30%

58 In a company, there are 2 sections A and B. The average salary of employees of both the sections put together is $14000. The average salary of employees in section A is $12000 and that of Section B is $24000. If there are 66 employees in both the sections put together, find the number of employees in section B.

(A) 11
(B) 13
(C) 15
(D) 17
(E) 19

59 If the average (arithmetic mean) of four distinct positive integers is 11, what is the greatest possible value of any one of the integers?

(A) 35
(B) 38
(C) 40
(D) 41
(E) 44

60 Sahana asked some people in her neighborhood how many times they visited the mall last month.

Trips to the mall last month	
Number of trips	Frequency
0	18
1	11
2	15
3	8
4	6

What was the median number of trips to the mall last month made by the people surveyed?

(A) 0.5
(B) 1.5
(C) 2
(D) 2.5
(E) 3

For Questions 61 and 62, refer to the figure below.

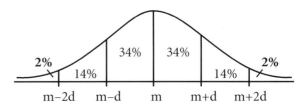

The figure above shows the bell curve or normal distribution curve with mean, m, and standard deviation, d. The percentages given refer to the approximate probability under the specified area. For example, the probability of an event occurring that is between the mean (m) and +1 standard deviation away from the mean ($m + d$) is 34%.

In a certain district, the heights of 1,000 high school students are normally distributed with a mean of 165 cm and standard deviation of 3 cm.

Chapter 6: Data Analysis

61. If a high school student is selected at random, what is, approximately, the probability that the student's height is less than 162 cm?

- A 14%
- B 16%
- C 34%
- D 56%
- E 84%

62. A high school student selected at random will have any of the following heights:

I. Less than 159 cm
II. Between 159 cm and 162 cm
III. Between 162 cm and 165 cm
IV Between 165 cm and 168 cm
V. Between 168 cm and 171 cm
VI. More than 171 cm

Which of the following pairs have equal probabilities?

Indicate all such options.

- A I and VI
- B II and V
- C III and IV
- D II and IV

63. Distribution of Employees in a Office

Department	Full Time	Part Time
Accounting	50	20
Sales	100	30
Marketing	120	50
Human Resources	30	10
Management	50	40

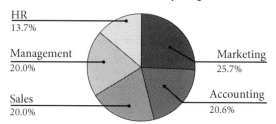

Healthcare Enrollment by Department

A round of new hires made it so that each department had at least 60% of their workers as full time employees. If 50 people were hired, how could the new hires be distributed?

Indicate all such solutions.

- A 10 hires to full time accounting, 15 hires to part time sales, and 25 hires to full time management.
- B 5 hires to full time management, 25 hires to part time marketing, and 20 hires to full time sales.
- C 5 hires to full time sales, 10 hires to full time management, and 35 hires to part time marketing.
- D 30 hires to full time management, 5 hires to part time accounting, and 15 hires to marketing full time.

Practice Set 2: Medium

64. The table below shows the revenue generated and the number of customers in three different store locations of a certain business over the last week.

Store Location	Revenue ($)	Number of customers
Princeton Street	31,144	458
St Agnes Road	58,320	720
Hayat Street	34,336	592

What is the average of the revenues generated per customer at the three locations?

Ⓐ 55
Ⓑ 58
Ⓒ 68
Ⓓ 69
Ⓔ 81

65. Let M and N be events such that $P(M)=\frac{1}{2}$, $P(M \text{ and } N)=\frac{1}{6}$ and $P(M \text{ or } N)=\frac{3}{4}$. Find $P(N)$.

Ⓐ $\frac{1}{12}$
Ⓑ $\frac{1}{4}$
Ⓒ $\frac{5}{12}$
Ⓓ $\frac{5}{6}$
Ⓔ 1

66. Of the 200 employees at PPP Appliansers, one half works in both the Marketing and the Sales department. If 160 employees work in the Marketing department, and the number of employees in Sales department is 3 times the number of employees that are neither in Marketing nor in Sales, how many of the employees work in the Sales department?

Ⓐ 35
Ⓑ 105
Ⓒ 140
Ⓓ 160
Ⓔ 180

67. A pair of dice is rolled. If the two numbers appearing on the dice are different, what is the probability that the sum of them is at most 4?

Ⓐ $\frac{1}{15}$
Ⓑ $\frac{1}{6}$
Ⓒ $\frac{2}{15}$
Ⓓ $\frac{13}{15}$
Ⓔ $\frac{14}{15}$

68. Kabir is hosting a contest attended by 200 people, 80 of whom are males and the rest females. At the end of the contest, one of the contestants will be chosen at random to win a prize. If 1/5 of male contestants and 1/6 of female contestants arrived late, what is the probability that the prize will be won by a contestant who arrived late?

Ⓐ 4/25
Ⓑ 6/35
Ⓒ 9/50
Ⓓ 9/80
Ⓔ 1/9

Chapter 6: Data Analysis

69 6" 2" 10" 2" 5"

Above are the measures of rainfall for five consecutive days during the winter. For the measure of those five days, which of the following is true?

I. The median equals the mode.
II. The median equals the arithmetic mean.
III. The range equals the median.

Ⓐ I only
Ⓑ II only
Ⓒ III only
Ⓓ I and II only
Ⓔ I and III only

For Questions 70 to 72, refer to the figure below.

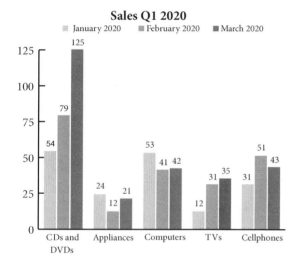

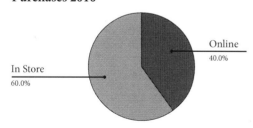

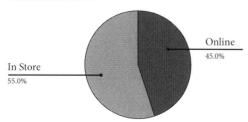

70 Of the products that had an increase in sales from January 2020 to March 2020, which ones had a percentage increase of over 100%?

Indicate all such answers.

Ⓐ CDs and DVDs
Ⓑ Appliances
Ⓒ Computers
Ⓓ TVs
Ⓔ Cellphones

71 If the sales in Q1 represent $\frac{1}{4}$ of the total sales of 2020, what is the difference in the number of products purchased in store compared to online in 2020?

72 In 2010, the company decided to switch to selling just CDs and DVDs and cell phones online whereas they previously only had an online store for video games. Only appliances, computers, and TVs were sold in the store. Based on this information which of the following must be true?

Indicate all such statements.

Ⓐ The amount of video games sold online more than doubled.
Ⓑ There was an increase in purchases of CDs and DVDs in 2020 that led to an increase in online purchases.
Ⓒ The number of appliances, computers, and TVs sold in stores did not increase drastically between 2010 and 2020.
Ⓓ The amount of appliances sold was greater in 2010 than 2020.

73 Set A consists of all three digit numbers that can be made with 1, 3, and 5. What is the median of Set A?

Ⓐ 315
Ⓑ 333
Ⓒ 351
Ⓓ 441
Ⓔ 531

Practice Set 2: Medium

74. A car dealership sold x amount of cars one month, twice as many cars the next month, and then twenty more cars than the first month the month after. If the average number of cars sold per month was 44 cars, what was the median number of cars sold over the time period?

    (A) 39
    (B) 44
    (C) 48
    (D) 59
    (E) 78

75. The average of 8 consecutive even integers is 21. What is the value of the lowest number in the data set?

    (A) 10
    (B) 12
    (C) 14
    (D) 16
    (E) 18

76. A fair coin is tossed 100 times. The probability of getting tails an odd number of times is

    (A) $\dfrac{1}{33}$
    (B) $\dfrac{1}{8}$
    (C) $\dfrac{3}{8}$
    (D) $\dfrac{1}{2}$
    (E) $\dfrac{3}{4}$

77. Three people stop for lunch at hot dog stand. If each person orders one item and there are three items to choose from, how many different combinations of food could be purchased? (Assume that order doesn't matter, e.g., a hot dog and two sodas are considered the same as two sodas and a hot dog.)

    (A) 6
    (B) 9
    (C) 10
    (D) 18
    (E) 27

78. In a certain examination 60% of the students passed in Mathematics, 74% passed in English and 18% failed in both English and Mathematics. If 416 students passed in both these subjects, then what will be the total number of students who took the exam?

    (A) 740
    (B) 770
    (C) 800
    (D) 820
    (E) 840

79. Data Set A contains the values x, y, and z where x, y, and z are all positive integers. Data Set B contains all of the values in Data Set A as well as the values w and t. If the mean of Data Set B is double Data Set A, which of the following expressions is equal to $w + t$?

    (A) $\dfrac{2(x+y+z)}{3}$
    (B) $\dfrac{7(x+y+z)}{3}$
    (C) $\dfrac{10(x+y+z)}{3}$
    (D) $2(x + y + z)$
    (E) $\dfrac{10}{3}x - (y + z)$

For more practice, visit www.vibrantpublishers.com

Chapter 6: Data Analysis

80 The median of a data set is x and its range is 2. If the data set contains 4 positive integers, which of the following could represent the average of the data set?

- A) $\frac{x}{4}$
- B) $\frac{3x}{4}$
- C) x
- D) $\frac{7x}{4}$
- E) $2x$

81

Fixed Cost	Frequency
$320	3
$450	4
$520	x
$650	7
$750	1

The frequency table shows the distribution of fixed production cost over a period of months. If the average fixed production cost was $533, what is the value of x?

- A) 5
- B) 10
- C) 12
- D) 15
- E) 20

82 If in an office $\frac{1}{2}$ of the staff commute by bus, $\frac{1}{3}$ commute by motorbike, $\frac{1}{12}$ commute by car and remaining 100 walk, then what is the total number of staff in that office?

- A) 100
- B) 300
- C) 600
- D) 1200
- E) 9000

83 A problem on probability in the GRE quantitative section is given to A, B C and D for solving independently. If the probabilities of solving the problem by A, B, C and D are 60%, 70%, 80% and 90% respectively, what is the probability that the problem will be solved?

- A) 0.9188
- B) 0.9326
- C) 0.9424
- D) 0.9820
- E) 0.9976

84 How many different eight digit numbers are possible from the numbers 1, 2, 5, 5, 5, 6, 6, 6?

- A) 8
- B) 1120
- C) 6720
- D) 20160
- E) 40320

85

Dataset A: -20, -15, 0, 5

Dataset B: 1, 2, 3, 4, 5

Dataset C: 99, 99, 99, 99, 99

Dataset D: -35, 42, 89, 300

Which of the following choices lists the four datasets above in order from least standard deviation to greatest standard deviation?

- A) ACBD
- B) CABD
- C) DABC
- D) BCDA
- E) CBAD

86 The average of four numbers is 3*x*. If three of the numbers are 3*x* + 2*y*, 4*x* − 5*y*, and −6*x*, what is the fourth number in terms of *x* and *y*?

Ⓐ 2*x*
Ⓑ 11*x* + 3*y*
Ⓒ 2*x* − 3*y*
Ⓓ *x* + *y*
Ⓔ −3*y*

87 A student's final grade was determined by the averages of their mid-term and their final; exams. If the student's final exam grade was a 40% grade increase from their midterm exam for a total average of 66% for their final grade, what was their final exam grade?

Ⓐ 40%
Ⓑ 55%
Ⓒ 58%
Ⓓ 66%
Ⓔ 77%

88

Theater Tickets

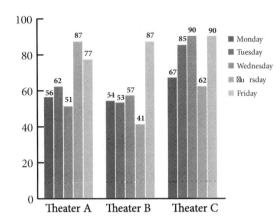

Friday Concession Sales

Concession Item	Sales
Popcorn	$1976
Drinks	$2400
Candy	$1325
Meals	$1634

A movie theater has a max capacity of 30 seats and can have up to 3 showings per day. On which days and in which theater was the theater likely to have been at least 60% full for all showings?

Indicate all such answers.

Ⓐ Theater A on Thursday
Ⓑ Theater B on Tuesday
Ⓒ Theater C on Wednesday

Chapter 6: Data Analysis

89

Sales Distribution by Region

Region	Sales Amount (USD) 2015	Sales Amount (USD) 2020
North America	25,090	36,050
Europe	18,520	23,170
Asia	15,000	13,950
South America	9,030	10,520
Africa	6,510	7,270

Sales Percentages in North America by Subregion in 2015

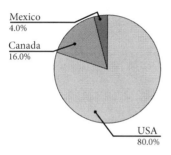

In 2015, if 45 percent of sales in South America were made to Brazil, what percent of total sales across all regions in 2015 would Brazil sales account for?

Give your answer to the nearest whole percent.

90

Units Sold for Different Types of Electronics Gadgets

Product Type	Units Sold
Smartphones	120
Laptops	180
Tablets	150
Headphones	250
Smartwatches	100

Percentage of Total Revenue Contributed by Each Gadget

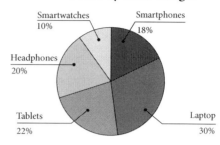

The figures shown above reflect how a retail shop that sells electronic gadgets performed last night. If their total revenue is $90,000, how much is the average cost of a tablet from this shop?

$

91 List B contains 10 integers with -6 being the lowest value in the list. If the average of List B is below 38, what is the greatest range possible for the numbers in the list?

Ⓐ 54
Ⓑ 433
Ⓒ 434
Ⓓ 439
Ⓔ 570

92 Two blueberry fields, field A and field B, had an average weight of 8.1 pounds. The average weight of blueberries gathered per bush in field A was 8.6 pounds. There are 94 blueberry bushes in field A and 86 blueberry bushes in field B. What was the approximate average weight of blueberries per bush in field B?

Ⓐ 7.55
Ⓑ 7.60
Ⓒ 7.81
Ⓓ 8.01
Ⓔ 8.63

93 Giovanni scored an 87, 93, 91, 94, 73, and a 84 on his recent tests. How many of his test scores were above the mean, but below the median?

- A) None
- B) One
- C) Two
- D) Three
- E) Four

For Questions 94 and 95, refer to the figure below.

Theater Tickets

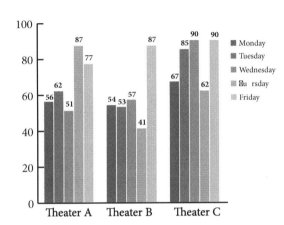

Friday Concession Sales

Concession Item	Sales
Popcorn	$1976
Drinks	$2400
Candy	$1325
Meals	$1634

94 If at least 75% of the people who went to the theater on Friday bought concessions, what could be the average amount spent per person?

Indicate all such answers.

- A) $27.50
- B) $29.00
- C) $34.62
- D) $37.25
- E) $41.54

95 Theater D was reserved for private rentals for events such as field trips and birthday parties. The theater held 2 viewings per day and averaged at most 57 tickets sold per day. If Theater D has a capacity of 30, what is the smallest group size possible that rented out Theater D during the entirety of the week?

Indicate all such answers.

- A) 8
- B) 15
- C) 20
- D) 25

96

Tax Revenue Allocation

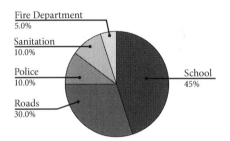

Funding Per School

School	Funding
Hawk Elementary	$150,400
Eaglewood Middle School	$210,300
Brighton High School	$226,550

A new school is being built which will require the tax revenue allocated to schools to increase a minimum of 5% and a maximum of 8%. What would be the expected funding needed for this new school?

Indicate all such answers.

- A) $50,000
- B) $60,000
- C) $70,000
- D) $80,000
- E) $90,000
- F) $100,000

Chapter 6: Data Analysis

97 Set K contains the terms {4, 13, 15, 21, x}. If the range of set K is 2x, which of the following could be the value of x?

- (A) 6.5
- (B) 8.5
- (C) 10
- (D) 17
- (E) 28

98 Martha measured her resting heart rate in beats per minute to be 65, 70, 68, 67, 66, x, and y over a one week period of random testing times. If her resting heart rate range was 7 and her average resting heart rate was 67 and $x > y$, what is the value of y?

- (A) 61
- (B) 67
- (C) 68
- (D) 71
- (E) 72

99 An engineering firm buys $6750 of microchips that cost $45 each. Later they find another distributor that is less expensive and the firm buys $6400 of microchips that cost $32 each. What is the approximate average price per microchip purchased?

- (A) $25.62
- (B) $28.45
- (C) $32.83
- (D) $37.57
- (E) $38.50

100

Product	Sales Price	Cost	Cases Ordered	Sell-Through Rate
Coke	$5.00	$4.25	1,500	80%
Bubly	$4.75	$3.50	1,000	75%
Pepsi	$5.50	$4.75	1,250	80%
Fanta	$6.00	$4.75	600	85%
Store Brand	$4.00	$2.00	1,500	70%

The above graph shows the breakdown of cases of drinks from the first quarter at a local gas station.

What is the profit, in dollars, the store made on Store Brand drinks?

- (A) $900
- (B) $1200
- (C) $3,000
- (D) $4,200
- (E) $6,000

101

Tax Revenue Allocation

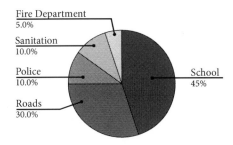

Funding Per School

School	Funding
Hawk Elementary	$150,400
Eaglewood Middle School	$210,300
Brighton High School	$226,550

The city was given a grant to cover 50%-75% of all police costs. The funding covered by the grant would be reallocated to the fire department, sanitation, and roads with no department outside of police seeing a decrease in funding. Which of the following is a possible tax revenue allocation with this grant covering some of police costs?

Indicate all such answers.

- A Sanitation 10%, Fire Department 10%, Roads 35%, Schools 45%
- B Schools 45%, Roads 30%, Sanitation 12.5%, Fire Department 7.5%, Police 5%
- C Schools 40%, Roads 40%, Fire Department 12.5%, Sanitation 5%, Police 2.5%,
- D Schools 45%, Roads 33%, Sanitation 12%, Fire Department 6%, Police 4%

102

Heating Methods utilized by residents of Region X

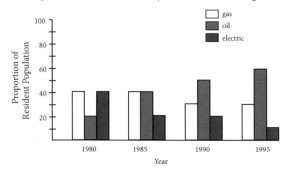

What year or years had the greatest increase in oil usage by residents from one set of years to the next?

- A 1980
- B 1985
- C 1990
- D 1995
- E 1990 and 1995

103 There are 300 students in the senior class. There are x amount of students in band and 140 students in choir. There are at least 50 students in both band and choir and there are some members of the senior class who do not participate in either. What could be a possible probability of choosing a student who is in band, but not in choir?

Indicate all such options.

- A $\frac{1}{3}$
- B $\frac{1}{2}$
- C $\frac{8}{15}$
- D $\frac{2}{3}$

Chapter 6: Data Analysis

104. In a sequence −3, 6, −12, 24,... each term is multiplied by −2 to get the next term. Which of the following could NOT be a term in the sequence?

Indicate all such numbers.

- [A] −1536
- [B] 96
- [C] 192
- [D] 384

105. In a certain examination 60% of the students passed in mathematics, 74% passed in English, and 18% failed in both English and mathematics. If 416 students passed in both the subjects, then what will be the total number of students who took the exam?

- (A) 740
- (B) 770
- (C) 800
- (D) 820
- (E) 840

Questions 106 to 108 are based on the following chart.

Heating Methods utilized by residents of Region X

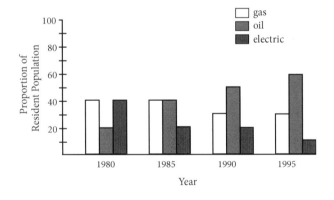

106. What is the mean percent of residents who use oil as their main heating source?

- (A) 22.5%
- (B) 35%
- (C) 37.5%
- (D) 42.5%
- (E) 50%

107. If 50,000 residents make up Region X, how many more residents chose oil heat over electric heat in 1995?

- (A) 5,000
- (B) 15,000
- (C) 25,000
- (D) 30,000
- (E) 55,000

108. What percentage of gas consumers from 1985 switched to alternative heating method in 1990?

- (A) 10%
- (B) 25%
- (C) 50%
- (D) 75%
- (E) 100%

Questions 109 to 111 are based on the following chart.

Most Expensive US Cities to Live in 2020

City	Median Income
Boston	$45,000
San Francisco	$65,000
New York	$40,000
DC	$66,000
Seattle	$63,000

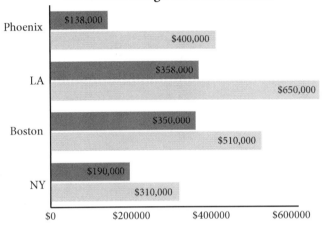

Median Housing Price 2010 vs. 2020

Phoenix: $138,000 / $400,000
LA: $358,000 / $650,000
Boston: $350,000 / $510,000
NY: $190,000 / $310,000

109. What is the positive difference in percentage of the average median income as a percentage of housing price in 2020 between Boston and NY rounded to the nearest percentage?

110. Which of the following is supported by the information in the table and graph?

    Indicate all such statements.

    A. The greatest percentage increase in median housing price between 2010 and 2020 was Phoenix at over 180% increase.

    B. The average income for the most expensive cities in 2020 was $55,800.

    C. The median of the median housing prices in 2010 was Boston at $350,000.

111. The most expensive city to live in worldwide in 2020 was Singapore with a median housing price of $4,200,000. The average median housing price in the US in 2020 for the cities given is what percent less than the median housing price in Singapore rounded to the nearest percent?

112. The average rainfall on the weekend was $\frac{2}{3}$ the average rainfall for the rest of the week. What fraction of the weekly rainfall happened on the weekend?

113. In a certain museum exhibit, 2/5 of the artifacts are Palaeolithic, and the remaining 45 are Neolithic. Of the Palaeolithic artifacts, 2/3 are Mediterranean. If 40 the artifacts are Mediterranean, how many Neolithic artifacts are not Mediterranean?

114. How many different numbers can be combined to create a 3 digit number with different digits that is divisible by 9?

115. Set A comprises all 3-digit numbers that are multiples of 9. Set B comprises all 3-digit numbers that are multiples of 3 but are not multiples of 6. How many elements does $(A \cup B)$ have?

Chapter 6: Data Analysis

Practice Set 3: Hard

Questions 116 to 118 are based on the following chart.

Job Growth Projected for Health Care Sector

Specialty	Job Growth Projected by 2025
Dietary Aide	7%
Physicians Assistant	28%
Hospice Nurse	6%
Patient Service Representative	-4%
Clinical Pharmacist	5%
Psychiatrist	9%

Degrees Held By Hospital Employess

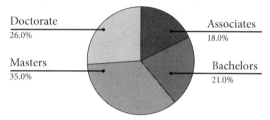

Doctorate 26.0%
Masters 35.0%
Associates 18.0%
Bachelors 21.0%

116. Patient services representative jobs require an associate's degree. Patient service representatives make up $\frac{1}{8}$ of the total hospital staff with associate's degrees. If the hospital adjusts their workforce according to the job growth predicted for patient service representatives, by how much will the associate's degree piece of the pie graph change?

    A) −4%
    B) −0.05%
    C) −0.009%
    D) 0.025%
    E) 4%

117. The job growth is estimated to have a margin of error of ±2%. For the specialties that will see a job growth of at least 5%, which of the following could be true?

    Indicate all such statements.

    A) Currently there are approximately 305,000 dietary aids in the US. In 2025, there could be 320,250.
    B) There are around 160,000 physician assistants that are board certified. Job growth will support the additional 50,000 students getting board certified by 2025.
    C) Some nurses and doctors decide to switch career paths and become clinical pharmacists. There are currently 185,000 clinical pharmacists and if 4,070 nurses and doctors switched careers, there would still be an estimated 60% of jobs available for others.
    D) If the ratio of women to men entering the field of psychiatry is estimated to be 4:5, this means 4% of new jobs will be held by women.

118. The hospital currently employs 12,500 staff members with 750 currently working on continuing their education to go from a masters to a doctorate and 20% of those with a bachelors working on a masters. What would be the percent change for the masters part of the pie once these staff members complete their degrees rounded to the next nearest percent?

    [   ]

119. A data set has the values of 30, 25, 34, 21, x, and y. The average value of this data set is 28. If there is no value greater than 34 and no value less than 21, what is the maximum possible average of 4 numbers in the data set?

    A) 30.5
    B) 30.75
    C) 32.25
    D) 33
    E) 34

120. Which of the following represents the median of four consecutive positive odd numbers *a*, *b*, *c* and *d* where $a < b < c < d$?

Ⓐ $\dfrac{a+b+c+d}{4}$

Ⓑ $\dfrac{a+d}{4}$

Ⓒ $\dfrac{d-1}{2}+1$

Ⓓ $a + 3$

Ⓔ $\dfrac{b+1}{2}+\dfrac{c-1}{2}$

121.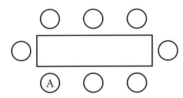

In this seating arrangement at a dinner table, there are 8 people. One of the dinner guests prefers to sit at either end of the table and seat A is reserved for one specific person. Based on these restrictions. What is the total possible number of ways to rearrange 8 people at this dinner table?

Ⓐ 36
Ⓑ 720
Ⓒ 1440
Ⓓ 5040
Ⓔ 40,320

Questions 122 to 124 are based on the following chart.

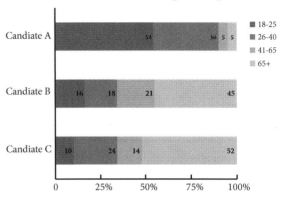

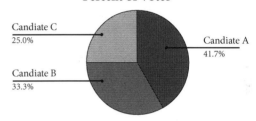

122. If a total of 1200 people voted which included no more than 35% of all 18-25 year olds in the town, what could be the total population size of 18-25 year olds?

Indicate all such answers.

A 300
B 360
C 580
D 1000
E 1100

Chapter 6: Data Analysis

123 If a total of 1200 people voted, which of the following are true statements?

Indicate all such statements.

- [A] Candidate C had the highest number of voters in the 65+ category than all other candidates.
- [B] Candidate A won the majority of votes in the age range of 41+.
- [C] The candidate that received the least amount of votes in the age range of 26-65, had the lowest percentage of all votes.

124 The ratio of in person voting to mail in ballots was 5:3. Of those who mailed in their ballots, 24% were 65+. If there were 1200 voters, what is the total number of 65+ voters who voted in person?

- (A) 24
- (B) 85
- (C) 108
- (D) 253
- (E) 361

125 Set A contains all integers divisible by 5 between 0 and 100. If the largest four values of the set were increased by a positive integer value x and the smallest four values of the set were decreased by x, which of the following would result?

Indicate all such statements.

- [A] The average would not change
- [B] The average would increase
- [C] The average would decrease
- [D] The standard deviation would not change
- [E] The standard deviation would increase
- [F] The standard deviation would decrease

126 Among the students in a high school $\frac{1}{5}$ have green eyes and $\frac{3}{7}$ have brown hair. Which of the following could be the probability of picking a random student with either green eyes or brown hair or both?

Indicate all such values.

- [A] $\frac{1}{5}$
- [B] $\frac{4}{7}$
- [C] $\frac{3}{5}$
- [D] $\frac{27}{35}$

127 A book must have a rating of 3.5 out of 5.0 or higher in order to showcase on the website's main selling page. One book has 42 ratings with an average of 3.4. Which of the following 5 ratings would allow for the book to be showcased?

Indicate all such values.

- [A] 4.3, 4.3, 4.3, 4.3, 4.5
- [B] 2.6, 3.8, 4.5, 5.0, 5.0
- [C] 3.2, 4.3, 4.5, 4.6, 4.2
- [D] 4.5, 3.8, 4.9, 5.0, 4.5

128

$$\text{Set A} = \{(1+x)^2, (2+x)^2, (3+x)^2\}$$
$$\text{Set B} = \{(1-x)^2, (2-x)^2, (3-x)^2\}$$

Based on sets A and B, which of the following are true?

Indicate all such statements.

- [A] For all $x > 0$, Set A has an average larger than Set B.
- [B] For all $x < 0$, Set A has an average larger than Set B.
- [C] Set A's range is equal to Set B's range.
- [D] Set B's range is greater than Set A's range.

Only when $x = 0$, the standard deviation of both sets is equal.

129.

List A: 5, x, y, z

List B: 3, 6, 8, x, y, z, w

If list A and list B both have an average of 8, what is the value of w?

130. There are 5 blue beads and 7 red beads in a jar. If the beads are randomly drawn one at a time and then not replaced, what is the probability of getting 3 blue beads in a row? Write your answer as a decimal rounded to the nearest thousandth.

Answer Key

Q. No.	Correct Answer	Your Answer
1	A	
2	C	
3	C	
4	D	
5	B	
6	B	
7	A	
8	E	
9	C,D	
10	B,C,D,E	
11	A	
12	C	
13	E	
14	B	
15	A	
16	A,B	
17	D	
18	B	
19	B	
20	C	
21	E	
22	D	
23	D	
24	B	
25	D	
26	D	
27	B,D	
28	A	
29	C,E,F	
30	D,E,F	
31	$\frac{8}{55}$	
32	$\frac{12}{55}$	

Q. No.	Correct Answer	Your Answer
33	A, C, E	
34	$\frac{55}{103}$	
35	C	
36	C	
37	$\frac{1}{3}$	
38	B	
39	C	
40	B	
41	B	
42	A	
43	C	
44	B	
45	B	
46	B	
47	A	
48	A	
49	C	
50	B	
51	B,D	
52	D,E,F	
53	22	
54	D	
55	C	
56	B	
57	B	
58	A	
59	B	
60	B	
61	B	
62	A,B,C	
63	A,D	
64	D	

Q. No.	Correct Answer	Your Answer
65	C	
66	B	
67	C	
68	C	
69	B	
70	A,D	
71	780	
72	B,C	
73	B	
74	C	
75	C	
76	D	
77	C	
78	C	
79	B	
80	C	
81	A	
82	1200	
83	E	
84	B	
85	E	
86	B	
87	E	
88	A,C	
89	5	
90	132	
91	D	
92	A	
93	A	
94	B,C,D	
95	A,B	
96	C,D,E,F	
97	B	
98	A	

Q. No.	Correct Answer	Your Answer
99	D	
100	B	
101	B,D	
102	B	
103	A,B	
104	A,C	
105	C	
106	D	
107	C	
108	A	
109	4.1	
110	A,B	
111	89	
112	$\frac{4}{19}$	
113	25	
114	76	
115	200	
116	C	
117	A,C	
118	7	
119	B	
120	E	
121	C	
122	C,D	
123	B,C	
124	D	
125	A,E	
126	B,C	
127	A,D	
128	A	
129	12	
130	0.046	

Practice Set 1 (Easy): Answers & Explanations

1 **Choice A is correct** because the maximum average amount the remaining 20 employees donated can be found to be $45. To find this, first identify the minimum amount donated by the 300 employees by multiplying by $15 to get 3000 × $15 = $4500. Find the minimum amount of the 180 employees by multiplying by $20 to get 180 × $20 = $3600. Add these two values together to get a total of $4500 + $3600 = $8100. Subtract from the total of $9000 to get $9000 − $8100 = $900. This can then be divided by 20 to get the maximum average of $45.

Choice B is incorrect because the maximum average is larger than $40. **Choice C is incorrect** because the maximum average does not equal $40. **Choice D is incorrect** because it is possible to solve for the maximum average.

2 **Choice C is correct** because the median and mean of consecutive number sets are always equal due to the distribution of the numbers. This would mean that the median of the 55 numbers is also 672 making the two quantities equal.

Choice A is incorrect because the median is equal to 672 and thus the two quantities are equal. **Choice B is incorrect** because the two quantities are equal. **Choice D is incorrect** because it is possible to solve for the median and compare.

3 **Choice C is correct** because the value of a can be identified to be 5 which is also the mode since there are two fives in the data set and the mode measures the most often occurring number.

To solve for the value of a, use the equation for mean = $\frac{sum\,of\,values}{number\,of\,values}$. Substituting what you know will give you $5 = \frac{4+5+6+a}{4}$. This simplifies to be $5 = \frac{15+a}{4}$. Multiply both sides by 4 to get $20 = 15 + a$. Subtract 15 from both sides and you will find $a = 5$.

Choice A is incorrect because the mode of the data set equals the same value as a. **Choice B is incorrect** because the two quantities are equal. **Choice D is incorrect** because it is possible to solve for mode and the value of a.

4 **Choice D is correct** because there is not enough information given about the data set in order to determine the average height of the data set. To find the average, you would need to know the number of people in the data set.

Choice A is incorrect because it is not possible to determine the average. **Choice B is incorrect** because it is unknown if the average is less than 66. **Choice C is incorrect** because it is not possible to know if the average is 66.

5 **Choice B is correct** because the probability of drawing a yellow candy, then a pink candy without replacement is found by multiplying $\left(\frac{5}{15}\right) \times \left(\frac{3}{14}\right) = \frac{15}{210}$. The probability of getting 2 white candies without replacement can be found by multiplying $\left(\frac{7}{15}\right) \times \left(\frac{6}{14}\right) = \frac{42}{210}$. Comparing the denominators of the fractions indicates that Quantity B is greater.

Choice A is incorrect because the Quantity B is greater. **Choice C is incorrect** because the two probabilities are not equal. **Choice D is incorrect** because it is possible to solve for and compare the probabilities.

6 **Choice B is correct** because the total combination of choices can be found to be 10. To find this, separate the two decision routes and then add them together. You will not use the two initial choices in your combination to solve because a choice has to be made to determine all options from it.

In the first instance, students will have 3 meal choices and 2 transportation choices. Multiply these numbers together 3 × 2 to get 6 choices if the first option for a field trip is decided.

For the second field trip choice, students have 2 meal choices and 2 transportation options. Multiply these options to get 2 × 2 to get 4.

Add the two results together to get 6 + 4 which equals 10. This is less than 20 making Quantity B the greater value.

Choice A is incorrect because the total combination of choices is less than 20. **Choice C is incorrect** because the total number of possible combinations is not 20. **Choice D is incorrect** because it is possible to solve for total combinations.

7 **Choice A is correct** because the percent of polygons that are not square quadrilaterals can be found to be greater.

To find this, identify how many polygons are quadrilaterals and squares. The percent of quadrilaterals is stated to be 45%. Of those 45%, 75% are squares. Multiply 0.45 by 0.75 to evaluate that there are 33.75% of polygons that are square quadrilaterals. Subtract this from 100% to find the percent of polygons that are not square quadrilaterals to be 66.25%.

Choice B is incorrect because the percent of polygons that are not square quadrilaterals is greater than 30%. **Choice C is incorrect** because the percent of polygons that are not square quadrilaterals does not equal 30%. **Choice D is incorrect** because it is possible to solve for the percent of polygons that are not square quadrilaterals.

8 **Choice E is correct** because looking at the chart the sales in Asia in 2020 were 13950 and the sales in Africa in 2020 were 7270. To create a ratio, divide the sales in Asia by the sales in Africa to get approximately 1.9. This would mean Asia's sales were about 2 times as much as Africa's sales. A ratio of 2 to 1 would be the closest to matching this result.

Choice A is incorrect because this would be the ratio of sales in Africa to sales in Asia which is the incorrect order. **Choice B is incorrect** because this over approximates the ratio. **Choice C is incorrect** because this is the incorrect ratio. **Choice D is incorrect** because this is the incorrect ratio.

9 **Choices C and D are correct.**
Choice C is correct because 22 falls within the range of 21–25. **Choice D is correct** because 24 falls within the range of 21–25.

To identify which range of values the median class size would fall, count up the total frequencies to determine there are 65 total classes listed (10 + 12 + 22 + 21 = 65). The median value would be the halfway point of the data. Divide 65 by 2 to get 32.5 which would mean the halfway point would be the value in the 33rd position. Counting the frequency until you reach the 33rd value would put you in the range of 21–25 (10 from 10–15, then 12 from 16–20, then 11 from 21–25 will get you 33 (10 + 12 + 11 = 33).

Choice A is incorrect because 12 is outside the range of 21–25. **Choice B is incorrect** because 20 is outside the range of 21–25. **Choice E is incorrect** because 26 is outside the range of 21–25. **Choice F is incorrect** because 31 is outside the range of 21–25.

10 **Choice B, C, D and E are correct.** Counting up the number of classes from the frequency table gives you 65 classes (10 + 12 + 22 + 21 = 65). Since 30.8% of courses are math courses, multiply 65 by 0.308 to get 20.02 which would round to 20 since it is not possible to have 0.02 of a course. Since there are 20 total math classes, at least 20% would mean that at least 4 courses are taught by a teacher (20 × 0.20 = 4)

Choice B is correct because 4 is a possible value since at least 4 were taught by student teachers. Choice C is correct because 8 is a possible value since at least 4 were taught by student teachers. Choice D is correct because 10 is a possible value since at least 4 were taught by student teachers. Choice E is correct because 12 is a possible value since at least 4 were taught by student teachers.

Choice A is incorrect because 2 is not a possible value since at least 4 were taught by student teachers. **Choice F is incorrect** because 21 is not a possible value since that is more than the number of math courses.

11 **Choice A is correct** because Michael recorded his successful product offers over a total of 31 days based on counting up the values from the chart. It can be determined that Michael made 7 successful offers once in the 31 days. To find the probability divide 1 by 31 to get approximately 0.032.

Choice B is incorrect because this is a higher probability than the actual value. **Choice C is incorrect** because this is a higher probability than the actual value. **Choice D is incorrect** because this is a higher probability than the actual value. **Choice E is incorrect** because this is a higher probability than the actual value.

12 **Choice C is correct** because the event of making 2 successful offers is mutually exclusive from the event of making 3 successful offers. The bars on the graph represent 31 days. Therefore, the number of days for each event can be read from the bar graph, and the probabilities can be added together.

P(2 offers) + P(3 offers) $= \frac{10}{31} + \frac{8}{31} = \frac{18}{31}$ which is approximately 0.581.

Choice A is incorrect because this is much lower of a probability than the actual value. **Choice B is incorrect** because this is much lower of a probability than the actual value. **Choice D is incorrect** because this is a higher probability than the actual value. **Choice E is incorrect** because this is a higher probability than the actual value.

Practice Set 1 (Easy): Answers & Explanations

13 **Choice E is correct** because the probability of having at least 1 successful offer is the complement (or opposite) of having 0 offers on a day. The equation P(at least 1 offer) = 1 – P(no offer) can be used to evaluate this. Therefore the probability would be $1 - \frac{1}{31} = \frac{30}{31}$ which is approximately 0.968.

Choice A is incorrect because this is a much lower probability than the actual value. **Choice B is incorrect** because this is the probability of 0 offers in a day. **Choice C is incorrect** because this is a much lower probability than the actual value. **Choice D is incorrect** because this is a much lower probability than the actual value.

14 **Choice B is correct** because the average weight of the family can be found to be 112 lb. To find this, first calculate the total weight of the family by first finding the total weight of all four kids. Multiply 4 by 60 to get 240 lb. The wife's weight was 210 lb, but she lost 2 lb each day for a week, making her final weight 210 – 2(7) = 196 lb. Add all of the weights together including the husband's to get a total of 196 + 240 + 236 = 672. Then divide this by 6 family members to get the average weight of 112 lb.

Choice A is incorrect because this is less than the average weight. **Choice C is incorrect** because this is greater than the average weight. **Choice D is incorrect** because this is greater than the average weight. **Choice E is incorrect** because this is greater than the average weight.

15 **Choice A is correct** because if the mean of 10 numbers is 16, the numbers in the data set can vary greatly. To get the lowest range, you will want to identify the lowest difference between the largest and smallest number. To get this, it is possible that all numbers are 16 since a data set of the same repeated value will always have a mean equal to that value. If the highest and lowest numbers are 16, then the range would be 16 – 16 which equals 0.

Choice B is incorrect because it is possible to get a smaller range than 1. **Choice C is incorrect** because it is possible to get a smaller range than 2. **Choice D is incorrect** because it is possible to get a smaller range than 3. **Choice E is incorrect** because it is possible to get a smaller range than 4.

16 **Choices A and B are correct.** A mathematical relationship based on the information can be found using the mean expression mean = $\frac{sum\ of\ values}{number\ of\ values}$. Filling this in with what is known gives you $17 > \frac{13+18+17+x}{4}$. This statement can be simplified to be $17 > \frac{48+x}{4}$.

Multiply both sides by 4 and you will get 68 > 48 + x. Subtract 48 and you will get 20 > x.

Choice A is correct because 0 < 20 and will get you an integer for the mean $\frac{48+0}{4} = \frac{48}{4} = 12$.

Choice B is correct because 8 < 20 and will get you an integer for the mean $\frac{48+8}{4} = \frac{56}{4} = 14$

Choice C is incorrect because if x = 10, you would not get an integer value for the mean. $\frac{48+10}{4} = \frac{58}{4} = 14.5$.

Choice D is incorrect because x must be less than 20 and cannot equal 20. **Choice E is incorrect** because x must be less than 20 to get a mean less than 17. **Choice F is incorrect** because x must be less than 20 to get a mean less than 17.

17 **Choice D is correct** because the average of each location can be found and then averaged. The average revenue generated per customer at the Princeton Street store would be $\frac{\$31,144}{458} = \$68$. For St Agnes Road, the average would be $\frac{\$58,320}{720} = \$81$. Finally, for Hayat Street, the average would be $\frac{\$34,336}{592} = \$58$. Add these averages together and divide to get the average of all three locations which is $\frac{\$68+\$81+\$58}{3} = \$69$.

Choice A is incorrect because this is less than the found average. **Choice B is incorrect** because this is less than the found average. **Choice C is incorrect** because this is less than the found average.

18 **Choice B is correct** because the P(B or L) is equal to 0.35. To find this, use the relationship that P(B or L) = P(B) + P(L) – P(B and L). Filling this relationship in will result in P(B or L) = 0.30 + 0.15 – 0.10. This adds to 0.35 for the final probability.

Chapter 6: Data Analysis

Choice A is incorrect because this is the result of incorrectly adding the probability of defective lights and defective lights and bad brakes. **Choice C is incorrect** because this is the result of incorrectly adding the probability of bad brakes and defective lights. **Choice D is incorrect** because this is the result of incorrectly adding all given probabilities. **Choice E is incorrect** because this is greater than the actual probability.

19 **Choice B is correct** because the total rainfall is 14% of the annual. This is found by adding up all of the values from the table by multiplying the number of days by the total rainfall and adding the products. The first row of 0 inches for 17 days will yield 0 so starting with the row of 1 in of rainfall, the equation would be 1(5) + 2(3) + 3(3) + 4(2) = 28 inches in total. Divide 28 by 200 and multiply by 100 to determine the percent. This will yield $\frac{28}{200} \times 100 = 14\%$

Choice A is incorrect because this is a much smaller percent than the actual value. **Choice C is incorrect** because this would be the result if the total rainfall in the 30-day period was divided by 100, not 200. **Choice D is incorrect** because this is a much greater percentage than the actual result. **Choice E is incorrect** because this would mean more than half the rainfall for the year was accounted for in one month which does not match the data.

20 **Choice C is correct.** Start from the condition, Adam has to be at the center.

| | | Adam | | |

There are four positions to be filled from the remaining 11 grandchildren, so the number of arrangements = $_{11}P_4$

$= \frac{11!}{(11-4)!}$

$= \frac{11!}{7!}$

$= 8 \times 9 \times 10 \times 11$

$= 7920$

Choice A is incorrect because there are more possible combinations. **Choice B is incorrect** because there are more possible combinations. **Choice D is incorrect** because this is greater than the number of possible combinations. **Choice E is incorrect** because this is greater than the number of possible combinations.

21 **Choice E is correct** because to find the total number of different combinations, multiply the number of ways for each item. Therefore, three different breads times four different meats times three different cheeses = 3 × 4 × 3 = 36.

Choice A is incorrect because this is just the number of options for bread or cheese. **Choice B is incorrect** because this is the number of options for meat. **Choice C is incorrect** because this results from incorrectly adding the number of each item to determine the combinations. **Choice D is incorrect** because this is less than the actual possible combinations.

22 **Choice D is correct** because the most the trip would cost is $33.60 and the least it would cost is $19.20. This can be found by multiplying the lowest cost by the best mileage to find the minimum cost of $\$0.96 \times \frac{480}{16} = \$19.20$. Then find the maximum cost with the expression of $\$1.12 \times \frac{480}{16} = \$33.60$. The difference would be $33.60 - $19.20 = $14.40

Choice A is incorrect because this is much lower than the actual difference in cost. **Choice B is incorrect** because this is much lower than the actual difference in cost. **Choice C is incorrect** because this is lower than the actual difference in cost. **Choice E is incorrect** because this is the result from incorrectly adding the maximum and minimum costs.

23 **Choice D is correct.** The probability that at least one of them arrives on time for work is the combination of the following events: Rob arrives on time but Tom arrives late, Rob arrives late but Tom arrives on time, and both Rob and Tom arrive on time. These 3 events combined are the complement of the event that both Rob and Tom arrive late for work.

P(at least one arrives on time)

=1−P(both Rob and Tom arrive late)

P(at least one arrives on time)=1−(0.12×0.16)

P(at least one arrives on time)=1−0.0192

P(at least one arrives on time)=0.9808

Choice A is incorrect because this would be the result if both were extremely likely to be late which is not the case. **Choice B is incorrect** because this would result from a higher probability they would be late. **Choice C is incorrect** because this is too low of a probability based on the given information. **Choice E is incorrect** because this is too high of a probability based on the given information.

Practice Set 1 (Easy): Answers & Explanations

24 Choice B is correct because you can find the sum of the terms and then use the average and number of terms to solve for the unknown. Average × number of terms = sum of terms. This would mean 16 × 6 = 15 + 37 + 19 + 9 + 23 + x. Simplifying would yield 96 = 100 + x which means $x = -4$.

Choice A is incorrect because this would lower than mean dramatically. **Choice C** is incorrect because a value of zero does not yield a mean of 16. **Choice D** is incorrect because this would make the mean greater than 16. **Choice E** is incorrect because this would make the mean greater than 16.

25 Choice D is correct because the sum of all of the numbers compared to the sum of the two numbers can help find the sum of the remaining numbers. The sum of all five numbers can be found with 8 × 5 = 40. The sum of the given two numbers would be –6 × 2 = –12. Now find the difference to be 40 – (–12) = 52.

Choice A is incorrect because this is not a large enough sum to find an average of 8. **Choice B** is incorrect because this is not a large enough sum to find an average of 8. **Choice C** is incorrect because this is not a large enough sum to find an average of 8. **Choice E** is incorrect because this is too large of a sum for the average of 8.

26 Choice D is correct. Let A be the set of students who like Mathematics and B be the set of students who like Science, thus $|A \cup B| = |A| + |B| - |A \cap B|$. Substituting the given into the formula yields $|A \cup B| = 12 + 15 - 5 = 22$.

It is given that the total number of students is 30. The probability that a student likes either Mathematics or Science is given by $P(A \cup B) = \dfrac{|A \cap B|}{Total\ number\ of\ students}$.

Substituting the given yields $P(A \cup B) = \dfrac{22}{30}$ or $P(A \cup B) = \dfrac{11}{15}$. Therefore, the correct answer is D.

Choice A is incorrect. This may result if the given is the probability that the student likes both Mathematics of Science. **Choice B** is incorrect. This may result if the given is the probability that the student likes Mathematics. **Choice C** is incorrect. This may result if the given is the probability that the student likes Science.

27 Choices B and D are correct.
Choice B is correct because the closing price of $35 on 01-06-2009 matches with 01-08-2009. **Choice D is correct** because the same closing price happened on 01-06-2009.

Choice A is incorrect because there is no other day with matching closing price. **Choice C** is incorrect because there is no other day with matching closing price. **Choice E** is incorrect because there is no other day with matching closing price.

28 Choice A is correct. The five gadgets have different price pointsl, hence, the difference in revenue despite the number of units sold. Now, to determine the ratio of products sold to revenue, simply divide the number of products sold by revenue percentage.

Smartphones: 120 / 10 = 12 : 1

Laptop: 180 / 30 = 6 : 1

Tablets: 150 / 22 = 6.8 : 1

Headphones: 250 / 20 = 12.5 : 1

Smartwatches: 100 / 18 = 5.6 : 1

By comparing their ratios, we can see that smartphones have the highest ratio of product sold to revenue.

Choice B is incorrect; laptops have the second to the lowest ratio of 6:1. **Choice C** is incorrect because headphones have the second highest ratio of 12.5:1 instead. **Choice D** is incorrect. Tablets have the second lowest ratio of 6.8:1. **Choice E** is incorrect and in fact, it has the lowest ratio.

29 Choices C, E and F are correct. The average number of millions of metric tons from the table can be found using the formula average = $\dfrac{sum\ of\ values}{number\ of\ values}$. Plugging in will give you the average = $\dfrac{2.6 + 1.5 + 1.4 + 2.3 + 0.8 + 0.4}{6}$. Simplifying the numerator yields $\dfrac{9}{6}$ which simplifies to be an average of 1.5.

Choice C is correct because Ethiopia is 1.4 which is less than 1.5. **Choice E is correct** because Kenya is 0.8 which is less than 1.5. **Choice F is correct** because Peru is 0.4 which is less than 1.5.

Choice A is incorrect because Brazil is 2.6 which is greater than 1.5. Choice B is incorrect because Columbia is 1.5 which equals and is not less than 1.5. Choice D is incorrect because Vietnam is 2.3 which equals and is not less than 1.5.

Chapter 6: Data Analysis

30 **Choices D, E and F are correct.** If the total coffee bean production for Brazil was 2.6 million metric tons, then the total amount of coffee bean production can be found using the ratio of $\frac{54.5}{100} = \frac{2.6}{x}$ because the total percentage of coffee bean production in Brazil compared to the total percentage of all coffee bean production is proportional to the amount of coffee beans produced in Brazil compared to coffee beans produced worldwide. Solving this proportion through cross multiplication would yield $54.5x = 260$. Divide both sides by 54.5 to get approximately 4.77. This means there were at least a total of 4.77 million metric tons of coffee beans produced.

Choice D is correct because 5.6 is greater than 4.77.
Choice E is correct because 6.8 is greater than 4.77.
Choice F is correct because 7.9 is greater than 4.77.
Choice A is incorrect because 3.8 is less than 4.77.
Choice B is incorrect because 4.2 is less than 4.77.
Choice C is incorrect because 4.7 is less than 4.77.

31 The correct answer is $\frac{8}{55}$.
There is a total of 275 travelers who participated in the survey. There are 40 people traveling to Asia (23+17). Hence, the probability is $\frac{40}{275} = \frac{8}{55}$.

32 The correct answer is $\frac{12}{55}$.
There is a total of 275 travelers who participated in the survey. The number of females going to Europe is 60. Hence, the probability is $\frac{60}{275} = \frac{12}{55}$.

33 **Choices A, C and E are correct.** All of the multiples of 90 will give you an odd number when added together so any whole number as an average is not possible. Then use the rule of averages to identify which multiples of 90 would get you each answer through guess and check. Multiples of 90 are 1 and 90, 2 and 45, 3 and 30, 6 and 15, 5 and 18, and 10 and 9. All multiples can be negative as well such as −1 and −90 since two negatives equal a positive when multiplied.

Choice A is correct because −45.5 would be the average if the two numbers were −1 and −90 because their product would be 90 and their average would be −45.5. **Choice C** is correct because 10 and 9 can be multiplied to be 90 and the average of 10 and 9 is 9.5. **Choice E** is correct because 5 and 18 are multiples that will give you an average of 11.5.

Choice B is incorrect because it is not possible to get a whole number average with the multiples of 90. **Choice D** is incorrect because it is not possible to get a whole number average with the multiples of 90.

34 The correct answer is $\frac{55}{103}$. This is a conditional probability question. There are 55 males going to North America, and there are a total of (55 + 48 = 103) people going to North America. Since the condition is that the traveler is going to North America, the probability that the traveler is a male is 55 out of 103, or $\frac{55}{103}$.

35 **Choice C is correct.** If we add the sales of old and new cars we will get the following information

Year	Old Cars	New Cars	Total Cars
2011	5	6	11
2012	6.2	7	13.2
2013	7	8.1	15.1
2014	8.1	9	17.1
2015	9	11.8	20.8
2016	12	12	24
2017	11	13	24
2018	10.5	16	26.5
2019	9	16.5	25.5
2020	9.2	17	26.2

From this, we will be able to see the answer as the years 2016 and 2017 (24,000 cars each)

Choice A is incorrect because in 2012 there were 13,200 cars sold and in 2013 there were 15,100 cars sold. **Choice B** is incorrect because in 2018 there were 26,500 cars sold and in 2019 there were 25,500 cars sold. **Choice D** is incorrect because in 2015 there were 20,800 cars sold and in 2019 there were 25,500 cars sold. **Choice E** is incorrect because in 2019 there were 25,500 cars sold and in 2020 there were 26,200 cars sold.

36 **Choice C is correct** because the years in which the old car sales were less than the previous year but the new car sales were more than the previous year are 2017, 2018, and 2019.

Choice A is incorrect because there were three years in this category. **Choice B** is incorrect because there were three years in this category. **Choice D** is incorrect because there were three years in this category. **Choice E** is incorrect because there were three years in this category.

37 The correct answer is $\frac{1}{3}$ or 0.33. The numbers that are greater than 4 on a six-sided die are 5 and 6. Thus, there are 2 favorable outcomes. The total number of possible outcomes when rolling a die is 6.

The probability of rolling a number greater than 4 is $\frac{number\ of\ favorable\ outcome}{total\ number\ of\ outcomes} = \frac{2}{6} = \frac{1}{3}$. Therefore, the probability of rolling a number greater than 4 is $\frac{1}{3}$.

Practice Set 2 (Medium): Answers & Explanations

38 Choice B is correct.

The sum of n numbers is their mean multiplied by n

The sum of the first 10 numbers = 10 × 83 = 830

The sum of the second group of 20 numbers = 20 × 65 = 1300

The mean of the 30 numbers is = $\frac{(830+1300)}{(10+20)} = \frac{2130}{30} = 71$

When k is added to the 10 numbers, the new mean is 82 and we have 11 numbers

The sum of the 10 numbers + k = 11 × 82 = 902

$k = 902 - 830 = 72$

72 is greater than 71. Hence the right column is greater than the left column.

Choice A is incorrect because 71 is less than 72. **Choice C** is incorrect because k and the mean are not the same values. **Choice D** is incorrect because it is possible to solve for Quantity A and Quantity B.

39 Choice C is correct. Remember, the median of a group of numbers is the number that is exactly in the middle of the group when the group is arranged from smallest to largest. To find the median of set A, you have to put the numbers in order: −4, −1, 2, 3, 7, and 11. Since there are only six numbers, you have to take the average of the two middle numbers, 2 and 3. The average of 2 and 3 is 2.5. To find the average of set B, add up all the numbers and divide by six, because there are six numbers. The sum of the numbers in set B is 15 divided by 6 is 2.5. So, the quantities are equal.

Choice A is incorrect because the two values are equal.
Choice B is incorrect because the two values are equal.
Choice D is incorrect because it is possible to compare the quantities.

40 Choice B is correct.

Average = $\frac{110 \cdot 26 + 140 \cdot 30 + 200 \cdot 23}{(110+140+200)} = 25.9111$

Compare 25.9111 with 26, we conclude that 25.9111<26, hence

Quantity B is greater than Quantity A.

Choice A is incorrect because 25.9111<26. **Choice C** is incorrect because 25.9111 is not equal to 26. **Choice D** is incorrect because all values can be determined from the given information.

41 Choice B is correct because the average Mandy made per day is less than $14.50. To determine this, follow these steps:

The average amount Mandy made per hour from Monday to Wednesday can be found by finding the sum of how much money she made per day and then dividing by the total hours worked on Monday, Tuesday, and Wednesday.

To find the sum of how much she made, multiply the hours worked by the amount made.

For Monday, she made $15 x 5 = $75.

For Tuesday, she made $12 x 6 = $72.

For Wednesday, she made $16 x 8 = $128.

Add $75 + $72 + $128 together to get a total of $275.

Divide by the total hours worked (5 + 6 + 8 = 19 hours) to get about $14.47 on average per hour.

Compare this average to Quantity B and see that $14.47 < $14.50, making Quantity B larger and choice B correct.

Choice A is incorrect because Quantity A is equal to $14.47 which is less than $14.50. **Choice C** is incorrect because the average amount Mandy made per hour is not $14.50 and therefore the two quantities are not equal. **Choice D** is incorrect because you can determine the value of Quantity A.

42 Choice A is correct. After the fourth test, Sarah and John's test scores were 91 and 90, respectively. This means that their total test scores are:

Sarah: $4 \times 91 = 364$

John: $4 \times 90 = 360$

This means that the sum of the four test scores is 364 and 360, respectively, for Sarah and John. First, let's take a look at the total test scores of Sarah and John for the first three tests:

Sarah: $88 + 92 + 93 = 273$

John: $85 + 90 + 95 = 270$

To find how Sarah and John performed during the fourth test, their total score from the scores of the three tests.

Sarah: $364 - 273 = 91$

John: $360 - 270 = 90$

This means that Sarah scored better than John on the fourth test, so Quantity A is greater.

Choice B is incorrect since John scored 90 and Sarah scored 91 on the fourth test. **Choice C** is incorrect because Sarah scored better than John. **Choice D** is incorrect because it is possible to find Sarah and John's test scores and compare them.

43 **Choice C is correct**. To find x in Set A, use the formula for the mean to get

$$\text{mean}_{\text{set A}} = \frac{2+5+7+10+x}{5} = 6.$$ Solving for x yields $\frac{24+x}{5} = 6$ or $x = 6$.

To find y in Set B, use the formula for the mean to get

$$\text{mean}_{\text{set B}} = \frac{3+4+8+9+y}{5} = 6.$$ Solving for y yields $\frac{24+y}{5} = 6$ or $y = 6$.

Therefore, $x = y = 6$.

Choice A is incorrect. The two quantities are equal; therefore, neither quantity is greater. **Choice B** is incorrect. The two quantities are equal; therefore, neither quantity is greater. **Choice D** is incorrect. There is enough data to determine the relationship between the two.

44 **Choice B is correct** because standard deviation is a measurement of the spread of a data set and if all numbers are multiplied by 10, the standard deviation would increase. For example, if the data set was 1, 2, 3, 4, and 5, the standard deviation can be calculated to be about 1.41. If those numbers were multiplied by 10, their new values would be 10, 20, 30, 40, and 50. The standard deviation of this data set would be about 14.14.

Choice A is incorrect because the standard deviation of the number set is not greater than the standard deviation if the numbers were multiplied by 10. **Choice C** is incorrect because the standard deviations are not equal. **Choice D** is incorrect because it is possible to compare the standard deviations.

45 **Choice B is correct** because to find the greatest possible value for w is 127, use the expression:

$$\text{average} = \frac{\text{sum of values}}{\text{number of values}}.$$

Plugging in what is known from the first idea that the average of x and y is 32 gives you the expression $32 = \frac{x+y}{2}$. Multiply both sides by 2 to get $64 = x + y$. Next, use the average equation again with the information that the average of x, y, z, and w is 48 to get $48 = \frac{x+y+z+w}{4}$. Multiply both sides by 4 to get $192 = x + y + z + w$.

Plug in $x + y = 64$ to get $192 = 64 + z + w$. Subtract 64 from both sides and you will find that $128 = z + w$. Since both numbers have to be integers, plug in 1 as the small value of z to get the largest value of w. Now subtract 1 from both sides of the expression $128 = 1 + w$ to get $127 = w$.

Choice A is incorrect because the value of w is 127 which is less than 128. **Choice C** is incorrect because the two quantities are not equal. **Choice D** is incorrect because it is possible to solve for the greatest value of w.

46 **Choice B is correct** because the probability of Quantity B is greater than the probability of Quantity A. To find the probability of picking a perfect cube when choosing any two digit positive integer, first identify the two digit positive integers between 10 and 99. There are a total of 90 possible outcomes and there are two perfect cubes: 27 and 64. This means the probability of picking a perfect cube when choosing any two digit positive integer is equal to 2 out of 90 or $\frac{1}{45}$.

For Quantity B, the probability of choosing a perfect square or a number divisible by 25 when choosing integers less than 100 can be found by solving for the probability of a perfect square or divisible by 25. This would be written as P(perfect square or divisible by 25) = P(perfect square) + P(divisibility by 25) - P(perfect square and divisible by 25). There are 99 numbers that are positive integers less than 100. There are nine perfect squares. There are three numbers divisible by 25 which

Practice Set 2 (Medium): Answers & Explanations

include 25, 50, and 75. There is one number that's both a perfect square and divisible by 25 which is 25. Therefore, the probability will equal $\frac{9}{99} + \frac{3}{99} - \frac{1}{99} = \frac{1}{9}$. For comparison purposes, $\frac{1}{9} = \frac{5}{45}$.

Since $\frac{5}{45}$ is greater than $\frac{1}{45}$, Quantity B is greater. **Choice A** is incorrect because $\frac{5}{45}$ is greater than $\frac{1}{45}$. **Choice C** is incorrect because the two probabilities are not equal. **Choice D** is incorrect because it is possible to compare the two quantities.

47 **Choice A is correct.** The total number of chocolates in the box is 17. But since there were already 2 almond-centered chocolates taken, only 15 are left. All 3 mint cream and 5 strawberry cream filled chocolates remain, but only 7 almond-centered chocolates remain. Quantity A is mint cream filled OR strawberry cream filled, so the probability is:

$$\frac{3}{15} + \frac{5}{15} = \frac{8}{15}$$

Quantity B is for almond-centered chocolates, which is $\frac{7}{15}$. Therefore, Quantity A is greater than Quantity B.

Choice B is incorrect because Quantity A is greater than Quantity B. **Choice C** is incorrect because the two quantities are not equal. **Choice D** is incorrect because it is possible to compare the quantities.

48 **Choice A is correct** because the probability of two independent events occurring is equal to the product of the individual event probabilities.

To find the probability of Quantity A, start with the fact that the chance of rolling a number greater than 1 is 5 out of 6. Then determine the probability of rolling a prime number is 3 out of 6. Multiplying these two probabilities together would give you $\frac{5}{6} \times \frac{3}{6} = \frac{15}{36}$.

Find the probability of Quantity B, first identify the probability of rolling an even number is 3 out of 6. Then the probability of rolling a factor of 6 would be equal to 4 out of 6. Multiplying these two probabilities would give you $\frac{3}{6} \times \frac{4}{6} = \frac{12}{36}$.

Therefore, Quantity A is greater than Quantity B.

Choice B is incorrect because Quantity B is less than Quantity A. **Choice C** is incorrect because the two probabilities are not equal. **Choice D** is incorrect because it is possible to solve for the given probabilities.

49 **Choice C is correct** because this is a simplified ratio of the laptop sold by shop one compared to the total laptop sold in 2019. To find the number of laptops sold by shop 1 in all the years add together 300 + 420 + 520 = 1,240. to find the total number of laptops sold in 2019 and all the shops together add together 420 + 400 + 200 + 320 + 600 = 1,940.

Choice A is incorrect because this is a different ratio than the actual number. **Choice B** is incorrect because this might result from mistakenly changing the order of the ratio. **Choice D** is incorrect because this answer results from a math error when simplifying. **Choice E** is incorrect because this is a different ratio than the actual result.

50 **Choice B is correct** because the number sold by shop 3 in all years and divided it by the number sold by shop 4 in all years would yield 129.4%. The total number of laptops sold by shop 3 in all the years together is equal to 400 + 200 + 280 = 880. The total number of laptops sold by shop 4 in all the years together equals 120 + 320 + 240 = 680. The percent can be found by dividing 880 by 680 and multiplying by 100 which yields 129.4%.

Choice A is incorrect because this percentage would result from a math error. **Choice C** is incorrect because this percentage would result from a math error. **Choice D** is incorrect because this is a much greater percentage than found. **Choice E** is incorrect because this is a much greater percentage than found.

51 **Choices B, D and E are correct.** Percentage increase = (Increase/Initial) × 100

Let's evaluate the options:

A. 2012 to 2014:
$\frac{300 - 220}{220} \times 100 = 36.36\%$ (not in the range asked)

B. 2011 to 2016:
$\frac{300 - 200}{200} \times 100 = 60\%$ (in the range asked)

C. 2013 to 2018:
$\frac{380 - 250}{250} \times 100 = 52\%$ (not in the range asked)

D. 2011 to 2019:
$\frac{400 - 200}{200} \times 100 = 100\%$ (in the range asked)

For more practice, visit www.vibrantpublishers.com

Chapter 6: **Data Analysis**

E. 2012 to 2020:
$\frac{400-200}{200} \times 100 = 100\%$ (in the range asked)

F. 2015 to 2019:
$\frac{400-310}{310} \times 100 = 29.03\%$ (not in the range asked)

Choice A is incorrect because the increase in price would be equal to 300 − 220 = 120. This would result in a percentage of 36.36% (120300 × 100 = 36.36%). This is not in the range of values possible. **Choice C** is incorrect because the difference would be found by subtracting 380 − 250 then dividing by 250 and multiplying by 100 to get 52%. This is not in the range of values possible. **Choice F** is incorrect because the increase in price would be equal to 400 - 310. then dividing this number by 310 and multiplying by 100 gets us 29.03% which is not in the range of values.

52 **Choices D, E and F are correct.**

Total revenue generated in 2019 = $40,000

Therefore, revenue generated from the sale of smart watches of this particular brand must be greater than 50% of $40,000.

In other words, the revenue generated from the sale of smart watches of this particular brand must be greater than $20,000

Price of the watch in 2019 = $400.

Therefore, to earn a revenue of $20,000, the number of watches sold = $20,000/$400 = 50

So the number of smart watches of the said brand sold in that year must be greater than 50, but less than or equal to 100 (as the total revenue is $40,000).

Only options (D), (E) and (F) are in this range.

Choice A is incorrect because it is not within the given range. **Choice B** is incorrect because it is not within the given range. **Choice C** is incorrect because it is not within the given range.

53 **The correct answer is 22%** because you will need to evaluate the percent of each department that works full time and enrolled in healthcare. To do this, take the number of full time workers from the table and multiply by the corresponding percent from the chart. For accounting, you would get 50 × 0.206 (20.6%) which equals 10.3. For sales, you would get 100 × 0.20 (20%) which equals 20. For marketing, you would get 120 × 0.257 (25.7%) which equals 30.84. For HR, you would get 30 × 0.137 (13.7%) which equals 4.11. For management, you would get 50 × 0.2 (20%) which equals 10. Adding these amounts together 10.3 + 20 + 30.84 + 4.11 + 10 will give you 75.25. Adding up all of the employees both full time and part time will get you 350 employees. Divide 75.25 by 350 and multiply by 100 to get around 21.5% which rounds to 22%.

54 **Choice D is correct.** The corporate sectors that decreased their support for Philanthropic causes from 2000 to 2005 are: Manufacturing, Retail, Wholesale and Others.

The total contribution by the Corporate Sectors towards Philanthropic Causes in the year 2005 was $570 million.

Amount contributed by the Manufacturing Sector in 2005 = 20% of 570 million

$= \frac{20}{100} \times 570 = \$114$ million

Amount contributed by the Retail Sector in 2005 = 8% of 570 million

$= \frac{8}{100} \times 570 = \$45.6$ million

Amount contributed by the Wholesale Sector in 2005 = 6% of 570 million

$= \frac{6}{100} \times 570 = \$34.2$ million

Amount contributed by the Other Sectors in 2005 = 18% of 570 million

$= \frac{18}{100} \times 570 = \$102.6$ million

The total amount contributed by these four sectors towards Philanthropic Causes in the year 2005
= 114 + 45.6 + 34.2 + 102.6 = $296.4 million = $300 million approximately.

Choice A is incorrect because this is just a partial amount of the total. **Choice B** is incorrect because this is less than the actual amount. **Choice C** is incorrect because this would be the result if you incorrectly rounded down. **Choice E** is incorrect because this is greater than the actual amount.

55 **Choice C is correct.** Amount contributed by the Finance, Insurance and Real Estate Sector in:

Year 2000 $= \frac{5}{100} \times 680 = \$34$ million

Year 2005 $= \frac{26}{100} \times 570 = \$148.2$ million

Amount contributed by the Service Sector in:

Year 2000 $= \dfrac{17}{100} \times 680 = \$115.6$ million

Year 2005 $= \dfrac{22}{100} \times 570 = \$125.4$ million

Amount contributed by the Manufacturing Sector in:

Year 2000 $= \dfrac{31}{100} \times 680 = \$210.8$ million

Year 2005 $= \dfrac{20}{100} \times 570 = \$114$ million

Amount contributed by the Retail Sector in:

Year 2000 $= \dfrac{19}{100} \times 680 = \$129.2$ million

Year 2005 $= \dfrac{8}{100} \times 570 = \$45.6$ million

Amount contributed by the Wholesale Sector in:

Year 2000 $= \dfrac{8}{100} \times 680 = \$54.4$ million

Year 2005 $= \dfrac{6}{100} \times 570 = \$34.2$ million

Amount contributed by the Other Sectors in:

Year 2000 $= \dfrac{20}{100} \times 680 = \$136$ million

Year 2005 $= \dfrac{18}{100} \times 570 = \$102.6$ million

We see that three sectors (Service, Manufacturing and Other) contributed more than $100 million in both 2000 and 2005.

Total amount contributed by the Service Sector in both years = 115.6 + 125.4 = $241 million

Total amount contributed by the Manufacturing Sector in both years = 210.8 + 114 = $324.8 million

Total amount contributed by the Other Sectors in both years = 136 + 102.6 = $238.6 million

Average amount contributed by these three sectors

$= \dfrac{241 + 324.8 + 238.6}{3} = \$268.13$ million

Choice A is incorrect because this is 20% of 570 which is not the total. **Choice B** is incorrect because this is a total amount contributed by the other sector, not the average. **Choice D** is incorrect because this is greater than the average. **Choice E** is incorrect because this is greater than the average.

56 **Choice B is correct.** Financial, Insurance and Real Estate Sector's 2005 contribution to Philanthropic Causes

$= \dfrac{26}{100} \times 570 = \$148.2$ million

Amount given for re-building homes $= \dfrac{1}{3} \times 148.2 = \$49.40$ million

Amount remaining = 148.2 − 49.40 = $98.80 million

Amount given for providing medical aid

$= \dfrac{1}{4} \times 98.8 = \$24.7$ million

Amount spent on rebuilding homes− Amount spent on medical aid

= 49.40 − 24.70 = $24.7 million = $25 million approximately.

Choice A is incorrect because this is lower than the actual amount. **Choice C** is incorrect because this is higher than the actual amount. **Choice D** is incorrect because this is higher than the actual amount. **Choice E** is incorrect because this is higher than the actual amount.

57 **Choice B is correct** because you will need to evaluate the percent increase or decrease for each of the sectors one at a time. The financial, insurance, and real estate sector had a total increase of 335.88% because from 2000 it was 34 million and in 2005 it was 148.2 million and the difference divided by the original would yield 335.88%. For services, in 2000 they had 115.6 million and in 2005 they had 125.4 million for a total percent increase of 8.48%. Manufacturing saw a percent decrease of −45.92%, retail had a decrease of negative −64.71%, wholesale saw a decrease of −37.13%, and others saw a decrease of −24.56%. These would be all found by taking the difference and dividing by the original. To find the average change in contributions not including financial, insurance, and real estate add up all the percentages and divide by five to get a total average of −33%.

Choice A is incorrect because this is higher than the actual percentage. **Choice C** is incorrect because this is lower than the actual percentage. **Choice D** is incorrect because this is lower than the actual percentage. **Choice E** is incorrect because this is lower than the actual percentage.

58 **Choice A is correct** because using the total salary and the values given you can solve for the total number of employees in section B. start by finding the total salary by multiplying $14,000 × 66 to get $524,000. Let x and y be the number of employees in section A and section B. you can create the statement $12,000x + 24,000y = 524,000$. This will simplify to be $x + 2y = 77$. You also know $x + y = 66$. Using elimination between these two equations you can determine $y = 11$.

Choice B is incorrect because this would result in an average salary greater than what is given. **Choice C** is incorrect because this would result in an average salary greater than what is given. **Choice D** is incorrect because this would result in an average salary greater than what is given. **Choice E** is incorrect because this would result in an average salary greater than what is given.

59 **Choice B is correct.** Use an Average Pie to solve this one. Write in the number of things, which is 4, and the average, which is 11.

Multiply to find the total, which is 44. Now you have to be careful with the vocabulary in the question. We know that the four distinct positive integers add up to 44. To find the greatest possible value of one of them, you need to figure out the smallest possible value of the other three. Since distinct means different, the other three numbers have to be the smallest positive integers: 1, 2, and 3. Those add up to 6, so the fourth number must be 44 − 6, or 38.

Choice A is incorrect because there is a larger value possible. **Choice C** is incorrect because it is not possible to get greater than 38. **Choice D** is incorrect because it is not possible to get greater than 38. **Choice E** is incorrect because it is not possible to get greater than 38.

60 **Choice B is correct.** Total number of people surveyed = 18 + 11 + 15 + 8 + 6 = 58

So the median will be the mean (average) of the 29th and 30th data points in the sorted list containing

18 – 0s, followed by 11 – 1s, followed by 15 – 2s, followed by 8 – 3s, followed by 6 – 4s.

The 29th data point is 1 and the 30th data point is 2, therefore median = (1 + 2)/2 = 1.5

Choice A is incorrect because this is too low of a median. **Choice C** is incorrect because this is the 30th data point not the median. **Choice D** is incorrect because this is greater than the actual median. **Choice E** is incorrect because this is greater than the actual median.

61 **Choice B is correct.** Given that $m = 165$ and $d = 3$, 162cm = 165 − 3 = $m - d$. Looking at the graph above, the sections on the bell curve to the left of $m - d$ represent the probabilities of 14% and 2%, which add up to 16%.

Choice A is incorrect because this is one of the probabilities but not the sum of both. **Choice C** is incorrect because this is greater than the probability given. **Choice D** is incorrect because this is greater than the probability given. **Choice E** is incorrect because this is greater than the probability given.

62 **Choices A, B and C are correct.** The probabilities can be given based on the standard deviation. In the order given, the probabilities are 2%, 14%, 34%, 34%, 14%, and 2%.

Choice A is correct because less than 159 is 2% in more than 171 is also 2%. **Choice B** is correct because between 159 and 162 is 14% and between 168 and 171 is 14%. **Choice C** is correct because between 162 and 165 is 34% and between 165 and 168 is also 34%.

Choice D is incorrect because between 159 and 162 is 14% and between $165 and 168 is 34%, which does not match.

63 **Choices A and D are correct.** For each department to have 60% or more in full time, make sure all departments have the correct ratio once all new hires are allocated. Before the new hires, all departments were greater than 60% except for management. So the answer needs to allocate employees to management full time.

Choice A is correct because 10 hires to full time accounting would make the percent of full time employees in that department 75% ($\frac{50+10}{50+20+10} = \frac{60}{80}$ = 75%). 15 hires to part time sales will still keep the full time ratio over 60% ($\frac{100}{100+30+15} = \frac{100}{145} = 69\%$). 25 hires to full time management will make that department go over the 60% requirement ($\frac{50+25}{50+40+25} = \frac{75}{115} = 65\%$).

Choice D is correct because 30 hires to full time management will put it over the 60% requirement ($\frac{50+30}{50+40+30} = \frac{80}{120} = 67\%$). 5 hires to part time accounting will keep the ratio over 60% ($\frac{50}{50+20+5} = \frac{50}{75} = 67\%$). An additional 15 hires to full time marketing will keep the ratio over 60% ($\frac{120+15}{120+50+15} = \frac{135}{185} = 73\%$).

Choice B is incorrect because 5 hires to full time management would not reach 60% full time for that department ($\frac{50+5}{50+40+5} = \frac{55}{95} = 58\%$).

Choice C is incorrect because 35 hires to part time marketing will make the ratio below 60% for full time in that department ($\frac{120}{120+50+35} = \frac{120}{205} = 59\%$)

64 **Choice D is correct.** Revenue generated per customer is given as Revenue/Number of customers

Revenue generated per customer at Princeton Street = $31,144/458 = $68

Revenue generated per customer at St Agnes Road = $58,320/720 = $81

Revenue generated per customer at Hayat Street = $34,336/592 = $58

Average of all three = ($68 + $81 + $58)/3 = $69

Choice A is incorrect because this is less than the found average. **Choice B** is incorrect because this is less than the found average. **Choice C** is incorrect because this is less than the found average. **Choice E** is incorrect because this is greater than the found average.

65 **Choice C is correct.** For combined events, the formula is

$P(A \text{ or } B) = P(A) + P(B) - P(A \text{ and } B)$

Substituting the given values,

$$\frac{3}{4} = \frac{1}{2} + P(N) - \frac{1}{6}$$

$$\frac{9}{12} = \frac{6}{12} + P(N) - \frac{2}{12}$$

$$\frac{9}{12} = \frac{4}{12} + P(N)$$

$$P(N) = \frac{5}{12}$$

Choice A is incorrect because this answer results from a math error. **Choice B** is incorrect because this answer results from a math error. **Choice D** is incorrect because this answer results from a math error. **Choice E** is incorrect because it is not possible for the probability to equal 1 based on the other probabilities given.

66 **Choice B is correct.** Number of employees who work in both Marketing and Sales = 1/2 of 200 = 100

As 160 employees work in the Marketing department, number of employees who work in Marketing only = 160 − 100 = 60

If x is the number of employees who work only in Sales, total number of employees who work in Sales = x + 100

Therefore, number of employees who work in neither Marketing nor Sales = (100 + x)/3

This is shown in the Venn Diagram below:

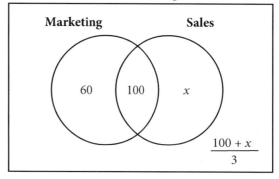

As the total number of employees = 200, we have

60 + 100 + x + (100 + x)/3 = 200

Or, 160 + x + (100 + x)/3 = 200

Or, x + (100 + x)/3 = 40

Multiplying throughout by 3 we have

3x + 100 + x = 120

Or, 4x = 20

Or, x = 5

Therefore, number of employees working in the Sales department = 100 + 5 = 105

Choice A is incorrect because this is too small of a number to match what is given. **Choice C** is incorrect because this is too large of a number to match what is given. **Choice D** is incorrect because this is too large of a number to match what is given. **Choice E** is incorrect because this is too large of a number to match what is given.

67 **Choice C is correct** because there are 4 out of 30 possible outcomes. When rolling two dice the possibility of getting a sum of at most 4 can be found with 1 and 1, 1 and 2, 2 and 1, 1 and 3, 3 and 1, 2 and 2. This means that there are 4 possible options out of 30 possible combinations, making the probability $\frac{4}{30} = \frac{2}{15}$.

Chapter 6: Data Analysis

Choice A is incorrect because this is too low of a probability. **Choice B** is incorrect because this probability results from a math error. **Choice D** is incorrect because this is too high of a probability. **Choice E** is incorrect because this is too high of a probability.

68 **Choice C is correct.**

Number of female contestants = 200 − 80 = 120

Number of male contestants arriving late = 1/5 of 80 = 16

Number of female contestants arriving late = 1/6 of 120 = 20

Total number of contestants arriving late = 16 + 20 = 36

Probability that the prize will be won by a contestant who arrived late

= Number of people arriving late/Total number of contestants

= 36/200 that simplifies to 9/50

Choice A is incorrect because this probability does not match. **Choice B** is incorrect because this probability does not match. **Choice D** is incorrect because this probability does not match. **Choice E** is incorrect because this probability does not match.

69 **Choice B is correct.** II only. The arithmetic mean is the average (sum divided by number of items), or 6 + 2 + 10 + 2 + 5 = 25 divided by 5 = 5.

The median is the middle number after the numbers have been ordered: 2, 2, 5, 6, 10.

The median is 5.

The mode is the most frequently appearing number: 2.

The range is the highest minus the lowest, or 10 − 2 = 8.

Therefore, only II is true: The median 5 equals the mean 5.

Choice A is incorrect because the median is 5 and the mode is 2, which are not equal. **Choice C** is incorrect because the range is 8 and the median is 5 which are not equal. **Choice D** is incorrect because the median does not equal the mode. **Choice E** is incorrect because the range does not equal the median.

70 **Choices A and D are correct.** The only categories that had an increase between January 2020 and March 2020 were CDs and DVDs, TVs, and cellphones. Use the percent increase formula $\left|\dfrac{initial - final}{initial}\right| \times 100$ to find which of these categories had over 100% increase.

Choice A is correct because $\left|\dfrac{54 - 125}{54}\right| \times 100 = 131\%$.

Choice D is correct because $\left|\dfrac{12 - 35}{12}\right| \times 100 = 192\%$.

Choice B is incorrect because appliances did not see an increase from January 2020 to March 2020.

Choice C is incorrect because computers did not see an increase from January 2020 to March 2020.

Choice E is incorrect because cellphones did not see more than 100% increase since using the formula yields $\left|\dfrac{31 - 43}{31}\right| \times 100 = 29.6\%$.

71 **The correct answer is 780** because if you add up all of the products you will get 650 total products sold between January 2020 and March 2020. This number is $\dfrac{1}{4}$ of 2600 which you can find by multiplying 650 by 4. Using the pie chart for 2020, you can find the difference in percentages between online and in store purchases that is 30%. To find 30% of 2600, multiply 2600 by 0.30 to get 780.

72 **Choices B and C are correct.** Online sales increased drastically between 2010 and 2020, while in store sales decreased. The statements chosen must match this idea based on the items sold online versus the items sold in store.

Choice B is correct because the table shows that in Q1 of 2020, CDs and DVDs saw an increase in purchases and since they were sold online they would account for an increase in online sales. Choice C is correct because the percent of products sold in store decreased meaning it is likely that the categories of items still sold in store did not increase enough to make a difference in the percent of sales in store.

Choice A is incorrect because this is a statement that could be true, but there is no evidence to directly support that video games were the sole cause of the percent increase from 2010 to 2020 for online sales. **Choice D** is incorrect because it is not possible to prove this based on the data and could be true, but does not have to be true.

73 **Choice B is correct** because to find the median, list off all of the three digit numbers that are possible with the digits 1, 3, and 5 from least to greatest: 135, 153, 315, 351, 513, and 531. Then find the middle number by counting in from the sides. Crossing off the numbers will get you

Practice Set 2 (Medium): Answers & Explanations

315 and 351 as the two middle numbers. The median will be the midpoint between these two numbers which is found by adding up the numbers and dividing by 2. This would give you $\frac{315+351}{2} = \frac{666}{2}$ which equals 333.

Choice A is incorrect because this is one number short of the median. **Choice C** is incorrect because this is one number greater than the median. **Choice D** is incorrect because this is the median of 351 and 513. **Choice E** is incorrect because this is the second to last number in the data set.

74 **Choice C is correct** because to find the median you need to first find the value of x. To do this, set-up the relationships for each month and then use the average to solve.

For the first month, the number of cars sold is x. For the second month, the number of cars sold would be $2x$. For the last month, the number of cars sold would be $x + 20$. Add these values together, divide by 4 and then set equal to 44 to use the average formula of $\frac{sum\,of\,values}{number\,of\,values} =$ average to find x. This would give you $\frac{x+2x+x+20}{3} =$ 44. Simplify the numerator and then multiply by 4 to get $4x + 20 = 132$. Subtract 20 and then divide by 4 to get $x = 28$.

Now you can plug this in to get the three month car sales as 28, 56 ($2x$), and 48 ($x + 20$). Reordering these values gives you 28, 48, and 56. The middle number in this data set is 48.

Choice A is incorrect because this is the value of x, not the median. **Choice B** is incorrect because this is the average, not the median. **Choice D** is incorrect because this results from a math error when calculating the average and accidentally adding 20 instead of subtracting. **Choice E** is incorrect because this is the largest number of cars sold, not the median.

75 **Choice C is correct** because if 14 is the lowest number in the data set, the mean would be $\frac{14+16+18+20+22+24+26+28}{8}$ which equals 21. To find this algebraically, use arithmetic series to solve for the sum of the data set with the formula $S = \frac{n}{2}(a_1 + a_n)$. Since you known n = 8, you can plug that into

the equation to get $S = \frac{8}{2}(a_1 + a_8)$ which simplifies to be $4(a_1 + a_8)$.

You also know that the set consists of even consecutive numbers which can be represented by the arithmetic formula $a_n = a_1 + d(n - 1)$ so in this case you can use 8 to find $a_8 = a_1 + 2(8 - 1)$ which simplifies to be $a_8 = a_1 + 14$. Plug this into the summation equation to get the sum is equal to $4(a_1 + a_1 + 14)$ which becomes $4(2a_1 + 14)$. Distribute to get $8a_1 + 56$.

Now, plug this into the average equation of average $= \frac{sum\,of\,values}{number\,of\,values}$ to get $21 = \frac{8a_1 + 56}{8}$. Multiply both sides by 8 to get $168 = 8a_1 + 56$. Subtract 56 and then divide by 8 to get 14 as your a_1 value.

Choice A is incorrect because this would give an average less than 21. **Choice B** is incorrect because this would give an average less than 21. **Choice D** is incorrect because this would give an average greater than 21. **Choice E** is incorrect because this would give an average greater than 21.

76 **Choice D is correct.** The total number of cases is 2^{100}. The number of favorable ways is $_{100}C_1 + {}_{100}C_3 + ... + {}_{100}C_{99}$ $= 2^{100-1} = 2^{99}$. Therefore, the probability of the required event is $\frac{2^{99}}{2^{100}} = \frac{1}{2}$

Choice A is incorrect because this is a fair coin so the probability should be equal to $\frac{1}{2}$. **Choice B** is incorrect because this is a fair coin so the probability should be equal to $\frac{1}{2}$. **Choice C** is incorrect because this is a fair coin so the probability should be equal to $\frac{1}{2}$. **Choice E** is incorrect because this is a fair coin so the probability should be equal to $\frac{1}{2}$.

77 **Choice C is correct.** To find the number, let's call the three items they can purchase A, B, and C. The possibilities:

All three order the same thing: AAA, BBB, CCC.

Two order the same thing: AAB, AAC, BBA, BBC CCA, CCB

All three order something different: ABC

So there are ten different ways the items could be ordered.

Chapter 6: Data Analysis

Choice A is incorrect because there are more than 6 possible options. Choice B is incorrect because there are more than 9 possible options. Choice D is incorrect because there are less than 18 possible options. Choice E is incorrect because there are less than 27 possible options.

78 **Choice C is correct.** Assume total number of students be 100.

Failed in Mathematics = 100 − 60 = 40

Failed in English = 100 − 74 = 26

Failed in both subjects = 18

Failed students in any of the subjects = 40 + 26 − 18 = 48

Students who pass in both the subjects = 52

If 52 passed, then total number of students = 100

If 416 passed, then total number of students

$= \left(\frac{100}{52}\right) \times 416 = 800$

Choice A is incorrect because 52% of this number is not 416. **Choice B is incorrect** because 52% of this number is not 416. **Choice D is incorrect** because 52% of this number is not 416. **Choice E is incorrect** because 52% of this number is not 416.

79 **Choice B is correct** because creating two average statements can help you isolate $w + t$.

Start with the average statement for Data Set A which would fill in the expression average

$= \frac{\text{sum of values}}{\text{number of values}}$ as $\frac{x+y+z}{3}$.

Then create an average statement for Data Set B which would be $\frac{x+y+z+w+t}{5}$.

You are told that Data Set B's average is double Data Set A's average. This will lead you to forming the expression $2(\frac{x+y+z}{3}) = \frac{x+y+z+w+t}{5}$. Multiply both sides by 5 to get $\frac{10(x+y+z)}{3} = x + y + z + w + t$. Subtract $x + y + z$ to get $\frac{10(x+y+z)}{3} - (x+y+z) = w + t$. The statement can then be simplified to be $(\frac{10}{3} - 1)(x+y+z)$ which equals $\frac{7(x+y+z)}{3}$.

Choice A is incorrect because this represents double the mean of Data Set A, but does not solve for $w + t$. **Choice C is incorrect** because this is not a complete isolation of $w + t$. **Choice D is incorrect** because this does not use the relationship of the averages to find $w + t$. **Choice E is incorrect** because this relationship does not convey the information from the problem correctly.

80 **Choice C is correct** because the data set has a small spread based on the range being 2. If you represented the data set as a, b, c, and d you can identify the average using the relationship $\frac{a+b+c+d}{4}$.

Since x is the median that means it must have been the value in between b and c so it could be concluded that $\frac{b+c}{2} = x$. Multiplying both sides by 2 would give you $b + c = 2x$.

Furthermore, it can be concluded that $d - a = 2$. This can be rearranged to give you $d = 2 + a$. Also note that $a \leq x$ since a is the smallest value in the data set.

All of these conclusions can be combined to get the statement that $\frac{a+b+c+d}{4} = \frac{a+2x+d}{4} = \frac{a+2x+2+a}{4} = \frac{2a+2x+2}{4} = \frac{a+x+1}{2}$. Noting that a cannot be greater than x, you can make the inequality that the average cannot be greater than $\frac{5x}{4}$.

If the average of a data set is the same as the median, the numbers must have an even distribution. This would likely mean b and c have to be equal and a would be 1 less than b and d would be 1 more than c. This would give you $x - 1$, x, x, and $x + 1$ as the data set.

Choice A is incorrect because this would not be possible with 4 positive integers to get an average with just x in the numerator. **Choice B is incorrect** because it is not possible given the range of values for the average to be x. **Choice D is incorrect** because the average must be less than $\frac{5x}{4}$.

Choice E is incorrect because the average must be less than $\frac{5x}{4}$.

81 **Choice A is correct** because you can use an average equation to solve for the missing frequency. To find the sum of all of the values, multiply the value by its frequency and then add each result to get 320(3) + 450(4)

+ 520x + 650(7) + 750(1). This simplifies to become 520x + 8060. Divide this by the number of values in the data set which is x + 3 + 4 + 7 + 1 which equals 15 + x. Now you will have the expression $\frac{520x+8060}{15+x} = 533$.

Multiply both sides by 15 + x to get 520x + 8060 = 7995 + 533x. Subtract 7995 and 520x from both sides to get 65 = 13x. Divide by 13 to get x = 5.

Choice B is incorrect because this would result in an average higher than 533. **Choice C** is incorrect because this would result in an average higher than 533. **Choice D** is incorrect because this would result in an average higher than 533. **Choice E** is incorrect because this would result in an average higher than 533.

82 **Choice D is correct** because you can use the total fraction of people who walk to evaluate the total number of people in the office. Add together the total fractions of the office accounted for by bus, motorbike, and car. This would yield $\frac{1}{2}+\frac{1}{3}+\frac{1}{12}=\frac{11}{12}$. Subtract from 1 to find the remaining fraction who walk which would be $1-\frac{11}{12}=\frac{1}{12}$. This means 100 people make up 112 of the total. Multiply by 12 to get the total of 100 × 12 = 1200.

Choice A is incorrect because this is the number of employees that walk, not the total. **Choice B** is incorrect because this is one-third of the office. **Choice C** is incorrect because this is half the size of the office. Choice E is incorrect because this results from a math error.

83 **Choice E is correct** because the probability that the problem will be solved is equal to the probability that at least one will be solved. This would equal 1 - probability that none of them solve which is 1 − [(1− 0.6)(1 − 0.7)(1 − 0.8)(1 − 0.9)] = 1 − 0.0024 = 0.9976.

Choice A is incorrect because this is too small of a probability. **Choice B** is incorrect because this is too small of a probability. **Choice C** is incorrect because this is too small of a probability. **Choice D** is incorrect because this is too small of a probability.

84 **Choice B is correct** because to determine the total combinations with repeats you would use 8!. Since 5 and 6 both repeat 3 times you will need to divide by 3! twice. This will get you the expression $\frac{8!}{3!3!}$ which equals 1120.

Choice A is incorrect because this is just the number of digits, not the possible combinations. **Choice C** is

Practice Set 2 (Medium): Answers & Explanations

incorrect because this only accounts for the repeating of one digit. **Choice D** is incorrect because this is the number of combinations divided by 2 which is not the correct method. **Choice E** is incorrect because this is the number of combinations without repeating values.

85 **Choice E is correct** because standard deviation is a measure of the spread of a dataset. Since Dataset C is all the same number, it would have the lowest spread and therefore the lowest standard deviation. Dataset D has the highest standard deviation because it has the largest spread from −35 to 300. Dataset A will have a larger standard deviation than dataset B because its numbers are more spread apart than just 1, 2, 3, 4 and 5. Therefore, the correct order is CBAD.

Choice A is incorrect because C has the lowest standard deviation and should be listed first. **Choice B** is incorrect because A's standard deviation is greater than B's so it should be listed third. **Choice C** is incorrect because this is the inverse order of the standard deviation. **Choice D** is incorrect because C has the lowest standard deviation and should be listed first.

86 **Choice B is correct** because the average is found by adding up all of the numbers and dividing by the total numbers. This would get you $\frac{3x+2y+4x-5y-6x+?}{4} = 3x$. Simplify this statement to get $\frac{x-3y+?}{4} = 3x$.

Multiply both sides by 3 to get x − 3y + ? = 12x. Since the expression ends up equaling 12x you need to remove the −3y by adding in another 3y and then add 11x to get to 12x. This means the missing value would be 11x + 3y.

Choice A is incorrect because this would leave y in the expression for average. **Choice C** is incorrect because this would leave a −6y in the expression. **Choice D** is incorrect because this does not match up with the average when plugged in. **Choice E** is incorrect because this would not simplify to be 3x when the average is taken.

87 **Choice E is correct** because you can use the average formula to determine the final exam grade. Set the midterm exam grade equal to x. This means that the final exam grade can be represented by 1.4x since it was 40% greater which means multiply by 1.4. Plug this into the average formula, average = $\frac{sum\ of\ values}{number\ of\ values}$ to get 0.66

Chapter 6: Data Analysis

$= \dfrac{x + 1.4x}{2}$. Simplify and multiply both sides by 2 to get $1.32 = 2.4x$. Divide both sides by 2.4 to get $0.55 = x$ which is 55%. This is the midterm exam grade, so make sure you multiply by 1.4 to get the final grade of $0.55 \times 1.4 = 0.77$ which is 77%.

Choice A is incorrect because this is the percent increase in the grade between the mid–term exam and final exam score. **Choice B** is incorrect because this is the midterm exam grade. **Choice C** is incorrect because this answer results from a calculation error. **Choice D** is incorrect because this is the final grade for the course.

88 **Choices A and C are correct.** Choice A is correct because if there were 87 tickets on Thursday, that means on average, theater A had 29 people in each of the three showings. This would be over 60% occupancy if the max occupancy was 30. Choice C is correct because the theater would have been at 100% occupancy at all 3 showings since 90 divided by 3 is 30 and that is the maximum occupancy.

Choice B is incorrect because theater B on Tuesday had 53 people which would be around 17 people per showing. This would only be $\dfrac{17}{30}$ which is around 57%.

89 **The correct answer is 5%** because to find the percentage of all sales that Brazil makes up, you first need to determine the amount of sales. Find 45% of South American sales in 2015 by multiplying 9,030 by 0.45 to get 4,063.50. To find what percent of all sales this makes up, add up all of the sales in 2015 to get 74,150 and then divide 4,063.50 by 74,150. This would give you around 0.05480, which when multiplied by 100 turns it into around 5%.

90 **The correct answer is $132.** First, determine the revenue contribute by tablets. Do this by multiplying the percentage from the pie chart by the total revenue generated by all gadgets.

$$22\% \times \$90,000 = 0.22 \times \$90,000 = \$19,800$$

From the table, we can see that the retail shop sold 150 tablets last month. To find the average cost of a tablet, divide the revenue by the total number of tablets sold.

$$\dfrac{\$19,800}{150} = 132$$

This means that the average cost of a tablet is $132.

91 **Choice D is correct** because if the average has to stay below 38 and the lowest number is −6, the greatest range will be from eight of the numbers being as low as possible and the last number being as high as possible. If all eight values are equal to −6, you would get a sum of −48, plus the lowest value of −6 would get you a total sum of −54. Since the average has to be below 38, create the statement $\dfrac{-54 + x}{10} < 38$. Multiply both sides by 10 to get $-54 + x < 380$. Add 54 to get the final conclusion that $x < 434$. This means the greatest value of x is 433. To get the range, now subtract −6 to get 439.

Choice A is incorrect because this results from a calculation error. **Choice B** is incorrect because it is possible to get a larger value for the range. **Choice C** is incorrect because it is possible to get a larger value for the range. **Choice E** is incorrect because this would not be possible with the 38 as a restriction for average.

92 **Choice A is correct** because the sum of the weights of the blueberries per bush in field A would be found by multiplying 8.6 by 94 which equals 808.4. This means to find the weights of the blueberries from field B, you can use the expression $\dfrac{808.4 + x}{94 + 86} = 8.1$. Simplify the denominator to 180 and then multiply both sides by 180 to get $808.4 + x = 1458$. Subtract 808.4 to get $x = 649.6$. Now divide this by 86 to get the approximate average of 7.55.

Choice B is incorrect because this is the average of the averages which is not the correct way to solve given that the fields do not have an equal amount of blueberry bushes. **Choice C** is incorrect because this would yield an average higher than 8.1. **Choice D** is incorrect because this would yield an average higher than 8.1. **Choice E** is incorrect because this would yield an average higher than 8.1.

93 **Choice A is correct** because the mean can be found to be 87 and the median is 89, so no test scores are above the mean and below the median. To find the median, put the numbers in order as 73, 84, 87, 91, 93, and 94. The middle two values will be 87 and 91. To find the exact median find the average of the two numbers with the equation $\dfrac{87 + 91}{2} = 89$. To find the mean, add up all of the numbers and then divide by 6. Adding up all of the numbers yields 522 which divided by 6 gets you 87.

Choice B is incorrect because there are no values in between the mean and median. **Choice C** is incorrect

Practice Set 2 (Medium): Answers & Explanations

because there are no values in between the mean and median. **Choice D** is incorrect because there are no values in between the mean and median. **Choice E** is incorrect because there are no values in between the mean and median.

94 **Choices B, C and D are correct.** There were a total of 254 people who went to the theater on Friday (77 + 87 + 90). The total spent on concessions is equal to 1976 + 2400 + 1325 + 1634 = 7335. If at least 75% bought concessions, that means there was a maximum average of $38.50 ($\frac{7335}{254 \times 0.75}$) spent and if everyone bought concessions there would be a minimum average of $28.88 spent ($\frac{7335}{254}$). Any value between $28.88 and $38.50 would work as the average amount spent per person on Friday.

Choice B is correct because it falls between $28.88 and $38.50. Choice C is correct because it falls between $28.88 and $38.50. Choice D is correct because it falls between $28.88 and $38.50.

Choice A is incorrect because it is less than $28.88. **Choice E** is incorrect because it is greater than $38.50.

95 **Choices A and B are correct.** To find the smallest group size possible, maximize everyday as much as possible to reach the average needed. If there is a capacity of 30 seats and 2 showings per day, that means each day would only be able to cover at most 60 people. If the average is at most 57 tickets per day then you could try setting 5 days at full capacity to get $\frac{60+60+60+60+x}{5}$ ≤ 57. Multiply by 5 to get 240 + x = 285. Subtract 240 and you will find the smallest possible number of people in one day is 45 people. Since the maximum occupancy is 30, 45 − 30 would give you the largest smallest group size of 15 people. Anything under this would work

Choice A is correct because this group size is possible if the average is under 57. Choice B is correct because it is possible that the smallest group size is 15 people.

Choice C is incorrect because you could not have a group size larger than 15 people. **Choice D** is incorrect because it is not possible to have 25 as the smallest group size since there could be instances where 25 is not the smallest.

96 **Choices C, D, E and F are correct.** Adding up all of the funds currently allocated to schools would get you $587,250. Since this is 45% of the total tax revenue allocation, divide by 0.45 to get $1,305,000 for the total. A minimum 5% increase in tax revenue would put the total fund allocation at 50% of all funds which would be $652,500. Subtract this from the funds already distributed to get a minimum funding of $65,250 for the new school. A maximum increase of 8% would be a total of 53% of the budget which would be $691,650 for schools total. Subtract the funds already distributed to schools to get a maximum funding of $104,400.

Choice C is correct because $70,000 is in the possible range. Choice D is correct because $80,000 is in the possible range. Choice E is correct because $90,000 is in the possible range. Choice F is correct because $100,000 is in the possible range.

Choice A is incorrect because $50,000 is below the minimum funding needed. **Choice B** is incorrect because $60,000 is below the minimum funding needed.

97 **Choice B is correct** because the range can be found by subtracting the largest number from the smallest number. Assume 21 is the largest number and 4 is the smallest number, then the range would be 21 − 4 which equals 17. If this is equal to 2x then x will equal 17 divided by 2 which is 8.5

Choice A is incorrect because it is not possible to get a range of 2x if x was 6.5. **Choice C** is incorrect because it is not possible to get a range of 2x if x was 10. **Choice D** is incorrect because it is not possible to get a range of 2x if x was 17. **Choice E** is incorrect because it is not possible to get a range of 2x if x was 28.

98 **Choice A is correct** because if the range was 7 and $x > y$, that means x must be the largest value in the data set since the current range is only 5 (70 − 65 = 5). To get a range of 7, add 7 to the lowest value of 65 to get 72. This means x = 72.

Now to solve for y, use the average formula average = $\frac{sum\, of\, values}{number\, of\, values}$. Plugging in you will get 67 = $\frac{65+70+68+67+66+72+y}{7}$. Simplifying and multiplying by 7 will get you the new equation 469 = 408 + y. Subtract 408 to get y = 61.

Chapter 6: Data Analysis

Choice B is incorrect because this would not result in an average of 67. **Choice C is incorrect** because this would not result in an average of 67 **Choice D is incorrect** because this would not result in an average of 67. **Choice E is incorrect** because this is the value of x.

99 **Choice D is correct** because to find the average you need to find out how many total microchips were bought. Divide $6750 by $45 to find the first purchase was for 150 microchips. Divide $6400 by $32 to find the second purchase was for 200 microchips. In total that would be 350 microchips bought for a total of $13,150. To find the average cost per microchip divide $13,150 by 350 to get approximately $37.57.

Choice A is incorrect because this value is too low of an average. **Choice B is incorrect** because this value is too low of an average. **Choice C is incorrect** because this value is too low of an average. **Choice E is incorrect** because this is the average of the two prices, but does not account for there being different amounts purchased each time.

100 **Choice B is correct** because the profit can be found by subtracting revenue minus cost. The revenue will be the sales price per unit times the number of units sold. for store brand drinks there was a 70% sell through rate of the 1,500 cases ordered. This means the revenue would equal 70% of 1,500 × 4 which equals $4,200.

The cost would equal the price times the number ordered which would be 2 × 1,500 which equals $3,000.
To find profit, complete the operation $4,200 − $3,000 which equals $1,200.
Choice A is incorrect because this is lower than the actual profit. **Choice C is incorrect** because this is equal to the cost. **Choice D is incorrect** because this is equal to the revenue. **Choice E is incorrect** because this number is greater than the revenue itself.

101 **Choices B and D are correct.** The range of possible allocation of percent could be determined by finding 50% of 10% and 75% of 10%. 50% of 10% would be 5% of funds covered and available to be reallocated. 75% of 10% would be 7.5% of funds covered and available to be reallocated.
Choice B is correct because schools and roads maintain their funding, while 5% of police is reallocated to sanitation and the fire department. Choice D is correct because schools maintain their funding percentage, while 6% of funds gets allocated between roads, sanitation, and the fire department.

Choice A is incorrect because this allocation removes 100% of police funding. **Choice C is incorrect** because sanitation and schools have a decrease in funding.

102 **Choice B is correct** because the greatest increase was in 1985. From the graph in 1980, 20% used oil; in 1985, 40% used oil; in 1990, 50% used oil; and in 1995, 60% used oil. This means the greatest increase was from 20% to 40% which occurred in 1985.

Choice A is incorrect because this was not the greatest increase. **Choice C is incorrect** because this was not the greatest increase. **Choice D is incorrect** because this was not the greatest increase. **Choice E is incorrect** because this was not the greatest increase.

103 **Choices A and B are correct.** A venn diagram can help visual the possible options based on the information given.

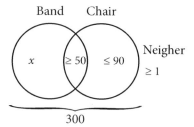

In this diagram, the amount of students in band is x, the overlap of band and choir is marked as ≥ 50 because at least 50 students need to be in that category. The choir category is marked as ≤ 90 since there will be a total of 140 between the overlap and the choir category. Neither is referenced as having at least 1 person since the prompt states there are students who do neither.

Choice A is correct because if $\frac{1}{3}$ of the students were in band then that would mean 100 students were in band and that would allow for 100 + 140 + 60 (neither) = 300.
Choice B is correct because if $\frac{1}{2}$ of the students were in band, but not in choir that means 150 students are in band. This is possible because 140 + 150 + 10 (neither) = 300.
Choice C is incorrect because this would not allow for any students in the neither category. **Choice D is incorrect** because this would be more than possible in the band category.

104 **Choices A and C are correct.**
The general expression for the geometric formula can be found using the expression $a_n = a_1 r^{n-1}$. Plugging in the

given information would yield $a_n = -3(-2)^{n-1}$. Plugging in each value will allow you to identify if it is a number in the sequence.

Choice A is correct because it is possible to get a positive 1536 as the 9th term in the sequence, but not a negative 1536. Choice C is correct because it is possible to get negative 192 as the 6th term in the sequence, but not a positive 192.

Choice B is incorrect because the fifth term in the series is 96. **Choice D** is incorrect because the 7th term in the series is 384.

105 **Choice C is correct** because the total number of students can be found to be 800. It can be determined that 40% of students failed mathematics since 100 − 60 = 40%. it can be determined that 26% failed in English because 100 − 74 = 26%. This means that a total of 48% failed in any one of the subjects as found by adding together 40 + 26 − 18 = 48%. This means 52% of students passed in both subjects.

If 416 students passed then that means 416 is equal to 52% of a number. To find this number you can divide 416 by 0.52 to get 800.

Choice A is incorrect because 52% of this number is not 416. **Choice B** is incorrect because 52% of this number is not 416. **Choice D** is incorrect because 52% of this number is not 416. **Choice E** is incorrect because 52% of this number is not 416.

106 **Choice D is correct** because to find the average add up all of the percentages and divide by the given years. The sum of the percentages would be 20 + 40 + 50 + 60 = 170. the average would be $\frac{170}{4}$ which equals 42.5%.

Choice A is incorrect because this is lower than the actual mean percentage. **Choice B** is incorrect because this is lower than the actual mean percentage. **Choice C** is incorrect because this is lower than the actual mean percentage. **Choice E** is incorrect because this is lower than the actual mean percentage.

107 **Choice C is correct** because The proportion of residents who used oil heat in 1995 was 60%. The percentage of people who used electric heat that year was 10%. The percent difference between these two types of heating method is 60% - 10% equals 50%. Therefore, 50% of 50,000 is 25,000.

Choice A is incorrect because this is less than 50%. **Choice B** is incorrect because this is less than 50%.

Choice D is incorrect because this is more than 50%. **Choice E** is incorrect because this is more than 50%.

108 **Choice A is correct** because the percentage of gas consumers in 1985 was 40%. In 1990, gas consumers made up 30% of the population. This means 10% of gas users from 1985 changed to alternative heating methods in the following time frame.

Choice B is incorrect because this is greater than the actual percentage. **Choice C** is incorrect because this is greater than the actual percentage. **Choice D** is incorrect because this is greater than the actual percentage. **Choice E** is incorrect because this is greater than the actual percentage.

109 **The correct answer is 4.1%** because the median income as a percentage of median home price in Boston is $\frac{45000}{510000} \times 100$ which is about 8.8%. For NY, the percentage is $\frac{40000}{310000} \times 100$ which is 12.90%. 12.9% − 8.8% = 4.1%.

110 **Choices A and B are correct.**

Choice A is correct because Phoenix had the greatest overall change in median housing price from 2010 to 2020. The exact percent increase can be found using $\left|\frac{initial - final}{initial}\right| \cdot 100$ which would become $\left|\frac{initial - final}{initial}\right| \times 100$. Filling this in would get you $\left|\frac{138000 - 400000}{400000}\right| \times 100 = 189\%$ increase between 2010 and 2020.

Choice B is correct because this can be found by adding up all of the median incomes and dividing by 5. $45,000 + $65,000 + $40,000 + $66,000 + $63,000 = $279,000. Dividing $279,000 by 5 gets you $55,800.

Choice C is incorrect because there are four values in the data set of the median house prices in 2010: $138,000 (Phoenix), $190,000 (NY), $350,000 (Boston), and $358,000 (LA). The median would be the average of NY and Boston which would be $\frac{190000 + 350000}{2}$ which equals $270,000 as the median.

111 **The correct answer is 89%** because the average median house price in the US for the cities listed in $467,500 which is found with the expression

Chapter 6: Data Analysis

$\frac{\$400,000 + \$650,000 + \$510,000 + \$310,000}{4} = 467,500.$
To find what percent less this is from $4,200,000, subtract the two numbers and divide by $4,200,000 to get $\frac{\$4,200,000 - \$467,500}{\$4,200,000}$ which equals about 88.8%. That means the average median house price in the US for the cities is 89% less than Singapore.

112 The correct answer is $\frac{4}{19}$ because if the average of the rainfall during the week is x, the average rainfall during the weekend is $\frac{2}{3}x$. The average of the whole week would be the average of each time the number of days that the average matches. For the days during the week that would be $5x$ and for the weekend that would $\frac{2*2}{3}x = \frac{4}{3}x$. Adding these together will get you $\frac{19}{3}x$. Now create the expression $\frac{weekend\,rainfall}{total\,rainfall} = \frac{\frac{4}{3}x}{\frac{19}{3}x}$ which simplifies to be $\frac{4}{19}$.

113 The correct answer is 25. The total number of artifacts are divided as either Palaeolithic or Neolithic. As 2/5 of the artifacts are Palaeolithic, 3/5 of them are Neolithic.
As there are 45 Neolithic artifacts, we have 3/5 of the total = 45
Therefore, the total = 45 × 5/3 = 75
Now let's create a table, enter the values and fill up the empty cells:

	Mediterr−anean	Not Mediterr−anean	Total
Palaeolithic	2/3 of 2/5 of 75 = 20	30 − 20 = 10	2/5 of 75 = 30
Neolithic	40 − 20 = 20	45 − 20 = 25	3/5 of 75 = 45
Total	40	75 − 40 (or 10 + 25) = 35	75

114 The correct answer is 76 because if the sum of the digits in a number add to 9, then it is divisible by 9. For a set of 3 digits, that means the possible combinations are 1, 8, and 0; 2,7, and 0; 3, 6, and 0; 5, 4, and 0; these four combination will have four arrangement for a total of 16 options and for 1, 2, and 6; 1, 3, and 5; 2, 3, and 4; these three combinations will have six(3!) arrangements for a total of 18 options. This would give us a total of 34 combinations..

You can also get a sum of 9 if the digits add to 18 since 1 + 8 = 9. This would work for the combinations of 9,8,1; 9,7,2; 9,6,3; 9,5,4; 8,7,3; 8,6,4; and 7,6,5. These seven combinations would each have six(3!)arrangements for a total of 42 options.

The 34 combinations from the first set of numbers and the 42 options from the other set give us a total of 76 total combinations.

115 The correct answer is 200. Set A = the set of all 3−digit numbers that are multiples of 9 = {108, 117... 999}.
Set B = the set of all 3−digit numbers that are multiples of 3 but not multiples of 6 = {105, 111, 117... 999}.
The common elements from both Set A and Set B = {117, 135... 999}.
The formula to find the number of elements of a set is given by $n = \frac{last\,term - first\,term}{difference} + 1.$
The number of elements in Set A = (999 − 108)/9 + 1 = 99 + 1 = 100
The number of elements in Set B = (999 − 105)/6 + 1 = 149 + 1 = 150
The number of common elements in sets A and B = (999 − 117)/18 + 1 = 49 + 1 = 50

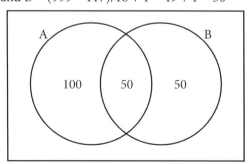

Hence A U B has 100 + 50 + 50 = 200 elements.

Practice Set 3 (Hard): Answers and Explanations

116 **Choice C is correct** because if patient service representatives make up $\frac{1}{8}$ of the total hospital staff, reducing them by 4% would lead to a decrease of 0.5%. To find this find the percentage that is $\frac{1}{8}$ of 18% to find that 2.25% of those with associate's degrees are patient service representatives. If the trend predicts a 4% decrease in jobs, that means 4% of 2.25% will be removed. This would be found by multiplying 0.025 by 0.04 to get 0.0009 or 0.009% decrease.
Choice A is incorrect because this is not accounting for $\frac{1}{8}$ of the staff. **Choice B is incorrect** because this is too large of a decrease. **Choice D is incorrect** because there would not be a positive increase. **Choice E is incorrect** because there would not be a positive increase.

117 **Choices A and C are correct.**
Choice A is correct because 320,250 is a 5% increase which fits in the 7% ±2% range.
Choice C is correct because a 5 ±2% would allow for at most a 7% increase in jobs which would be a maximum of 12,950 additional positions. If 4,070 of those jobs were taken, that would leave 8880 jobs which is 69% of the available positions.
Choice B is incorrect because if job growth is 30% (28% + 2%) than at most there would only be 48,000 jobs available which is less than the 50,000 students.
Choice D is incorrect because the margin of error is ±2% so the percentage of new jobs held by women could also vary.

118 **The correct answer is 7.** because there are currently 4,375 members that hold a masters (12,500 × 0.35). If 750 staff members will be getting their doctorate, that leaves 3565 staff members with masters. Currently there are 2625 staff with bachelors (12,500 × 0.21). This would mean 525 (2625 × 0.20) will receive a masters degree. This means 3565 + 525 = 4090 master degree holders once everyone has completed their degree.
To find percent change, use $\left|\frac{initial - final}{initial}\right| \times 100$. This would be $\left|\frac{4375 - 4090}{4375}\right| \times 100 = 6.5\%$ which rounded would be 7%.

119 **Choice B is correct** because to find x and y use the average formula: average = $\frac{sum\ of\ values}{number\ of\ values}$. Plugging into this expression will get you $28 = \frac{30 + 25 + 34 + 21 + x + y}{6}$. Simplify the denominator and multiply by 6 to get $168 = 110 + x + y$. Subtract 110 from both sides of the equation to get $58 = x + y$. Since no value can be greater than 34, this means x can be 34 and y can be 58 − 34 = 24. This would make the greatest four values 34, 34, 30, and 25.
Plug these back into the average formula to get average = $\frac{34 + 34 + 30 + 25}{4}$ which simplifies to be 30.75.
Choice A is incorrect because this is the average if you use 29 for x and y which is not the greatest possible number. **Choice C is incorrect** because this results from a math error when taking the average. **Choice D is incorrect** because this results from a math error when taking the average. **Choice E is incorrect** because this would only be possible if there were four 34s in the number set and there is not.

120 **Choice E is correct** because this would be simplified to be $\frac{b+1+c-1}{2}$ which further simplifies to be $\frac{b+c}{2}$ which is the median. You can also test out numbers like 1, 3, 5, and 7 to find the median of 4 and plug in to see $\frac{b+c}{2}$ does equal 4 with 3 and 5 plugged in: $\frac{3+5}{2} = 4$.

Choice A is incorrect because the expression is not representative of the median. **Choice B is incorrect** because the expression is not representative of the median. **Choice C is incorrect** because the expression only gives a median for the first set of consecutive positive odd integers but not in general. **Choice D is incorrect** because the expression is not representative of the median.

121 **Choice C is correct** because if you first identify the limits on the seating, then you can identify how many people are possible in each spot. Assign either end of the table as being taken and then calculate the arrangements in that position. Then add the arrangements based on the person sitting at the other end of the table.

Chapter 6: Data Analysis

Scenario One:

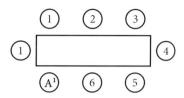

In this scenario, multiply the numbers in each spot to get 6! which equals 720.

Scenario Two:

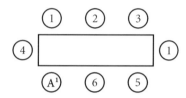

In this scenario, multiply the numbers in each spot to get 6! which equals 720. Add to the previous 720 to get a total of 1440 combinations possible.

Choice A is incorrect because there are more possible combinations. **Choice B** is incorrect because this does not account for all combinations. **Choice D** is incorrect because this only accounts for chair A being set. **Choice E** is incorrect because this does not account for restrictions and is just solving using 8!.

122 **Choices C and D are correct.** To find the maximum number of 18–25 year olds, use the fact that no more than 35% of all 18–25 year olds voted. Identify how many 18–25 year olds there are in each group by finding the number of people who voted per candidate and then the number of 18–25 year olds who voted for that candidate.

For Candidate A, the total number of people who voted would be 1200 × 0.417 which is about 500 votes and the total number of 18–25 year olds who voted for candidate A would be 500 × 0.54 which is 270.

For Candidate B, the total number of people who voted would be 1200 × 0.333 which is about 400 votes and the total number of 18–25 year olds who voted for candidate B would be 400 × 0.16 which is 64.

For Candidate C, the total number of people who voted would be 1200 × 0.25 which is about 300 votes and the total number of 18–25 year olds who voted for candidate A would be 300 × 0.10 which is 30.

Add all of these numbers together to get 270 + 64 + 30 = 364 as the maximum number of 18–25 year olds who voted. Now set up the proportion $\frac{364}{x} = \frac{35}{100}$ and cross multiply to find the total maximum population of 1040. Any value between 364 and 1040 works.

Choice C is correct because 580 is in the possible range. **Choice D** is correct because 1000 is in the possible range.

Choice A is incorrect because 300 is below the possible range. **Choice B** is incorrect because 360 is below the possible range. **Choice E** is incorrect because 1100 is above the possible range.

123 **Choices B and C are correct.**

Choice B is correct because candidate A won the most votes and the age range of 41+ makes up 46% of their votes. This means it is likely that they won the most votes in that age range with a total of 1200 × 0.417 × 0.46 which is approximately 230. Choice C is correct because candidate C is the candidate that received the lowest amount of votes in the age range of 26–65 with only 38% of its total votes compared to 39% of all votes for candidate B and 41% of all votes for candidate A.

Choice A is incorrect because even though Candidate C had 52% of its votes from the age range of 65+, they did not have the most voters in that category. Candidate B did since the total votes for candidate B was 1200 × 0.333 which is about 400 votes and the total votes for 65+ would be 400 × 0.45 which is about 180 votes. Candidate C only had 156 votes (1200 × 0.25 × 0.52).

124 **Choice D is correct** because to find the number of 65+ mail ballots for candidate A, start with dividing the 1200 ballots into the 5:3 ratio by dividing by 8 (5 + 3) and then multiplying by 3. This would get you $\frac{1200}{8}$ × 3 = 450. Next, find 24% of 450 by multiplying by 0.24 to get 108 total 65+ voters who used mail in ballots.

The total number of 65+ voters can be determined by each candidate's percentage of votes. Candidate A would have 1200 × 0.417 × 0.05 which is about 25 votes. For candidate B, the total number of 65+ voters would be 1200 which is about 180 votes. Candidate C has 156 votes (1200 × 0.25 × 0.52). Adding these together will get you 361.

Subtract the number of total 65+ voters by the number who mailed in their ballot to get the total who voted in person which would be 361 − 108 = 253.

Choice A is incorrect because this would result from a math error. **Choice B** is incorrect because this would result from a math error. **Choice C** is incorrect because this is the total number of ballots mailed in by 65+ and this is more than the amount of votes received by 65+ voters for candidate A. **Choice E** is incorrect because this is the total number of 65+ voters.

Practice Set 3 (Hard): Answers & Explanations

125 **Choices A and E are correct.**

Choice A is correct because if the increase in the highest four values is offset by an equal decrease in the lowest four values, then the average will not change since the sum of the numbers remains the same. Choice E is correct because the spread of the numbers will increase which directly impacts the standard deviation.

Choice B is incorrect because the average does not change. **Choice C** is incorrect because the average does not change. **Choice D** is incorrect because the standard deviation increases. **Choice F** is incorrect because the standard deviation increases.

126 **Choices B and C are correct.** To determine the range of possibilities aim to find the maximum and minimum overlap. The minimum overlap between the two groups would be if no students had both green eyes and brown hair. The maximum overlap would be if all students with brown hair had green eyes.

For the minimum overlap, find a value that could be divided evenly amongst the probabilities such as $35x$. This would mean $\frac{1}{5}$ of $35x$ students would have green eyes which equals $7x$. If $\frac{3}{7}$ of students had brown hair, this would mean $15x$ ($35x \times \frac{3}{7}$) would represent the number of people with brown hair. Add these together to get $22x$ students with either brown or green hair assuming no overlap. This would be a probability of $\frac{22}{35}$.

For maximum overlap, assume all students with green eyes have brown hair. The possibility of a student with green eyes and brown hair would be $\frac{1}{5}$. The probability of green eyes or brown hair would be the probability of each individual event minus the probability of both to prevent overlap. This would be $\frac{1}{5} + \frac{3}{7} - \frac{1}{5} = \frac{3}{7}$.

Any values within the range of $\frac{3}{7} \leq P \leq \frac{22}{35}$.

Choice B is correct because it falls within the range of possible probabilities. Choice C is correct because it falls within the range of possible probabilities.

Choice A is incorrect because it is outside the range of possible probabilities. **Choice D** is incorrect because it is outside the range of possible probabilities.

127 **Choices A and D are correct.** Currently with an average of 3.4 with 42 ratings, the book has a total of 142.8 rating points. It needs an average of 3.5 over 47 ratings (42 + 5) so that means it needs a total of 164.5 rating points. The difference between the ratings is 21.7 points so any combination that adds to this would get the book to be showcased.

Choice A is correct because 4.3 + 4.3 + 4.3 + 4.3 + 4.5 = 21.7 which is just enough points. Choice D is correct because 4.5 + 3.8 + 4.9 + 5.0 + 4.5 = 27.2 which is more points than needed to get into the 3.5 range.

Choice B is incorrect because 2.6 + 3.8 + 4.5 + 5.0 + 5.0 = 20.9 which is less than the points needed. **Choice C** is incorrect because 3.2 + 4.3 + 4.5 + 4.6 + 4.2 = 20.8 which is less than the points needed.

128 **Choice A is correct** because for all positive values of x, Set A will have larger values since it is being added and then squared.

Choice B is incorrect because all the values in Set B will be larger since it has a double negative within the parenthesis if $x < 0$ which would make a larger average. **Choice C** is incorrect because set A's range is greater than set B's range. **Choice D** is incorrect because set A's range is greater than set B's range.

129 **The correct answer is 12** because if the average of list A is 8, then you can set-up an average statement that $\frac{5+x+y+z}{4} = 8$. Multiplying both sides by 4 will get you the statement $5 + x + y + z = 32$. Subtract 5 to get the statement $x + y + z = 27$.

Now create an average statement for list B of $\frac{3+6+8+x+y+z+w}{7} = 8$. Simplify the numerator and multiply by 7 to get $17 + x + y + z + w = 56$. Subtract 17 to get $x + y + z + w = 39$. Then plug in $x + y + z = 27$ to get $27 + w = 39$. Subtract 27 to find $w = 12$.

130 **The correct answer is 0.046** because to find the probability of drawing three blue beads in a row find the probability of a blue bead each draw and then multiply. The probability of a blue bead in the first draw is $\frac{5}{12}$. For the second draw the probability is $\frac{4}{11}$ since there is no replacement of beads. The third draw would have a probability of $\frac{3}{10}$. Multiplying $\frac{5}{12} \times \frac{4}{11} \times \frac{3}{10} = 0.046$.

Before You Begin the Test

Please Read the Instructions Carefully

This practice test is designed to mirror the structure and rigor of the GRE Quantitative Reasoning section. Treat it as a formal simulation. The more seriously you take this exercise, the more accurately it will reflect your current preparedness—and guide your next steps.

The number of questions and the time limits in each section are aligned with those on the actual GRE, providing you with a realistic and reliable measure of your readiness.

Once you complete the test, refer to the answer key to check your responses. You'll also find detailed instructions for calculating your Quantitative Reasoning score, along with explanations for each question. Be sure to review these explanations thoroughly—especially for the questions you got wrong—to gain insight into the reasoning behind the correct answers and to sharpen your test-taking strategies.

Set Up Your Testing Environment

To replicate real testing conditions:

- Choose a quiet, uninterrupted space to work in.
- Have the following materials at hand:
  - ❑ Rough paper
  - ❑ A few sharpened pencils
  - ❑ A timer, stopwatch, or clock to track your time (if you are simulating test-day pacing)
- Ensure that you remain free of distractions throughout the session.
- Avoid checking your phone, notes, or external resources during the test.

Why This Matters

Your performance on this test is more than just a score—it's a diagnostic tool. It will help you identify question types you excel at and those that need reinforcement. The explanations provided are a valuable resource—use them to deepen your understanding and refine your test-taking strategy.

Chapter 7
Practice Test #1

IMPORTANT
READ THE INSTRUCTIONS BEFORE BEGINNING THE TEST

1. Take this test under real-like testing conditions. Put away any distractions and sit in a quiet place with no disturbances. Keep a rough paper, some pencils, and a calculator beside you.
2. Begin with **Section 1** of the Verbal Reasoning test.
3. Refer to the **Answer Key** on page 251 and note down the number of questions you got right.
4. Based on your score:
   ❑ If you answered fewer than 7 questions correctly, proceed to **Section 2 (Easy)** on page 246.
   ❑ If you answered 7 or more questions correctly, proceed to **Section 2 (Hard)** on page 248.
5. Note down the number of correct answers you got right on **Section 2**.
6. Calculate your **Scaled Score** on page 284 for the test.
7. Review the **detailed explanations** for all questions beginning on page 252.

Chapter 7: Practice Test #1

SECTION 1 | 21 MINUTES

1

$a \leq 0.66\overline{49}$

$b \leq 0.6\overline{649}$

Quantity A	Quantity B
a	b

- Ⓐ Quantity A is greater.
- Ⓑ Quantity B is greater.
- Ⓒ The two quantities are equal.
- Ⓓ The relationship cannot be determined from the information given.

2 In the *xy*-plane, the point (2,3) is on line l, and the point (3,2) is on line m. Each of the line has a positive slope.

Quantity A	Quantity B
Slope of line *l*	Slope of line *m*

- Ⓐ Quantity A is greater.
- Ⓑ Quantity B is greater.
- Ⓒ The two quantities are equal.
- Ⓓ The relationship cannot be determined from the information given.

3 The radius of circle *E* is 4 times greater than the radius 1 of circle *F*.

Quantity A	Quantity B
The circumference of circle *E* minus the circumference of circle *F*	4π

- Ⓐ Quantity A is greater.
- Ⓑ Quantity B is greater.
- Ⓒ The two quantities are equal.
- Ⓓ The relationship cannot be determined from the information given.

4 *n* is an integer for which $\frac{1}{2^{(1-n)}} \leq \frac{1}{8}$

Quantity A	Quantity B
n	-1

- Ⓐ Quantity A is greater.
- Ⓑ Quantity B is greater.
- Ⓒ The two quantities are equal.
- Ⓓ The relationship cannot be determined from the information given.

5 This year, *x* athletes won an Olympic medal for water competitions. $\frac{1}{3}$ of the winners earned a medal for swimming and $\frac{1}{4}$ of those who earned a medal for swimming also earned a medal for diving. How many people won an Olympic medal for water competitions but did not receive a medal for swimming and a medal for diving?

- Ⓐ $\frac{11x}{12}$
- Ⓑ $\frac{7x}{12}$
- Ⓒ $\frac{5x}{12}$
- Ⓓ $\frac{6x}{7}$
- Ⓔ $\frac{x}{7}$

Section 1

Questions 6 to 8 are based on the following data.

6 What is the percentage of candidates qualified to that of the candidate appeared when the states C and D are combined in 2001?

The table shows the number of candidates who applied and qualified over the years from various states.

Year	2000		2001		2002	
State	Applied	Qualified	Applied	Qualified	Applied	Qualified
A	6300	740	5600	650	6200	1150
B	5200	850	4500	980	5800	1300
C	3500	950	4000	780	4100	1250
D	2500	650	3500	690	3200	1650

- (A) 15%
- (B) 18%
- (C) 20%
- (D) 30%
- (E) 35%

7 What is the average number of candidates from state B who appeared in the provided years?

- (A) 5160
- (B) 5166
- (C) 5360
- (D) 6166
- (E) 6206

8 What is the percentage of applicants qualified from State A for all years compared to the number of candidates who appeared from State A for all years?

- (A) 9%
- (B) 11%
- (C) 12%
- (D) 13%
- (E) 14%

9 Which of the following is equal to the expression $\dfrac{(ab)^4 c^0}{a^4 b^5}$ such that $a, b, c \neq 0$?

- (A) ab
- (B) $\dfrac{1}{a}$
- (C) abc
- (D) $\dfrac{1}{b}$
- (E) $\dfrac{c}{ab}$

10 Working at the same constant rate, m workers can lay a total of n bricks per hour. At this rate, how many bricks could 4 workers lay in 8 hours?

- (A) $\dfrac{2m}{n}$
- (B) $\dfrac{2n}{m}$
- (C) $\dfrac{32m}{n}$
- (D) $\dfrac{m}{2n}$
- (E) $\dfrac{32n}{m}$

11 Two 4-sided fair dice number 1 to 4 are rolled once. Find the probability that the absolute value of the difference between the numbers is less than 3.

- (A) $\dfrac{1}{8}$
- (B) $\dfrac{3}{8}$
- (C) $\dfrac{5}{8}$
- (D) $\dfrac{7}{8}$
- (E) $\dfrac{9}{8}$

12 Find the value of angle z in the parallelogram below.

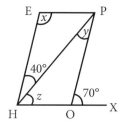

SECTION 2 (EASY) | 26 MINUTES

1 The length of one side of equilateral triangle S is 3 times the length of one side of equilateral triangle T. The ratio of the area of equilateral triangle S to the area of equilateral triangle T is *a:b*.

Quantity A	Quantity B
a	6

Ⓐ Quantity A is greater.
Ⓑ Quantity B is greater.
Ⓒ The two quantities are equal.
Ⓓ The relationship cannot be determined from the information given.

2 Four artists have an average of 18, and none of them are older than 30 and younger than 12.

Quantity A	Quantity B
Range of the four artist's age	25

Ⓐ Quantity A is greater.
Ⓑ Quantity B is greater.
Ⓒ The two quantities are equal.
Ⓓ The relationship cannot be determined from the information given.

3
$$\frac{2}{3}\left|r - \frac{4}{3}\right| = \frac{17}{9}$$

Quantity A	Quantity B
r	5

Ⓐ Quantity A is greater.
Ⓑ Quantity B is greater.
Ⓒ The two quantities are equal.
Ⓓ The relationship cannot be determined from the information given.

4
Set A comprises multiples of 2.
Set B comprises multiples of 3.
Set C comprises multiples of 6.

Quantity A	Quantity B
Least common multiple of Set A, B and C	12

Ⓐ Quantity A is greater.
Ⓑ Quantity B is greater.
Ⓒ The two quantities are equal.
Ⓓ The relationship cannot be determined from the information given.

Section 2: (Easy)

5

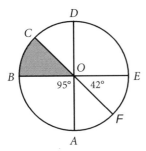

In the circle with radius 2, line segments AD, BE and CF all pass through the center of the circle O.

Quantity A	**Quantity B**
The area of shaded sector COB	$\dfrac{2\pi}{5}$

Ⓐ Quantity A is greater.
Ⓑ Quantity B is greater.
Ⓒ The two quantities are equal.
Ⓓ The relationship cannot be determined from the information given.

6 Which of the following describes all values of x for $1 - x^2 \geq 0$?

Ⓐ $x \geq 1$
Ⓑ $0 \leq x \leq 1$
Ⓒ $-1 \leq x \leq 1$
Ⓓ $x \leq -1$
Ⓔ $x \leq -1$

7 Julian has received 8 of her 12 evaluation scores. So far, his average is 3.75 out of a possible 5. If Jill needs an average of 4.0 points to get a promotion, which list of scores will allow Julian to receive her promotion?

Indicate all such answers.

☐ A 3.5, 4.75. 4.75. 5.0
☐ B 3.25, 4.5. 4.75. 5.0
☐ C 3.0, 3.5. 4.75. 4.75
☐ D 3.75, 4.5. 4.75. 5.0
☐ E 3.0, 4.0. 4.0. 4.75

8 A small, rectangular park has a perimeter of 560 feet and a diagonal measurement of 200 feet. Which system of equations is used to find its area, in square feet?

Ⓐ $L + W = 560$, $L^2 + W^2 = 200^2$
Ⓑ $L + W = 280$, $L^2 - W^2 = 200^2$
Ⓒ $2L + 2W = 560$, $L^2 + W^2 = 200$
Ⓓ $L + W = 280$, $L^2 + W^2 = 40,000$
Ⓔ $L + W = 560$, $L + W = 200$

9 In a garden, there are only red, yellow, and blue flowers. One–fourth of the flowers are red, and 40 percent are blue. One flower is chosen at random. What is the probability that the chosen flower is not red?

Ⓐ 25%
Ⓑ 30%
Ⓒ 40%
Ⓓ 75%
Ⓔ 80%

10 Ten years ago, when Alice was born, Martin was twice as old as Joseph. Now, Martin is twice as old as Alice. How old is Joseph?

Ⓐ 10
Ⓑ 12
Ⓒ 14
Ⓓ 15
Ⓔ 20

11 The volume of water inside a pool doubles every hour. If the pool is filled to its full capacity within 8 hours, how many hours was it filled to one quarter of its capacity?

Ⓐ 2
Ⓑ 4
Ⓒ 5
Ⓓ 6
Ⓔ 7

Chapter 7: Practice Test #1

12 What are two consecutive even numbers whose sum is 94 and whose squared difference equals 188? What is the smaller of the two numbers?

- Ⓐ 36
- Ⓑ 38
- Ⓒ 42
- Ⓓ 46
- Ⓔ 48

13 If Alex has $100 to spend and was unable to buy a watch before the price was reduced by 25%, but can afford it after the reduction, what was the maximum possible price of the watch prior to the price reduction?

- Ⓐ $110.00
- Ⓑ $120.00
- Ⓒ $125.00
- Ⓓ $133.00
- Ⓔ $150.00

14 If $f(x) = \frac{1}{4}x + 2$, what is x if $f(x) = 8$?

☐

15 If $y - 3x > 12$ and $x - y > 38$, which of the following are possible values of x?

Indicate all such answers.

- A −60
- B −30
- C −6
- D 4
- E 20
- F 40
- G 60

SECTION 2 (HARD) | 26 MINUTES

1 A jar is filled with x pound of grain. The jar has a hole at the bottom and each day 1% of the grain is lost from the tank through the hole.

Quantity A	Quantity B
Percentage of grain lost in the three days	3%

- Ⓐ Quantity A is greater.
- Ⓑ Quantity B is greater.
- Ⓒ The two quantities are equal.
- Ⓓ The relationship cannot be determined from the information given.

2 Sequence A: 107, 101, 95 ...., −61

Quantity A	Quantity B
Number of terms in Sequence A	29

- Ⓐ Quantity A is greater.
- Ⓑ Quantity B is greater.
- Ⓒ The two quantities are equal.
- Ⓓ The relationship cannot be determined from the information given.

3

$x > 0$

Quantity A	Quantity B
$\dfrac{(390 + x)}{600}$	$\dfrac{(400 + x)}{590}$

- Ⓐ Quantity A is greater.
- Ⓑ Quantity B is greater.
- Ⓒ The two quantities are equal.
- Ⓓ The relationship cannot be determined from the information given.

Section 2: (Hard)

4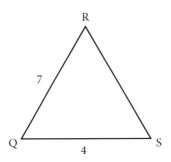

Each angle in $\triangle RSQ$ has a degree measurement of either a or b and the angles are expressed by the equation $2a + b = 180$.

Quantity A	Quantity B
Perimeter of $\triangle RSQ$	18

Ⓐ Quantity A is greater.
Ⓑ Quantity B is greater.
Ⓒ The two quantities are equal.
Ⓓ The relationship cannot be determined from the information given.

5 The length of the rectangle is increased by 10% and breadth is decreased by 20%.

Quantity A	Quantity B
% decrease in area of the rectangle	8%

Ⓐ Quantity A is greater.
Ⓑ Quantity B is greater.
Ⓒ The two quantities are equal.
Ⓓ The relationship cannot be determined from the information given.

6 A used-car salesman has 28 cars in his inventory. These cars were sold across various price ranges. The breakdown of cars sold is as follows:

  Under $15000: 9 cars
$15000-$16999: 5 cars
$17000-$18999: 8 cars
  Over $19000: 6 cars

Identify all potential median price ranges given this distribution.

Indicate all such answers.

Ⓐ $12000
Ⓑ $13000
Ⓒ $15500
Ⓓ $16500
Ⓔ $17500
Ⓕ $18000
Ⓖ $19500
Ⓗ $21000

7 If x is an integer, which of the following is even?

Ⓐ $x^2 + 2x + 10$
Ⓑ $x^2 - x - 1$
Ⓒ $x^2 + 3x + 8$
Ⓓ $x^2 - 4x + 6$
Ⓔ $x^2 - 5x + 11$

8 Arnold takes x seconds to swim y meters at a constant rate from point S to point T in a pool. Dexter can swim the same distance in z seconds at a constant rate. If Arnold leaves point S the same time that Dexter leaves point T, how many fewer meters will Arnold have swum than Dexter when the two swimmers pass each other?

Ⓐ $y(z-x)/(x+z)$
Ⓑ $y(x-z)/(x+z)$
Ⓒ $y(x+z)/(x-z)$
Ⓓ $xy(x-y)/(x+y)$
Ⓔ $xy(y-x)/(x+y)$

Chapter 7: Practice Test #1

9. James and Tina working separately can do a piece of work in 9 and 11 days respectively. If they work together, in how many days, will the work be completed?

- A) 5
- B) 6
- C) 7
- D) 8
- E) 10

10. What is the least integer n such that $\frac{1}{5^n} < 0.01$?

- A) 2
- B) 3
- C) 4
- D) 10
- E) 11

11. The following are the seven angles in a nonagon, 154°, 147°, 138°, 130°, 145°, 132°, 128°. The other two angles are equal. Find the exterior angle of the two unknown angles.

☐

12. The average (arithmetic mean) of three different numbers r, s, t is 100. The smallest number is r and the largest number is $t = 120$ What is the least possible value of r? Note that $r, s, t \neq 0$.

- A) 1
- B) 4
- C) 10
- D) 61
- E) 80

13. Five kilograms of melon contained 98% of water. If the next day the concentration of water decreased by 2%, what was the new weight of the melon, in kilograms?

- A) 2.0
- B) 2.5
- C) 3.0
- D) 3.5
- E) 4.0

14. The function is defined for all number x by $f(x) = x^2 + x$. Let t be a number such that $f(2t) = 30$.

Indicate the possible values of t.

- A) −5
- B) −3
- C) −0.5
- D) 2
- E) 2.5

15. If in a set of numbers, the numbers are $2x + 3, x - 3, 3x - 7, 2x + 11$, which equation is equivalent to the mean of the given data?

- A) $5x + 7$
- B) $3x - 2$
- C) $x + 5$
- D) $2x - 1$
- E) $2x + 1$

Answer Key

Section 1		
Q. No.	Correct Answer	Your Answer
1	B	
2	D	
3	A	
4	B	
5	A	
6	C	
7	B	
8	E	
9	D	
10	E	
11	D	
12	30	

Section 2 (Easy)		
Q. No.	Correct Answer	Your Answer
1	A	
2	B	
3	B	
4	B	
5	A	
6	C	
7	A,D	
8	D	
9	D	
10	D	
11	D	
12	D	
13	D	
14	A,B	
15	A,B	

Section 2 (Hard)		
Q. No.	Correct Answer	Your Answer
1	B	
2	C	
3	B	
4	C	
5	A	
6	C,D,E,F	
7	C	
8	B	
9	A	
10	B	
11	87	
12	A	
13	B	
14	B,E	
15	E	

For more practice, visit www.vibrantpublishers.com

Chapter 7: Practice Test #1

SECTION 1: Answers & Explanations

1 **Choice B is correct** because the obtained value of Quantity B is greater than Quantity A.

Analyze the given quantities.

Quantity A:

$a \leq 0.66\overline{49}$

$a \leq 0.6649494949$

The maximum value of a is 0.66495

Quantity B:

$b \leq 0.664\overline{9}$

$b \leq 0.6649999999$

The maximum value of is 0.66499

Choice A is incorrect because Quantity A is not greater than Quantity B. **Choice C** is incorrect because Quantity A and Quantity B are not equal. **Choice D** is incorrect because a relation can be obtained from the given information.

2 **Choice D is correct.** The question gives only one point from each line

l and m. Hence, there are many possible values of the slope of the lines such that the slope is positive.

Analyze the possible slope of each line.

If the lines intersect at $(0,0)$, the slope of line l is $\frac{3}{2}$ while the slope of line m is $\frac{2}{3}$. The slope of line l is greater than line m.

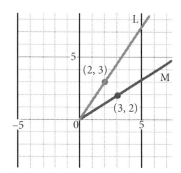

If the lines intersect at $(5,5)$, the slope of line l is $\frac{2}{3}$ while the slope of line m is $\frac{3}{2}$. The slope of line l is less than the slope of line m.

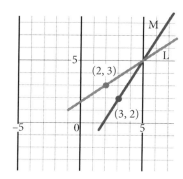

If the lines are parallel, the slope of line l is equal to the slope of line m.

Hence, the correct answer is Choice D because the relationship cannot be determined from the given information.

Choice A is incorrect because Quantity A is not greater than Quantity B. **Choice B** is incorrect because Quantity B is not greater than Quantity A. **Choice C** is incorrect because Quantity A and Quantity B are not equal.

3 **Choice A is correct** because Quantity A is greater than Quantity B.

Find the circumference of each circle.

circle F Let $r = 1$.

   Circumference $= 2\pi r$

   $= 2\pi(1)$

   $= 2\pi$

circle E Let $r = 4$.

   Circumference $= 2\pi r$

   $= 2\pi(4)$

   $= 8\pi$

Analyze the quantities

Quantity A

The circumference of circle E minus the circumference of circle F.

$8\pi - 2\pi = 6\pi$

Quantity B

4π

Choice B is incorrect because Quantity B is not greater than Quantity A. **Choice C** is incorrect because Quantity A and Quantity B are not equal. **Choice D** is incorrect because a relation can be obtained from the given information.

Section 1: Answers & Explanations

4 **Choice B is correct.** Find the possible values of n.

$$\frac{1}{2^{(1-n)}} \leq \frac{1}{8}$$

$$\frac{1}{2^{(1-n)}} \leq \frac{1}{2^3}$$

$$2^{-(1-n)} \leq 2^{-3}$$

$$-(1-n) \leq -3$$

$$n - 1 \leq -3$$

$$n \leq -3 + 1$$

$$n \leq -2$$

Analyze the quantities.

Quantity A: n

Values of includes $-2, -3, -4$ ...

Quantity B: -1

Hence, Choice B is correct because Quantity B is greater than Quantity A.

Explanation for Incorrect Choices:

Choice A is incorrect because Quantity A is not greater than Quantity B. **Choice C** is incorrect because Quantity A and Quantity B are not equal. **Choice D** is incorrect because a relation can be obtained from the given information.

5 **Choice A is correct** because the obtained answer for the number of athletes who did not earned a medal for both swimming and diving is $\frac{11}{12}x$.

Let x be the number of athletes.

Find the number of athletes who earned a medal for both swimming and diving.

$$\frac{1}{3} \text{ of } x \text{ and } \frac{1}{4} \text{ of } (\frac{1}{3} \text{ of } x)$$

$$= \frac{1}{3}x\left(\frac{1}{4}\right)$$

$$= \frac{1}{12}x$$

Find the number of athletes who did not earn a medal for both swimming and diving.

$x-$ the number of athletes who earned a medal for both swimming and diving

$$= x - \frac{1}{12}x$$

$$= \frac{11}{12}x$$

Choice B is incorrect because $\frac{7x}{12}$ is less than the obtained answer. **Choice C** is incorrect because $\frac{5x}{12}$ is less than the obtained answer. **Choice D** is incorrect because $\frac{6x}{7}$ is not the equivalent to $\frac{11}{12}x$ in simplest form. **Choice E** is incorrect because $\frac{x}{7}$ is not the equivalent to $\frac{11}{12}x$ in simplest form.

6 **Choice C is correct** because the obtained percentage is 20%.

Take the needed information.

State C – year 2001 – Applied : 4000 , Qualified: 780

State D – year 2001 – Applied : 3500 , Qualified: 690

Find the percentage of candidates qualified to that of the candidate appeared when the states C and D are combined in 2001

$$\frac{(780 + 690)}{(4000 + 3500)}(100) = \frac{1470}{7500}(100) = 19.6\% \text{ or}$$

approximately 20%

Choice A is incorrect because 15% is lower than the obtained percentage. **Choice B** is incorrect because 18 % is lower than the obtained percentage. **Choice D** is incorrect because 30 % is greater than the obtained percentage. **Choice E** is incorrect because 35 % is greater than the obtained percentage.

7 **Choice B is correct** because the obtained answer is 5166.

The average number of candidates from State B over the given years is the number of candidates who applied from year 2000, 2001 and 2002.

$$Average = \frac{5200 + 4500 + 5800}{3}$$

$$Average = \frac{15500}{3}$$

$$Average = 5166$$

Choice A is incorrect because 5160 is not the average obtained. **Choice C** is incorrect because 5360 is not the average obtained. **Choice D** is incorrect because 6166 is not the average obtained. **Choice E** is incorrect because 6206 is not the average obtained.

For more practice, visit www.vibrantpublishers.com

8 **Choice E is correct** because the obtained answer is 14%.

The percentage of applicants qualified from State A for all years compared to the number of candidates who appeared from State A for all years

$$\frac{(740+650+1150)}{(6300+5600+6200)}(100) = \frac{2540}{18100}(100) = 14.03\%$$

or approximately 14%

Choice A is incorrect because 9% is less than the obtained percentage. **Choice B** is incorrect because 11% is less than the obtained percentage. **Choice C** is incorrect because 12% is less than the obtained percentage. **Choice D** is incorrect because 13% is less than the obtained percentage.

9 **Choice D is correct** because the simplified form of the expression is $\frac{1}{b}$.

Simplify the expression $\frac{(ab)^4 c^0}{a^4 b^5}$ using the law of exponents.

Apply Zero Exponent Rule $\quad x^0 = 1 \ldots\ldots\ldots\ldots \frac{(ab)^4 \cdot 1}{a^4 b^5}$

Apply Power of a Product Rule $(xy)^m = x^m y^m \ldots\ldots \frac{a^4 b^4}{a^4 b^5}$

Apply Quotient Rule $\quad \frac{x^m}{x^n} = x^{m-n} \ldots\ldots\ldots a^{4-4} b^{4-5}$

$\ldots\ldots\ldots\ldots a^0 b^{-1}$

Apply Negative Exponent Rule $x^{-m} = \frac{1}{x^m} \ldots\ldots\ldots\ldots \frac{1}{b}$

Choice A is incorrect because ab is not the simplified form of the given expression. **Choice B** is incorrect because $\frac{1}{a}$ is not equivalent to the given expression. **Choice C** is incorrect because abc is not the simplified form of the given expression. **Choice E** is incorrect because $\frac{c}{ab}$ the simplified form of the given expression.

10 **Choice E is correct** because the obtained number of bricks is $\frac{32n}{m}$.

Let m be the number of workers and n be the bricks per hour.

Rate per worker is $\frac{n}{m}$.

Rate of 4 workers is $4\left(\frac{n}{m}\right) = \frac{4n}{m}$

The number of bricks in 8 hours is $\frac{4n}{m}(8) = \frac{32n}{m}$.

Choice A is incorrect because $\frac{2m}{n}$ is not the obtained number of bricks. **Choice B** is incorrect because $\frac{2n}{m}$ is not the obtained number of bricks. **Choice C** is incorrect because $\frac{32m}{n}$ is not the obtained number of bricks. **Choice D** is incorrect because $\frac{m}{2n}$ is not the obtained number of bricks.

11 **Choice D is correct** because the obtained value of x is $\frac{7}{8}$.

Outcomes of rolling a 4-sided die are 1, 2, 3, and 4. Rolling two 4-sided dice will have an outcome of 16. Find the probability that the absolute value of the difference between the numbers is less than 3.

Let x be the absolute value of the difference between the numbers is less than 3.

Assign values to x.

x is the absolute value of the difference between the two numbers on the dice and x should be less than 3.

When $x=0, |x|=|0|=0$. The possible outcomes are (1,1), (2,2), (3,3), (4,4)   **Outcomes: 4**

When $x=1, |x|=|1|=1$. The possible outcomes are (1,2), (2,3), (3,4), (2,1), (3,2), (4,3)   **Outcomes: 6**

When $x=2, |x|=|2|=2$. The possible outcomes are (1,3), (3,1), (2,4), (4,2)   **Outcomes: 3**

Find the total outcomes: $4+6+4=14$.

Solve for the probability when $x<3$.

$$\frac{Total\ outcomes\ when\ x<3}{Total\ possible\ outcomes\ of\ drawing\ two\ dice} = \frac{14}{4(4)} = \frac{14}{16} = \frac{7}{8}$$

Choice A is incorrect because $\frac{1}{8}$ is lower than the obtained probability. **Choice B** is incorrect because $\frac{3}{8}$ is lower than the obtained probability. **Choice C** is incorrect because $\frac{5}{8}$ is lower than the obtained probability. **Choice E** is incorrect because $\frac{9}{8}$ is more than 1.

12 The correct answer is 30° because it is the obtained value of z.

∠POH and ∠POX are supplementary angles. Hence, ∠POH + ∠POX = 180°.

$$\angle POH + \angle POX = 180°$$
$$\angle POH = 180° - \angle POX$$
$$\angle POH = 180° - 70°$$
$$\angle POH = 110°$$

HOPE is a parallelogram, hence, HE||PO and EP||HO, diagonal Hp acts as a transversal making the opposite angles congruent.

Hence, $y = 40°$

Use Triangle Sum Theorem to find z.

$$z + y + \angle POH = 180°$$
$$z + 40° + 110° = 180°$$
$$z + 150° = 180°$$
$$z = 180° - 150°$$
$$z = 30°$$

SECTION 2 (EASY): Answers & Explanations

1 **Choice A is correct.**

Find the ratio of the area of equilateral triangle S to the area of equilateral triangle T.

All equilateral triangles are similar to each other. The ratio of its sides is $\frac{m}{n}$ meanwhile the ratio of its area is $(\frac{m}{n})^2$.

If one side of equilateral triangle S is 3 times the length of one side of equilateral triangle T, then the ratio of its side is $\frac{3}{1}$ or 3:1. From this, the ratio of its area is $\frac{9}{1}$ or 9:1.

Hence, $a = 9$ and $b = 1$.

Analyze the quantities.

Quantity A: $a = 9$

Quantity B: 6

Hence, Choice A is correct because Quantity A is greater than Quantity B.

Choice B is incorrect because Quantity B is not greater than Quantity A. **Choice C** is incorrect because Quantity A and Quantity B are not equal. **Choice D** is incorrect because a relation can be obtained from the given information.

Section 2 (Easy): Answers & Explanations

2 **Choice B is correct** because Quantity B is greater than Quantity A.

Analyze the quantities.

Quantity A Range of the four artist's age

Range = Maximum Age − Minimum age

Range = 30 − 12

Range = 18

Quantity B 25

Choice A is incorrect because Quantity A is not greater than Quantity B. **Choice C** is incorrect because Quantity A and Quantity B are not equal. **Choice D** is incorrect because a relation can be obtained from the given information.

3 **Choice B is correct** because Quantity B is greater than Quantity A.

Solve for the value of r.

$$\frac{2}{3}\left|r - \frac{4}{3}\right| = \frac{17}{9}$$

$$\left(\frac{3}{2}\right)\frac{2}{3}\left|r - \frac{4}{3}\right| = \frac{17}{9}\left(\frac{3}{2}\right)$$

$$\left|r - \frac{4}{3}\right| = \frac{17}{6}$$

Apply the absolute value rule.

$$r - \frac{4}{3} = -\frac{17}{6} \qquad\qquad r - \frac{4}{3} = \frac{17}{6}$$

$$r = -\frac{17}{6} + \frac{4}{3} \qquad\qquad r = \frac{17}{6} + \frac{4}{3}$$

$$r = \frac{-17 + 8}{6} \qquad\qquad r = \frac{17 + 8}{6}$$

$$r = \frac{-9}{6} \qquad\qquad r = \frac{25}{6}$$

$$r = \frac{-3}{2} \qquad\qquad r = \frac{25}{6}$$

Analyze the quantities:

Quantity A: r

There are two possible values of r.

$$r = \frac{-3}{2} \text{ or } r = -1.5$$

$$r = \frac{25}{6} \text{ or } r = 4.17$$

Quantity B: 5

Choice A is incorrect because Quantity A is not greater than Quantity B. Choice C is incorrect because Quantity B is not equal to Quantity A. Choice D is incorrect because a relation can be obtained from the given information.

4 **Choice B is correct** because Quantity B is greater than Quantity A.

Identify the numbers in each set.

Set A comprises multiples of 2............ {2, 4, 6, 8, 10…}
Set B comprises multiples of 3............ {3, 6, 9, 12, 15…}
Set C comprises multiples of 6............ {6, 12, 18, 24, 30..}

Analyze the quantities.

Quantity A: Least common multiple of Set A, B and C

Set A — 2, 4, **6**, 8, 10, 12,14
Set B — 3, **6**, 9, 12, 15, 18, 21
Set C— **6**, 12, 18, 24, 30, 36, 42

The least common multiple is 6.

Quantity B: 12

Choice A is incorrect because Quantity A is not greater than Quantity B. Choice C is incorrect because Quantity A and Quantity B are not equal. Choice D is incorrect because a relation can be obtained from the given information.

5 **Choice A is correct** because Quantity A is greater than Quantity B.

Find the measure of $m\angle COB$.

$m\angle COB$ and $m\angle EOF$ are vertical angles.

$m\angle COB = m\angle EOF = 42°$

Find the area of the sector COB.

$$A = \frac{n}{360}\pi r^2$$

$$A = \frac{42}{360}\pi (2)^2$$

$$A = \frac{7}{15}\pi$$

Analyze the quantities.

Quantity A   The area of shaded sector COB

$$A = \frac{7}{15}\pi$$

Quantity B

$$\frac{2\pi}{5} = \frac{2(3)\pi}{5(3)} = \frac{6\pi}{15}$$

Choice B is incorrect because Quantity B is not greater than Quantity A. Choice C is incorrect because Quantity A and Quantity B are not equal. Choice D is incorrect because a relation can be obtained from the given information.

6 **Choice C is correct** because the obtained value of x is $-1 \le x \le 1$.

Find x.

$$1 - x^2 \ge 0$$
$$-x^2 \ge -1$$
$$x^2 \le 1$$

For $u^n \le a$, if n is even then $-\sqrt[n]{a} \le u \le \sqrt[n]{a}$.

$$x^2 \le 1$$
$$-\sqrt{1} \le x \le \sqrt{1}$$
$$-1 \le x \le 1$$

Choice A is incorrect because $x \ge 1$ is not the obtained value of x. Choice B is incorrect because $0 \le x \le 1$ is not the obtained value of x. Choice D is incorrect because $x \le -1$ is not the obtained value of x. Choice E is incorrect because $x \le -1$ or $x \ge 1$ is not the obtained value of x.

7 **Choice A and D are correct** because the sum of the scores is 18.

Calculate Julian's current total score.

$$8(3.75) = 30$$

To get an average of 4, he needs a total score of

$$12(4.0) = 48$$

The additional score he needs to get is $48 - 30 = 18$.

Evaluate each choice.

Choice A: 3.5 + 4.75 + 4.75 + 5.0 = 18.0
Choice B: 3.25 + 4.5 + 4.75 + 5.0 = 17.5
Choice C: 3.0 + 3.5 + 4.75 + 4.75 = 16.0
Choice D: 3.75 + 4.5 + 4.75 + 5.0 =18.0
Choice E: 3.0 + 4.0 + 4.0 + 4.75 = 15.75

Choice B is incorrect because 17.5 is lower than the obtained sum of the remaining scores. Choice C is incorrect because 16.0 is lower than the obtained sum of the remaining scores. Choice E is incorrect because 15.75 is lower than the obtained sum of the remaining scores.

Section 2 (Easy): Answers & Explanations

8 **Choice D is correct** because to solve the area of the rectangle $= LW$, the system equation to use to solve for the value of L and W are $L + W = 280$ and $L^2 + W^2 = 40,000$.

Use the given information to write an equation.
Let L be the length and W be the width.

Perimeter is said to be 560 feet.

Hence, $2L + 2W = Perimeter$
$2L + 2W = 560$
$2(L + W) = 560$
$L + W = 280$

Diagonal is 200. Use the Pythagorean theorem.
$L^2 + W^2 = D^2$
$L^2 + W^2 = 200^2$
$L^2 + W^2 = 40,000$

Choice A is incorrect because $+W = 560$, $L^2 + W^2 = 200^2$ is not the obtained answer. **Choice B** is incorrect because $+W = 280$, $L^2 - W^2 = 200^2$ is not the obtained answer. **Choice C** is incorrect because $2L + 2W = 560$, $L^2 + W^2 = 200$ is not the obtained answer. **Choice E** is incorrect because $+W = 560$, $L + W = 200$ is not the obtained answer.

9 **Choice D is correct** because the obtained answer is 75%.

Identify the percentages of each flower.

One-fourth of the flowers are red .... $\frac{1}{4}(100) = 25\%$

40% of the flowers are blue 40%

% of the flowers are yellow ..... $100\% - (25\% + 40\%) = 35\%$

Find the probability that the chosen flower is not red.
This means that he chose either blue or yellow flowers.

$40\% + 35\% = 75\%$

Choice A is incorrect because 25% is less than the obtained answer. **Choice B** is incorrect because 30% is less than the obtained answer. **Choice C** is incorrect because 40% is less than the obtained answer. **Choice E** is incorrect because 80% is greater than the obtained answer.

10 **Choice D is correct** because Joseph's age is 15.

Let A be Alice's age, M be Martin's age and J be Joseph's age.

Write the equations based on the given information.

Ten years ago, Alice was born .... $A - 10 = 0$

Ten years ago, Martin was twice
as old as Joseph .... $M - 10 = 2(J - 10)$

Now, Martin is twice as old as Alice ..…........…… $M = 2A$

Find J.

$A - 10 = 0$
$A = 10$
$M - 10 = 2(J - 10)$
$2A - 10 = 2(J - 10)$
$2(10) - 10 = 2(J - 10)$
$20 - 10 = 2J - 20$
$10 + 20 = 2J$
$30 = 2J$
$15 = J$

Choice A is incorrect because 10 is less than the obtained age of Joseph. **Choice B** is incorrect because 12 is less than the obtained age of Joseph. **Choice C** is incorrect because 14 is less than the obtained age of Joseph. **Choice E** is incorrect because 20 is more than the obtained age of Joseph.

11 **Choice D is correct** because the obtained answer is at 6th hour.

Let C be the capacity of the pool.

At 8 hours, it is at full capacity C.

It says that the volume of the pool doubles every hour, hence, at 7th hour capacity is at $\frac{C}{2}$.

At which hour is the capacity at $\frac{C}{4}$?

At 6th hour, the capacity is at $\frac{C}{4}$.

Choice A is incorrect because 2 is lower than the obtained time. **Choice B** is incorrect because 4 is lower than the obtained time. **Choice C** is incorrect because 5 is lower than the obtained time. **Choice E** is incorrect because 7 is not the obtained answer.

Chapter 7: Practice Test #1

12 **Choice D is correct** because the obtained answer for x is 46.
Write the equation.
Let x be the small number.
$x+2$ be the bigger number.
Sum of the numbers is 94............. $x+(x+2)=94$
Squared difference of the numbers...... $(x+2)^2 - x^2 = 188$
Find the value of x.
$$x+(x+2)=94$$
$$2x=94-2$$
$$2x=92$$
$$x=46$$
Use the second equation to confirm.
$$(x+2)^2 - x^2 = 188$$
$$(46+2)^2 - 46^2 = 188$$
$$(48)^2 - 46^2 = 188$$
$$188 = 188$$
Choice A is incorrect because 36 is less than the obtained answer. **Choice B** is incorrect because 38 is less than the obtained answer. **Choice C** is incorrect because 42 is greater than the obtained answer. **Choice E** is incorrect because 48 is greater than the obtained answer.

13 **Choice D is correct** because the obtained maximum value of P is $133.00.
Alex has $100. He can't afford the watch hence, the price of the watch P is greater than $100.
$$P > \$100$$
He can already afford it when the price was reduced to 25%.
$$0.75\ P \leq \$100$$
Solve for P.
$$0.75\ P \leq \$100$$
$$P \leq \frac{\$100}{0.75}$$
$$P \leq \$133.33$$
Choice A is incorrect because $110.00 is less than the value of P. **Choice B** is incorrect because $120.00 is less than the value of P. **Choice C** is incorrect because $125.00 is less than the value of P. **Choice E** is incorrect because $150.00 is less than the value of P.

14 The correct answer is 24.
$$f(x) = \frac{1}{4}x + 2$$
$$8 = \frac{1}{4}x + 2$$
$$8 - 2 = \frac{1}{4}x$$
$$6 = \frac{1}{4}x$$
$$24 = x$$

15 **Choice A and B are correct** because −60 and −30 are less than the obtained value of x.
Solve for y in the first equation in terms of x.
$$y - 3x > 12$$
$$y > 12 + 3x$$
Substitute it into the second equation.
$$x - y > 38$$
$$x - (12 + 3x) > 38$$
$$x - 12 - 3x > 38$$
$$-2x > 50$$
$$x < -25$$
Choice C is incorrect because −6 is not less than the obtained value of x. **Choice D** is incorrect because 4 is greater than the obtained value of x. **Choice E** is incorrect because 20 is greater than the obtained value of x. **Choice F** is incorrect because 40 is greater than the obtained value of x. **Choice G** is incorrect because 60 is greater than the obtained value of x.

SECTION 2 (HARD): Answers & Explanations

1 **Choice B is correct** because Quantity B is greater than Quantity A.
Find the percentage of grain lost in the first three days.
Day 1:
  Lost grain: 1% of x or $0.01x$
  Remaining grain: $x - 0.01 = 0.99x$
Day 2:
  Lost grain: 1% of $0.99x = 0.0099x$
  Remaining grain: $0.99x - 0.0099x = 0.9801x$

Day 3:

Lost grain: 1% of $0.9801x = 0.009801x$

Remaining grain: $0.9801x - 0.009801x = 0.970299x$

Sum of the total lost grain for 3 days:

$$0.01x + 0.0099x + 0.009801x = 0.029701x$$

Percentage of the lost grain for 3 days:

$$\left(\frac{0.029701x}{x}\right) * 100 = 2.9701\%$$

Analyze the quantities.

$$2.9701\% < 3\%$$

Choice A is incorrect because Quantity A is not greater than Quantity B. **Choice C** is incorrect because Quantity A and Quantity B are not equal. **Choice D** is incorrect because a relation can be obtained from the given information.

2 **Choice C is correct** because Quantity A is equal to Quantity B.

Use the arithmetic sequence formula and identify the terms.

$$a_n = a_1 + (n-1)d$$
$$a_1 = 107, \; d = -6, \; a_n = -61$$

$$-61 = 107 + (n-1)(-6)$$
$$-61 - 107 = -6n + 6$$
$$-168 = -6n + 6$$
$$-168 - 6 = -6n$$
$$-174 = -6n$$
$$29 = n$$

Choice A is incorrect because Quantity A is not greater than Quantity B. **Choice B** is incorrect because Quantity B is not greater than Quantity A. **Choice D** is incorrect because a relation can be obtained from the given information.

3 **Choice B is correct** because Quantity B is greater than Quantity A.

Take note that making the numerator bigger makes the fraction bigger and making a denominator smaller makes the fraction bigger.

Analyze the quantities.

Compare the numerators of the fractions

Numerator of Quantity A   Numerator of Quantity B
$(390 + x)$ $(400 + x)$

Making the numerator bigger makes the fraction bigger, hence,

Quantity A < Quantity B

Quantity B

Denominator of Quantity A   Denominator of Quantity B
600   590

Making the denominator smaller makes the fraction bigger, hence,

Quantity A < Quantity B

Hence, based on the result, Quantity A < Quantity B

Choice A is incorrect because Quantity A is not greater than Quantity B. **Choice C** is incorrect because Quantity A and Quantity B are not equal. **Choice D** is incorrect because a relation can be obtained from the given information.

4 **Choice C is correct** because Quantity A and Quantity B are equal.

Find the perimeter of the triangle.

The equation $2a + b = 180$ indicates that two angles have equal degree measurement thus it is an isosceles triangle.

Using the Isosceles triangle theorem which states that, if two angles of an isosceles triangle are equal, then the sides opposite to the equal angles will also have the same measure. Hence, looking at the figure, side RS has an equal length with side RQ.

Analyze the quantities.

Quantity A: Perimeter of $\triangle RSQ = 7 + 7 + 4 = 18$

Quantity B: 18

Choice A is incorrect because Quantity A is not greater than Quantity B. **Choice B** is incorrect because Quantity B is not greater than Quantity A. **Choice D** is incorrect because a relation can be obtained from the given information.

5 **Choice A is correct** because Quantity A is greater than Quantity B.

Let L be the length and B be the breadth.

Area of the rectangle is $A = LB$

Apply the changes in length and breadth.

Increase in length is $(100 + 10)\%$ of $L = 110L/100 = 1.1L$

Decrease in breadth is $(100 - 20)\%$ of $B = 80B/100 = 0.8B$

Find the new Area of the rectangle.

$A = LB$

$A = 1.1L(0.8B)$

$A = 1.1L(0.8B)$

$A = 0.88LB$

Find the percentage change.

$$\frac{(0.88LB) - LB}{LB}(100\%)$$

$$\frac{-0.12LB}{LB}(100\%)$$

$-0.12(100\%)$

12% decrease

The length of the rectangle is increased by 10% and breadth is decreased by 20%.

Choice B is incorrect because Quantity B is not greater than Quantity A. **Choice C** is incorrect because Quantity A and Quantity B are not equal. **Choice D** is incorrect because a relation can be obtained from the given information.

6 **Choice C, D, E, F are correct** because these values are within the median price $15000–$18999.

Find the median.

There are 28 cars, median is at $\frac{n+1}{2} = \frac{28+1}{2} = \frac{29}{2} = 14.5$.

The median is between the 14th and 15th car sold.

Car 1 to 9 –   Under $15000

Car 10 to 14 – $15000–$16999

Car 15 to 22 – $17000–$18999

Car 23 to 28 – Over $19000

The 14th car falls at $15000–$16999 and the 15th car falls at $17000–$18999. Hence, the median price is at $15000–$18999.

Choice A is incorrect because $ 12000 is below the median price. **Choice B** is incorrect because $13000 is below the median price. **Choice G** is incorrect because $ 19500 is above the median price. **Choice H** is incorrect because $21000 is above the median price.

7 **Choice C is correct** because it is even.

Analyze the choices. Since x is an integer, it can be positive or negative. Substitute $x = 1$ and $x = -1$ into the equations and identify if the result is even or odd.

Choice A: $x^2 + 2x + 10$

when $x = 1$ .... $x^2 + 2x + 10$

$(1)^2 + 2(1) + 10 = 12$ even

when $x = -1$ .... $x^2 + 2x + 10$

$(-1)^2 + 2(-1) + 10 = 9$ odd

Hence, choice A is odd.

Choice B: $x^2 - x - 1$

when $x = 1$ .... $x^2 - x - 1$

$(1)^2 - (1) - 1 = -1$ odd

when $x = -1$ .... $x^2 - x - 1$

$(-1)^2 - (-1) - 1 = 1$ odd

Hence, choice B is odd.

Choice C: $x^2 + 3x + 8$

when $x = 1$ .... $x^2 + 3x + 8$

$(1)^2 + 3(1) + 8 = 12$ even

when $x = -1$ .... $x^2 + 3x + 8$

$(-1)^2 + 3(-1) + 8 = 6$ even

Hence, choice C is even.

Choice D: $x^2 - 4x + 6$

when $x = 1$ .... $x^2 - 4x + 6$

$(1)^2 - 4(1) + 6 = 3$ odd

when $x = -1$ .... $x^2 - 4x + 6$

$(-1)^2 - 4(-1) + 6 = 11$ odd

Hence, choice D is odd.

Choice E: $x^2 - 5x + 10$

when $x = 1$ .... $x^2 - 5x + 11$

$(1)^2 - 5(1) + 11 = 7$ odd

when $x = -1$ .... $x^2 - 5x + 11$

$(-1)^2 - 5(-1) + 11 = 17$ odd

Hence, choice E is odd.

Choice A is incorrect because $x^2 + 2x + 10$ is odd.

Choice B is incorrect because $x^2 - x - 1$ is odd.

Choice D is incorrect because $x^2 - 4x + 6$ is odd.

Choice E is incorrect because $x^2 - 5x + 11$ is odd.

8 **Choice B is correct** because the obtained expression is $\frac{y(x-z)}{(x+z)}$.

Write the equations for the rate.

Arnold's rate: $\frac{y}{x}$ Dexter's rate: $\frac{y}{z}$

Both Arnold and Dexter swim in opposite directions. The rates can be added.

Mutual rate = Arnold's rate + Dexter's Rate

$$= \frac{y}{x} + \frac{y}{z}$$

$$= \frac{yz + yx}{xz}$$

$$= \frac{y(x+z)}{xz}$$

Find the time at which both Arnold and Dexter pass each other from opposite directions.

Mutual time = distance covered / mutual speed

$$= \frac{y}{\frac{y(x+z)}{xz}}$$

$$= y\left(\frac{xz}{y(x+z)}\right)$$

$$= \frac{xz}{(x+z)}$$

Find the difference between Dexter's distance and Arnold's distance after they pass each other.

Dexter's distance − Arnold's Distance = (Dexter's rate * mutual time) − (Arnold's rate * mutual time)

$$= \frac{y}{z}\left(\frac{xz}{(x+z)}\right) - \frac{y}{x}\left(\frac{xz}{(x+z)}\right)$$

$$= \left(\frac{xz}{(x+z)}\right)\left(\frac{y}{z} - \frac{y}{x}\right)$$

$$= \left(\frac{xz}{(x+z)}\right)\left(\frac{yx - yz}{zx}\right)$$

$$= \left(\frac{xz}{(x+z)}\right)\left(\frac{y(x-z)}{xz}\right)$$

$$= \frac{y(x-z)}{(x+z)}$$

Choice A is incorrect because $y(z-x)/(x+z)$ is not the obtained expression. **Choice C is incorrect** because $y(x+z)/(x-z)$ is not the obtained expression. **Choice D is incorrect** because $xy(x-y)/(x+y)$ is not the obtained expression. **Choice E is incorrect** because $xy(y-x)/(x+y)$ is not the obtained expression.

Section 2 (Hard): Answers & Explanations

9 **Choice A is correct** because the obtained answer is approximately 5.

Use the work problem formula $\frac{1}{t_1} + \frac{1}{t_2} = \frac{1}{t}$.

Let J be the number of days James can finish the work.
Let T be the number of days James can finish the work.

$$\frac{1}{J} + \frac{1}{T} = \frac{1}{t}$$

$$\frac{1}{9} + \frac{1}{11} = \frac{1}{t}$$

$$\frac{9+11}{99} = \frac{1}{t}$$

$$\frac{20}{99} = \frac{1}{t}$$

$$\frac{99}{20} = t$$

$$t \approx 5$$

Choice B is incorrect because 6 is greater than the obtained answer. **Choice C is incorrect** because 7 is greater than the obtained answer. **Choice D is incorrect** because 8 is greater than the obtained answer. **Choice E is incorrect** because 10 is greater than the obtained answer.

10 **Choice B is correct** because the obtained value is 3.

Assign values to n.

Let $n=1$, $\frac{1}{5^n} < 0.01$

$$\frac{1}{5^1} < 0.01$$

$$0.2 < 0.01 \quad \text{not true}$$

Let $n=2$, $\frac{1}{5^n} < 0.01$

$$\frac{1}{5^2} < 0.01$$

$$0.04 < 0.01 \quad \text{not true}$$

Let $n=3$, $\frac{1}{5^n} < 0.01$

$$\frac{1}{5^3} < 0.01$$

$$0.008 < 0.01 \quad \text{true}$$

Hence, the least value for the inequality to be true is when $n=3$.

Choice A is incorrect because 2 does not give a true statement for the given inequality. **Choice C is incorrect** because 4 is greater than the obtained answer. **Choice D is** incorrect because 10 is greater than the obtained answer. **Choice E is incorrect** because 11 is greater than the obtained answer.

11 **The correct answer is 87°** because it is the obtained exterior angle of the nonagon.

Sum of the Interior Angles of a Nonagon.
$$(n-2)(180°)=(9-2)(180°)=1260°$$
Sum of the 7 Interior Angles of a Nonagon.
$$154° +147° +138° +130° +145° +132° +128° =1074°$$
Find the unknown interior angles.
$$1260° =1074° +2x$$
$$186° =2x$$
$$93° =x$$
Find the exterior angle of the two unknown angles.
$$\text{Exterior angle} = 180° - \text{interior angle}$$
$$=180° -93°$$
$$=87°$$

12 **Choice A is correct** because all the given choices are less than 90 but $r=1$, is the least value that satisfies the given conditions.
Set up the mean equation.
$$\frac{r+s+t}{3}=100$$
Find the possible values of r.
$$\frac{r+s+120}{3}=100$$
$$r+s+120=100\,(3)$$
$$r+s+120=300$$
$$r+s=300-120$$
$$r+s=180$$
Since $r<s$ and $s=180-r$,
$$r<s$$
$$r<180-r$$
$$2r<180$$
$$r<90$$
Considering the condition, $r,s,t \neq 0$, $0<r<90$.

Choice B is incorrect because 4 is not the least value that satisfies the given conditions. **Choice C is incorrect** because 10 is not the least value that satisfies the given conditions. **Choice D is incorrect** because 61 is not the least value that satisfies the given conditions. **Choice E is** incorrect because 80 is not the least value that satisfies the given conditions.

13 **Choice B is correct** because the obtained answer is 2.5.
Initial weight of the melon   – 5 kg
Water content in kg   – 5(0.98)=4.9 kg
Solid content in kg   – 5(0.02)=0.1 kg
Water has decreased by 2%.
$$98\% - 2\% = 96\%$$

The new weight of the melon is
$$x = 0.096x + 0.1$$
$$x - 0.096x = 0.1$$
$$0.04x = 0.1$$
$$x = 2.5$$
Choice A is incorrect because 2.0 is less than the obtained value of x. **Choice C is incorrect** because 3.0 is greater than the obtained value of x. **Choice D is incorrect** because 3.5 is greater than the obtained value of x. **Choice E is incorrect** because 4.0 is greater than the obtained value of x.

14 **Choice B and E are correct** because the obtained values of t are $\frac{5}{2}$ or -3.
Find t.
$$f(x) = x^2 + x$$
$$f(2t) = (2t)^2 + 2t$$
$$30 = 4t^2 + 2t$$
$$30 = 4t^2 + 2t$$
Use the quadratic formula to solve for t.
$$4t^2 + 2t - 30 = 0$$
$$a=4, b=2, c=-30$$
$$t = \frac{-b \pm \sqrt{b^2 - 4ac}}{2a}$$
$$t = \frac{-2 \pm \sqrt{2^2 - 4(4)(-30)}}{2(4)}$$

Section 2 (Hard): Answers & Explanations

$$t = \frac{-2 \pm 22}{8}$$

$$t = \frac{-2 + 22}{8} = \frac{20}{8} = \frac{5}{2}$$

$$t = \frac{-2 - 22}{8} = \frac{-24}{8} = -3$$

Choice A is incorrect because -5 is not the obtained value of t. **Choice C is incorrect** because -0.5 is not the obtained value of t. **Choice D is incorrect** because 2 is not the obtained value of t.

15 **Choice E is correct** because the obtained equation of the mean is $2x + 1$.

Find the mean of the given data
$2x + 3, x - 3, 3x - 7, 2x + 11$.

$n = 4$

$$\text{Mean} = \frac{(2x+3)+(x-3)+(3x-7)+(2x+11)}{4}$$

$$= \frac{(2x + x + 3x + 2x) + (3 - 3 - 7 + 11)}{4}$$

$$= \frac{8x + 4}{4}$$

$$= \frac{4(2x + 1)}{4}$$

$$= 2x + 1$$

Choice A is incorrect because $5x + 7$ is not equivalent to the mean of the given data. **Choice B is incorrect** because $3x - 2$ is not equivalent to the mean of the given data. **Choice C is incorrect** because $x + 5$ is not equivalent to the mean of the given data. **Choice D is incorrect** because $2x - 1$ is not equivalent to the mean of the given data.

Before You Begin the Test

Please Read the Instructions Carefully

This practice test is designed to mirror the structure and rigor of the GRE Quantitative Reasoning section. Treat it as a formal simulation. The more seriously you take this exercise, the more accurately it will reflect your current preparedness—and guide your next steps.

The number of questions and the time limits in each section are aligned with those on the actual GRE, providing you with a realistic and reliable measure of your readiness.

Once you complete the test, refer to the answer key to check your responses. You'll also find detailed instructions for calculating your Quantitative Reasoning score, along with explanations for each question. Be sure to review these explanations thoroughly—especially for the questions you got wrong—to gain insight into the reasoning behind the correct answers and to sharpen your test-taking strategies.

Set Up Your Testing Environment

To replicate real testing conditions:

- Choose a quiet, uninterrupted space to work in.
- Have the following materials at hand:
    - ❑ Rough paper
    - ❑ A few sharpened pencils
    - ❑ A timer, stopwatch, or clock to track your time (if you are simulating test-day pacing)
- Ensure that you remain free of distractions throughout the session.
- Avoid checking your phone, notes, or external resources during the test.

Why This Matters

Your performance on this test is more than just a score—it's a diagnostic tool. It will help you identify question types you excel at and those that need reinforcement. The explanations provided are a valuable resource—use them to deepen your understanding and refine your test-taking strategy.

Chapter 8
Practice Test #2

IMPORTANT
READ THE INSTRUCTIONS BEFORE BEGINNING THE TEST

1. Take this test under real-like testing conditions. Put away any distractions and sit in a quiet place with no disturbances. Keep a rough paper, some pencils, and a calculator beside you.
2. Begin with **Section 1** of the Verbal Reasoning test.
3. Refer to the **Answer Key** on page 273 and note down the number of questions you got right.
4. Based on your score:
   - ❏ If you answered fewer than 7 questions correctly, proceed to **Section 2 (Easy)** on page 268.
   - ❏ If you answered 7 or more questions correctly, proceed to **Section 2 (Hard)** on page 270.
5. Note down the number of correct answers you got right on **Section 2**.
6. Calculate your **Scaled Score** on page 284 for the test.
7. Review the **detailed explanations** for all questions beginning on page 274.

SECTION 1 | 21 MINUTES

1. a and b are both positive integers $64^a = \left(\dfrac{1}{16}\right)^b$

Quantity A	Quantity B
a	b

- (A) Quantity A is greater.
- (B) Quantity B is greater.
- (C) The two quantities are equal.
- (D) The relationship cannot be determined from the information given.

2. The average temperature of Monday through Friday was 75 degrees. The weekend temperature averaged x degrees, bringing the total average temperature for the week to 77 degrees.

Quantity A	Quantity B
x	76

- (A) Quantity A is greater.
- (B) Quantity B is greater.
- (C) The two quantities are equal.
- (D) The relationship cannot be determined from the information given.

3. The solution for the system of equations $y = x^2 + x - 6$ and $x + 2y = 15$ is the coordinate pair (x, y).

Quantity A	Quantity B
0	x

- (A) Quantity A is greater.
- (B) Quantity B is greater.
- (C) The two quantities are equal.
- (D) The relationship cannot be determined from the information given.

4.
$$\dfrac{xy}{x+y} = \dfrac{1}{7}$$

Quantity A	Quantity B
$\dfrac{1}{x} + \dfrac{1}{y}$	7

- (A) Quantity A is greater.
- (B) Quantity B is greater.
- (C) The two quantities are equal.
- (D) The relationship cannot be determined from the information given.

5. A circular photograph is surrounded by a square frame. The diagonal of the frame is 20 inches and the radius of the photograph is 5 inches. Which expression gives the area of the frame?

- (A) $100 - 25\pi$
- (B) $100 - 5\pi$
- (C) $200 - 5\pi$
- (D) $200 - 25\pi$
- (E) $400 - 25\pi$

6. One bell sounds every 15 minutes and another bell goes off every 40 minutes. What is the probability that the two bells will be going off at the same time if a random time is chosen within a 24 hour time period?

- (A) $\dfrac{1}{1440}$
- (B) $\dfrac{1}{400}$
- (C) $\dfrac{1}{120}$
- (D) $\dfrac{1}{90}$
- (E) $\dfrac{1}{24}$

7. Triangle ABE is what fraction of the area of square ABCD?

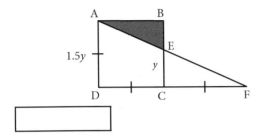

Questions 8 to 10 are based on the following data.

Regional Store Locations and Sales

Region	2000	Sales (Thousands $)	2020	Sales (Thousands $)
West Coast	127	3563	242	3541
Midwest	412	4233	241	2310
East Coast	512	6560	351	7120
South	463	5324	213	5125

East Coast Sales by State 2000

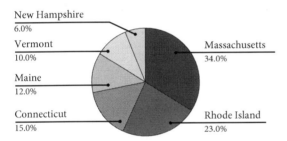

8. What fraction of all sales in 2000 were made in Connecticut?

A) 5%
B) 12.5%
C) 15%
D) 24%
E) 30%

9. Which regions in which year earned a higher average sales per store than the South's average sales per store in 2000?

Indicate all such answers.

A) South in 2020
B) East Coast in 2020
C) West Coast in 2000
D) Midwest in 2020

10. The percent decrease in the number of stores in the Midwest from 2000 to 2020 was approximately how much greater than the percent decrease in the number of stores in the East Coast from 2000 to 2020?

A) 7.1%
B) 10.8%
C) 30.3%
D) 31.4%
E) 41.5%

11. A car traveled 25 mph for ⅓ of its distance traveled, 50 mph for ¼ its distance, and 70 mph for the remaining distance. Which of the following must be true?

Indicate all such statements.

A) The car's average speed was below 50 miles per hour.
B) The car spent less than half its time going 70 miles per hour.
C) The total time it took to complete the journey was 15 hours.
D) The time taken to drive 50 mph was $\frac{3}{8}$ the time taken to drive 25 mph.

12. The price of a stock increased 23% one year and then decreased 12% the following year. The final value of the stock was what percent of the original price of the stock?

Chapter 8: Practice Test #2

SECTION 2 (EASY) | 26 MINUTES

1. The number of students in the class is an odd integer. The ratio of girls to boys in the class is 6:5.

Quantity A	Quantity B
The smallest possible number of students in the class	33

   Ⓐ Quantity A is greater.
   Ⓑ Quantity B is greater.
   Ⓒ The two quantities are equal.
   Ⓓ The relationship cannot be determined from the information given.

2. Square ABCD has a perimeter of 36 in and Cube x has a volume of 64 in^3.

Quantity A	Quantity B
Side length of Square ABCD	Edge length of Cube x

   Ⓐ Quantity A is greater.
   Ⓑ Quantity B is greater.
   Ⓒ The two quantities are equal.
   Ⓓ The relationship cannot be determined from the information given.

3.
   $$0 < x < 1$$

Quantity A	Quantity B
$\dfrac{1}{x^7}$	$\left(x^{-4}\right)^3$

   Ⓐ Quantity A is greater.
   Ⓑ Quantity B is greater.
   Ⓒ The two quantities are equal.
   Ⓓ The relationship cannot be determined from the information given.

4.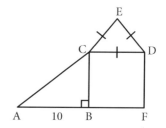

   The area of square BCDF is 49 cm.

Quantity A	Quantity B
Perimeter of ABC	Perimeter of DCE

   Ⓐ Quantity A is greater.
   Ⓑ Quantity B is greater.
   Ⓒ The two quantities are equal.
   Ⓓ The relationship cannot be determined from the information given.

5. In a rectangular plane, equilateral triangle ABC is graphed with vertex A at (2, 2), vertex B at (5, 6), and vertex C at (x, y).

Quantity A	Quantity B
x	0

   Ⓐ Quantity A is greater.
   Ⓑ Quantity B is greater.
   Ⓒ The two quantities are equal.
   Ⓓ The relationship cannot be determined from the information given.

6. For positive numbers, a, b, and c, $\dfrac{ab}{c} = 2$ and $\dfrac{c}{b} = 2$.

Quantity A	Quantity B
b	3

   Ⓐ Quantity A is greater.
   Ⓑ Quantity B is greater.
   Ⓒ The two quantities are equal.
   Ⓓ The relationship cannot be determined from the information given.

Section 2: (Easy)

7. A company must pay a tariff of 34% per pound on their supplies ordered from overseas and a flat rate of $550 in shipping costs. How many pounds of supply did they order if they paid $1501.40 for the most recent shipment?

   A) 642
   B) 710
   C) 803
   D) 951
   E) 2798

8. A car went 75 meters in 8 seconds and then accelerated to travel 180 meters in 10 seconds. Approximately, how much faster was the car going after it accelerated? (use 1 mile = 1.6 kilometers)

   A) 15
   B) 20
   C) 25
   D) 30
   E) 35

9. Set A contains points of (x, y) where x and y are positive integers such that $3x + 4y \leq 10$. What is the total number of points within set A?

   [ ]

10. A car was purchased for $29,999 with a simple interest rate of r over a period of 6 years. If the amount of interest paid after 4 years was $4199.86, what is the value of r?

    A) 3.5%
    B) 5%
    C) 14%
    D) 16%
    E) 35%

11. Set A consists of all prime numbers from 1 to 100. Set B consists of all numbers from Set A that contain the number 3.

    How many terms are in Set B?

    A) 5
    B) 6
    C) 7
    D) 8
    E) 9

12. The number x is a three-digit value that has a remainder of 4 when divided by 6. Which of the following could be the unit digit of x?

    A) 0
    B) 1
    C) 2
    D) 4
    E) 5

13. List K contains consecutive positive integers 1 through x inclusive. For the standard deviation of List K to decrease, which of the following must occur?

    Indicate all such options.

    A. 1 is subtracted from all numbers in the set.
    B. The largest number increases by 1 and the smallest number decreases by 1.
    C. All numbers get divided by 2.
    D. All numbers are square-rooted.

14. Which of the following characteristics of a data set would have the largest standard deviation?

    A) Median > Mean
    B) Mean > Median
    C) Mean = Median
    D) Range = 0
    E) Range > Median

15. An event company had a certain amount of chairs to distribute evenly amongst tables at a banquet. If they distributed 6 chairs per table, they would have 2 chairs left. If they distributed 9 chairs per table, they would have 8 chairs left. Which of the following is a possible number of chairs?

Indicate all such answers.

- [A] 26
- [B] 32
- [C] 45
- [D] 54
- [E] 62

SECTION 2 (HARD) | 26 MINUTES

1. The average test score for the morning class, which has 30 students, was 85. The average test score for the afternoon class, which had 25 students, was 90.

Quantity A	**Quantity B**
The average test score for both classes	87.5

- (A) Quantity A is greater.
- (B) Quantity B is greater.
- (C) The two quantities are equal.
- (D) The relationship cannot be determined from the information given.

2.
$$a < b \text{ and } |a| > |b|$$

Quantity A	**Quantity B**
$\dfrac{b}{a}$	$\dfrac{|a|}{b}$

- (A) Quantity A is greater.
- (B) Quantity B is greater.
- (C) The two quantities are equal.
- (D) The relationship cannot be determined from the information given.

3. A sequence starts with positive integer x and is multiplied by -2 each time to get the next number in the series.

Quantity A	**Quantity B**
The eleventh number in the series	The twentieth number in the series

- (A) Quantity A is greater.
- (B) Quantity B is greater.
- (C) The two quantities are equal.
- (D) The relationship cannot be determined from the information given.

Section 2: (Hard)

4

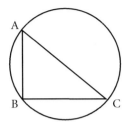

Triangle ABC is inscribed in a circle with a circumference of 26π with the diameter of the circle as the hypotenuse of the triangle. The sides of the triangle are in the ratio 5:12:13.

Quantity A	Quantity B
Perimeter of triangle ABC	60

Ⓐ Quantity A is greater.
Ⓑ Quantity B is greater.
Ⓒ The two quantities are equal.
Ⓓ The relationship cannot be determined from the information given.

5

Quantity A	Quantity B
The area of a regular octagon with side lengths of 6	The area of a square with side lengths of 10

Ⓐ Quantity A is greater.
Ⓑ Quantity B is greater.
Ⓒ The two quantities are equal.
Ⓓ The relationship cannot be determined from the information given.

6 From a group of 10 employees that includes 3 people with over 20 years of experience at the company, a 4-person committee is going to be formed so that exactly one member is experienced. How many different combinations are possible that meet this requirement?

Ⓐ 105
Ⓑ 350
Ⓒ 840
Ⓓ 1020
Ⓔ 5040

7

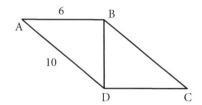

What is the area of parallelogram ABCD?

Ⓐ 30
Ⓑ 36
Ⓒ 48
Ⓓ 80
Ⓔ 100

8 Workers A and B can work together to complete a task in 20 hours. Workers B and C can complete the same task in 40 hours. Workers A and C would take 8 hours to complete the same task. How long would it take to complete the task if workers A, B, and C all work together?

Ⓐ 5
Ⓑ 10
Ⓒ 15
Ⓓ 20
Ⓔ 25

Chapter 8: Practice Test #2

9. If x and y are positive integers such that $\frac{x}{y}$ is an odd integer, then $x - y$ can equal which of the following?

- A) 11
- B) 13
- C) 27
- D) 30
- E) 49

10. A product is marked up 45% from cost but then goes on sale to allow for a 15% profit. What is the approximate percent difference in cost between the original markup and the final sale price?

- A) 10%
- B) 15%
- C) 20%
- D) 30%
- E) 80%

11. The price of gold varied between $2582 per ounce and $2875 per ounce over a 30 day period. Eliza bought 50 ounces of gold at a price of $2680 per ounce during some point in the month and then sold all 50 ounces later in the month. Which of the following could be the percentage profit Eliza made on the gold?

Indicate all that apply.

- A) A loss of 25%
- B) A loss of 38%
- C) A gain of 5%
- D) A gain of 12%

12. A sequence is defined by the expression $a_n = a_{n-1} - 5$ where $a_1 = 405$. What is the sum of the first 100 terms in the sequence?

- A) 405
- B) 1000
- C) 4050
- D) 10,125
- E) 15,750

13. Given $-10 < x < 8$ and $15 < y < 23$, what is the range of xy?

☐

14.

Library Budget 2018	
Staff	$345,000
Equipment	$546,000
Books	$34,250
Events	$25,100
Maintenance	$327,010
Supplies	$13,520
Subscriptions	$159,120

If a pie chart was made to show the percent of the budget that went to equipment was compared to all non-salary related areas, what would be the approximate degree measure of the pie chart for the category?

- A) 50°
- B) 88°
- C) 165°
- D) 178°
- E) 220°

15. If $x < y < 0 < z$ and x, y, and z are integers, which of the following could be $\frac{xy}{z}$?

Indicate all possible answers.

- A) −4
- B) 0
- C) 1
- D) 10

Answer Key

\	Section 1	\
Q. No.	Correct Answer	Your Answer
1	B	
2	A	
3	D	
4	C	
5	D	
6	C	
7	$\frac{1}{9}$	
8	A	
9	A,C	
10	A	
11	A,B,D	
12	108.24	

\	Section 2 (Easy)	\
Q. No.	Correct Answer	Your Answer
1	B	
2	A	
3	B	
4	A	
5	D	
6	D	
7	E	
8	B	
9	2	
10	A	
11	C	
12	D	
13	C,D	
14	E	
15	A,E	

\	Section 2 (Hard)	\
Q. No.	Correct Answer	Your Answer
1	B	
2	D	
3	A	
4	C	
5	A	
6	A	
7	C	
8	B	
9	D	
10	C	
11	C	
12	E	
13	414	
14	D	
15	C	

Chapter 8: Practice Test #2

SECTION 1: Answers & Explanations

1 **Choice B is correct** because rewriting both values are powers of 4 can help you identify the relationship between a and b to find that a is $-\frac{2}{3}b$.

The expression 64^a can be rewritten as 4^{3a} and $\left(\frac{1}{16}\right)^b$ can be rewritten as 4^{-2b}. Now that the expressions have the same base, the exponents can be set equal to each other.

If $3a = -2b$ this would mean a is $-\frac{2}{3}b$, making Quantity B greater.

Choice A is incorrect because a is a negative fraction of b so it would not be greater. **Choice C** is incorrect because a does not equal b. **Choice D** is incorrect because it is possible to create a comparison between the numbers.

2 **Choice A is correct** because you can use the average formula to evaluate the average weekend temperature.

If the average temperature was 75 degrees from Monday to Friday, this means the sum of the week's temperature can be found by multiplying the average by 5 days. This would get you a total of $75 \times 5 = 375$.

The sum of all temperatures during the week can be found by multiplying the second average by 7 days to get $77 \times 7 = 539$.

Subtract these two values to find the sum of the weekend temperatures: $539 - 375 = 164$.

To get the average for the weekend, divide the sum by the number of days to get $\frac{164}{2} = 82$. This number is greater than 77 so Quantity A is greater.

Choice B is incorrect because 77 is less than 82. **Choice C** is incorrect because x does not equal 77. **Choice D** is incorrect because it is possible to solve for the value of x.

3 **Choice D is correct** because there are two possible solutions for x, $x = -4.5$ and $x = 3$ which means it is not possible to compare the two quantities.

To solve for x, rearrange the linear equation into slope–intercept form by subtracting x and dividing by 2 to get $y = -0.5x + 7.5$.

Set the two expressions equal to each other to evaluate their solution set. You will get the expression $x^2 + x - 6 = -0.5x + 7.5$. Add $0.5x$ and subtract 7.5 to get all terms on one side. This will give you $x^2 + 1.5x - 13.5 = 0$.

For easier factoring, multiply everything by a factor of 2 to get $2x^2 + 3x - 27 = 0$. To factor, split the middle term into $-6x$ and $9x$ to get $2x^2 - 6x + 9x - 27 = 0$. Now factor in pairs to get $(2x + 9)(x - 3) = 0$.

Set each expression equal to zero and you will get $2x + 9 = 0$ and $x - 3 = 0$. Solving for x in both terms gets you -4.5 and 3. If $x = -4.5$ Quantity A would be greater. If $x = 3$, then Quantity B would be greater.

Choice A is incorrect because Quantity B can be greater than Quantity A. **Choice B** is incorrect because Quantity A can be greater than Quantity B. **Choice C** is incorrect because the two quantities cannot equal each other.

4 **Choice C is correct** because simplifying the given expression will get you the value of Quantity A. The given expression of $\frac{xy}{x+y} = \frac{1}{7}$ can be cross multiplied to get $7xy = x + y$. Divide both sides by xy to get $7 = \frac{x+y}{xy}$. This can be expanded to get $7 = \frac{x}{xy} + \frac{y}{xy}$ which simplifies to be equal to $7 = \frac{1}{y} + \frac{1}{x}$. This would make both Quantity A and Quantity B equal to 7.

Choice A is incorrect because Quantity A equals 7. **Choice B** is incorrect because Quantity A equals 7. **Choice D** is incorrect because it is possible to solve for Quantity A.

5 **Choice D is correct** because the area of the frame can be found by finding the area of the square with a side length of $10\sqrt{2}$ and then subtracting the area of a circle with a radius of 5.

To find the side length of the picture frame, use the diagonal of 20 and a 45–45–90 right triangle ratio of x, x, and $x\sqrt{2}$. Since the hypotenuse of the triangle would be 20, that means that $x\sqrt{2} = 20$. Solving for x by dividing would get you $\frac{20}{\sqrt{2}} = x$. Rationalize the denominator to find that $x = 10\sqrt{2}$.

To get the area of the square use the formula $A = s^2$. For a square with a side length of $10\sqrt{2}$, the area would be $A = \left(10\sqrt{2}\right)^2$ which equals 200.

To get the area of the circle use the formula $A = \pi r^2$. Plugging in a radius of 5 will give you an area of 25π.

Subtract the area of the circle from the area of the square

274 | GRE Quantitative Practice Questions

Section 1: Answers & Explanations

to get the expression 200 − 25π.

Choice A is incorrect because it solves with the wrong area values. **Choice B is incorrect** because 100 is not the area of the square. **Choice C is incorrect** because it solves with the wrong area values. **Choice E is incorrect** because it solves with the wrong area values.

6 **Choice C is correct** because there is a 1 in 120 chance that within a 24 hour time period the bells will ring at the same time.

Determine the least common multiple of 15 and 40 to evaluate at what minute both bells will ring. The least common multiple of 15 and 40 is 120.

Now, evaluate how many minutes there are in 24 hours by multiplying 24 by 60 to get 1440.

Divide 1440 by 120 to determine the amount of times in 24 hours both bells would sound off. Since this is 12, the probability would be $\frac{12}{1440}$ which simplifies to be $\frac{1}{120}$.

Choice A is incorrect because this would mean they go off together just once. **Choice B is incorrect** because this results from a math error. **Choice D is incorrect** because this results from a math error. **Choice E is incorrect** because this would mean that at least once an hour the two bells go off at the same time which is not true.

7 **The correct answer is** $\frac{1}{9}$ because the area of the square can be found to be 9 and the area of the shaded triangle is 1 for a fractional area of $\frac{1}{9}$.

To find the area of the square use the ratio of the larger triangle ADF to the smaller triangle ECF. It is given that the shorter side lengths have a ratio of 1.5y to y. Use this to create the ratio $\frac{1.5y}{y}$ which simplifies to be $\frac{3}{2}$. This means the larger triangle is $\frac{3}{2}$ the size of the smaller triangle.

Using the given side length of 6 you can create the ratio $\frac{1.5y}{y} = \frac{6+1.5y}{6}$. Cross multiply to get $6y + 1.5y^2 = 9y$. Subtract 6y and divide by 1.5y to get y = 2.

Length BE would be 1.5y − y so it would equal 1.5(2) − 2 = 1. The area of the shaded triangle will be $A = \frac{1}{2}bh$ which would be $A = \frac{1}{2}(2)(1)$ which equals 1.

The area of the square can be found with $A = s^2$. The side length would be 1.5(2) = 3 so the area would be $3^2 = 9$. The triangle can be found to be $\frac{1}{9}$ of the total area of the square.

8 **Choice A is correct** because in 2000 Connecticut was 5% of all sales. Since the pie chart shows Connecticut was 15% of all East Coast sales in 2000, multiply 6560 by 0.15 to get 984. Then add up the total sales in 2000 to get 3563 + 4233 + 6560 + 5324 = 19680. Divide 984 by 19680 to get 5%.

Choice B is incorrect because this would result from a calculation error. **Choice C is incorrect** because this is just the percent of east coast sales, not of all sales. **Choice D is incorrect** because this would result from a calculation error. **Choice E is incorrect** because this would result from a calculation error.

9 **Choices A and C are correct.** The approximate average sales per store in the South in 2000 can be found by dividing the number of sales by the number of stores: $\frac{5324}{430} = 12.38$. Use the process of elimination to see which answer is greater than this.

Choice A is correct because $\frac{5125}{213} = 24.06$ which is greater than 12.38. **Choice C is correct** because $\frac{3563}{127} = 28.06$ which is greater than 12.38.

Choice B is incorrect because $\frac{4120}{351} = 11.73$ which is less than 12.38. **Choice D is incorrect** because $\frac{2310}{241} = 9.59$ which is less than 12.38.

10 **Choice A is correct** because the percent difference between the two values can be found by using the percent decrease formula of $\left|\frac{initial - final}{initial}\right| \times 100$ and then subtracting the percentage for the East Coast from the Midwest.

To find the approximate percent decrease in the number of stores in the East Coast from 2000 to 2020 use the values of 512 and 351. This would make the expression $\left|\frac{512 - 351}{512}\right| \times 100 = 31.4\%$.

Chapter 8: Practice Test #2

To find the approximate percent decrease in the number of stores in the Midwest from 2000 to 2020 use the values of 412 and 241. This would make the expression $\left|\frac{412-241}{412}\right| \times 100 = 41.5\%$.

Now subtract the two percentages to get approximately $41.5 - 31.4 = 7.1\%$.

Choice B is incorrect because this results from a calculation error. **Choice C is incorrect** because this results from a calculation error. **Choice D is incorrect** because this is the percent decrease for the Midwest stores. **Choice E is incorrect** because this is the percent decrease for the East Coast stores.

11 **Choices A, B and D are correct**.

Choice A is correct because the average speed is less than 50 miles per hour. This can be calculated by using the equation, average speed $= \frac{total\ distance}{total\ time}$. To find the total time, divide each distance by its speed and then add to get $\frac{\frac{1}{3}x}{25} = \frac{x}{75}$, $\frac{\frac{1}{4}x}{50} = \frac{x}{200}$, and $\frac{\frac{5}{12}x}{70} = \frac{x}{168}$. Adding these values together would get you a total time of $\frac{x}{75} + \frac{x}{200} + \frac{x}{168} = \frac{x}{41.18}$. Now plug this in to the expression for average speed to get $\frac{total\ distance}{total\ time} = \frac{x}{\frac{x}{41.18}} = 41.18$ miles per hour which is less than 50 miles per hour.

Choice B is correct because to find the fraction of the time spent going 70 miles per hour, subtract the given fractions from 1. $1 - \frac{1}{3} - \frac{1}{4} = 1 - \frac{7}{12} = \frac{5}{12}$. This is less than half the time.

Choice D is correct because if the total distance was hypothetically 240 miles, that means the car traveled for 80 miles at 25 mph ($\frac{1}{3} \times 240 = 80$) and 60 miles at 50 mph ($\frac{1}{4} \times 240 = 60$). To find the time it took to travel these distances use the formula $t = \frac{d}{r}$. For 25 mph, it would take $t = \frac{80}{25} = 3.2$ hours. For 50 mph, it would be $t = \frac{60}{50} = 1.2$ hours. Divide these numbers to get $\frac{1.2}{3.2} = \frac{3}{8}$.

Choice C is incorrect because there is no time mentioned in the question.

12 **The correct answer is 108.24%** because to find the total percentage, convert 23% to a decimal of 0.23 and add to 1 to indicate an increase. This would get you 1.23 as the first multiplier. Then convert 12% to a decimal of 0.12 and subtract from one since it is a decrease to get $1 - 0.12 = 0.88$. The expression to find what percent the final value of the stock is in comparison to the original value would be $(1.23)(0.88)x$. Multiply to get 1.0824 meaning the new price is 108.24% of the original price.

SECTION 2 (EASY): Answers & Explanations

1 **Choice B is correct** because if the ratio of girls to boys in class is 6:5, then the number of students in the class must be divisible by 6 +5 = 11. The smallest odd number integer that is divisible by 11 is 11. This makes Quantity B greater than Quantity A.

Choice A is incorrect because Quantity A is less than Quantity B. **Choice C** is incorrect because the two quantities are not equal. **Choice D** is incorrect because it is possible to compare the two quantities.

2 **Choice A is correct** because the edge length of the cube can be found to be 8 in. while the side length of the square is 9 in.

To find the side length of the square, use the perimeter formula for a square of P = 4s. If the perimeter is 36 in, that means each side's length is 9 in.

To find the edge length of the cube, use the volume formula for a cube of $V = s^3$. This would give you an edge length of 4 in since $4^3 = 64$.

Choice B is incorrect because the edge length of the cube is not greater than the side length of the square. **Choice C** is incorrect because Quantity A does not equal Quantity B. **Choice D** is incorrect because it is possible to compare the quantities.

3 **Choice B is correct** because if you simplify Quantity B it equals $x^{-12} = \frac{1}{x^{12}}$. Then if $0 < x < 1$, it can be argued that $\frac{1}{x^{12}} > \frac{1}{x^7}$ since dividing a fraction by 1 always results in its reciprocal. For example, if $x = \frac{1}{2}$ then $\frac{1}{x^{12}} = \frac{1}{\left(\frac{1}{2}\right)^{12}} = 2096$ and $\frac{1}{x^7} = \frac{1}{\left(\frac{1}{2}\right)^7} = 128$. This shows that $\frac{1}{x^{12}} > \frac{1}{x^7}$.

Choice A is incorrect because $\frac{1}{x^{12}} > \frac{1}{x^7}$. **Choice C** is incorrect because the two quantities do not equal each other. **Choice D** is incorrect because it is possible to compare the two values based on the possible x values.

4 **Choice A is correct** because the perimeter of ABC is approximately 29.2 while the perimeter of DCE is 21.

To find the perimeter of DCE, use the area of the square to determine that each side length is 7 since $A = s^2$. This means the perimeter of the equilateral triangle is 7 + 7 + 7 = 21.

To find the perimeter of ABC, use the two side lengths of 7 and 10 and the Pythagorean theorem of $a^2 + b^2 = c^2$. Plugging in you would get $7^2 + 10^2 = c^2$ which becomes $49 + 100 = 149 = c^2$. Take the square root of both sides to get c as approximately 12.2. Add up the side lengths to get 12.2 + 10 +7 = 29.2 for the perimeter of ABC.

Choice B is incorrect because the perimeter of ABC is greater. **Choice C** is incorrect because the perimeters are not equal. **Choice D** is incorrect because it is possible to solve for the perimeters.

5 **Choice D is correct** because x can equal 0 or 7. Graph the given points in the coordinate plane and determine the distance between vertex A and B to evaluate where vertex C can be located.

This diagram shows (2,2) and (5,6) plotted and the two potential locations of vertex C.

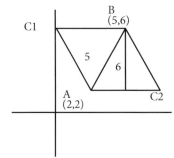

Since ABC is an equilateral triangle, that means the distance between all three vertices is the same. To find the distance, you can create a right triangle with the side lengths of 3 (5 − 2 = 3) and 4 (6 − 2 = 4). Then use the Pythagorean theorem $a^2 + b^2 = c^2$ to determine the hypotenuse (and therefore the distance) is $3^2 + 4^2 = c^2$ which simplifies to be $9 + 16 = 25 = c^2$ or $c = 5$.

The x–coordinate of C can be 5 to the right of A or 5 to the left of B. This would get you two possible locations of 7 (2 + 5 = 7) or 0 (5 − 5 = 0). Since 7 is greater than 0 and 0 is equal to 0 it is not possible to determine the relationship.

Choice A is incorrect because x is only greater than 0 for one of its values, not both. **Choice B** is incorrect because 0 is never greater than x. **Choice C** is incorrect because x can equal 0, but it can also be 7.

6 **Choice D is correct** because b can be equal to, less than, or greater than 3.

For example, $b = 3$ is possible if $a = 4$ and $c = 6$ because $\frac{ab}{c} = \frac{4(3)}{6} = 2$ and $\frac{c}{b} = \frac{6}{3} = 2$.

It is possible for $b < 3$ if $b = 1$, $a = 4$, and $c = 2$ since $\frac{ab}{c} = \frac{4(1)}{2} = 2$ and $\frac{c}{b} = \frac{2}{1} = 2$.

It is also possible for $b > 3$ if $b = 4$, $a = 4$, and $c = 8$ since $\frac{ab}{c} = \frac{4(4)}{8} = 2$ and $\frac{c}{b} = \frac{8}{4} = 2$.

Choice A is incorrect because b can also be less than or equal to 3. **Choice B** is incorrect because b can also be greater than or equal to 3. **Choice C** is incorrect because b can also be greater than or less than 3.

7 **Choice E is correct** because to determine the total pounds, identify the expression that represents the scenario. The equation C = 0.34P + 550 can be created to represent cost where P is pounds of supplies.

Set this equation equal to 1501.40 to solve and get 1501.40 = 0.34P + 550. Subtract 550 from both sides and then divide by 0.34 to find P = 2798.

Choice A is incorrect because this results from a calculation error. **Choice B** is incorrect because this is the result if you used 1.34 and not 0.34. **Choice C** is incorrect because this results from a calculation error. **Choice D** is incorrect because this is the answer if you do not divide by 1.34.

8 **Choice B is correct** because the speeds can be converted to find the initial speed of approximately 21 mph and the final speed of around 41 mph.

To find the initial speed, multiply to convert from meters per second to miles per hour with the following sequence

$$\frac{75\,m}{8\,s} \times \frac{60\,s}{1\,min} \times \frac{60\,min}{1\,hour} \times \frac{1\,km}{1000\,m} \times \frac{1\,mile}{1.6\,km} = 21 \text{ mph.}$$

Convert the final speed to mph:

$$\frac{180\,m}{10\,s} \times \frac{60\,s}{1\,min} \times \frac{60\,min}{1\,hour} \times \frac{1\,km}{1000\,m} \times \frac{1\,mile}{1.6\,km} = 40.5 \text{ mph.}$$

Subtract for a difference of 40.5 − 21 = 19.5 which is closest to 20 mph.

Choice A is incorrect because this results from a calculation error. **Choice C** is incorrect because this results from a calculation error. **Choice D** is incorrect because this results from a calculation error. **Choice E** is incorrect because this results from a calculation error.

9 **The correct answer is 2** because rearranging the expression into the slope–intercept form will reveal that only two points within the inequality are integer values (1,1) and (2,1).

To rearrange the equation subtract 3x and divide by 4 to get $y \leq \frac{5}{2} - \frac{3}{4}x$. Graphed, this line would have a y-intercept of $(0, \frac{5}{2})$ and an x-intercept of $(\frac{10}{3}, 0)$. This means two possible integer combinations of 1s and 2s fall in this range.

10 **Choice A is correct** because to find the interest rate use the simple interest formula of I = PRT. Plugging in the given information gives you $4199.86 = $29,999(r)(4) which simplifies to be 4199.86 = 119996r. Divide by 119996 to get r = 0.035 which would be equal to 3.5%.

Choice B is incorrect because this results from a calculation error. **Choice C** is incorrect because this is what percent $4199.86 is of $29,999 which is not the same as the interest rate over 4 years. **Choice D** is incorrect because this results from a calculation error. **Choice E** is incorrect because this would be based on incorrectly interpreting the decimal value of 0.035 as 35%.

11 **Choice E is correct** because there are 9 prime numbers between 1 and 100 that contain a 3. First, identify all primes between 1 and 100: 2, 3, 5, 7, 11, 13, 17, 19, 23, 29, 31, 37, 41, 43, 47, 53, 59, 61, 67, 71, 73, 79, 83, 89, 97. Then isolate the ones that contain a 3: 3, 13, 23, 31, 37, 43, 53, 73 and 83.

Choice A is incorrect because there are more than 5 numbers. **Choice B** is incorrect because there are more than 6 numbers. **Choice C** is incorrect because there are more than 7 numbers. **Choice D** is incorrect because there are more than 8 numbers.

Section 2 (Easy): Answers & Explanations

12 **Choice D is correct** because it can be discovered through trial and error which unit digits will leave a remainder of 4 for any three–digit number being divided by 6. For example, 110 divided by 6 would be 18 remainder 2. For the other values such as 1, 101 divided by 6 leaves a remainder of 5. For 2, the remainder of 102 divided by 6 is 0. For 4, 124 divided by 6 is 20 remainder 4. For 5, 105 divided by 6 is the remainder 3.

Choice A is incorrect because this leaves a remainder of 2.
Choice B is incorrect because this leaves a remainder of 5.
Choice C is incorrect because this leaves a remainder of 0
Choice E is incorrect because this leaves a remainder of 3.

13 **Choice C and D are correct.** For the standard deviation to decrease, the values of the numbers must get closer together since standard deviation is a measurement of the spread of the data set.

Choice C is correct because the numbers would become closer if they were all divided by 2. For example, if the data set was 1 through 5, the new data set would be $\frac{1}{2}$ to $\frac{5}{2}$ which are closer in value. **Choice D is correct** because if all numbers are squarely rooted, the spread of the numbers would decrease. For example, if the data set was 1 to 5, the new data set would become 1 to around 2.236.

Choice A is incorrect because if all numbers were manipulated in the same way, the standard deviation would not change. **Choice B** is incorrect because this would increase the standard deviation because the spread of the numbers would increase.

14 **Choice E is correct** because if the range is greater than the median, that would indicate a large spread of values within the data set. Since standard deviation is a measurement of spread, the range is often used as an indicator of the size of the standard deviation of a data set.

Choice A is incorrect because this could indicate a large standard deviation, but not always. **Choice B** is incorrect because in some cases this could indicate a large standard deviation, but not always. **Choice C** is incorrect because this would indicate an evenly distributed data set that does not have a large standard deviation typically.
Choice D is incorrect because this would mean the data set is all of the same number and this would lead to the smallest standard deviation.

15 **Choices A and E are correct.** The number of chairs cannot be divisible by 6 or 9 since there are chairs left over in either case. This would eliminate answers C and D. Of the remaining answers, test out their divisibility to see what remainders you get.

Choice A is correct because 26 divided by 6 is 4 remainder 2 and divided by 9 is 2 remainder 8 which means this number of chairs works. **Choice E is correct** because 62 divided by 6 is 10 remainder 2 and divided by 9 is 6 remainder 8 which also works.

Choice B is incorrect because 32 does not leave a remainder of 8 when divided by 9. **Choice C** is incorrect because 45 is divisible by 9. **Choice D** is incorrect because

For more practice, visit www.vibrantpublishers.com

Chapter 8: Practice Test #2

SECTION 2 (HARD): Answers & Explanations

1 **Choice B is correct** because to find the average for both classes, find the sum of all test scores from both classes then add them together and divide by the number of students to get the average of 87.27. This can be seen with the expression $\frac{(30 \times 85) + (25 \times 90)}{30 + 25} = \frac{4800}{55} = 87.27$. Since 87.5 is greater than 87.27, Quantity B is greater.

Choice A is incorrect because the average is less than 88. **Choice C** is incorrect because the two values are not equal. **Choice D** is incorrect because it is possible to compare the two quantities.

2 **Choice D is correct** because based on the given statement it can be concluded that a must always be negative and its absolute value must always be greater than b which sometimes makes Quantity A larger and sometimes makes Quantity B larger.

If a and b are both negative, Quantity A would be greater. For example, if $a = -2$ and $b = -1$, then Quantity A would be $\frac{b}{a} = \frac{-1}{-2} = \frac{1}{2}$ and Quantity B would be $\frac{|a|}{b} = \frac{|-2|}{-1} = -2$. Since $\frac{1}{2} > -2$, then Quantity A would be greater.

If a was negative and b was positive, Quantity B would be greater. For example, if $a = -2$ and $b = 1$, then Quantity A would be $\frac{b}{a} = \frac{1}{-2} = \frac{-1}{2}$ and Quantity B would be $\frac{|a|}{b} = \frac{|-2|}{1} = 2$. Therefore, $2 > \frac{-1}{2}$, making Quantity B greater.

Choice A is incorrect because only when both values are negative is Quantity A larger. **Choice B** is incorrect because Quantity B is larger only when a is negative and b is positive. **Choice C** is incorrect because the two quantities cannot be equal.

3 **Choice A is correct** because if you start a sequence with a positive integer, then every odd number will be positive and every even number will be negative if you multiply by a negative. This means the eleventh number in the series will be positive and the twentieth number in the series will be negative, making Quantity A the larger value.

Choice B is incorrect because it is a negative value that will never be greater than a positive value no matter which positive value of x you begin at. **Choice C** is incorrect because the two terms cannot be equal to each other. **Choice D** is incorrect because it is possible to compare the two values.

4 **Choice C is correct** because the perimeter of triangle ABC can be found to be 60. Use the circumference of 26Π to determine the diameter of the circle to be 26. This would mean the hypotenuse of the triangle is 26. Since the ratio of the side lengths at 5:12:13, compare the ratio with x:y:26 to get 10:24:26. Add these side lengths to get a total perimeter of 10 + 24 + 26 = 60.

Choice A is incorrect because the perimeter is equal to 60. **Choice B** is incorrect because the perimeter is equal to 60. **Choice D** is incorrect because the perimeter can be solved for.

5 **Choice A is correct** because to find the area of an octagon use the formula $A = 2s^2(1 + \sqrt{2})$ and to find the area of a square use the formula $A = s^2$.

The area of the octagon would be $A = 2s^2(1 + \sqrt{2}) = A = 2(6)^2(1 + \sqrt{2})$. This simplifies to equal $72 + 72\sqrt{2}$ which is approximately 173.82.

The area of the square would be $A = s^2 = 10^2 = 100$. This means the area of the octagon is greater.

Choice B is incorrect because the area of the octagon is greater than the area of the square. **Choice C** is incorrect because the areas are not equal. **Choice D** is incorrect because it is possible to solve for the areas and compare..

6 **Choice A is correct** because you can use combinations to solve. For the first spot, you have 3 people to choose from so you would use the expression $_3C_1$ which equals 3. Then for the next stop, you have 7 people to choose from who are not experienced and 3 spots so the expression would be $_7C_3$ which equals 35. Multiply these two values together (3 × 35) to get 105.

Choice B is incorrect because this would be the answer if you chose 1 out of 10 in the first combination. **Choice C** is incorrect because this would be if you still chose from all remaining crew including the experienced members. **Choice D** is incorrect because this would result from a math error. **Choice E** is incorrect because this is the number of total combinations without accounting for limitations on experienced members.

Section 2 (Hard): Answers & Explanations

7 **Choice C is correct** because to get the area of a parallelogram you will multiply the base times the height. To find the height use the Pythagorean theorem $a^2 + b^2 = c^2$ with hypotenuse of 10 and leg of 6 to get $6^2 + b^2 = 10^2$. Simplifying this would yield $36 + b^2 = 100$. Subtract 36 to get $b^2 = 64$ and square root to find the missing height of 8. Now multiply the base of 6 by the height of 8 to get 48 as the area.

Choice A is incorrect because this is the answer if you multiplied incorrectly. **Choice B is incorrect** because this is the answer if you multiplied 6 by 6. **Choice D is incorrect** because this is the answer if you multiplied 8 by 10. **Choice E is incorrect** because this is the answer if you multiplied 10 by 10.

8 **Choice B is correct** because using the given rates, you can solve for the combined rate through fractional statements. Let the rate of workers A and B equal $\frac{1}{a} + \frac{1}{b} = \frac{1}{20}$. Let the rate of workers B and C equal $\frac{1}{b} + \frac{1}{c} = \frac{1}{40}$. Finally, let the rate of workers A and C equal $\frac{1}{a} + \frac{1}{c} = \frac{1}{8}$.

Now add these statements together to get $\frac{1}{a} + \frac{1}{b} + \frac{1}{b} + \frac{1}{c} + \frac{1}{a} + \frac{1}{c} = \frac{1}{20} + \frac{1}{40} + \frac{1}{8}$ which simplifies to be $\frac{2}{a} + \frac{2}{b} + \frac{2}{c} = \frac{1}{5}$. Divide by to to find $\frac{1}{a} + \frac{1}{b} + \frac{1}{c} = \frac{1}{10}$ meaning all three workers can complete the task in 10 hours.

Choice A is incorrect because this is faster than possible. **Choice C is incorrect** because this would result from a math error. **Choice D is incorrect** because this is slower than possible. **Choice E is incorrect** because this is longer than it would take.

9 **Choice D is correct** because to get an odd integer when dividing, you have to divide two odd numbers or two even numbers. Then two odd numbers being subtracted will yield and even number and two odd numbers being subtracted will also equal an even number. The only even number is 30.

Choice A is incorrect because it is not possible to get an odd number. **Choice B is incorrect** because it is not possible to get an odd number. **Choice C is incorrect** because it is not possible to get an odd number. **Choice E is incorrect** because it is not possible to get an odd number.

10 **Choice C is correct** because if the original cost was 100 dollars a 45% mark–up would be $145 (100 + 100(0.45) = $145). If the price was then decreased to allow for a 15% profit, the discounted price would need to be $115 (100 + 100(0.15)). This means the percent difference in cost would be $\frac{145-115}{145} = 0.207 = 20.7\%$. The closest choice to this is Choice C.

Choice A is incorrect because this results from a calculation error. **Choice B is incorrect** because this results from a calculation error. **Choice D is incorrect** because this is the difference in percent. **Choice E is incorrect** because this is the percent of the original price.

11 **Choice C is correct.** Eliza spent a total on $2680 × 50 = $134,000 on gold. On the high end, Eliza could have sold for $2875 per ounce which for 50 ounces would mean she profited (2875 × 50) − $134,000 which equals $9750. On the low end, she would have lost (2582 × 50) − $134,000 = −$4900. Her percent profit would be anything between $\frac{9750}{134000}$ and $\frac{-4900}{134000}$ which would be around 7.27% and −3.65%.

The possible percentage profit or loss is within the range of approximately **−3.65% to +7.27%**.

Choice C is correct because it falls within the range.

Choice A is incorrect because it falls outside the range. **Choice B is incorrect** because it falls outside the range. **Choice D is incorrect** because it falls outside the range.

12 **Choice E is correct** because to find the sum of an arithmetic series you can use the expression of $S = \frac{n}{2}(a_1 + a_n)$. In this case $a_n = a_{100}$ which can be found by multiplying −5 by 99 and adding to a_1. This will get you −495 + 405 = −90. Now plug this into the sum expression to get $S = \frac{100}{2}(405 + -90)$ to get a sum of 15,750.

Choice A is incorrect because this is just the first term in the sequence, not the sum. **Choice B is incorrect** because this results from a math error. **Choice C is incorrect** because this results from a math error. **Choice D is incorrect** because this results from a math error.

13 **The correct answer is 414** because the lowest possible value for *xy* is found with −10 × 23 which equals −230. The largest possible value of *xy* is found with the values 8 × 23 which equals 184. The difference between these values would be 184 − (−230) = 414.

14 **Choice D is correct** because to find the degree measure add up all budget areas except for staff. This would get you $546,000 + $34,250 + $25,100 + $327,010 + $13,520 + $159,120 = $1,105,000. Divide the equipment budget by this total budget to get the fraction of the pie chart that would be made up by this category:

$\frac{\$546,000}{\$1,105,000} = 0.494$. Multiply this by 360° to get approximately 178°.

Choice A is incorrect because this results from a calculation error. **Choice B** is incorrect because this results from a calculation error. **Choice C** is incorrect because this results from a calculation error. **Choice E** is incorrect because this results from a calculation error.

15 **Choices C and D are correct.**

Choice C is correct because if $x = -3$, $y = -1$, and $z = 3$ then this would be $\frac{(-3)(-1)}{3} = 1$.

Choice D is correct because $x = -5$, $y = -4$, and $z = 2$ then this would be $\frac{(-5)(-4)}{2} = 10$.

Choice A is incorrect because it is not possible to get a negative if both *x* and *y* are negative and are being divided by a positive. **Choice B is incorrect** because it is not possible to get 0 from dividing integers.

Know Your Scaled Score

This table can be used to calculate your scaled score. Use a pencil to note down your scores for Section 1 and Section 2 (Easy or Hard).

Input the number of questions you got right for both sections and add them in the adjacent columns. To get your scaled score for each section, refer to the table on page 284. Lastly, add both sections' scaled scores to get your total score for all tests.

If you attempted the Easy Section, check your scaled scores in the Quantitative (Easy) column.

If you attempted the Hard Section, check your scaled scores in the Quantitative (Hard) column.

Section 1 (Number of correct answers)	Section 2 (Number of correct answers)	Total (Section 1 + Section 2)	Scaled Score

For more practice, visit www.vibrantpublishers.com

SCALED SCORE TABLE

Raw Score	Quantitative (Easy)	Quantitative (Hard)
27	160	170
26	159	167
25	157	164
24	155	162
23	154	161
22	153	159
21	152	158
20	151	157
19	150	155
18	149	154
17	148	153
16	147	153
15	146	152
14	145	151
13	144	150
12	143	149
11	142	148
10	141	147
9	140	146
8	139	145
7	137	
6	136	
5	135	
4	133	
3	131	
2	130	
1	130	
0	130	

Made in United States
Orlando, FL
19 September 2025